Praise for Gerard Straub and
Reading Thomas Merton and Longing for God in Haiti

"Merton would be pleased and humbled to know he accompanied Gerry Straub into the most appalling circumstances of Haiti, and to afford motivation throughout such hopeless daily experiences encountered here with bald honesty and raw faith."

—Brother Paul Quenon, OCSO, Abbey of Gethsemani, and Author of *In Praise of the Useless Life*

"The power of contemplation and action to beacon hope for our world's dark journeys shines out in Gerry Straub's fascinating tale of his adventures in Haiti as the founder of the Santa Chiara Children Center. Merton would have been avid to read the story of this married, secular Franciscan who gave up a New York media career to serve the poor. Gerry's witness in this book would have mentored Merton on how faith in action can triumph in hiding over despair and violence."

—Guerric Heckel, OCSO, Director of St. Francis Retreat Center at Mepkin Abbey, South Carolina

"This is how mature adults put together a life of the gospel. . . ."

"The writing in Gerry Straub's book Reading Thomas Merton and Longing for God in Haiti *reminds me of Merton's writing in its honesty. I would use this book for adult faith formation. It's an easy book to read. There is so much spiritual wealth scattered throughout, including a wide range of quotes from great spiritual writers. What you will find in this book is an imperfect but deep lay person trying to put his struggles with life and faith together, which is what Merton did in his writing.*

When I look at Merton's writing and I step back from it, it depicts a guy trying to put the pieces together. Merton was wrestling with himself. Of course, now that Merton's diaries have been released, one can see the raw material. It's not a finished book where we get the idea that this guy's having lunch with God and floating on clouds in Kentucky. It's a guy struggling through all his stuff. We all have stuff we wrestle with. Gerry Straub read Merton when he was an atheist because he was a deep person and game recognizes game.

In Reading Thomas Merton and Longing for God in Haiti, *Gerry shows us a lot of his struggles and doubts, his stuff, as he wrestles with real-life problems. This is how mature adults put together a life of the gospel. The book is a manual in the sense that we see a model of what it's like to do one's homework and to put it into practice the demands of the gospel. Gerry's book is a lesson in how to do it for any adult who's serious about their faith.*

Gerry's maturing faith took him to Haiti to care for abandoned kids. But you don't have to go to Haiti. Pick a pile and grab a shovel; there's plenty to do in your neighborhood.

I am going to give Reading Thomas Merton and Longing for God in Haiti *the Deacon Dolan money back guarantee. If you buy this book and you don't like it, just send it to me and I personally will give you your money back."*

—DEACON DENNIS DOLAN, PAULIST DEACON AFFILIATE
SERVING IN ST. PETERSBURG, FLORIDA

Deacon Dennis Dolan has been a permanent deacon since August, 1993. He spent many years as a Catholic chaplain with the Connecticut Department of Corrections. Deacon Dennis became a Paulist Deacon Affiliate in 2018. Deacon Dennis currently serves in a parish in the Diocese of St. Petersburg, Florida. He and his wife, Deborah, have three children and five grandchildren.

"Where did I come from? Where am I now? Where am I going?"

Reading Thomas Merton and Longing for God in Haiti *found me at a pivotal moment in my life, when I was seeking answers to deep questions about spirituality and poverty—especially in light of my experiences spending time in Haiti during and after college.*

Any person of faith who has ever been to a place of unconscionable poverty, violence, or lack of infrastructure (and these places exist in the United States too) knows the deep, uncomfortable dissonance it provokes. Haiti, though beautiful with its people, culture, and food, is also marked by a reputation for poverty and instability, especially in the southern regions near the capital, Port-au-Prince. For many Americans visiting for the first time, the encounter is jarring and unforgettable.

As I see it, Americans who visit Haiti for humanitarian reasons often face two choices: live it while you are there and then try to forget it when you return home or embrace the struggle and fight for a reconciled conscience—listening to what God might be asking and responding courageously. That response looks different for each person, but it always requires a deeper dive into one's spiritual life, guided by others who walk that same journey. For me, Reading Thomas Merton and Longing for God in Haiti *became a crucial companion along that path.*

For a while I tried to shift my focus away from Haiti, but it remained written on my heart. God was asking me to do something—though I didn't yet know what. I read academic studies, sociological works, and personal accounts from both Haitians and Americans, but nothing touched the spiritual core of what I was wrestling with. That's when I realized what I was really searching for: a book through the lens of Christian spirituality, rooted in the Haitian experience, that explored meaning, purpose, materialism, and both material and spiritual poverty. Gerry Straub's book was exactly that.

It took me nearly a year of on and off reading, because the book demanded serious reflection. But throughout that journey, Straub's insights— together with Thomas Merton's—helped me find a more practical response to my own "longing for God in Haiti." Halfway through, I decided to leave a very stable and enjoyable teaching and coaching job in Denver to pursue a role at a new Cristo Rey school in North Miami, serving a predominantly Haitian and Latin American community. Cristo Rey schools serve families with limited access to high-quality, college-preparatory education, while also offering students unique work experience. They seek a systemic response to injustice, while grounding students in spiritual formation.

Straub's vulnerable storytelling guided my discernment and self-reflection in ways I don't think anyone else could have. This was not only because of his experiences in Haiti, but because he drew on the wisdom of St. Francis of Assisi and Thomas Merton—two spiritual giants in the Catholic tradition, and two of my personal favorites—to unpack what Haiti revealed to him. Many missionaries and humanitarians return home without the resources or accompaniment needed to process what they've seen. Straub gives language to that struggle.

Material poverty is devastating, but it is not the deepest root of evil. Spiritual poverty is. This is not to justify material poverty but to recognize that greed, power, and indifference perpetuate it—in Haiti, in the United States, in the Philippines, in the Congo, and beyond. Humanity's deepest questions cannot be reduced to economics or sociology. They are spiritual questions—and Reading Thomas Merton and Longing for God in Haiti invites us to ask them.

A Haitian friend, Agnaud, once shared with me a saying from his culture that Straub's book also embodies: "Ki kote mwen te soti? Ki kote mwen ye? Ki kote m'ap ale?"—"Where did I come from? Where am I now? Where am I going?"

My time living in various parts of Haiti and Jamaica, spending time at the Tijuana-San Ysidro border with migrants, even now in Miami, where I live, have forced me to ask serious questions about my life and its relationship to the world around me. In college, I was thrown into a week-long trip to Haiti without much preparation or resources to unpack the profound encounter with myself, with humanity, and with God there. While I am still unpacking that story–knowing that Gerry Straub had been on a similar journey, from Hollywood to Haiti, was comforting to know I wasn't crazy and alone, but it also provided a sort of mentorship, one that I have a feeling might be used to help others unpack these experiences, too.

Whether you have been to Haiti and wrestled with these questions, whether you live amid poverty and violence and are struggling to make sense of it, whether you have lived in comfort but still feel the weight of life's spiritual challenges, or whether you are simply wondering, "Where is God in all this?"—this book has something to say to you. If you read it with an open heart, I believe you will discover something beautiful about yourself, about God, and about the world around you—even in the midst of a world full of violence, anger, chaos, and despair.

DEREK EDWARDS, THEOLOGY DEPARTMENT CHAIR,
CRISTO REY MIAMI HIGH SCHOOL

Reading Thomas Merton *and* Longing *for* God *in* Haiti

Learning Wisdom in the School of My Life

GERARD THOMAS STRAUB
with His Study Partner Jonathan Montaldo

Published by:

Pax et Bonum Communications

VERO BEACH, FLORIDA

ISBN-13:
979-8-9860888-1-5 (Paperback)
979-8-9860888-7-7(Ebook)

Edited by
Carol Killman Rosenberg

Cover & interior design by
Gary A. Rosenberg

www.thebookcouple.com

Cover photo by
Gerard Straub

Printed in the United States of America

Other Books by Gerard Thomas Straub

Salvation for Sale

Dear Kate (a novel)

The Sun & Moon Over Assisi

When Did I See You Hungry?
(photo/essay)

Thoughts of a Blind Beggar

Hidden in the Rubble

The Loneliness and Longing
of Saint Francis

The Sunrise of the Soul

A Journey to Meekness

The Cross of Love, The Pain of Poverty

Films by Gerard Thomas Straub

We Have a Table for Four Ready

Room Enough for Joy

Glidepath to Recovery

When Did I See You Hungry?

Embracing the Leper

Holy Pictures

Rescue Me

Endless Exodus

Poverty and Prayer

The Patience of a Saint

Where Love Is

The Faces of Poverty

Room at the Inn

The Narrow Path

The Fragrant Spirit of Life

Poverty and Prayer II

A Distressing Disguise

Cathedrals of the Poor

Mud Pies & Kites

We Anoint Their Wounds

The Wings of Love

The Smile of a Sick Child

Rooted in Love

Silenzio

The Loneliness and Longing
of St. Francis of Assisi

Dedicated to
The Abandoned Kids
of the
Santa Chiara Children's Center
in
Port-au-Prince, Haiti

Especially the Straub Kids
Bency Clare
Peter Francis
Clare Marie
Teresa Regina
Judeline
Isnaïda
Moïse

and in Loving Memory of
Tamysha
and
Kenja

*"Mystics see through a lens of paradox: dazzling darkness,
beautiful wound, the longing that is the remedy for longing.
Paradox points beyond itself to a truth that both transcends
and includes logic, a truth that is alive, generative, and whole."*

—Mirabai Starr, "Dazzling Darkness"[1]

*"Faith . . . is always contradicting itself, because everything we say about
God is so inadequate that it always runs us head first into a paradox."*

—Thomas Merton, Run to the Mountain[2]

*"There is only one true flight from the world; it is not an escape
from conflict, anguish, and suffering, but the flight from disunity
and separation, to unity and peace in the love of other men."*

Thomas Merton, New Seeds of Contemplation[3]

Exterior of Thomas Merton's Hermitage, December 2000; *Photo by Gerry Straub*

"December 5 [1964]. In the hermitage, one must pray or go to seed. The pretense of prayer will not suffice. Just sitting will not suffice. It has to be real. Yet, what can one do? Solitude puts you with your back to the wall, or your face to it, and this is good. So you pray to learn to pray."

—Thomas Merton, *A Vow of Conversation*[4]

"How clearly I see and experience, this morning [December 1, 1964], the difference and distance between my own inertia, weakness, sensitivity, stupidity and the love of Christ which instantly pulls all things in me together so that there is no longer any uncertainty or misdirection or lassitude. What a shame and what dishonor to Christ if I let my life be such a mess of trivialities, such silly concerns that are in reality a mask for despair."

—Thomas Merton, *A Vow of Conversation*[5]

"O God, teach me to be satisfied with my own helplessness in the spiritual life. Teach me to be content with Your grace that comes to me in darkness and works things I cannot see. Teach me to be happy that I can depend on You. That should be enough for an eternity of joy. That by itself ought to be infinitely greater than any joy my own intellectual appetite could desire."

—Thomas Merton, *Entering the Silence*[6]

Thomas Merton

1915–1968

Thomas Merton lived out his longing for God. In the river of words that he left behind, we are able to follow the flow of Merton's inner life as he searched for a God who is beyond words. In a world growing ever more falsely sophisticated, yet unable to find its God and largely incapable of experiencing the simple joys of living, Thomas Merton, more than fifty years after his untimely, accidental death in Asia, is still relevant.

A born writer with a prodigious gift of expression, the multifaceted monk was a true renaissance man who became a mythological figure whose richly diverse life was both the medium and the message for the universal search for the Ultimate. More than a legend, Merton was a relentless seeker and part-time prophet.

Photo credit: John Howard Griffith. Or Ed Rice.
Permission from Paul PEARSON at MERTON Center, pmpearson@bellarmine.edu

No book could even hope to capture the fullness of such a brilliant, complex man. This humble book simply tries to enter the stillness and silence of Merton's prayer life in hopes that it might point the way for us. Merton himself freely admitted he had no answers. All he had, he said, were his experiences. *Reading Thomas Merton and Longing for God in Haiti,* following Merton's example, only hopes to prompt you to penetrate your own silence, no matter how frightening, and discover your own Light.

> *"Merton was above all a man of prayer, a thinker who*
> *challenged the certitudes of his time and opened new horizons*
> *for souls and the Church. He was also a man of dialogue,*
> *a promoter of peace between peoples and religions."*
>
> —POPE FRANCIS, IN HIS 2015 ADDRESS TO THE U.S. CONGRESS

Contents

A Friendly Warning
before Reading My Book

I've made more than twenty films on poverty around the world. I've filmed in some of the worst slums on earth, witnessing unimaginable misery and deprivation. The films did not shy away from confronting the injustice of global poverty where more than 10,000 children a day die of starvation or diseases related to hunger. Produced by my ministry, Pax et Bonum Communications, the films are a strong, consistent, and prophetic voice speaking out on behalf of the poor and encouraging people to enter more deeply into prayer and to be more compassionate to those in dire need. Besides fostering compassion for the homeless, hungry, marginalized, and oppressed, the films (and now books) inspire a genuine and respectful fraternity among all people and promote the importance of genuine interfaith dialogue.

Rooted in Franciscan spirituality, along with the mystical traditions of all faiths, Pax et Bonum Communications champions the importance of contemplation and action. We believe the best way to love God is through acts of love, mercy, compassion, and kindness, especially for those living in acute poverty. We believe that care for the chronically poor is an essential component of the spiritual life, especially for the followers of the nonviolent Christ. We believe everyone is called to a life of sharing, caring, and giving. Our films stress the necessity of prayer, peace, harmony, humility, and social justice. In the ecumenical spirit of Saint Francis of Assisi, we hope to show the connectedness of all creation, which will promote a deeper understanding and appreciation of the common good and our essential need to become nurturers, healers, and consolers.

My film ministry eventually led to my opening a home for abandoned children on the periphery of a slum in Port-au-Prince, Haiti. I went from filming the poor to living among them. While I was drawn to monastic contemplation, and even was graced with the chance of living in the stillness and silence of Thomas Merton's hermitage for a week, my journey to God took me to a noisy, violent, rat-infested slum. My hermitage, my path to God and myself, became compassion. My external journey through horrific slums around the world is documented in my films. My interior journey is exposed in the pages of this book.

The manuscript of this book was essentially finished (after years of work and three different incarnations of it) in January 2021. Even after having eight books published by four traditional, venerable publishing houses, it was rejected by two publishers. Because I was consumed with running the orphanage in Haiti, the book laid dormant for over a year. In January 2022, a friend convinced me to gently put my foot into the waters of independent publishing, which would require a steep learning curve. The world of traditional book publishing was shrinking and becoming more difficult to enter. I was tired of knocking on doors that no longer easily opened, unless you were an author whose name alone would sell books and reduce the publisher's risk of having a warehouse filled with unsold books. The projected profit margin for Christian book publishers was the determinate factor in publishing a book. The vastly changing digital world made publishing on demand a new reality. When a person orders a book, it is printed and shipped inside of a day. No warehouse, no inventory of unsold printed books. This is the second book published by Pax et Bonum Communications. The first was *A Journey to Meekness*, which consists of prayer poems and reflections. It was essentially a practice run before attempting to publish the book that filled my heart . . . *this book.*

In his introduction to my photo/essay book *When Did I See You Hungry?* (published in 2002), Giacomo Bini, OFM, then the Minister General of the Order of Friars Minor, wrote: "The book you are holding in your hands is dangerous and should probably carry a government health warning. Gerry Straub is a modern-day Francis, jolting us into the truth by the power of images. You may be glad or sorry you opened this book, but you can't leave it down and remain as you were before you picked it up: whatever you do now is a decision. There's no neutral option. You will either do something—or you reject your truth, our truth, the truth at the heart of everything."

Be warned: even more so, the same can be said for this book.

I want to offer you something to think about before you read any further. As you read this book, the book is reading you. That might sound strange, but think about it for a moment. Anytime you read a text, be it in the bible or a poem or a novel, the text is actually inviting you to enter into a different world, to move beyond the limits of yourself. Merton's words did that to me. As I read Merton in Haiti and in numerous slums around the world, I felt as if he had kidnapped me. I couldn't escape, couldn't put down whatever Merton book I was reading. My point is: allow this book, which is heavily sprinkled with Merton's words and the impact they had on me, to open up for you new vistas of understanding. Read it with more than your eyes. Read it with your broken heart. Read it with an open mind.

Interior of Merton's Hermitage, 2000;
Photo by Gerry Straub

Longing & Writing for God in Haiti

by Jonathan Montaldo

Gerry Straub writes and prays with his Guardian Angels, 2021;
Photo by Walencia, one of the kids

"Doesn't everything die at last and too soon?
Tell me, what are you going to do
with your one, wild and precious life?"

—MARY OLIVER, FROM "THE SUMMER DAY"[7]

In 1933, when newly eighteen and making a tour of Rome before going up to Cambridge University, Thomas Merton tossed on his bed in the cramped, dimly lit room of a pensione. An avid bookworm from boyhood, his new appreciation of the Christ depicted in Byzantine mosaics as he visited Rome's churches prompted his buying a Latin New Testament. He set aside the poems he had been reading of his favorite, D. H. Lawrence, and allowed the aisles and arches of these shrines to become, as he would later write in his autobiography *The Seven Storey Mountain*, a "refuge for his mind." But that night he was sick with yet another infected tooth. He later thought it delirium that ushered the presence of his dead father, Owen, to his imagination. There were tears and recognition of infidelities to his father's integrity of vision, his sole dedication to his art since the death of Merton's mother when he was six:

> The sense of his presence was as vivid and as real and as startling as if he had touched my arm or spoken to me. The whole thing passed in a flash, but in that flash, instantly, I was overwhelmed with a sudden and profound insight into the misery and corruption of my own soul, and I was pierced deeply with a light that made me realize something of the condition I was in, and I was filled with horror at what I saw, and my whole being rose up in revolt against what was within me, and my soul desired escape and liberation and freedom from all this with an intensity and urgency unlike anything I had known before. And now I think for the first time in my whole life I really began to pray—praying not with my lips and with my intellect and my imagination, but praying out of the very roots of my life and my being, and praying to the God I had never known, to reach toward me out of His darkness and to help me to get free of the thousand terrible things that held my will to their slavery.[8]

Eight more years of wildly distracted and wavering dedication to any one thing would pass before Merton, in 1941, would enter the Abbey of Gethsemani in Kentucky and flesh out his avid longing to live solely for God. By nature, nurture, and obedience to monastic duties ordered by his Abbot, he would continue to write his heart out in books, magazines, poems, letters, and private journals so that perhaps he might realize what it meant to make a spiritual journey of his life, his quite ordinary and tedious life in a monastery but inflected by an experience-rooted, personally ardent longing for the ultimate meaning of what it could mean to be a more completely human being, knowing in the dark but surely that the kingdom of God was being born within him.

> *"There are people one meets in books or in life*
> *whom one does not merely observe, meet, or know.*
> *A deep resonance of our entire being is immediately set up*
> *with the entire being of the other.*
> *Heart speaks to heart in the wholeness of the language of music.*
> *True friendship is a kind of singing."*
>
> —Thomas Merton, Conjectures of a Guilty Bystander[9]

I met Gerard Straub and his books more than twenty years ago. He is no Thomas Merton—no one else could be—but everything I know about Gerry resonates for me with that same passionate attention to the exact contours of his singular receptions of his life's experiences as alternating light and dark traveling to being consumed with knowing Christ in the faces of his neighbors. Gerry, too, had a conversion experience in a Franciscan church in Rome that instigated his leaving Manhattan and Los Angeles behind to write books and make films about the economically poor all over the world. The lens of his unwavering attention gave flesh to the faces he unveils for us behind our abstractions, the statistics of those who are hungry, thirsty, and impoverished by the face-averring negligence of we who live better-off and better-served. His photography collected and annotated in *When Did I See You Hungry?* continues to be for me the centerpiece witness to his continuing conversion to compassionate living with the least and lost.

Not to be overly harsh on myself, I confess my gift for cheap sentiment, especially when an author requests a blurb for a new book. For four of Gerry's many other books, I wrote blurbs that cost me nothing from my library rocking chair. Taste my talent:

This contemporary parable of conversion sings of exile from the fake highs of a soap-opera life to the hard roads of finding the one thing necessary to ground the human heart. With perfect pitch for what fails us in our culture of consuming, Gerard Thomas Straub takes us with him down the Franciscan path to an inner peace and simplicity that costs him nearly everything.

Gerard Straub's transparency will bring our affluent and insulated hearts to their knees. *Thoughts of a Blind Beggar* provokes prayer and instigates action to repair our world's brokenness. A profoundly simple but dangerously honest book destined to change lives.

Gerard Straub's harrowing account of his voluntary descent into the agony of Haiti's suffering, his choosing to become lost among and with the lost, disallows his readers to remain comfortable on the sidelines.

An atmosphere of prayer pervades Gerard Thomas Straub's prose in his new work on Saint Francis of Assisi. In his engagingly contemplative text, he interweaves meditations about his own inner experiences and personal biography while discussing the legacy of the medieval saint. Straub shows us the only realistic way to create culture of prayer and action that transforms our self-centered loneliness to a more exacting way of communion with everyone through which all truly long for God.

Yes, taste and see how I easily from afar patted Gerry's incendiary, call-to-action books on their covers. I am easily disgraced by my bad-faith, uneasy distance from the witness and living text of his mature Christian commitments. I have not made the efforts and thus not attracted enough grace to eat the diet of meat and strong drink of Gerard Straub's Franciscan life. I support his work at the Santa Chiara Children's Center in Haiti, but Saint Augustine only knows I am comfortable but often miserable in my safe room with my milk and crackers. "Help my friend, Lord, but as for me, not yet please not yet."

> *"Monks pray by entering deeply into the school of life itself,*
> *to make their whole lives a meditation, a learning from God, a school of wisdom,*
> *a clear-sighted and humble cooperation with the*
> *wisdom of divine providence in their lives,*
> *a ceaseless effort to please the Heavenly Father by*
> *receiving His secret instruction, in all events,*
> *by learning from His holy will and living constantly under His gaze.*
> *Meditation is not just playing with ideas but is fed by realities.*
> *We reflect on the action of grace and detecting as best we can*
> *the innumerable movements of divine love in our lives,*
> *trying to respond faithfully.*
> *This prayer is characterized by great simplicity*
> *and by simple, silent cries going up to God from the depths of our heart."*
>
> —THOMAS MERTON, MONASTIC OBSERVANCES[10]

Thomas Merton prayed in diverse fashion, but his private journals testify to his own practice of entering the school of life itself to find God's presence there. He taught his novices to enter the school of their lives, just as he did. He urged them to pray by remembering all the graces they received in all their relationships with persons, places, and important, life-changing moments. This kind of prayer is one of gratitude and love for one's life just as it is. Writing in general, but writing journals, prayers, and poems specifically was Merton's way of being attentive and alive to God's grace within and through all his life's many things.

Like Saint Francis of Assisi, although to a secondary extent, Merton has mentored Gerry Straub's spiritual exercises of remembering, of being awed by, and of obeying the commands of God's love, received throughout his community's days at the Santa Chiara Children's Center. His prose is always undergirded with the poetry of his longing for God's presence in and for Haiti hour by hour. Gerry's prose and life resonate with Merton's texts. This book befriends Merton's own searching for God. Straub and Merton sing together, adding their voices to the chorus of God's beloved community in Haiti.

Ostensibly to make this book more obviously "Mertonesque," Gerry asked me to contribute some notes from my own studies of Merton's life, my easy contemplative studies in a rocking chair. My contribution is unnecessary. Maybe Gerry hoped that, by my interfacing with his own life-study of God's more fearsome presence in his life, more grace might tap me on my shoulders. Perhaps Gerry wants me to join his praying the presences of Saint Francis, Thomas Merton, and his community of children and staff in Haiti, by my asking, just as Gerry does in Haiti hour by hour, "Lord, what is it *You* want me to do with my one, wild and precious life?"

Jonathan Montaldo
Feast of Mary, August 15, 2022

The Gate of Heaven Is Everywhere

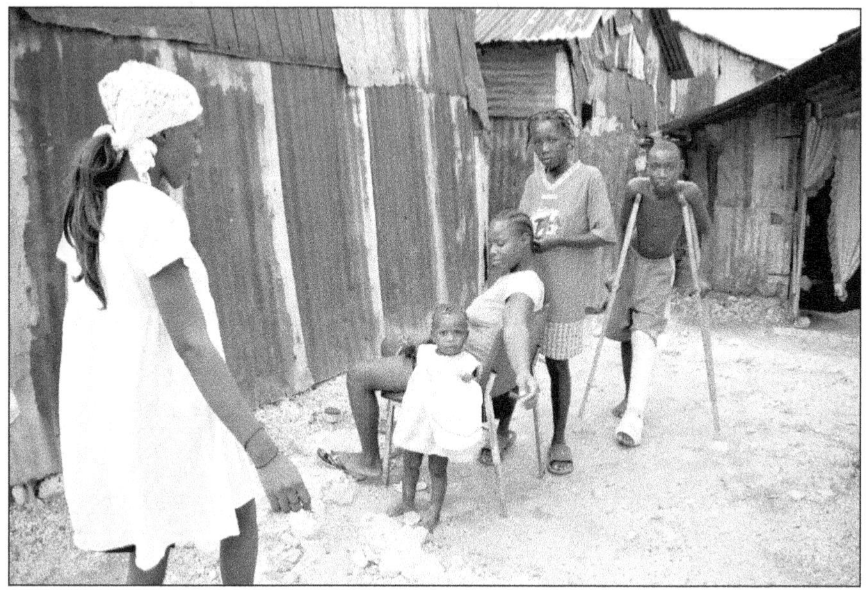

Cité Soleil, December 2009; *Photo by Gerry Straub*

Much of this book was written during a tumultuous year when both the global pandemic and the rise of the Black Lives Matter movement captured the nation's attention. Covid-19 had me in its deadly grip. Fortunately, I escaped. Pervasive, structural, and systemic racism in the United States has a firmer grip on all of us. When I travel to Haiti from Florida, I never bother to check which gate the flight departs from because all I need to do is walk down the one concourse that remained open during the curtailment of flights at the small Fort Lauderdale airport until I see the gate with all the black people waiting for the boarding time. In Haiti, I spend days on end without seeing another white person. In the last seven years, I've entered deeply into the Black experience. In doing so, my attention was and is often drawn to the prophetic and dangerous words of Thomas Merton.

The bombing of a Black church in Birmingham on September 15, 1963, that killed four young, innocent girls shocked Merton. I'm shocked by the number of kids killed by bullets during gang warfare in Cité Soleil. In 1963, Merton called the Civil Rights Movement "the most providential hour, the Kairos not merely of the Negro, but of the white man." One can only wonder what Merton would have said about the deaths of Michael Brown, Eric Garner, Freddie Gray, Rayshard Brooks, George Floyd, Breonna Taylor, Elijah McClain, and Andres Guardado, all of whom died during encounters with law enforcement.

Merton claimed the "gate of heaven was everywhere." Even Haiti. In Haiti, I went from being a "guilty bystander" in the Black struggle for equality to an inner space where the "dream of separateness" and the "noise of othering" died. I'm not superior to or better than the people I live with and serve in Haiti. There is one snippet of Merton's voluminous writing that really resonated with me, as I had a very similar experience in Haiti as Merton had in a visit to Harlem in 1964. On June 16 of that trip to the very poor Black section of New York City, the monk in the hood wrote:

> The noise of traffic and uninterrupted cries of children playing, crises of life and joy coming out of purgatory, loud and strong the voice of a great living organism. Shots too—and there is no rifle range. Frequent shots—at what? More frequent than in the woods behind the hermitage in hunting season. And drums, bongos, and the chanting of songs, and dogs barking and traffic, buses like jet planes. Above all the morning light, then the afternoon light, and the flashing windows of the big new developments.[11]

So many phrases hit home for me: "uninterrupted cries of children playing" is part of my daily reality. I would substitute "screams" for "cries." It is hard for most of my friends and family in the States to comprehend just how much noise five dozen kids can make.

". . . cries of life and joy coming out of purgatory." Purgatory is a place of purging. Most of my kids came not from purgatory but from the pit of hell that is the massive, violent slum of Cité Soleil. One of our kids, a four-year-old boy, went back to Cité Soleil to visit his mom and he was shot in the arm. It takes years to purge the kids from the horrible life lessons they learned in the slum. Many of our kids still want to pick through our garbage, still want to store leftover food under their beds, still want to use profane language, and still want to punch or slap rather than settle differences in a nonviolent, peaceful manner. It takes time to teach them to use a toilet, as they never had one. They come garden trained, not toilet trained. One girl was nine years old when she was brought to us, and she already had many sexual partners.

". . . loud strong voice of a great living organism." The choice of the word "great" to describe the living organism of the playing children is wonderful. Many if not most of our adult staff at Santa Chiara Children's Center have been so beaten down by poverty and oppression that they seem lifeless and demoralized. I find hope in the unbounded energy of the kids and their full embrace of life.

"Shots too—and there is no rifle range. Frequent shots—at what?" Oh my, does this ring true in my experience in Haiti. I hear gunfire most nights. It is the sound of anguish.

In October 2020, I was within a hundred feet of gunfire on the street on two occasions. It was horrifying. One was a gun battle between police and protestors just outside a hospital I had just entered with a sick child. Not knowing where the gunfire came from, I dropped to the floor as people ran screaming in all directions. The second was outside a store I was about to enter. A man was fatally shot. I saw his lifeless body on the street. Scary stuff.

"And drums, bongos, and the chanting of songs, and dogs barking and traffic, buses like jet planes." Yikes, that's the soundtrack of my life in Haiti. There are packs of wild dogs that go crazy at night, barking ceaselessly, chasing phantoms. It took me over a year before the nonstop barking kept me from falling asleep. Mix in the early morning loud sounds generated by chickens and goats. I had no idea goats made such annoying noises. If you want to experience loud music, come to a slum in Haiti. Friday and Saturday nights the loud music goes on until nearly dawn. There are occasional festivals when the neighborhood people rent speakers the size of a Buick. There is no hope of sleeping on those nights.

Finally: "Above all the morning light, then the afternoon light, and the flashing windows of the big new developments." In this last sentence we see the mystic's gift of insightful seeing on full display. Merton looks upon the ugly, tall, prison-like housing projects and sees the beauty of the sunlight bouncing off the windows of the cramped apartments. To see beauty in everything, even commonplace things, is a gift of grace. I often gaze out my second-floor office/living room window and see the beauty of the distant mountain range. In this master "wide shot," Port-au-Prince seems tranquil, harmonious, and inviting. But zoom down into the streets, you see in close-up the misery, pain, and violence of a city in chaos. Yet when I drive around the city and come face to face with the struggle and suffering, I also see the inner beauty of the people who persevere and still manage to smile. In their endless struggle for survival, for finding their daily bread, they are grateful for the extraordinary gift of life, even a ridiculously hard, even tortured, life of overwhelming want. Sadly, many of us have lost the ability to see the true beauty of life.

Merton had his famous "4th and Walnut" epiphany. Most of the streets in Haiti have no signposts, so I never know the name of the street I'm on. But on many of the nameless streets, I'm touched by a deep awareness of God and how that awareness must be made visible by my own personal acts of mercy and compassion. Sometimes that means simply wiping a tear from the face of a child or embracing a crying child. It means paying the rent of a pregnant woman who was about to be evicted from her shack of a home, a home without indoor plumbing or running water, so she is not evicted and homeless when she gives birth to another child of God. If you want to grow in mercy and compassion, go to a place where suffering and struggle are a daily reality.

I don't know how many days Merton was in the three-square mile Black ghetto of Harlem, probably not more than a few days. As I pen these words in December 2020, I've been in Haiti for nearly six years. It's taken that long to really appreciate, understand, and live Merton's truth about racial healing, justice, and restoration.

Merton was an early theological voice speaking out against the injustice of segregation. He read and communicated with Black writers such as James Baldwin, who knew that white liberals lacked any perception of black peoples' lives. Baldwin wrote: "They could deal with a Negro as a symbol or a victim, but had no sense of him as a man."[12] In Haiti, I came to know, understand, respect, and love many Black people as people, as friends. This has made a huge difference in my life in terms of the Black Lives Matter movement and Trump's broadening the racial divide and sparking racial tensions and violence. I came to see firsthand the intelligence, creativity, spirituality, and beauty within the Black community. In his "Letter to a White Liberal," Merton urged, "the white man understand his sin [of racism], repent of it, and atone for it." Amen.

In *Passion for Peace: The Social Essays*, edited by William H. Shannon, Merton writes:

> The Negro children of Birmingham, who walked calmly up to the police dogs that lunged at them with a fury capable of tearing their small bodies to pieces, were not only confronting the truth in an exalted moment of faith, a providential Kairos. They were also in their simplicity, bearing heroic Christian witness to the truth, for they were exposing their bodies to death in order to show God and man that they believed in the just rights of their people, knew that those rights had been unjustly, shamefully and systematically violated, and realized that the violation called for expiation and redemptive protest, because it was an offense against God and His truth. They were stating clearly that the time had come where such violations could no longer be tolerated. These Negro followers of Dr. King are convinced that there is more at stake than civil rights. They believe the survival of America is itself in question. . . . [They] are not simply judging the white man and rejecting him. On the contrary, they are seeking by Christian love and sacrifice to redeem him, to enlighten him, so as . . . to awaken his mind and his conscience, and stir him to initiate the reform and renewal which may still be capable of saving our society.[13]

That was written in the 1960s. Some sixty years later, the time is more than ripe to initiate the reforms and renewal needed to bring about true racial justice.

I clearly remember what prompted my slow, long slide from the Catholic faith of my youth. As a teenager, I'd attend Mass on Sunday and heard about God's love and mercy and then afterward heard on the streets of my white neighborhood in the Queens section of New York City how the "niggers" (forgive me for using such a horrible, ugly word) had crossed 103rd Avenue and would soon be invading 97th Avenue where we lived. The message was clear: once the Blacks infiltrated our block, the property values would quickly decline. I saw no evidence of God in people's lives. I heard lots of hate-filled words as my little corner of New York City became racially integrated. In my twenties, I slowly lost my faith and quietly slipped into an unsettled atheism. It would take about thirty years to reembrace my Christian faith after an epiphany in an empty church in Rome. But twenty-five years later, I'm still struggling with the challenge of becoming more Christ-like. There are days, I'm more like Judas.

Over the years, I learned that Christ-like transformation isn't concerned with acquiring more but in letting go of more and becoming more present to those with less. Merton felt that materialism and fear sparked by mass consumption played a vital role in white racism. In *Seeds of Destruction,* he stated, "Our trouble is that we are alienated from our own personal reality, our true self. We do not believe in anything but money and the power of enjoyment which comes from the possession of money."[14]

The pandemic has made us all poorer and kept us apart. Having caused the deaths of 377,014 Americans by January 12, 2021 (and over a million by January 2022), the virus has also intensified our awareness of our innate vulnerability and the ever-present threat of death from an accident or illness. While Covid-19 does present a legitimate threat to our lives, even if the risk of dying from it is low, the pandemic should cause us to realize we don't want to live a senseless life. We should be desiring to live a life that is stretched out toward an ever-greater awareness of the common good, the realization of the unity of all life. The welfare of one is bound up with the welfare of all. We are all responsible for each other, bound closely together for good or ill by the choices we make, even when no one is watching us or when we are doing something that seems insignificant. The pandemic ordeal the entire would is enduring could make us harsher or more sensitive to the suffering of others, more indifferent or more compassionate. If more and more Christians breathe in the love of Christ and embrace the risen body of Christ, we'll experience a surge in compassion and mercy.

God's message begins and ends with gracious mercy. God's "No" to sin is always in service of the divine "Yes" to a relationship with humanity and all of Creation.

Just to be clear, I don't believe my ministry to abandoned kids in Haiti will save my soul. Only God can do that. While the spiritual discipline required to live in a deeply impoverished area of Port-au-Prince is personally very beneficial, it doesn't make God love me any more than he/she already does. God loves us no matter what we do or don't do. However, if we do right and express true sorrow when we do wrong, we can live and die in peace, trusting fully in God's extravagant, unwarranted mercy. I pray:

> *You alone, my God, are faithful to Your promises. I know You are with me, walking beside me, and I have no reason to fear or doubt . . . but I am weak and need Your strong arm. I appeal to Your gentleness, O God of mercy. I seek Your divine help, O God of compassion. I cling to Your faithfulness, O God of endless love.*
>
> *O Lord, help me to renew my innermost being. I stumble and fall often. My many failures disappoint me. But You never treat me as I deserve. You close your eyes to my faults. I trust in Your endless mercy and compassion. But I*

need Your help to truly purify my deepest being, to create there a more suitable chamber for Your spirit to reside.

The best way you can show your love of God is to be merciful to others. Every act of mercy and kindness brings us closer to the reality of God. Growing closer to God is our real job in life. We need to open our eyes and see the many blessings God has given us and then we must share them freely with others. Don't be afraid of enjoying the full freedom of giving your life away. In *New Seeds of Contemplation*, Thomas Merton reminds us: "We do not detach ourselves from things in order to attach ourselves to God, but rather we become detached from ourselves in order to see and use all things in and for God."[15]

Merton's compassion was bred in solitude. Mine was bred in slums around the world. From his hermitage, Merton reached out to the world, to people of all faiths, people of no faith, and all people on the peripheries of life, all people suffering from injustice. From my brief time of solitude in my Florida hideout each month, I try to minister to my own inner poverty.

> *"There is not much use talking to men about God if they are not able*
> *to listen. The ears with which one hears the message of the Gospel*
> *are hidden in man's heart, and these ears do not hear anything unless*
> *they are favored with a certain interior solitude and silence."*
>
> —THOMAS MERTON, CHOOSING TO LOVE THE WORLD[16]

—Gerry Straub
Port-au-Prince, Haiti, December 10, 2021
The 53rd anniversary of the death
of Thomas Merton in Bangkok

Living in a War Zone

As I was writing this book, the violence and chaos that is part of the fabric of life in Haiti weighed heavily on my mind and occasionally found its way into the pages of the book. But literally just as the book was about to move from the hands of the editor and into the hands of the book designer, the level of insane violence began to dominate all facets of life in Haiti. Many Haitians fleeing the violence died at sea when their rickety, old, overcrowded boats sank during the desperate voyage to Florida. In the first six months of 2022, the United Nations Human Rights office in Haiti documented 934 killings, 684 injuries, and 680 kidnappings across the city of Port au Prince, the capital of Haiti. As gangs took over poor neighborhoods and blocked the roads that connect the capital city with the rest of the country, it became impossible to know how many are being killed across the country. According to the UN office in the capital, 234 more were killed just in the Port au Prince neighborhood of Cité Soleil between July 8, 2022, and July 12, 2022. Most of the kids living in my orphanage came from Cité Soleil, which is the largest, most violent slum in Haiti.

Since the assassination of the President—in his own bed—in July 2021, Haiti has been in a long, slow slide into anarchy. Protestors set fire to a wall of tires at key intersections of Port-au-Prince, stifling all movement and commerce. Businesses were burned to the ground. The inept and corrupt government had no response to the ongoing chaos. In the vacuum of power, heavily armed gangs ruled the country. They blocked the roads from the port, thereby cutting off the supply of fuel, food, and goods. There was a severe gas shortage. The price of virtually everything skyrocketed. The poor were being choked to death.

Most of the poor had no steady supply of electricity, no running water, no indoor plumbing or toilets. Mountains of rotting garbage were rising throughout the city; people burning garbage added to the noxious pollution. In the largest slum in the city, rats outnumber people. Even before the president was brutally killed, many people lived in poorly constructed shacks with porous roofs and dirt floors; when it rained, the floor became a bed of mud. I could not imagine surviving in such harsh conditions. By the spring and early summer of 2022, Haiti had become a living nightmare. Each day was a struggle for survival. By August 2022, Haiti was in extreme turmoil. The escalating gang violence, which included barbaric beheadings and burning people alive, had gripped the profoundly impoverished nation in crippling fear. In the previous two months, nearly 200 people had been kidnapped in Port-au-Prince. People were afraid to leave their homes. Shacks in Cité Soleil were burned to the ground, forcing thousands to flee. Pope Francis said at the time, "I fear that it [Haiti] is falling into a pit of despair."

How we managed to create a safe place of peace and kindness amidst such barbarity is nothing short of a miracle. I cry for Haiti. I cry for my kids, especially the older girls who will one day in the not-too-distant future venture out of Santa Chiara. No one can prepare them for the reality beyond our walls.

On August 22, 2022, I was in Florida for a week. I was consumed with reviewing the edited manuscript that the book's editor had sent to me. I had spent two long days, from well before sunrise until deep into the night working on her revisions and corrections, and I was not even halfway through the book. At 8:30 in the morning, I received a phone call from Haiti giving me some horrific news. Two days earlier, on a Saturday, a mother and her two older teenage daughters were driving to an Adventist church when their car was surrounded by gang members. They shot the three women and then set their car on fire, cremating the remains of their innocent victims. Normally, the father would have been in the car. He is alive because he wasn't in the car. Later in the day, in the same area, three more people walking on the street were shot to death.

This easily could have been me. I often drive to a store in the area. It is not too far from Aristide's home. The point is that anything can happen to any of us when we leave the Santa Chiara Children's Center. I had a hard time returning to my review of the corrected manuscript. After looking at the photo of the family who did not deserve such a brutal fate, I could not begin to comprehend the grief and torment of the father who lost everything in one act of extreme madness. I'm sure he wishes he had been with his wife and daughters, because without them he is surely lost.

Clearly, the police, the military, the government are all impotent when it comes to stopping the madness of the gangs controlling the city and deciding who lives and who dies. The living are slowly being choked to death by high prices and food and fuel shortages that are a direct result of the unchecked violence.

I called the editor to discuss the changes. I mentioned to her that I felt as if I needed to add something about the increased level of violence over the past six months even though the book already contained information about the assassination of the president that had touched off a wave of violent protests. But this new outbreak of extreme barbaric violence was so far off the charts that it was pushing Haiti dangerously close to a state of complete anarchy.

Just days before I returned to Florida for a week of air-conditioning and hot water, I encountered this news headline: "52 Haitian Women Were Victims of Gang Rape in Cité Soleil." I shared the details of the news report with the editor. The National Network for the Defense of Human Rights presented a report with testimonies from fifty-two women who were victims of gang rape. It indicated that more than twenty women were raped in the presence of their children, another in the presence of her parents, and two in front of their spouses. Six women witnessed the execution of their husbands before being raped, and four were abused while pregnant. One of the victims was a fourteen-year-old adolescent.

I realize all this is very hard to read, but I felt I had to mention the depth of the barbarity at the top of the book as a frame of reference for what follows. Reading Merton in Haiti was very different than reading the monk in the peaceful tranquility of my home in America. My cherished and often fanciful ideas about God got blown to bits in the hell of Haiti, where there is no Mertonesque stillness and silence.

PART ONE

Entering into Silence & Solitude

Merton's Hermitage, December 2000;
Photo by Gerry Straub

CHAPTER 1

Wounded with the Wounded

A Tale from Two Radically Different Cities

I live on a picturesque, sparsely populated island off the coast of Fort Pierce, Florida. I live on the island during the one week a month I'm in America. During the other three weeks, I live in a place that is the absolute opposite of the tranquility and beauty of the island. In Florida, my neighbors are pelicans. In stark contrast, my other home is in a nation paralyzed by a pandemic of poverty and violence and ruled by a government awash in corruption and where the elite of society finance brutal roving gangs that put a chokehold on daily life.

That second home is in a deeply impoverished section of Port-au-Prince, Haiti, where I run a home for about fifty abandoned kids, a dozen of whom are still in diapers, called the Santa Chiara Children's Center, which opened in May 2015. Some of our kids have spent their entire lives inside the walls of Santa Chiara. One child was a day-old when his mother left him on a garbage dump where someone found him and brought him to us. His name is Peter Francis Straub. He turned four in January 2022. Crying babies, screaming kids, and loud gunfire are the soundtrack of my life in Haiti. Burning rubbish contributes to the dreadful, choking pollution.

The heart-wrenching story of another child who was abandoned virtually minutes after his birth became the two lead paragraphs of a story about me and Santa Chiara titled "An Unscripted Life" written by Joe Heil, which was published in *Notre Dame Magazine* in their Spring 2022 issue:

> Moïse Straub, two weeks old, arrived at the front gate of Santa Chiara Children's Center in Port-au-Prince, Haiti, on the Ides of March, 2021. He was cradled in the arms of a woman who was not his mother. The real mother, after giving birth in the notorious slum of Cité Soleil, gave Moïse to a stranger. Blood and fluid still covered the newborn. The distressed, teenage mother had begged the woman to tend the infant until she returned. She never did.
>
> There was some reluctance among Santa Chiara's staff to accept the child. Nevertheless, the founder, Gerard Thomas Straub, decided to keep the baby boy, even though Santa Chiara's primary mission is caring for and educating girls. To

turn Moïse away would send him to certain death in one of the world's most impoverished, dangerous, filthy and degrading slums. Straub named the child, giving him his own surname and filing to adopt him. Moïse, Haitian Creole for Moses, thus joined five other abandoned children also named Straub.

In Haiti, my neighbors don't have electricity or running water or even a toilet. They live in fear of being kidnapped or robbed. I know people in Haiti who have been killed or wounded by gun violence. One was a doctor who was shot to death minutes after withdrawing money from a bank. I know people who have been robbed at gunpoint. I was thrown to the ground during a robbery. I know a woman who was pregnant when she took a motorcycle taxi and the driver turned down an isolated road, stripped her of her clothing, and beat her.

My life has been threatened a few times. My car was once surround by protestors, one of whom held high a jug of gasoline, threatening to pour it on my car and set it on fire—with me and an eight-year-old girl inside. It was beyond frightening. I thought my life was going to end in a horrific fashion. I pleaded with them to let the girl go. Mercifully, they let us drive away. On another occasion, a mob of protestors threw rocks at my car, forcing me to back up at a high speed to escape injury. I once drove through a barricade of burning tires to get to a hospital, where I had a MRSA infection the size of a golf ball lanced without anesthesia. Before cutting me, the doctor simply said they had no anesthesia. The pain was so bad two medical assistants had to hold me down. I've seen how a simple infection becomes a death sentence or a loss of limb due to the woefully inadequate public hospitals. The tragedy of Haiti is that the poor experience so much deprivation that they are left with no support to defend themselves or create a better life for themselves, and so some desperate people, sadly, resort to violence as a means of survival.

In Florida, I experience the beauty of nature. In Haiti, I experience some of the worst of human nature. Yet in Haiti, I also see more clearly the beauty of all life and the healing balm of mercy and compassion. I need to be in both places . . . just more time in Haiti. Haiti is a crucible for transformation.

Before entering the bloated belly of poverty, my center of gravity was New York City and Los Angeles, the two centers of television production. I was a network television producer whose credits include three popular soap operas; a few actors who worked for me became major movie stars, including Alec Baldwin. I left that world to eventually devote myself to filming poverty around the world. While making over twenty feature-length documentary films, I visited some of the worst slums in India, Kenya, Uganda, Brazil, Peru, Honduras, El Salvador, Mexico, Jamaica, and the Philippines. I also filmed the homeless in Los Angeles, Detroit, San Francisco, and Budapest, Hungary. As I traveled to all those distant, horrific slums and especially during my life in Haiti since 2015, the common thread was reading Thomas Merton. The Trappist monk has had a tremendous impact on my life and how I live it.

Pope Francis said, "Only those not ashamed to touch the wounded flesh of those on the margins will be admitted to God's kingdom."[17] I'm not so sure about that. However, to truly follow Christ, I knew I personally needed to go where there was brokenness and profound need. I had to be with the hungry and the hurting. I had to be with the weak and the vulnerable. I had to be with the powerless, the lost, and the lonely. I had to be with the outcast, the abandoned, and the refugee. I had to embrace the leper and walk with the homeless. I had to be with people struggling with mental and physical limitations, to be with the "wounded flesh." I had to be where Christ would be: on the periphery of society and far from the centers of power and money.

To follow Christ more closely, I felt I personally had to be wounded with the wounded. I had to turn my back on the life I had lived in Hollywood and enter the tormented world of excruciating poverty—and film what I had witnessed in dozens of slums around the world.

Eventually, I had to be in Haiti, living among people who live in shacks without indoor plumbing, among people who live with rats and festering piles of rotting garbage, among people who dress in rags. I had to be in a place where many kids never make it to their fifth birthday, dead from curable illnesses . . . or a bullet. I had to be with people who endure breathing in the toxic smoke from burning garbage and the stench of open sewers. I had to be among people who live in fear of gang violence. I slowly learned that Haiti was a land of dirt and blood, a land of tears and agony, a land of broken families and abandoned kids, a land of monstrous, barbaric cruelty and violence. Haiti is a land of deep despair and debilitating hopelessness.

Haiti is the personification of an unscripted life. The "script" we had planned for most days is often tossed before the sun gets very high in the sky. Emergencies are so frequent they become commonplace. Every day is an exercise in crisis management.

I knew my personal salvation was intrinsically tied to trying to emulate Christ's self-emptying love, that I had to become a candle of hope, the embodiment of mercy and compassion. I'm still working on that. Some days, I succeed a little. Most days, I fail. On those days when I fall short, I bow my head in prayer, forgive myself, and keep walking down poverty road, trusting that God will see the good intention in my heart and generously shower me with the graces needed to radically trust the spark of divinity within me in order to truly see and embrace my own weakness and vulnerability and totally depend upon God for everything.

Love in the Time of Coronavirus

I never read *Love in the Time of Cholera*, the famous novel written by Nobel Prize–winning Colombian author Gabriel García Márquez. I have the book. Someone sent it to me when I was filming in Haiti after the 2010 earthquake when a cholera outbreak took the lives of thousands of mostly poor Haitians. It occurred to me I could've titled this book *Love in the Time of Coronavirus*, as I was writing it when the deadly pandemic was gripping the world in fear, killing more than 70,000 Americans by May 6, 2020. By mid-November, the pandemic had reemerged with a vengeance. On December 3, 2020, 2,802 people died. That is one person every thirty seconds. But it kept getting worse. On January 7, 2021, 4,110 Americans died. Living in an atmosphere of widespread fear, panic, and confusion taught me about love and what it really means.

The following comes from the March 22, 2020, edition of my *Haiti 2020 Journal*, which was sent to 178 of my supporters and donors of the Santa Chiara Children's Center in Port-au-Prince. The names you'll encounter in this entry are all children or staff members of our home for sixty-one abandoned kids (at that time), including one boy and four girls who were given my last name (to go with the first names I gave them) because they were unnamed infants when they were brought to me.

Before the Haitian government decided to close the airport in Port-au-Prince, I'd decided not to travel to Florida. My decision doesn't mean I'm a heroic person. I'm mostly a frightened wimp. While I did think going to Florida would increase my chances of contracting the virus before I cleared customs in Ft. Lauderdale that isn't the reason I elected to stay in Haiti. The last place you want to be when you are sick is Haiti. The simple, unvarnished truth is that I couldn't leave Bency Clare, Peter Francis, Clare Marie, Naïve, Teresa Regina, Judline, Baby Ruth, Izzy, Ally, Jinette, Naïca, Walencia, Vanderson, Isidore, Orlane, Carla, and the dozen or more kids who have lived at Santa Chiara for at least five years, kids like Adele whom I've known and supported since the day of her birth. She still radiates when she sees me.

I couldn't sit in a comfortable apartment on an isolated and beautiful island off the coast of Ft. Pierce, Florida, and not be concerned about all of the Santa Chiara staff, especially Nurse Rose and all those staff members who have been with me since the very beginning back in May 2015. I'd deeply miss the children, especially Peter and Clare. My heart simply would not let me leave.

What is this thing we call love? Perhaps in this time of global crisis where many Americans are forced to stay at home we can think less about fear and worry and more about entering more fully into the saving grace of love. I can't begin to estimate the number of times in the last 20 years that I've used the term "self-emptying" love in my books, films, and public speaking events. I understood the term and its importance. But did I really live it? Not so much. Was there someone, anyone, I would give my life for in order to protect them?

The suffering God is everybody.

Yesterday morning, I stood like a still point in the midst of swirling chaos. Kids were tugging at me, hugging me, kissing me, holding my hand. Social distancing wasn't possible. Some said, "Apples," others said, "Cookies." One little girl said, "Fromage" (cheese). The place was abuzz with activities. On Saturday morning there was a deep cleaning. All the furniture from the first floor, including the three refrigerators and all the beds and cribs were moved outside. The guys, most of whom were wearing masks, were scrubbing the floors and walls with a strong disinfectant. Mackenson was wielding his power spray gun that dislodged layers of dirt. I simply stood silent, almost motionless, taking it all in. It was life in all its beauty and complexity. Ally said Isidore hurt her arm. Isidore denied it. Isidore said Jinette stole two of his toy cars. Jinette denied the crime, even though the two cars were on her bed. I spoke simply and softly telling Jinette to give the cars back to Isidore.

I'm learning that the contemplative life doesn't require me to live in a monastery. St. Francis saw the world as his cloister. Merton believed the monastery wasn't an escape from the world. He wrote: "On the contrary by being in a monastery I take my part in all the struggles of the world."[18] In the midst of virtual nonstop activity at Santa Chiara, it is imperative for me to carve out a few hours for stillness and silence. Perhaps this time of "staying home" for many Americans will give them time to look more deeply inside themselves and find the true richness of life that comes from the supreme richness of God planted in all of us.

Now that a week away from Haiti will not be possible for the foreseeable future, I'm going to try to create more alone space on the second floor during the day so I might concentrate on my writing . . . which will go a long way to relieving the stress of caring for so many kids and adults.

Merton wrote: "Our job is to love others without stopping to inquire whether or not they are worthy. That is not our business. What we are asked to do is to love and this will render both ourselves and our neighbors worthy, if anything can."[19] I've had to put this into practice in Haiti. It wasn't easy. I failed often. I've become angry at the very people I've wanted to help.

In unpublished notes for a conference Merton had prepared for his monastic novices on "prayer," he urged them to meditate by entering "the school of their lives," to meditate upon the events of their lives as a "school of wisdom" in which they were being taught to become their truest selves. As I worked on this manuscript, over a period of many years, it slowly dawned on me that as I wrote about Merton's prayer life, I was simultaneously entering the school of my own life, and becoming, with Jonathan's sure-handed guidance, one of Merton's novices seeking to advance in the "school of wisdom."

A Medieval Saint and a Modern Monk

*"Our real journey in life is interior: it is a matter
of growth, deepening and an ever greater surrender
to the creative action of love and grace in our hearts."*

—Thomas Merton, *The Asian Journal of Thomas Merton*[20]

For as long as I can recall, I've been searching for God. On a few occasions, I thought I was getting close . . . then, in a flash, I was back to thinking there is no God. Through the ups and downs of my faith, and even through the dry, barren years of claiming to be an atheist, Thomas Merton, the eloquent monk who longed for solitude even though he had friends of all faiths from all over the world, somehow managed to speak to me, no matter my confused state of mind or lack of faith.

Even though I was part of the Hollywood film and television industry that manufactures dreams and illusions, I longed to visit a rural, wooded part of Kentucky and spend time in a monastery that is steeped in stillness and silence, a place where one very unique monk made solitude a virtue. Metaphorically speaking, you can't get much further from loud and louche Hollywood than in a tranquil and unadorned monastery in Kentucky.

Thomas Merton is, more than likely, the most famous Christian monk of the last hundred years, which I suppose is something he both liked and loathed. After all his writing, all his years as a monk, all his vast expenditure of energy on a wide range of actions on behalf of peace, civil rights, social justice, and interfaith dialogue, Merton realized that none of it brought him his own interior peace.

I was—and still am—thirsting for what Merton found in the woods of the Abbey of Our Lady of Gethsemani in the bucolic rolling hills of Kentucky. The Sufi mystic Rumi said: "I have a thirsty fish in me that can never find enough of what it's thirsty for!" I feel as if I have a school of fish within me . . . and they are all lousy students.

I needed a place to kneel in silence.

I first walked the grounds of Gethsemani Abbey twenty-two years ago. In 2000, I made three trips to the monastery: In May, I was given permission to photograph Merton's hermitage for a few hours. In August, I spent a weekend in the monastery. Having finished writing *The Sun & Moon Over Assisi*, I came to Gethsemani to enter more fully into the life of Thomas Merton. In December, I was graced with the rare privilege of spending a week alone in Merton's hermitage. I didn't enter the hermitage to encounter Merton. I entered it, as Merton did, to encounter God.

During that amazing week living in Merton's hermitage, I did what he did: I kept a detailed journal of my time there. On the surface, I was filled with a pious passion for God; inwardly, it was a different story as I secretly clung to my old, far-less-than-godly ways. My

Hollywood showbiz life made ungodly things easily attainable. While I was no Harvey Weinstein, my behavior often was far from angelic. In my hermitage journal I wrote: "Oh sweet Lord, I pray for the grace to empty myself of all that is only me so that I may be filled with what is only You." While I truly meant those words, they remained merely words as I rushed off after years of self-imposed solitude to slums around the world thinking I needed to do good in order to be good. Meanwhile, in God's eyes, no matter how ungodly my behavior occasionally was, I was good. It is extremely hard to admit, but the same is true for Harvey as he sits in prison for his multiple misguided misdeeds.

From 2000 to 2014, I spent a great deal of time filming in some of the worst slums on earth. In 2010, during the aftermath of the earthquake, I even briefly lived in a dreadful slum in Haiti. My small cinder block home in the midst of the crippling poverty of postapocalyptic Port-au-Prince was far removed from the small cinder block hermitage, surrounded by a luxuriant forest, which was once occupied by Thomas Merton.

Thomas Merton saw the spiritual journey as a metaphorical "going forth into strange countries." For Merton, even going nowhere required travel. Day by day, our entire lives are a journey, a journey to nowhere, a journey to God. I've been around the world, traveled to many "strange countries" in order to get nowhere, in order to arrive at an empty place within me where, according to Merton, the fullness of life is hidden. Some days, that is hard to believe. I guess that's where faith comes in.

My spiritual journey has been influenced by two towering figures, one a medieval saint, the other a modern monk—Saint Francis of Assisi and Thomas Merton. Both were flawed men whose greatness increased with their own recognition of their personal flaws and realizing their ultimate dependency upon God.

Twenty-five years ago, after I had a dramatic conversion experience in an empty Franciscan church in Rome, Saint Francis became my spiritual guide. Day after day, the medieval saint showed a modern skeptic how to enter the heart of God. The walled, hillside town of Assisi became my spiritual home and opened the mystical windows of my soul. In those early and often lonely days of reconnecting to my Catholic faith, Merton was my main companion and inspiration. For me, Francis and Merton were brothers . . . my brothers.

Following Saint Francis led me to the worst slums on earth, and I always brought Thomas Merton with me. I carried books by or about Merton into the massive slums and refugee camps of Uganda and Kenya crammed with kids with bloated bellies on the verge of death from malnutrition, into a leper colony in Brazil housing hundreds of people with mutilated faces, whose arms and legs had been eaten away by a vile disease, into the dire squalor in the Philippines where people lived on a mountain of garbage, scavenging like vultures off the rotting waste of others, into a home for seriously ill and impoverished children in Peru, into the barrios of Mexico, El Salvador, and Honduras, into darkest corners of India and Jamaica. The horrors of the sprawling slums in those faraway places often brought me to tears. Entire families squeezed into one room without electricity or a toilet.

Naked kids being bathed in the streets with water laced with bacteria, women defecating in public. The stench of open sewers was nauseating. Seeing so much needless suffering left me with a case of post-traumatic stress disorder . . . which I still endure.

I also took Merton with me to the bleakest and most violent neighborhoods of Philadelphia, Detroit, and Los Angeles while making films on the homeless and addicted. In those cities, I witnessed an endless parade of misery, pain, rejection, and loneliness. People sleeping on the streets, in cardboard boxes, under tarps, or in small tents. Kids without shelter forced to share space with the mentally ill and drug addicts in overcrowded missions. People freezing to death while sleeping in abandoned buildings. After all the agony I witnessed and filmed during the day, I often turned to Merton at night for some comfort. Reading Merton was not an escape or distraction from the poverty and suffering I saw each day; it was a mode of communion with a man who endeavored to understand the human condition and its relationship with God. Merton helped me see my own inner poverty and the importance of compassion.

After the earthquake in Haiti that killed over 300,000 people and left well over a million people homeless, I lived for two weeks in a huge slum, the only white face in a sea of black faces; I had no running water or electricity, and I shared my humble, dirt-floored abode with rats and mice. I read Merton by candlelight at night and on crowded, dilapidated buses during the day.

Saint Francis led me to poverty. Thomas Merton led me to prayer.

Thomas Merton introduced me to a spiritual reality far bigger, far deeper, and far more profound than I ever imagined existed. He also showed me that faith can be tinged with doubt and darkness. When I first picked up a book by Merton, I was in my late twenties and dealing with a very adult crisis with a religious faith that hadn't grown beyond adolescence. My immature faith offered no guidance, no assurance, no support; what it offered was lifeless formulas, dogmatic assertions, harsh judgments, and condemnation. My childhood faith was no match for the hopeless nihilism I encountered as an adult. So, I dropped the fairytale-like faith of my youth and opted for the only alternative that made any sense: atheism. Yet even in my atheist days, when I enjoyed the sport of debunking religion and making fun of televangelists, Merton intrigued me and prompted me to look at things differently. In his journals and numerous letters, I saw a real man, not a pious, plastic saint. In him, I saw very faint echoes of myself and my daily struggles to make sense of life. Merton was my only connection to the Catholic faith into which I was born.

Somehow, I intuitively knew there was much good in the faith I had discarded, but I had no way to connect with it; nor did I see any real evidence of it in the lives of "practicing" Catholics who seemed no different or no better than the rest of our self-centered, consumer-crazed society that callously ignored the poor and easily embraced war. Jesus and the litany of saints who tried to emulate him seemed to be relics from the dustbin of history and their lives just some pious legends that had no relevance to my modern, secular, skeptical life. Still, there seemed to be something poetically beautiful in the way Christ and the saints confronted the ugly reality of life and turned human expectations and experiences upside down. I hungered for a spirituality that had the transformative power to make all things new . . . which seemed like a fairytale. Even the Church had fallen into the unholy state of denial and corruption in the wake of the many revelations of the sexual abuse of children by priests.

Over the years, Merton showed me that real satisfaction comes from giving, not taking, that real love requires real sacrifice, that thinking about or striving for success is useless, that I had to look within myself for answers to the questions that tormented me. Merton taught me the value of stillness and silence, where I could discover and accept my true self and find authentic love and deep peace. But the lesson didn't really take root, didn't sink down deeply enough within me to change my life in any significant way for a long time. It was hard for me to move past my own deep questions, my own nagging doubts and inner contradictions—and my own sin.

It wasn't until I put down my cameras in May 2015 and began living in Haiti in order to care for abandoned children that I really began to learn how to pray—and see the true beauty in all of life, even suffering. In a letter written in April 1965, Merton wrote:

> The religion of our time, to be authentic, needs to be the kind that escapes practically all religious definition. Because there has been endless definition, endless verbalizing, and words have become gods. There are so many words that one cannot get to God as long as He is thought to be on the other side of words . . . . One's whole being must be an act for which there can be found no word.[21]

I loved that. I'm not sure how, but somehow it made sense to me. All the words spoken in different religious tongues often divide us or judge us. I cannot explain why I am in Haiti. I am there because it is the place for me to move beyond words, to live the truth I felt welling up within me . . . and to go deeper into prayer.

Note: It is OK to distance yourself from spiritual spaces that are more concerned with what doctrine you believe than accepting, protecting, and loving you. It is OK to find a space to exhale.

The Long, Winding Road to Publication

Channeling my fascination with Thomas Merton into a publishable book has been a long, lonely journey. In May 2000, I had a flash of inspiration to write a book about Thomas Merton and Saint Benedict, in which the ancient and modern monks would function as my surrogate spiritual directors. My hunch was that Saint Benedict and Thomas Merton could help me satisfy my hunger for a deeper relationship with God. The idea for the book came just a week before I was about to embark on a trip to Kenya to photograph the plight of the poor. The massive Kibera slum in Nairobi was part of a yearlong project that took me to thirty-nine cities in eleven nations. All those trips into the bloated belly of severe, chronic poverty gave birth to both a photo/essay book and a short film titled *When Did I See You Hungry?*, which was narrated by Martin Sheen.

Over the course of the next fourteen years, during which I made more than twenty feature-length documentary films on poverty around the world, percolating in the back of my mind was this book on Merton and Benedict. I used all my free time to work on it. Over the years, the book had three incarnations, none of which really worked and they never reached the point of submitting them to a publisher. During that same span of time, three other books I'd written were published. They were *Thoughts of a Blind Beggar*, which consisted of a series of spiritual reflections in poetic form; *Hidden in the Rubble*, which documented the aftermath of the devastating earthquake in Haiti; and *The Loneliness and Longing of Saint Francis*, which took a deeper look at the spirituality of the saint and his love of the poor, which won a prestigious award from the Catholic Press Association. In the Fall of 2020, as I was writing this book, Paraclete Press published *The Sunrise of the Soul*, which consisted of a series of short reflections on stillness, silence, solitude, and service. Merton had a strong presence in each of those books; moreover, he was frequently quoted in my poverty films.

The three incarnations of the Merton-Benedict book ate up nearly two thousand pages. What doomed the three books was that each of them focused too much attention on the external events of not only my life, but also the troubled times in which I lived. I was trying to filter the events of my life and the events in our society that either confused or infuriated me through the prism of monastic spirituality. Each version of the book grew fatter and fatter, but they were lean on the kind of spiritual substance for which I hungered. Much of this fourth attempt was written as I rode out the trauma of the global pandemic while stranded in Haiti. I'd been in Haiti since February 29, 2020. When the coronavirus hit, I had the option to leave on one of the few evacuation flights in March. But, as I mentioned earlier, if I left, I wouldn't be allowed to return, as the Haitian government banned all flights from America. I elected to stay with my kids—and it nearly cost me my life.

In late May 2020, my world nearly came to an end. I fell perilously ill. I was in dire need of oxygen. Fortunately, friends in Haiti, the Missionaries of Charity, had a spare tank. They told my staff where they could refill it and purchase others. After a few days of fever, with the aid of a portable oxygen tank, I was taken to a hospital for tests. It was wrongly determined that I only had bronchial pneumonia. I was put on a strong antibiotic and was on oxygen around the clock for seven days. I insisted on staying at the Santa Chiara Children's Center, as hospitals in Haiti are breeding grounds for all kinds of germs, some deadly. A friend of mine in Haiti is a Passionist priest and doctor. He runs two huge hospitals for the poor, one for kids, the other for adults. He had a Covid ward with 500 beds, all filled. He was working around the clock. I spoke with him on the phone, and he said I couldn't rule out the virus. He wanted me to come to his hospital, as he feared I had Covid-19. I opted to stay at Santa Chiara, where I had plenty of oxygen and access to medical consultation. I felt safe and loved inside the walls of Santa Chiara. Thanks to the two nurses and a female doctor who worked in our medical clinic, I was visited by three internists who examined me on a regular basis.

There were some very dark moments during the illness. I thought I was going to die. The superior of the Missionaries of Charity tried to get a priest to come to give me the Last Rites. A friend was so deeply concerned about me, he arranged for a private jet to fly me to Florida. But there was no way I could fly, as I was too sick to even stand. Besides, in Florida, where there was a spike in Covid cases, I would be on my own. Mercifully, asthma medication administered through a nebulizer and the strong antibiotics began to work, and I slowly started to recover. An emergency evacuation became unnecessary. During the two weeks when I was really sick, I lost twenty-seven pounds. When fully recovered, I was able to travel commercially back to Florida on June 25, nearly four months after coming to Haiti. An antibody test in Florida revealed I actually had Covid-19. I also learned I had many of the pandemic's symptoms. Two years later, I learned that the woman doctor who treated me assumed I would die on the couch.

Now as this book is on the cusp of being published, I shake my head in a mixture of both disbelief and wonder at it taking twenty years to see the "flash of inspiration" materialize. I marvel at how I went from spending a week of solitude in Merton's hermitage to living in a crowded slum in Haiti. That quiet, isolated hermitage and the noisy chaos of Haiti are both part of the reality of my life.

A photo of me taken on May 28, 2020, while I was fighting for my life

Black Kids

This might sound strange. It was a warm August evening in the late summer 2022. I was down in the yard. I was dealing with the aftereffects of a PTSD-related panic attack. The pounding in my head had begun to subside. I just wanted to stretch my legs and hopefully catch a slight breeze after a scorching hot day. I did not want to talk with anyone or engage any of the kids. I stood silently and watched from afar the kids playing. Suddenly, I had this strange thought: *All these kids are black.* The thought snapped me to attention: *Of course, you idiot.* But the point was that I no longer see "black kids"; I only see kids. I've become blind to the color of their skin. In the normal course of the day, I never see a white face . . . unless I'm in an upscale supermarket in Pétionville, a toney slice of the deeply impoverished capital city, which is a forty-minute drive from Santa Chiara.

Black lives mattered to me long before the slogan became necessary. Still, Black lives matter no more than any other life, no matter the race, religion, or social status—nor any less than any other life. In the eyes of God, we are all equal, all equally loved. Yet we have this huge racial divide . . . and the insidious rise of White Nationalism, whose members cling to their whiteness because they have nothing else, no spiritual core, no moral core, no ethical core. They are bigots and haters, yet they claim to be Christians. Guess they never heard what Jesus taught. They back laws that are shamefully passed to make it especially hard for Blacks to vote.

Yes, my Santa Chiara kids are Black. I love them. I'm proud of them.

> *"There is only one true flight from the world; it is not an escape*
> *from conflict, anguish, and suffering, but the flight from disunity*
> *and separation, to unity and peace in the love of other men."*
>
> —THOMAS MERTON, *NEW SEEDS OF CONTEMPLATION*[22]

Merton reminds us of the importance of compassion:

> I cannot treat other men as men unless I have compassion for them. I must have at least enough compassion to realize that when they suffer they feel somewhat as I do when I suffer. And if for some reason I do not spontaneously feel this kind of sympathy for others, then it is God's will that I do what I can to learn how. I must learn to share with others their joys, their sufferings, their ideas, their needs, and their desires. I must learn to do this not only in the cases of those who are of the same class, the same profession, the same race, the same nation as myself, but when men who suffer belong to other groups, even to groups that are regarded as hostile. If I do this, I obey God. If I refuse to do it, I disobey God.[23]

Through our own relationship with God, compassion invites us to create a sanctuary of peace for another who suffers.

CHAPTER 2

Merton and Me, Wearing Pants

No Idea

"My Lord God, I have no idea where I am going." So began Merton's most famous prayer. As the prayer continues, Merton moves hopefully forward in his darkness:

> I do not see the road ahead of me. I cannot know for certain where it will end. Nor do I really know myself, and the fact that I think I am following Your will does not mean that I am actually doing so. But I believe that the desire to please You does in fact please You. And I hope that I have that desire in all that I am doing. I hope that I will never do anything apart from that desire.[24]

So many things flash before my mind as I read the words of that prayer. Up until the last few years, I had no idea of God's will for my life, but I felt whatever it was, I knew I had done many things that couldn't possibly be in harmony with God's will, countless little acts of selfishness, endless moments of unloving behavior. Mine has been a messy, imperfect life, littered with missteps and mistakes. In 2015, I felt I was supposed to be in Haiti.

Merton's prayer goes on to say that if he continues to strive to do God's will, no matter how often he fails, God will lead him down the right road, even if he knows nothing about it. Merton prays: "I will trust You always though I may seem to be lost and in the shadow of death. I will not fear, for You are ever with me, and You will never leave me to face my perils alone."[25]

I've taken great comfort from those honest words. But more than comfort, in the last few years, especially during one densely dark period of my life about ten years ago, I came to feel and know the truth of those words: I am never alone; God is always with me, no matter how dark, no matter how bad any situation is. Even so, sometimes I forget or ignore this truth.

Merton knew it was in darkness that we find the Light.

Montaldo Study Note 1

Thomas Merton's Contemplative Prayer of Waiting,
A Dialogue of His Longing to Hear God's Voice in Silence

He came into the world, like all of us, captive to a tainted ancestry of selfishness and violence inexorably etched into his own heart. Through a monastic life of prayer, he would escape the thicket of Western culture's materialism into which he was born. He would rediscover in a singular and different style a traditional, even medieval road of selflessness and nonviolence. Becoming a monk, he would become another witness for his generation of the way out of self-defeating individualism.

He possessed a critical mind. His passions were prodigal. He inordinately loved books, women, jazz, art, argument, and making his judgments heard. Yet, at twenty-three, he chose baptism as a Roman Catholic, and then, going further at the age of twenty-six to the puzzlement of friends, he became a Trappist monk. He might have become "beat," always on the road, and writing in rebellion against an American society of squares and gray suits. Once a well-heeled and swinging citizen of Manhattan, he placed himself in a subsistence farming community marked by routine, prayer, silence, and anonymity. By becoming a monk, he rebelled against his elitist perspectives to forge a character more complex than wearing a blue-jeaned playboy's mask and striking merely literary poses.

On December 10, 1941, under a canopy of cold stars, Thomas Merton arrived in rural Kentucky at the Abbey of Gethsemani and immediately loved its walls. His monastic life for twenty-seven years would be a hard therapy for the wanderlust he had inherited from his father. Staying in one limiting place and becoming a Christian philosopher and writer at prayer, he would excavate and mine another meaning for his life within the unfolding history of his times.

Through an institutionalized life of effort at spiritual exercises, he would finally learn that waiting for a salvific "word" he could never speak to himself was the essence of true prayer. In one of the last books that he had prepared for publication before his accidental death in Bangkok, Thailand, *The Climate of Monastic Prayer*, he finally defined contemplation as essentially having to wait and listen through silence:

> The true contemplative is not one who prepares his mind for a particular message that he wants or expects to hear but remains empty because he knows that he can never anticipate the words that will transform his darkness into light. He does not even anticipate a special kind of transformation. He does not demand light instead of darkness. He waits on the Word of God in silence, and, when he is 'answered,' it is not so much by a word that bursts into his silence. It is by his silence itself, suddenly, inexplicably revealing itself to him as a word of great power, full of the voice of God.[26]

Before entering a monastery, he had already practiced keeping a vigil in silence, his heart's eye concentrated on the horizon of the next moment. The next moment could reveal the presence of God's "word" for him. Waiting without projecting his own needs into the next moment became his dark form of hope. He was a monk only for two weeks in 1941 when he wrote this prayer before Midnight Mass at Christmas:

> *Your brightness is my darkness. I know nothing of You and, by myself, I cannot even imagine how to go about knowing You. If I imagine You, I am mistaken. If I understand You, I am deluded. If I am conscious and certain I know You, I am crazy. The darkness is enough.*[27]

> Darkness kept Merton waiting sober and watchful for the graces of an open doorway to a presence he could not recognize by himself. Longing for God in silence was the road he traveled to arrive and live in Wisdom's house.[28]

Merton intuited that not loving God was the primary source of our unhappiness. Loving God requires prayer. Prayer helps us to be alert to the possibilities of the hour. Most of us are stuck either in the past or the future, making the present moment lost time. We're too busy to be present—present to each other, present to the poor, present to God.

Within the monastery walls, Merton learned the art of attentiveness. The monastic stability of being rooted in one place freed Merton to delve ever more deeply by reflection and prayer into the meaning of his unfolding life in the evolving history of his times. He steadfastly honed his writing craft, which became an instrument of confession and witness in a prolific outpouring of poetry, journals, letters, and books on a wide range of interests, everything from civil rights and war to Zen Buddhism. From his perch in a rural forest of Kentucky, Merton explored a galaxy of ideas in an effort to become a better, more God-like, human being. In the darkness of humanity, he discovered the Light of God.

Merton learned how to sit in the darkness. The darkness scares us. Religious terrorism, which threatens us today, might disappear if the fundamentalists of all faiths, those willing to kill for "their" God, had the inner honesty to pray that prayer Merton penned long ago. In honestly communicating the darkness that became his rite of passage into God's presence, Merton gave countless readers over the last sixty years a great gift. He freely admitted the complexity and the paradoxes of his own life. In his book *Contemplation in a World of Action*, Merton confessed he was "a self-questioning human person who struggles to cope with the turbulent, mysterious, demanding, exciting, frustrating, confused existence."[29] That was comforting for me to learn. Merton saw the contemplative life as a life of relationships informed by love in search of freedom. Down through the ages, mystics of all faiths understood that silence is the place where time and eternity embrace.

Like us, Merton had no idea where he was going on his journey to God. Unlike most of us, he simply followed where he thought God was leading him, trusting that if he was mistaken, God would gently give him a course correction . . . and all would be well in the end, no matter where he ended up. Merton didn't just see things; he saw God in everything.

> *It does not matter where I am going*
> *if I am not going to God.*

A Prayer at Santa Sabina

For Thomas Merton, it was a very long journey to reach the point where he could see God in everything. That journey began, in earnest, with a few halting steps inside a huge, centuries-old basilica in Rome many years before the idea of becoming a monk even entered his consciousness. During one of my trips to Rome, I made a concerted effort to visit that very same basilica where Merton once prayed.

In an attempt to recover from the post-traumatic stress disorder that plagued me after filming intense suffering in Uganda, I made a month-long pilgrimage to Assisi and all the places in Italy that were important in the life of Saint Francis. The trip began in Rome in 2008. The following comes from a diary I kept during the journey:

> Today I'm making a little side pilgrimage to the Basilica of Santa Sabina. In the silence of the ancient church a great modern spiritual writer quietly began his inner journey to God.
>
> In his autobiography, *The Seven Storey Mountain,* Thomas Merton vividly described the impact of his stay in Rome in 1933. The future monk and world-famous author was only 18 years old when he visited Rome, and, as he would later write, at the time he believed "in nothing." It was not the usual tourist sites that moved him. He found much of the city's ancient statuary and monuments "vapid and boring" and was equally unimpressed with the art and ecclesiastical monuments of the Renaissance and Counter-Reformation. What truly astonished him were the city's most ancient churches, in which so much of the iconography of Christianity's first millennium was still to be seen. "I was fascinated by these Byzantine mosaics," he wrote. "I began to haunt the churches where they were to be found, and without knowing anything about it, I became a pilgrim."[30] Eager to understand the iconography of the mosaics, Merton purchased a Bible. He wrote: "I read more and more of the Gospels, and my love for the old churches and their mosaics grew from day to day."[31] Without fully realizing it, Merton was on the road to a genuine encounter with God.
>
> On one memorable day, Merton climbed the Aventine Hill to visit Santa Sabina, one of Rome's oldest and least modified churches. He decided it was time

to pray and to do so on his knees, yet prayer in a public place was intensely embarrassing. Merton later would write, "That day in Santa Sabina, although the church was almost empty, I walked across the stone floor mortally afraid that a poor devout old Italian woman was following me with suspicious eyes."[32] Despite his self-consciousness, he managed to cross himself with blessed water as he entered the church and then, kneeling at the communion rail, recited the Our Father over and over again.

Thomas Merton loved St. Francis. In fact, he almost became a Franciscan friar before he entered a Trappist monastery in Kentucky. Tomorrow I leave for Assisi. Today is a day to pray where Merton prayed, to pray that my pilgrimage brings me closer to the heart of God.

Absent or Present

God never seems to be where I expect God to be. I want God to lead me where I want to go. We seem content to be near God but have no genuine interest in being with God because that would mean changing everything. When I really examine my life, I see clearly how God is absent during long stretches of my day. If that is the case, and it surely is, then how can I say I am following God. (Of course, God is never absent, but God's presence amounts to absence if we elect not to be open to it. God never forcefully intrudes on our freedom to accept or reject God's presence.) I guess there is a reason Paul instructs us to pray always. To be a true contemplative is to learn how to be praying while doing other stuff, to continually strive to be in the presence of God. To be absent from God is to be near death. Often our prayers seem to go unheard or unanswered. Sometimes things go so horribly wrong in our lives that we truly feel as if God is not only absent, but that God has actually abandoned us. In 2010, during a very dark time in my life, that is exactly how I felt.

A decade later with the surge of Covid-19, the entire world was in a dark, frightening, isolated time, yet I didn't feel fearful or alone even as I sat sequestered in Haiti surrounded by five dozen squirming kids who depend upon me and who didn't understand social distancing—they just wanted hugs and kisses.

Brother Corona

There is a Franciscan priest who is a highly regarded writer and poet. He is the author of many books on Franciscan spirituality. One of his books was instrumental in helping me fall in love with the mendicant little brother who, back in the thirteenth century, took Lady Poverty as his bride. I spent long stretches of time with the priest on three different monthlong pilgrimages to all the places in Italy that Saint Francis loved. The friar's gentle, poetic being radiated with the spirit of Saint Francis. He is a friend who holds a special place in my heart. His name is Murray Bodo. A mutual friend of ours told me that Fr.

Murray called the coronavirus Brother Corona. That sounded so absurd, I said that for me Brother Corona was a Mexican beer. But within seconds, I realized the Franciscan truth in giving the deadly virus that had spread fear and death all around the world such a familiar and friendly name.

For Saint Francis, all of creation was his brother or sister. In his exquisite *Canticle of Creation*, which was the saint's poetic summation of his spirituality, written near the end of his life when he was exhausted by fasting and illness and was completely blind, he cried out to the Lord. He felt God told him that his sufferings were nothing compared to the immeasurable treasure waiting for him in heaven. Francis was instantly filled with joy, as if a brilliantly bright sun had risen in the darkness of his soul. Francis responded to the message with a poem meant to be sung. In the poem, he calls the sun his brother, the moon and stars his sisters. There was also Brothers Wind and Air, Sister Water, Brother Fire, and Sister Earth, who is our mother. He ends the poem by praising Sister Death.

Francis had left his self by integrating his entire being into everything he could see, hear, touch, feel, and smell. All of creation was united in the mind of God, in the heart of Jesus. Francis was telling us that all of creation is united with God, the creator of all, and the essence of that mystical union is best expressed and fully realized in the spirit of fraternity in which all of creation forms an unseen oneness. For Francis, all division and separateness had dissolved. The canticle eloquently expressed the saint's attitude of grateful dependency on all things as gifts from God. *All things:* good and bad.

Francis's poetry, as well as his life, grew out of his love of poverty, which helped him penetrate the mystery of God-incarnate. Even though Francis could no longer see or enjoy the beauty of creation, could no longer see other creatures, even though his eyes were so diseased that they couldn't even be exposed to the light of a fire let alone the glorious light of the sun, he was still able to express his innermost joy through material things, through the sun, the moon, and the stars, through the wind and air, the water and fire, through the flowers and herbs and all of earth, and he could do so only because all of nature was being illuminated from within. For Francis, the sacred had electrified the cosmos, and the cosmos was manifested within him. For Francis, there could never be a separation between the Creator and the creation.

But Brother Corona? It seems impossible to see anything good coming from so much widespread death and immeasurable suffering. Where it hasn't ended life, this insidious virus has turned life upside down. People are feeling anxious, trapped, vulnerable, isolated, confused, lost, and angry.

But at the same time, this new virus is uniting us in unexpected ways. The only war you hear about is not between nations but a war on humanity's common enemy: a lethal virus we do not fully understand. People are being kinder to each other. The pandemic has slowed life down, has forced us to really see what is essential and what is not. It has forced us to our rooms to ponder our lives. The coronavirus has opened our eyes to just how connected all of creation is.

Really staring at my own mortality in the face is changing me. I see more beauty than I normally do. I think about how I can be more loving, more compassionate. Still, on Saturday (March 28, 2020), I became so angry at one staff member I fired her without really looking at her point of view. On Sunday, I rescinded her firing. I see more clearly my own pettiness and how easily I can tumble from being filled with joy to feeling a sense of despair and hopelessness.

In all of this, I didn't pray so much to be spared from being touched by the virus as I did to be infused with wisdom and love during the day ahead of me. The day ahead of me is all that I have. Through the day I strive to be present to the sacrament of the present moment . . . though I don't often succeed.

On March 28, late on a Saturday afternoon, Santa Chiara was filled with laughter and pure joy. The staff organized a sack race. It was hysterical. Kids jumping to the finish line. One little girl was trailing her opponent badly. She simply shed the sack and ran to the finish line. The biggest roars of laughter came when adults fell to the ground. Staffers Carla, Orlane, and others all crashed and tumbled onto the concrete pavement. For about thirty minutes, all the pandemic tension was chased away by pure silliness. As I looked over all the staff and kids truly enjoying themselves, I thought Santa Chiara was just one big, crazy, unusual family. For once I felt a sense of—not pride—accomplishment that somehow my naivete and inability to see all the pitfalls of such a huge undertaking had nonetheless created something beautiful yet still flawed.

I don't know what the future holds for me, for Santa Chiara, or the world. When the virus is finally conquered, it will have left in its wake a completely changed world. The global economic collapse will visit more suffering upon the poorest of the poor. We'll have to do a much better job of coming together as a human family. There will be no room for division.

Note: Sadly, over the next few years, the division deepened as the racism and gun violence increased, and the on-going war in Ukraine caused greater economic hardships. By early June 2022, after the back-to-back massacres in a supermarket in Buffalo, New York and an elementary school in Uvalde, Texas took the lives of dozens of elderly Blacks and innocent children (more on those mass shootings later) and the pending televised Congressional hearings into the assault on the Capital by angry Trump supporters on January 6, 2021, the divisions between us were intensified.

Our self-centered way of life has been killing the planet for many decades. Far from our view or interest people living on the margins of life in such faraway places as Africa, the Middle East, and South America have had the life squeezed out of them. Species of life have become extinct. We are destroying the water, the air, and earth. Someone on a progressive Jewish website wrote: ". . . we [thought] we were safe, we thought, our ways, our things, our technology, our systems, our money would protect us. We couldn't conceive they would fail us."

But today is here. The sun will rise as it always does, but it will shed its warm, life-giving light on a very different world—a world ready for a renewal. Once the fear and anxiety are behind us, once we've properly mourned for the dead, we'll have a chance to recreate the world in which the foundation is love, compassion, mercy, forgiveness, kindness, mutuality, and fraternity. In this new world, all religious faiths will walk arm in arm, walk in mutual respect and understanding, will walk with listening ears and hearts, dropping the stupid game of "my religion is better than your religion." If that happens, generations to come will thank Brother Corona. Let it be so. Amen.

PS: I wrote "Brother Corona" very early on a Sunday morning, well before sunrise. Around 7:30 am, I printed it out and went downstairs. I sat alone on a bench at the back of the property. I greeted Brother Rat as he raced by after stealing some bird seed. Before Haiti, the sight of a rat scared me. Some kids brought me flowers they had picked. My plan was to read "Brother Corona" and make any needed corrections and maybe add a fresh insight. Soon there were four kids sitting next to me. The dog tried to eat my pen. Walencia took my cell phone from my pocket and took some photos.

If I am not in my second-floor apartment, I am always surrounded by kids (Haiti, 2021);
Photo by one of the kids, Walencia.

Waking Up to Crying Injustices

Sadly, in time, absurd conspiracy theories about Covid-19, the preventative shutdown, and even masks promulgated by the radical far right began to divide Americans in very ugly ways. Armed men, carrying assault rifles and waving Nazi flags stormed state capitals protesting the shutdown. There are legitimate reasons for opening up the economy, but on May 7, 2020, I saw a news clip of a man carrying a sign proclaiming: "I'm selfish and proud of it."

Within weeks, the murder of George Floyd by Minneapolis police officers sparked waves of massive protests and civil unrest that lasted for weeks and highlighted the unchecked pandemic of racial injustice. The president tried to fan the flames of division by sending the military to Washington, DC, to disperse the crowd so he could walk to a nearby church for a photo op, but he was sternly rebuked by former top military brass, and he was forced to withdraw the troops.

By June 9, 2020, on the day George Floyd was buried, the death toll from Covid-19 in the States had reached 111,635.

Within a week of George Floyd's burial, the police in Atlanta shot and killed another Black man. The man, Rayshard Brooks, was sleeping in his car in a Wendy's parking lot. He was reportedly drunk. The police tapped on his window. He woke up. As requested by the police, he got out of the car. There was some discussion. Sleeping in your car is not a crime. Brooks failed a sobriety test. There was more discussion. The two police officers started to handcuff him. When his hands were behind his back but before the cuffs could be closed, Brooks suddenly resisted. Perhaps the vivid memory of George Floyd's murder by the police, who kept their knee on his neck for eight minutes and forty-one seconds as Floyd said, "I can't breathe," entered Brook's mind and he panicked. Whatever the reason, Brooks suddenly resisted having the handcuffs put on him. He began to wrestle with the two police officers. Within seconds the three of them were on the parking lot pavement rolling about. Two cops and an unarmed inebriated man should not have been a fair match.

Amazingly, somehow Brooks managed to escape, grabbed a TASER gun from one of the cops, and started running. The cops got up and started running after Brooks. Again, a large, drunk man running from two police officers should not have been a problem. There are police procedures to handle a foot chase, which never ends in the fleeing suspect escaping. Yet, seemingly for no reason, one of the officers shot Brooks in the back. Two of the fired bullets entered Brook's back; a third bullet entered a car in the drive-in lane. All of this was caught on numerous cameras from six angles. When I first saw the video, I thought perhaps the fact that Brooks had one of their TASERS caused the cops to be justified in shooting. A police expert who was a former police officer said that cops are trained to know that a TASER can only reach about 20 feet; beyond that distance they are useless. As he was being shot, the video shows Brooks trying to fire back with the TASER.

The outrage and protest at this incident were instant and widespread. This was little more than a traffic stop—only the car was not even moving. There was absolutely no reason for it to have ended in a fatal shooting, even given Brooks's resisting arrest, taking the cop's TASER, and fleeing. The police had his car and his driver's license. Rayshard Brooks was never going to get far. There was no need for deadly force. Capture him and charge him with resisting arrest. End of story. This all started because a Wendy's employee spotted a guy asleep in his car in (or near) the drive-through lane and he called the police. How this ended with the sleeping man being shot in the back has only one root cause: he was Black. The entire incident lasted just under forty-five minutes.

I had two cousins who were policemen; one was a captain, the other a lieutenant. My nephew was a detective sergeant before retiring. So, I don't like second-guessing a police officer who makes a split-second decision under a stressful, dangerous situation. But the Rayshard Brooks case is an exception. As details emerged from all the video and audio recordings, the more it became clear Rayshard's death was unnecessary. For instance, Brooks passed a field eye test in which he followed the officer's finger as he repeatedly moved it from left to right and back again for about two minutes. Brooks followed the finger as if his life depended upon it. He also passed walking the straight-line test, as well as the standing on one leg test. We heard Brooks say, "I don't want to be in violation with anyone." He spoke of his daughter's birthday, which was the next day. He was not aggressive. He was even humorous. Brooks begged to be allowed to walk to his sister's home, which was only two blocks away, offering to do so under the officer's supervision after he locked his car. Had Brooks been white and lived in the right zip code, this simple, reasonable request would have been granted.

Why wasn't Brooks given a break? There was no reason to handcuff Brooks, essentially for sleeping in his car. The situation could've easily been defused, especially considering Brooks's demeanor. He hadn't committed a crime, nor was he armed. Furthermore, the police didn't face a life-threatening risk, which is required for the use of deadly force. Systemic racism is the only explanation for the shooting. It's assumed that fear of prison during the pandemic caused Brooks to panic when the cuffs where being applied. Perhaps he didn't want to screw up his daughter's birthday. Blacks have a legitimate fear of the police. Within a minute for his unwise fleeing, Rayshard Brooks was dead. Two bullets to the back. Senseless. Disgraceful. Murder.

With stunning quickness, within two weeks, the officer who shot Brooks was charged with murder. It was revealed that after the officer killed Brooks, he kicked his corpse. The other officer stood on the shoulder of Rayshard Brooks; he too was arrested. Brooks's Black life did not matter.

As I mentioned in the "Overture," some sixty years ago, Thomas Merton was deeply disturbed by the bombing of a Black church in Birmingham in which four children perished. Merton identified with those who were victims of violence. He put the photo of one eleven-year-old girl in his journal. In his book *Seeds of Destruction*, published in 1964, Merton wrote:

> The race question cannot be settled without a profound change of heart, a real shakeup and deep reaching metanoia on the part of White America. It is not just a question of a little more good will and generosity; it is a question of waking up to crying injustices and deep-seated problems which are engrained in the present set-up and which instead of getting better are going to get worse.[33]

The murders of Brooks and Floyd were spawned by slavery's legacy of racism.

Note: The blatant racism has increased in the last two years since the above was written, as many states instituted new voting regulations that made it harder for Blacks to vote.

That Time of Day

In the Spring of 2010, I was plunged into a severe crisis, which I'll share a little more about soon, that tore my life asunder and thrust me into a pit of darkness and despair. All seemed lost. I didn't think I would survive. There were days I didn't want to survive. In that darkness, Thomas Merton became a beacon of light that guided me through the storm.

In his book *No Man Is an Island*, Merton wrote: "There must be a time of day when the man who makes plans forgets his plans, and acts as if he had no plans at all. There must be a time of day when the man who has to speak falls very silent. And his mind forms no more propositions, and he asks himself: *Did they have any meaning?* There must be a time when a man of prayer goes to pray as if it were the first time in his life he had ever prayed; when the man of resolutions puts his resolutions aside as if they had all been broken, and he learns a different wisdom: distinguishing the sun from the moon, the stars from the darkness, the sea from the dry land, and the night sky from the shoulder of a hill."[34]

The crisis made one thing perfectly clear: I was at that time of day. It was a time to fall silent and be still, a time to look deeply into the essence of my life, the essence of life itself, so much of which made absolutely no sense. Because it made no sense, I kept moving, kept doing in order not to be overcome by the apparent meaninglessness of it all.

I was at that time of day when I had to sit alone . . . and ponder and pray.

I've had within me for a long time a faint desire for genuine solitude, but my extremely active life and ministry to the poor always prevented me from fully embracing solitude. My life was very much public, constantly surrounded by people, often on a stage where I was the center of attention. But when I found myself on the verge of exhaustion and suffering from the emotional impact of seeing so much human suffering around the world, I was confronted with a personal crisis that left me with no choice but to do what I needed to do. Stop!

I was at that time of day when I could give the day the time it deserved; the time required to allow something real to happen. I was at that time of day when I could be both silent and attentive . . . attentive to birds flying around my yard, and attentive to the flock of thoughts flying around inside my head.

I was at that time of day when I was free, free to find and love myself . . . and God. All the things that had been pulling at me for years, demanding my full attention, such as the nonstop responsibility of running a non-profit charity trying to right the injustice of chronic poverty, had suddenly vanished like a poorly constructed building in Haiti toppled by an earthquake.

I was at a Kairos time of day, a time when I could give myself a chance to let go of everything I knew in order to be carried along by the flow of all I did not know, the very flow of the hidden mystery and raw reality of life.

Speaking about prayer and the essence of what we truly need, Thomas Merton said, "We don't have to rush after it. It's there all the time, and if we give it time, it will make itself known to us."[35]

I gave it time. For six months, I entered the invisible chamber of my soul where I tried to shut out all cares, worries, distractions, idle thoughts . . . shut out all but God as I waited for God. Oddly enough, all the saints and mystics would say, God was already there. It was me who was missing, hidden in the rubble of my own life, buried under the weight of my countless faults, failures, mistakes, illusions, and capricious desires. Suddenly, the time was ripe to cast off the burden of the past, with all its stupid missteps, and caste off the useless anxiety over the future, with all its uncertainty, and to seek to see the face of God.

While I can't say I saw the face of God, in stopping everything for six months, I was given the grace and strength to move forward. I felt the tender mercy of God, felt God's love embrace my entire being. But most important, I learned to trust God. For the first time in my life, I felt a faint sense of wholeness. In the stillness and silence, I was able, in time, to enter the fullness of life and slowly learn to love afresh with a new, rejuvenated heart, as I continued my education, for I'm still in kindergarten when it comes to spirituality.

So much of life is contradiction and chaos. Only in stillness and prayer can harmony emerge from the confusion. I pray the emptiness and darkness that still occasionally consumes my inner life does not overcome me, does not prompt me to seek the false light of the world and all its empty promises and illusions. My past experience has taught me that whenever the Light of God truly penetrates my disordered inner being, I'm able to see clearly how far I am from God, how great the contrast is between who God is and who I am.

It is in stillness that we find our emptiness,
the emptiness that can only be filled
by welcoming God into our hearts.

A Blessing in Disguise

Note: *While I'm reluctant to dig up the past, to open old wounds, for the sake of clarity and transparency I need to "name" the crisis that forced me to "stop." I have no interest in exposing* *or hurting the very people who hurt me. I know the truth of what happened; moreover, my own actual failures, missteps, and venial sins connected with the crisis were forgiven by God long ago. My recovery, thank God, has been full and complete. Here is a generalized and capsulized portrait of what happened that sent me into exile.*

In the Spring of 2010, while in the midst of suffering from a severe case of post-traumatic stress disorder after witnessing unimaginable carnage (such as streets lined with rotting corpses and medical procedures —including amputations—performed without anesthesia) in the wake of the devastating earthquake in Haiti that killed more than 300,000 people, I was falsely accused of doing something I didn't do. It created an opening for some disingenuous "friends" and ministry officials to formally investigate my private life, and then exaggerate and distort things they uncovered to force me out of my own ministry.

Even after a thorough investigation (conducted by a board member who was a journalist) into the actual charge revealed that nothing happened and that the alleged incident was fabricated by an unstable woman with an overactive imagination and an ax to grind, the inquisition into my private life continued unabated. It was a nightmare. I was treated like a moral leper beyond redemption for a few minor unrelated lapses in judgment. I was betrayed and destroyed in what amounted to a hostile takeover of my ministry. I was fired by the very people I'd hired. I felt as if I'd been stabbed in the back. I was plummeted into such a deep state of despair that I questioned the merit of continuing to live.

In time, through prayer, and with Merton's written words as guidance, I was able to forgive those who conspired to oust me and was then set free from my anger and able to move on and establish a new, more effective ministry to the poor. Today I consider the entire ugly, mean, and demeaning incident to be a blessing in disguise that gave me the time, space, solitude, and opportunity to deal with some inner things that had been crying out for attention for some time. Before the false accusation, I used my busyness and the "importance" of my work to ignore my own inner pain and conflicts, my own inner poverty.

We each have a dark side. My dark side scares me. The more I actively engage in the difficult work of self-knowledge, the more clearly I see how I've been a prisoner of my own blind instincts, compulsions, and illusions. In prayer, my dark side has been illuminated, and I'm slowly learning to act from my true center, not from the shadows. What we need to become whole is hidden in our brokenness. I'm still struggling to enter more fully into this reality.

Humility increases with self-knowledge.

Note: *I want to mention that during the crisis, the persecution, there were three priests who called me almost every day. The supported me and never lost their faith in me. For them, I'm eternally grateful.*

CHAPTER 3

Sacred Heart

A Kiss of Death

At 5:45 am on March 23, 2020, I was startled by the sound of a loud gunshot outside my window. It sounded too close for comfort. In Haiti, anything can happen at any time. The pandemic of violence trumps the pandemic of coronavirus. Or so I initially thought. The threat from the virus is more insidious. Every person you meet becomes a threat to your life. Every person, in effect, is carrying a concealed weapon. No trigger to pull to do you in; they simply need to shake your hand and a few weeks later you're a goner. Later that morning, a woman on my staff reflexively kissed me on my cheek. It was a fleeting, gentle kiss, a simple sign of affection. About thirty minutes later, I was driving a malnourished infant to the Missionaries of Charity for treatment. Suddenly, a great fear took hold of me. Was the woman carrying the virus? Did she just transmit it to me? Was it a kiss of death?

A Prison

How sad that we often decide to abstain from life, to hide ourselves because we've been hurt or rejected. Our inner cell of self-protection soon becomes a prison that robs us of the vitality of life. Our very woundedness is waiting to be transformed into compassion. Our emotional and physical pain helps us understand and respond to the suffering of another. Compassion is as elegant as any cathedral.

> *"God lives outside the comfort zone, beyond the hedged bets,*
> *in risks accepted, in dangers embraced."*
>
> —JOHN KIRVAN, GOD HUNGER:
> DISCOVERING THE MYSTIC IN ALL OF US[36]

A Duck in a Chicken Coop

As Pico Iyer wrote in *The Art of Stillness*, Merton was a "gregarious traveler, heavy drinker, and wounded lover" before he stepped into "a Trappist monastery in Kentucky and became Father Louis, taking his restlessness in a less visible direction."[37] In *The Sign of Jonas,* Thomas Merton wrote: "An author in a Trappist monastery is like a duck in a chicken coop. And he would give anything in the world to be a chicken instead of a duck."[38] Being both a writer and monk was hard. I doubt Merton could've been a monk instead of a writer. He had to be both, even if that made his life more difficult. I think being a monk made Merton a better writer. As a filmmaker running an orphanage, I feel like a duck in a chicken coop.

I think there are lots of ordinary people who feel out of place or misplaced or even displaced, who feel like a duck in a chicken coop. This feeling, often unexpressed, speaks to our inner longing . . . for something beyond what we know or have experienced. It speaks to our need to belong, to be loved and accepted. I never feel at home anywhere. I have this deep longing within me that I can't seem to satisfy. Oddly enough, I feel somewhat at home writing this book, while simultaneously feeling I have no right to write it because I'm so woefully unqualified to say anything of substance about Merton or prayer. However, I'm so powerfully drawn to Merton the searcher that I'm able to muster the confidence to keep writing, to keep trying to understand not only the monk but his—and my—relentless search for a deeper meaning.

When Merton writes about the true or real self and the false or illusionary self, I'm better able to recognize and feel those two dimensions within me. He speaks to the deepest yearnings of my spirit, while at the same time boldly confronting the complex problems within society. Merton writes from his inner experience and, in the process, helps me connect with and verbalize my own inner experience, my own inner conflicts and confusions. His individual search for God became symbolic of the universal search for God, which is why his writing touched a wide range of people, including non-Christians, on their own individual journeys.

> *Allow God to turn your life upside down and inside out.*
> *Allow God to topple your expectations.*
> *Journey beyond your comfort zone.*

The Difficult Journey

Everyone experiences heartbreak; everyone needs tenderness and compassion. At some point in our lives, we all have to face the difficult journey of coming to terms with feelings of rejection, humiliation, and fear. These very real and very painful feelings, which I know all too well, in time and in prayer, become an authentic path from despair to hope. Tragedies and disasters become places of courage, of perseverance, places where we learn to plumb the depths of our inner life, our true essence, and are able, by God's grace, to move from rejection and terror to healing and hope. Love grows from that deep-rooted pain within the universe where God is present, and ever willing to embrace us and bless us.[39]

A byproduct of our fast-paced modern life is that most of us are so fully engaged in an endless stream of activities and endeavors that we have lost the aptitude for deep listening and as a result have alienated ourselves from the very source of our being. We have forgotten the clear biblical instruction: *Be still and know I am God.* Thomas Merton anchored his life in stillness and silence. In my overly active life in Haiti, I need to learn how to periodically, perhaps even on a daily basis, silence my intellect and senses. In doing so, I'm not briefly fleeing the world but attempting to experience the essential reality of a full life in God. The "life in abundance," which Jesus promises, is blocked by our whirlwind of activity, which only leaves us feeling tired and impoverished.

> *The universal lack of an interior life is a key element behind*
> *the rash of violent political and religious conflicts*
> *that plague so many nations.*

Making All Things New

The interior life is the beginning of eternal life. Heaven does not begin after we die. It starts here and now as we respond to God's grace by making all things new and creating paradise on earth. Today, sadly, many people seem to have forgotten or have dismissed heaven, thereby ignoring the idea of eternally living with God. We're so preoccupied with the surface of life, we don't pay attention to the divine call to enter more deeply into the silent streams of a God-energized life of the Spirit, which transforms us into more loving and compassionate beings who see beauty in everything, who love the truth, who thirst for justice, and who embrace and protect all of creation. We watch TV, we shop, we fight, we ignore the common good, we applaud the rich and the powerful, we snub the poor and the weak, and we rape the environment.

Not Having, Not Knowing

It seems that lots of people today not only know God, but they also seem to possess God. They've got God in their pocket. I once rejected Christianity because, in part, Christians seemed to possess God. How is that possible? I mean, how can God be possessed? At best, all we can do, as Merton suggested, is wait for God. Once a year, during Advent, we're reminded of that simple reality.

I certainly feel as if "I have God" in my life. I can talk about God, share my experiences of God with friends and strangers alike, but I also must admit at the same time—and this is the really tough part—that "I do not have God," that I too am merely waiting for God. It's confusing. I have God and at the same time I don't have God. I possess God, and I am waiting for God. I know God and at the same time I don't know God. When it comes to

God, there must be, as Paul Tillich suggests in *The Shaking of the Foundations*, "an element of not having and not knowing, and of waiting."[40]

Merton was the guru of waiting.

Transformation is not possible where we, not God, are secretly in control, arrogantly pretending we "know it all." Prayer brings me face to face with the ultimate darkness. Prayer challenges me to enter the darkness. In the darkness, I'm able to see my own insecurity. In the darkness, I learn I need light from someone else. I cannot provide light for myself. Light is a gift that needs to be received.

> *For the most part, the life of prayer*
> *is lived in darkness.*

Intimate Communion

Waiting, waiting, waiting. Our spiritual lives are a vigil of waiting. We wait with hope for the advent of God. Yet as we wait for God, God is already here with us. And we are with God, yet not fully so, and so we wait, living with paradox and expectancy. Spiritual transformation never ends . . . it's always new, forever beginning, constantly evolving.

Each of us is on a lifelong journey to wholeness. We all want to overcome the fractures and divisions we feel within ourselves and among our circle of family and friends. Our lives are like puzzle parts, and we can't see the full picture. Wholeness and completeness are ultimately only found in intimacy with God. And intimacy with God is only found through desire and surrender. When we desire God above all else and when we let go of our clinging egos and destructive religions, God is free to enter into intimate communion with us.

> *The world demands more and more from us.*
> *God only asks for empty hands.*

Note: June 12, 2022, Port-au-Prince, Haiti. *Two years down from when I wrote the above, I still like what I had written. Yet so much has changed since I penned those honest words. I now understand there is more to it. Impermanence is a fact of life. There is constant change. We are ever-changing. God comes to us, speaks to us in the present moment of our lives. God comes to us as we are, where we are. God takes on the form, the voice, to meet us precisely where we are now. We are not static, nor is God. There is, in Zen, no last word. The soul and God are unknown.*

According to Christian tradition and theology, through the Incarnation Christ came into the world to bring us into a fuller communion with God. Yet we are starving to death because of a lack of authentic communion with God and each other. Sadly, shamefully, we tear each other apart. We divide, judge, and condemn. We isolate and imprison. We hinder and hate. We need to recapture our oneness. We need communion, not division.

Empty Hands

Twenty-two years ago, after I finished writing *The Sun & Moon Over Assisi*, I approached God with my hands full . . . and asked for more. Saint Francis of Assisi was willing to go to God with empty hands. For him, the only thing that really mattered was utter trust in God, and his adult life was a continual witness to the realization that total trust cannot exist until we have lost all self-trust and are rooted in poverty. Francis was a tough act to follow.

The deepest levels of self-denial, which Francis reached, present us with a huge gap in comparison to our feeble efforts at approaching perfect trust in God. What is it that keeps me from total surrender into the loving embrace of God? I know what God seeks, yet I hesitated. I believed God loved me, and this love did not spring from a reluctant heart; God stood always willing and waiting to love me even more deeply . . . yet I hesitated in accepting this love out of fear of losing myself and being buried in God. For many years, rather than following the self-emptying example of Francis and the saints, I tried the latest spiritual shortcuts to God. And I bought books. All I did was go around in circles, getting nowhere, slowly. The spinning still continues, albeit to a lesser degree.

Francis said the road to God is straight and narrow: The road is poverty. I was looking for an easier road, one that gently wound its way up the mountain to the summit where God dwelt.

Today, I'm certainly not on an easy road. At long last, I'm living on poverty road, with all its uncertainty and suffering. The dusty, violent, litter-strewn roads of Haiti have opened my eyes. Nonetheless, I still gobble up books. However, I've learned that there are no shortcuts to God. There is only ongoing, hard work. There are days, many of them, when I become weary from the work. I just must keep going, keep working, trusting I'll keep discovering breadcrumbs of wisdom and keep learning how to let go of more and more. I doubt self-emptying will ever end, that up to my last breath I'll hold on to something I know is not good. I hope I'm wrong.

> *All that is "self" must be abandoned if we are to follow Jesus.*
> *The road he travels is the road of self-emptying.*

A Nun, a Farmer, and a Priest

In August 2009, I spent a week in Paray-le-Monial, France, where I spoke and showed film clips to a gathering of 4,500 Catholic young people from all over Europe. Centuries earlier, a nun from Paray, which is located in the heart of the Burgundy region, had a remarkable vision that gave birth to deep devotion to the heart of Jesus. She was a simple nun. She lived in a small, rural town surrounded by lush fields and rolling hills far from the centers of human power. She lived the hidden life of a cloistered nun, a dedicated life of prayer and adoration. Yet, she saw something no one else had seen. What she saw is still touching and transforming lives more than 325 years after her first vision.

In so many ways our sophisticated, modern world is so vastly different from hers; yet, in the most essential ways, life today is still very much the same as it was for this obscure, humble, veiled sister living long ago and far away in a monastery in Paray-le-Monial in the 1670s. We all still seek communion; we all need something beyond ourselves. We need to know the heart of God, to give our hearts to God and to each other.

Note: Actually, we don't need to look beyond ourselves for anything; the whole universe is within us. We need to look within, then reach out in the love we discover what animates everything.

Through a series of visions, Jesus revealed his most precious heart to Saint Margaret Mary Alacoque, a divine heart beating and overflowing with endless love for humanity, a human heart bowed and broken by the suffering endured by countless humans around the world because of poverty and violence, unjust and chronic poverty, unwarranted and brutal violence.

Because I loved the famous story about another saint who lived near Paray-le-Monial, I used a free day to travel to the village of Ars. Long ago, in this remote village in the south of France, Saint John Marie Vianney (1786–1859), known as the Curé of Ars, noticed an old farmer who used to sit for hours in the humble, empty church. When the saint asked him what he was doing, the farmer replied: "He looks at me and I look at him." It really is that simple, but modern life is so connected to so much, we are easily disconnected from the All. Television and the internet have turned our interior dwellings into shanty towns. Instead of looking in, they prompt us to look outward, and we become what we gaze upon. When praying, we turn away from ourselves and turn toward God.

I think Thomas Merton would remind us that contemplation cannot be relegated to some secluded corner of our life, dualistically existing apart from other tasks. Contemplation lives and breathes in the recognition of the divine possibility contained in the present moment. This takes lots of practice and a daily effort.

For me, it was interesting to find the following paragraph in *No Man Is an Island*: "Great priests, saints like the Curé d'Ars, who have seen the hidden depths of thousands of souls, have, nonetheless, remained men with few intimate friends. No one is more lonely than a priest who has a vast ministry. He is isolated in a terrible desert by the secrets of his fellow men."[41]

It's impossible to imagine the tremendous ache in the Sacred Heart of Jesus.

> *The more aware we become of*
> *the divine presence within us,*
> *the more we shall forget ourselves*
> *and become more serene*
> *and pure of heart.*

Heal Me

"Jesus have pity on me," the blind man cried out as Jesus passed by. Touched by the blind man's faith, Jesus healed him. We may not be physically blind or even hurting, but we are all blind and injured, all in need of Jesus's healing touch or word. Life is an ever-flowing stream of injuries, and frequently the injuries are inner or spiritual wounds that can cripple us. Melancholy, depression, abuse, betrayals, and bitter disappointments can blind us to the fullness of life, trapping us in a dark corner of despair. The inner injuries we accumulate and allow to go unhealed can rip apart the fabric of our existence. Our spiritual maladies become who we are. These injuries can prevent us from seeing Jesus, from reaching out our hand to him for a healing. The power to heal still resides within the risen Lord. Jesus can still turn to us and say, "Have sight; your faith has saved you." But first, we must reach out to him.

> *Jesus, heal me of all the inner hurts which I don't even recognize, buried hurts which have influenced me in ways I cannot even imagine. Heal me, sweet Jesus, of the destructive behavior that allows me to choose poorly as I navigate my way through the day. Lord Jesus, heal me . . . heal me of all bitterness, all resentment, all anger, all impurity, all unloving tendencies, all behavior that does not reflect the love, compassion, and mercy which is ever flowing from your Sacred Heart. Come, Lord Jesus, heal me, make me whole, help me love.*

All Is Grace

"All is grace," are the last words of a dying fictional priest in France. The priest had struggled from day to day, strengthened only by the belief that what he was doing was right, but sometimes even that abandoned him. When I first read those words, written by Georges Bernanos in *The Diary of a Country Priest*, I could not imagine saying them. "All is meaningless chaos" seemed, at the time, closer to the truth. (And still is, especially in Haiti.)

Most of the last twenty years of my life have been a struggle to pray and be faithful to the self-sacrificing love that Christ calls us to do on a daily basis in the midst of our everyday life. I'm often far too harsh on myself. My faith often wavers and wobbles. I often feel an anguished uncertainty. I'm slowly understanding that God wants me to be merciful to myself as well as to others. This is a hard won truth. I need to humbly embrace my own humanity.

I love the following passage from *The Diary of a Country Priest* in which the unnamed dying, despondent parish priest finds God in the very stuff of everyday life, the daily round of concrete events, feelings, and suffering:

> I have not lost my faith. I have found it again, though not in my poor brain . . . nor my feelings, nor even my conscience. It sometimes seems to me that it has

withdrawn, that it lives on in a place where I certainly would not have looked for it, in my flesh, in my miserable flesh, in my blood and in my flesh, in my perishable, but baptized flesh.[42]

Through the Incarnation, divinity entered the physical domain and made them one. Holiness comes through our humanness, not in opposition to it. All *is* grace.

Despite his deep suffering, the curé carries on, often in doubt and confusion, because of his sure, yet elusive, conviction that we are loved by a God who also suffered rejection and loss. Incarnation points him toward community and the world—with love, kindness, and respect for everything and everyone. His was not a life of cheap grace. He fought every day to overcome his faults and failures. Every day we must choose love—over and over again—in daily concrete ways in the face of pain, rejection, and despair. The country priest's flirtations with despair showed him that the true meaning of hell was to give up on love.

In Haiti I must face the dark underside of humanity. Every day I see innocence and vulnerability, death and loss. The evil that surrounds us can only be transformed by love.

Amazing Grace

Sin is saying no to grace. Sin closes my eyes to the truth. Sin erodes the will and renders it impossible to stand against the tyranny of lust in all its alluring manifestations. Sin weakens us, then kills us. Yet I continue to sin.

I'm beginning to understand how Christ's resurrection turned disgrace into grace—how grace opens the door to the possibility of change. Grace changes a person. Conversion is about being changed. Grace is the breath of love. As Bono and U2 proclaimed in song, grace makes everything beautiful.

Beg God for the grace of prayer.

A More Loving Heart

Setting aside the actual reception of the Eucharist, my attendance at the daily 6:30 am Mass at the Missionaries of Charity has a marked benefit to my daily life. It sets the foundation upon which the remainder of the day rests. Some of the benefit flows from the faith of the sisters. Yet, I confess that some days the benefit is short lived. On more occasions than I'd like to admit, within an hour of getting home, a staff member does something that makes me so angry that I say or do something I regret. Still, even on the worst of days, something from the daily liturgical celebration recenters me on the hidden life of Jesus. It could be the scripture reading, the homily, or my nearly daily conversation with Sr. Immacula, who is the regional superior, or simply the living example of the prayerful way the sisters love and serve the poor.

Normally, I'm the only person in attendance with the sisters. When I had Covid, I missed many weeks with the sisters. Before becoming sick, the pandemic caused a lack of priests to celebrate the Mass. Over that time, I got out of the habit of rising at 4:00 am and leaving the house at 6:00 am. Ah, the soft life has its appeal.

As soon as I recovered from the illness and was free of the oxygen tanks, I had the impulse to return to daily Mass—and I did so on June 16, 2020. A few days later, on July 19, the Church celebrated the Solemnity of the Most Sacred Heart of Jesus. I brought with me a prayer I wrote, as I wanted to give it to Sr. Immacula. It was written twenty-five years ago on a train that was traversing the South of France. Not long before, I had my dramatic conversion experience in an empty church in Rome. I was headed for all the locations in France where Vincent van Gogh had lived as part of my research for the novel I was writing. But something was different inside me—a new longing. I'm not sure how writing the prayer happened. It just flowed out of me. Here it is:

A Prayer for a More Loving Heart

O Most Sacred Heart of Jesus
create in me a pure heart,
a heart that doesn't lust or hate,
a heart that isn't proud or envious.

O Most Sacred Heart of Jesus
help me purify my polluted heart,
help me soften my hardened heart,
help me warm my frigid heart.

O Most Sacred Heart of Jesus
help me transform my heart
into a heart that beats
more in rhythm with your Sacred Heart.

Jesus my Lord, you are the source
Let my contrite heart beat with love,
the way your Most Sacred Heart does.

CHAPTER 4

A Response to a Call

Montaldo Study Note 2

Thomas Merton's Uncaged Mind

In an appreciative article for *Newsweek* (September 14, 1998), Kenneth Woodward called Thomas Merton, a "man with an uncaged mind." Merton wrote in various genres: poetry, meditative prose, scholarly articles, political polemics, dramatic pieces, song cycles, autobiography, letters, and personal journals. Merton was among the first Christian American writers with a popular audience to share his enthusiasm for contemplative traditions other than his own. His study of world religions included personal contacts with an international spectrum of contemplatives and scholars. His Christian philosophy and spiritual exercises supported his life's project to free himself from the "obligatory answers" proscribed and enforced by his Western education, social class, and cultural norms.

In his book *Conjectures of a Guilty Bystander*, Merton considered personal freedom the mark of true spirituality. A "true religion" nurtures freedom:

Freedom from domination, freedom to live one's own spiritual life, freedom to seek the highest truth, unabashed by any human pressure or any collective demand, the ability to say one's own "yes" and one's own "no" and not merely to echo the "yes" and the "no" of state, party, corporation, army or system. This is inseparable from authentic religion. It is one of the deepest and most fundamental needs of the human person, perhaps the deepest and most crucial need of the human person as such: for without recognizing he challenge of this need, no man [sic] can truly be a person, and therefore without it he cannot fully be a man either. The frustration of this deep need by irreligion, by secular and political pseudoreligion, by the mystiques and superstitions of totalitarianism, have made man morally sick in the very depths of his being. They have wounded and corrupted his freedom, they have filled his love with rottenness, decayed it into hatred. They have made man a machine geared for his own destruction.[43]

He rarely minced words as he pierced through the patina of American claims to exceptionalism and innocent idealism. He identified himself as a "marginal person" to a Western materialistic society's dominant paradigms. Yet, he never renounced his citizenship nor his responsibility to shift North American society's priorities:

> We have a responsibility to our own time, not as if we could seem to stand outside it and donate various spiritual and material benefits to it from a position of compassionate distance. We have a responsibility to find ourselves where we are, in our own proper time and place, in the history to which we belong and to which we must inevitably contribute either our response or our evasions, either our truth and act, or mere slogan and gesture.[44]

He balanced his prophetic, haranguing public essays on social justice, nuclear war, and protests for peace with more personal writing in private journals and letters. His autobiographical prose revealed his character as a poet of his inner experiences. He was acutely aware of his fragile, often one-sided grasp on truth. A loner at heart who needed to think independently, he attended to a diverse chorus of other voices through voracious reading and personal contacts. He was never fundamentalist as he exposed in his private journals the paradoxical complexities of his life. He renounced any obsession to nail every ethical question to the floor. He was conscious of the need for lifelong learning and revision of his preconceived notions of human experience. He exuded enthusiasm for tracking God's presence in all things: people, nature, and the flow of events, the "stream of reality and of life itself."

In active contemplation, there is a deliberate and sustained effort to detect the will of God in events and to bring one's whole self into harmony with that will. Active contemplation depends on an ascesis (an inner work and discipline) of abandonment, a systematic relaxation of the tensions of the exterior self and a renunciation of its tyrannical claims and demands, in order to move in a dimension that escapes our understanding and overflows in all directions our capacity to plan. The element of dialectic in active contemplation is centered on the discovery of God's will, that is to say, the identification of the real direction events are taking, especially in our own life. But along with this there is a deep concern with the symbolic and ritual enactment of those sacred mysteries that represent the divine actions by which the redemption and sanctification of the world is affected. In other words, active contemplation rests on a deep ground of liturgical, historical, and cultural tradition—but a living tradition, not dead convention. And a tradition still in dynamic growth and movement.[45]

He taught that contemplative prayer and reflection are for everyone and that the context for seeking God's presence is our everyday lives. He taught the novice monks at Gethsemani to contemplate by entering "the school of their lives." Contemplative prayer perceived all the events of their lives as a "school of wisdom." In *New Seeds of Contemplation,* he wrote:

> Contemplation is a response to a call: a call from Him [sic] Who has no voice, and yet Who speaks in everything that is, and Who, most of all, speaks in the depths of our own being: for we ourselves are words of His. But we are words that are meant to respond to Him, to answer Him, to echo Him, and even in some way to contain Him and signify Him. Contemplation is this echo. It is a deep resonance in the inmost center of our spirit in which our very life loses its separate voice and resounds with the majesty and mercy of the Hidden and Living One.[46]

Thus, contemplation was attentiveness to the "words" God was always speaking through their most personal experiences. To hear God's voice, they needed to ruminate on the daily direction of their hearts' desires. This way of praying, however, would never be automatic. They would have to make conscious decisions to instigate their contemplative lives.

> Either you look at the universe as a very poor creation out of which no one can make anything, or you look at your own life and your own part in the universe as infinitely rich, full of inexhaustible interest, opening out into the infinite further responsibilities for study and contemplation and interest and praise. Beyond all and in all is God.[47]
>
> Perhaps the Book of Life, in the end, is the book one has lived. If one has lived nothing, one is not in the book of life.[48]

Reversing the Flow

Thomas Merton believed contemplation was "a response to a call: a call from Him Who has no voice, and yet Who speaks in everything that is, and Who, most of all, speaks in the depths of our own being: for we ourselves are words of His."[49]

Wow. If you thought of yourself as a word of God, it would mean that the entire way in which you lived and acted would have to dramatically change. It changed Merton. Deep within himself, Merton touched the flow and ultimate source of life. His stability ultimately came not from the monastery but from the only stable source there is . . . God.

Merton shows us the need to reverse the flow of life, from receiving to giving. The fruit of contemplation is that it exposes and transforms our basic selfishness and egocentricity by showing us that we must serve others. The unmerited gift of love within us increases as we give it away. The saints and mystics down through the ages knew on a cellular level that God dwelt within them and that God's spirit needed to flow out of them to others.

Faith is a pilgrimage to compassion.

A Culture of Compassion

Jesus is a physician not a judge. Jesus wanted to end the superficial conflicts of his day by inaugurating a culture of compassion. Jesus desired that love would so permeate our being that compassion for all would become a normal part of our behavior—that every act of our lives, no matter how small or insignificant, would be life giving.

In *New Seeds of Contemplation,* Thomas Merton wrote: "The function of faith is not to reduce mystery to rational clarity, but to integrate the unknown and the known together in a living whole, in which we are more and more able to transcend the limitations of our external self."[50]

A State of Flux

Life is laced with inconsistencies and contradictions. Life is a constant state of flux. Life is filled with ambiguity, failure, and false starts . . . and that's OK. Life throws things at you . . . some good, some bad. Life is a school; you keep learning until graduation, which comes at death.

It's in failure and rejection that we're given the chance to truly face our inner demons. What we need to become whole is hidden in our brokenness.

Nada

Note: *A few years before my time in Merton's hermitage, I spent some time in Italy working on my first book on Saint Francis. The following was penned in 1997 in Assisi. My prayer life has improved since then, but what I wrote was still pretty close to an accurate portrayal of my prayer life until a few years ago.*

There is one area of my life where poverty is very real: my prayer life is impoverished. If I had to choose one word to describe my prayer life, it would be *empty.* A big, fat nada. Perhaps the reason my experience of prayer is empty is because Jesus is still outside of me—not within me in an existentialist way which I can feel. So, my prayer seems "outward" and lacks the true intimacy of being "inward," a sweet communion within me, as I imagine it was for Francis and all the other saints. I often experience prayer as a blank inertia. Once in a great while, the blankness or void gives way—ever so fleetingly—to something more substantive, as if God, though still hidden, is really present. When I experience prayer as a void, I lack the trust in God to continue anyway. I flee the darkness, the emptiness.

I've tried setting more time aside for quiet prayer—just sitting still before the Lord— but the noise of my own thinking, my own consciousness, makes it virtually impossible for me to sit still for more than a few minutes. Saint Teresa of Ávila may have had an interior castle, but I have an interior prison—blank, cold, barren. Even though I love God and sincerely long for a deeper relationship, I consider myself a spiritual failure because of my inability to pray more effectively, to feel more connected to God on a daily basis. Sin seems nearer than God does. A lot nearer.

Saint Francis de Sales said something to the effect that to continually get up after a fall, over and over again, was more pleasing to God than if we had not fallen at all. His point: faith that persists, despite continual failure, must please God. I hope so.

> *Oh dear God, please give me the courage to trust fully in You when my prayer leaves me feeling alone; give me, sweet Lord, the grace of perseverance to sit still in my inner prison until you unlock the door. St. Augustine writes: "Go back inside yourself, for truth dwells in the inner man." Come, Lord Jesus, enter my heart with your Presence and Fullness.*

Note: The prayer has slowly been answered over the last twenty-five years, increasingly so in the last four years. While formal prayer still is a struggle, I'm nonetheless now more aware of God's presence in my daily life. Actually, it would be more accurate to say that I'm more aware of God's presence as I go about my day. While I do set a modest amount of time aside each day for prayer and reflection (usually the first one to two hours of each day), I most often feel God's presence when I have a camera in my hands and I'm in the middle of a slum.

In a slum, I'm far removed from the normal concerns of my life, and I'm truly able to see the other. A slum is where God "speaks" to me, usually about my own personal weaknesses and my need to be more merciful, more compassionate, and less judgmental. (Being less judgmental is the hardest part.) During my prayer time, external words from my devotional reading occasionally come alive and seem to enter into my very being, and their truth becomes my truth. But it is different with a camera in my hands. It is then that something within me speaks to me.

Oh . . . how words fail when trying to articulate things of the Spirit. Merton wrote very little about his own prayer life. I once made a very simple statement, which actually catches the essence of what I'm struggling to say: I pray with my camera. The camera helps me see . . . and, hopefully, what I film or photograph helps others see also.

Where the King Dwells

> *"If we neglect prayer we are like the unweaned child taken*
> *from its mother's breast and given no substitute."*
>
> —RUTH BURROWS, *INTERIOR CASTLE EXPLORED*[51]

For most of the last two decades, my problem wasn't neglecting prayer; it was advancing in prayer. *Advancing* isn't exactly the right word; perhaps, understanding prayer better describes my frustration with prayer. I couldn't understand why prayer had become difficult and unrewarding, a task rather than a joy. In the late 1990s when I was still teaching a month-long annual course on writing at the Pontifical Gregorian University in Rome and was struggling with prayer, I had dinner with a Jesuit priest who was professor of systematic theology at the university. Our conversation briefly touched on prayer. He told me to read the second chapter of the fourth mansion in Saint Teresa of Ávila's spiritual masterpiece, *Interior Castle*.

The next day, I went to a bookstore near the Vatican and bought the book. I read it and shrugged. The idea of God as a king residing in a castle didn't connect with me. A year later, home in Los Angeles, I was still struggling with prayer, when I came across Saint Teresa's book again. I recalled the Jesuit's advice and read the recommended section again. This time, the saint's words roused my interest and found a tentative home in my heart.

The seven mansions or dwelling places within Teresa's imaginative castle represent stages of prayer. The first thing I learned from the book, which Saint Teresa began writing in 1577, is that the spiritual journey is slow and long. There are no express lanes to the seventh mansion. The trip takes time and energy. When you embark upon the journey, you will slowly begin to put distance between yourself and everything you once thought to be important. Your travel companions are silence and solitude; contemplation is your walking stick.

The Interior Castle is not the gospel on prayer; it is merely the saint's way of describing her path to God. There are many paths. Saint Teresa is telling us that our souls were made for God, that we have the capacity to enter into union with the Creator. God is dwelling in the depths of your soul, and prayer is how you communicate with the Majesty of All.

We are all invited to the interior castle and to find our way to the innermost room where God dwells . . . waiting for us. Continual prayer is the door through which you enter. All that you need is within you . . . where the unity of all life exists.

Cosmic Bellhop

Over the years, I've learned that prayer is not about asking God for favors, as if God were a cosmic bellhop picking up put bags of need. Prayer is simply a path to an inner life.

God is in your prayer; God is the essence of prayer.

When you pray, you are not praying to a far-off God, who may or may not be listening to your prayer. God is within you. Prayer, therefore, is within you. Prayer is the gateway to that place deep within you where you experience the oneness of God . . . and see the beauty of God everywhere, even in the midst of a slum. Prayer brings us into the presence of the inner light.

Silence Is Still Preferable

Silence is also a form of prayer that may lead us to an inner experience of God. Rabbi Dov Ber of Mezeritch (Ukraine)—a disciple of the Baal Shem Tov—commends contemplative silence as a way to meet God:

> "He who speaks too much brings sin."
> (*Pirkei Avot* 1:5).
> The meaning of this teaching is as follows:
> the word sin means deficiency.
>
> Even when you speak with others about the wisdom
> of the Torah,
> silence is still preferable.
>
> Silent contemplation offers greater possibilities for
> connection with the Divine
> than does discussion or speech.[52]

Paradoxes and Inconsistencies

From the moment of his baptism at the age of twenty-three, Merton's sole desire was to encounter God's living presence in his own imperfect life and in the chaotic times in which he lived. This deep yearning for God was the ground of both his monastic life and his writing life. Nonetheless, his life did not have a happy, neat ending. His life was a pilgrim's march down a dark, lonely path toward God. During his sustained, probing journey, Merton heard God's "voice" beckoning him, though often muffled, through all his experiences. This is the Merton I can understand, because it has been through the experiences of my life—especially the bad experiences—that I came to "know" God a little better. (Also, over the years, my exploration into other religions, reading great Jewish writers, Islamic writers, and Buddhist writers, greatly expanded my understanding of the Christian tradition into which I was born.)

My own life, once I began to really examine it, has taught me more than any dogma or article of faith. Through my sin I learned what sin really was, and I saw my own weakness. The magic of Merton's autobiographical writing is that in it he often manages to seduce the reader into thinking they are having an actual conversation with him as one human to another. In the preface to a translation of one of his books, he wrote: "I seek to speak to you, in some way, as your own self."

Merton incites personal engagement and response. All kinds of people have made Merton's journals their own. I obliquely saw many aspects of myself in them. I remember reading once that Merton "felt out of place everywhere." So do I. Someone also said he was "all tumult and tranquility." That sounds like me also. Like Merton, I can shift gears emotionally and intellectually in a heartbeat. Merton showed us his heart so we in turn could see our own hearts. His flashes of envy and anger resonated with me. He admits to backsliding; backsliding was second nature to me. Through the mirror of his autobiographical art, Merton prompted me to reflect more deeply on the mystery of my life.

Like Merton, we all struggle with conflicting desires that prevent true inner peace. We're all confronted with temptations we occasionally can't resist. Merton's best creation was the molding of his inner life. The goal of the spiritual life is to find peace within ourselves and then share that peace with others.

> *Recognized or not, the greatest reality in life is*
> *our desire to know and be united with God.*
> *Sadly, our natural desire for God*
> *has been so distorted by false desires*
> *that we must purify from our hearts*
> *before we can come close to God.*

My Soul Is Thirsting for You

My soul has been wounded, gravely so. I am unable to heal myself. You, O God, alone know the source of my hidden ailments. You know all my doubts, all my confusions, and the endless contradictions that spring from my meager life. You know my weaknesses, my faults and my many failures. You, O God, alone know how parched and dry my inner life is, how I desperately thirst for the only water that can quench my intense longing.

I truly do want to be one with You and to please You always. But through my fault, my most grievous fault, I do not always act as I wish to act. I am not always aware of Your presence because I am too focused on myself, on my own wounds, my own ideas, my own selfish desires. The path to Your door and the fullness of life is straight and narrow, yet I keep veering off onto cul-de-sacs of empty promises and phantom illusions.

My God, my God your way is so confusing and hard to follow. Yet it is so clear and so easy to follow. You simply and only want me to love, always, everywhere, everyone. You want me to do as You do, to make myself invisible and silent, to make myself weak and poor, to give myself away, completely and without reservation, so that only You can shine.

So begins a long prayer that came at the end of my book *The Sunrise of the Soul.*

I love this amazingly hopeful line in Paul's Letter to the Romans: "The spirit comes to the aid of our weakness for we do not know how to pray as we ought, but the Spirit himself intercedes with inexpressible groanings ["sighs" is a better translation]." (Romans 8:26) The point: When I earnestly began my journey to God I didn't even have to know how to pray. I just needed to begin in my own poverty and weakness.

Merton summed it up best: "Love is the epiphany of God in our poverty. The contemplative life . . . is the search for peace . . . in the openness of love. It begins with the acceptance of my own self in my poverty."[53]

In *The Sign of Jonas*, Merton told himself that he needed to "shut up" and "be simple and poor" if he ever wanted to experience real peace.

Jesus was born in poverty and simplicity. How can I reject (or dishonor) the birth condition of my savior? On the road to God, words eventually dissolve into silence.

CHAPTER 5

A Radical Message

Dark Cellars

Merton is not always easy to understand. For me it has been a blessing to have a friend like Jonathan who has been so willing to freely share his hard-earned insights into Merton's life that he garnered from years of study. So much of what has been written on Merton is too densely academic for most people to understand. The so-called "Merton experts" seem to write expressly for other "Merton experts," leaving the rest of us to fumble around in the dark.

Montaldo Study Note 3

Always Stretching Forward toward Christ: Thomas Merton's Restless Journey

"All I want is to know Christ and the power of his resurrection and to share his sufferings by reproducing the pattern of his death. That is the way I can hope to take my place in the resurrection of the dead. Not that I have become perfect yet: I have not yet won, I am still running, trying to capture the prize for which Christ Jesus captured me. I can assure you . . . I am far from thinking that I have already won. All I can say is that I forget the past and I strain ahead [epektesein] for what is still to come. I am racing to finish, for the prize to what God calls us upwards to receive in Christ Jesus." (Philippians 3:10–14)

Merton remained a monk of Gethsemani for twenty-seven years because he never abandoned his love for the journey of becoming a monk. In spite of decades of monastic routine (perhaps precisely because of it), he could muster a poet's joy for the smallest turns of difference in time or temperature that marked an ordinary day as singular and new. His private joys in living his monastic life—often muffled below the public voicing of his cares, especially in the middle 1960s—situated him among those rare human beings who love the life they are leading and who have found their own true place. Listen to his joy in private prayer as he gazes out at his monastery's natural setting:

This marvelous vision of the hills at 7:45 A.M. The same hills as always, as in the afternoon, but now catching the light in a totally new way, at once very earthly and very ethereal, with delicate cups of shadow and dark ripples and crinkles where I had never seen them before, the whole slightly veiled in mist so that it seemed to be a tropical shore, a newly discovered continent. A voice in me seemed to be crying, 'Look! Look!' For these are the discoveries, and it is for these that I am high on the mast of my ship (have always been) and I know that we are on the right course, for all around is the sea of paradise.[54]

Monastic life and a poetic sensitivity inculcated in him this heightened awareness and attention, this alertness to the possibilities of the hour, what he called "the grip of the present on him" Alert expectancy to the speech a day makes was a habit he cultivated for a fruitful examined life. Paradoxically his monastic stability over two decades and its cloistered, narrow horizons made keener his temperament to be more ready to depart rather than to settle down in fixed ideas or perspectives that prevented his continuing growth in seeking God more authentically. Merton was never afraid to walk away from himself when, through experience, prayer, and study he found himself still too narrow and noninclusive to be a monk who was called to be a thoroughly Catholic human being.

Originally published in his book *Thoughts in Solitude*, Thomas Merton's most famous prayer names ignorance and insecurity as two of the generative guardian angels who attended his hope-filled monastic life and his literary career:

My Lord God, I have no idea where I am going. I do not see the road ahead of me. I cannot know for certain where it will end. Nor do I really know myself. But I believe that the desire to please you does in fact please you. And I hope I have that desire in all that I am doing and I hope I never do anything apart from that desire. And I know, that if I do this, you will lead me on the right road though I may know nothing about it. Therefore, I shall trust you always, though I may be lost and in the shadow of death, I shall not fear. For you are ever with me and you will never leave me to face my perils alone.[55]

Not to know where his life was going was always to begin again every day to take up his life of loving learning and desiring God. His ignorance was a stimulus to his continuing education in how to seek God. His insecurity animated his transcending limitations of his past experiences to incarnate new and more inclusive ways of living. Knowing he was ignorant was a wisdom that poised Merton to reach out to his life's "next thing" and to turn the next corner in his search for the "secret of God's Face" (*The Seven Storey Mountain*). Merton's acute restlessness of heart and mind, so striking in his completely published journals, was, therefore, foundational in his intensely personal search for God's presence in his life. Restlessness and insecurity kept him sober and watchful, although never perfectly it is true, so that he might not miss a moment in which his Christ might pass by for him.

Scholars have called Thomas Merton a "spiritual master," and the back covers of his books proclaim him one of the most significant spiritual writers of the twentieth century; however, Merton's own assessment of his identity was more modest. He wrote in his private journal in 1965, after twenty-four years of spiritual celebrity and monastic life, a pithy judgment about his "true self": "I am nobody's answer, not even my own." No matter our ascetic practices and how much we pray, no matter how many books we read or books we publish, no matter our status as pope or international celebrity, we will eventually need to find that place in our restless hearts where we can kneel and wait for a mercy that we know we cannot give to ourselves. We must eventually find that place in our restless hearts where we are deeply conscious that "all is grace."

One of Merton's conscious goals in writing private journals and in legally ensuring their complete publication after his death was to demolish any future for his guru status as a "spiritual master" and to insure a more complex reception of his literary and spiritual legacy. And while that legacy is indeed an authentic testament to an evangelical way of living based on imitation of Christ, particularly as transmitted by a Benedictine monastic rule, he knew his private journals would prove a stumbling block, even a cause for scandal, for readers expecting to find in his journals a holy man to emulate.

Merton's private journals have been fully published in seven volumes. They do not reveal his ascent to ever-higher stages of spiritual attainment. They reveal instead his gradual descent into a spiritual poverty that fully turned him toward God's mercy, like a hollowed-out tree turns toward the lightening that is about to strike it. Many a paragraph in his private journals are saturated with his tears, with his realization that he was not the monk, not even the human being, that his public books had led readers to think he was. His interior journey, which he claimed was more important than his exterior successful career, was often struggling. To the very end, he acknowledged himself always stumbling forward and imperfect. Read from this perspective, Merton's private journals are a narrative of how he was gradually being liberated from his aspirations to be a spiritual celebrity as a result of writing an autobiography, *The Seven Storey Mountain,* that misguided many a reader into thinking Thomas Merton was a monk who had fully arrived and was assured of continuing spiritual attainments.

In writing journals, Merton is acutely conscious of his intended reader: he incites his reader to identify with his words and his journey. He invites a personal involvement with major moments in his life that reminded him to more deeply become a person who prays and seeks God. He considered his best work to be autobiographical, what he called his "art of confession and witness."

Reflecting on my long experience of reading Merton since I was thirteen and keeping company with his books now into my seventies, I seem in retrospect almost destined to have heard his "voice" so early in my life. His voice has always educated me. His words still open my heart's inner ear. He still animates me to lead an "examined life." Through my long dialogues with Merton's texts, I have recognized our codependence on a providential divine mercy attending our interior journeys.

To expose the fault lines between his ideals and his day-to-day struggles to achieve them, to mind the gap between his published pious rhetoric and his struggling practice, was a major motive that impelled Merton to write and publish his private journals.

Precisely because his world-famous autobiography *The Seven Storey Mountain* had freeze-framed for his readership a glowing portrait of his pious self, his decision to continue with private journals, publishing an edited version as *The Sign of Jonas* in 1952, became a spiritual practice of honesty with regard to the crooked road his life had taken by the pursuit of both monastic vows and the exigencies of a literary career. His journals became, he wrote, "part of a documentation that is demanded of me--still demanded, I think—by the Holy Ghost." Merton allowed his journals to reveal the contradictions and inconsistencies that had always attended his monastic journey. His journals expose the otherwise hidden sins that truly mar his reputation as a public holy man. His journals became a means for him to practice what I call the virtue of his compassionate transparency. Let this journal entry be a case in point:

> Someone accused me of being a "high priest" of creativity. Or at least of allowing people to think me so. The sin of wanting to be heard, of wanting converts, disciples. Being in a cloister, I thought I did not want this. Of course I did and everyone knows it. . . . St William, says the breviary this night, when death approached, took off his pontifical vestments (what he was doing with them on in bed I can't imagine) and by his own efforts got to the floor and died. So I am like him, in bed with a miter on. What am I going to do about it? I have got to face the fact that there is in me a desire for survival as pontiff, prophet and writer, and this has to be renounced before I can be myself at last.[56]

Merton was first to admit that any treasures of spiritual insight embedded in his writing were a harvest from graced poor soil. His journals expose the real fissures in his character that rendered him a weak vessel in which by God's grace important lessons for others were contained. This is, of course, a theme in the Pauline corpus of the New Testament. And while Merton is no Saint Paul, how Protestant theologian Karl Barth judged the value of Saint Paul's vocation in his *Epistle to the Romans* could as well be said of Merton's value for his readers:

When pilgrims on the road to God meet one another, they have something
to say. A man may be of value to another man, not because he wishes to be
important, not because he possesses some inner wealth of soul, not because of
something he is, but because of what he is not. His importance may consist in
his poverty, in his hopes and fears, in his waiting and hurrying, in the direction
of his whole being towards what lies beyond his horizon and beyond his power.
The importance of an apostle is negative rather than positive. In him a void
becomes visible.[57]

The deep significance for us of Merton's legacy of "confession and witness" as contained in his private journals consists in his errors and in his acknowledged and exposed
failures. He exposes our shared human fate to stand with our feet straddling a divide
between who we long to be and who we actually are. Merton's self-confessed limitations
and errors illuminate. As Merton elaborates the contradiction of his desiring purity of
heart, while witnessing in himself the ability to evade the humility for its procurement,
he places before his reader's eyes everyone's struggles with conflicting desires that attend
everyone's interior life.

Merton focuses for his readers the inadequacy of confining religious experience to
the esthetic, or to the intellectual and academic, so as to hide from others and even
from oneself one's deeply conflicted personal experience when seeking God. Writing to
philosopher Étienne Gilson, Merton had pleaded:

Please pray for me to Our Lord that instead of merely writing something I may
be something, and indeed that I may so fully be what I ought to be that there
may be no further necessity for me to write, since the mere fact of being what
I ought to be would be more eloquent than many books.[58]

Merton confessed what all of us know: one can write and speak beautifully about the
spiritual life while not being able to live a beautiful spiritual life. Merton publicly exposed
his spiritual poverty so that he could own it. His practice of writing journals is thus akin
to the practice of confession urged by Gregory of Nazianzus: "He who manifests his
thoughts is soon healed. He who hides them makes himself sick." The confession of his
clay feet not only subverts the admiration of his readers but was an invitation to realize
with him that we must always be stretching forward toward the Father, through Christ
Jesus and with the Holy Spirit, the Holy Spirit who alone should be acknowledged as the
only Spiritual Master.

Now having entered my seventh decade, the tone and content of Merton's private
journals in his maturity captures my attention most. His voice from his longed-for hermitage, as he entered his fifties, has a more broken and uncertain modulation that strikes

me, from where I am hearing it now, as utterly honest and convincing. After finally getting everything, he always thought and said he wanted—being solitary in a hermitage—Merton was taken aback at finding himself still capable of acting much like the same young man he was on Perry Street in New York's Greenwich Village. Away from his monastic community, Merton, though never leaving off the daily disciplines, discovered himself much too easily and once more acting wild.

Merton's voice from the hermitage rivets me as he writes journals through encounters with seasons of insecurity that tore away at the disguises he had worn to hide the hard truths about his more visceral self. In his long-hoped-for hermitage, Merton experienced a "dread" for which his prayer, he did not know it fully until then, had always been preparing him. After decades of publicly theorizing on the spiritual life and of practicing monastic disciplines, Merton in his hermitage found himself humbled, his back to the wall, as he experienced himself making a mess of his "answered prayers" for a solitary life. Sitting on his hermitage porch in 1966, realizing that he had fallen deeply in love with a young woman, we read his words with eyes wide open, as he cries out to God into a dark night, calling out in his loneliness for mercy and the grace to realize that a broken, opened heart is the final destiny of a monastic vocation.

Merton appeals at this end-game stage of his interior journey because his hermitage experience allowed him no more mirrors to reflect upon himself garbed in the saffron robes of a "spiritual master." His journals of the late sixties profess the defeat for the plans of his self-idealizing personality as a hermit. His readers witness a void opening in him that attests to anyone reading closely that only God's mercy can transfigure a broken heart into a final blessing.

At the early age of thirty, having just completed the final draft of the autobiography that would make him famous, Merton had already realized that his interior contradictions and paradoxes formed by his conflicting desires would not be problems he would ever be able to solve. His life's contradictions were rather personal mysteries of faith through which he truly sought God. He wrote of this dynamic of traveling through contradictions and paradox in *The Seven Storey Mountain*:

> In one sense we are always traveling, and traveling as if we did not know where we were going. In another sense we have already arrived. We cannot arrive at the perfect possession of God in this life, and that is why we are traveling and in darkness. But we already possess Him by grace, and therefore, in that sense, we have arrived and are dwelling in the light, But oh! How far have I to go to find You in whom I have already arrived![59]

Jonathan always gives me something to ponder. Merton didn't pretend to have all the answers. More important than answers were the depth and quality of the questions Merton relentlessly asked on his spiritual journey, questions that arose out of foundational human discontentment that never allow us to settle without deep anxiety for easy, unexamined answers. Of course, we hate not having definite, black-and-white answers. We want the heroes and villains to be clearly delineated, that the right and the wrong ways to approach religious questions be clearly exposed. But insecurity is the guardian angel at the continuing presence of mysteries that attend our experience of being alive. These foundational mysteries, to paraphrase the French philosopher, author, and playwright Gabriel Marcel, can never be reduced into solvable problems. They remain painful despite any efforts to anesthetize our seemingly primal mental wounds.

The essential Transcendence of God is found in God's ultimate unknowability. Yet, we grasp at whatever we can know, and this leads us on in what, in the eyes of many, is a futile pursuit. But the "pursuit" is the point! Every day I'm confronted with the question: *Does God exist and if so what difference does it make in my life?* As I pen these words (in 2018), violent atrocities in Gaza, Syria, and Iraq are causing global dismay and creating a sense of absolute hopelessness. (Today, we see innocent civilian lives killed in Ukraine.) Here in America, the humanitarian crisis along our southern border caused by thousands upon thousands of kids fleeing extreme violence and poverty in Central America streaming into the United States, many unaccompanied by their parents, is bringing out a shameful, mean-spirited ugliness within many Americans—as members of one political party turn their backs on these suffering children and do absolutely nothing. I saw firsthand the violence in Honduras when I filmed there in February 2014, witnessing someone being shot. We say we worship Jesus, but following him is another story. We've turned the life, message, and truth of Jesus into a toothless religion instead of a persistent journey toward union with God, all people, and all creation.

In all humility, we need to fall to our knees in prayer. And, as Merton suggested, keep our mouths shut.

Jesus Was a Radical

Jesus was a radical. He thought there was something radically wrong with the entire Jewish notion that God intended to bring nationhood back to the Hebrew people, of which he was one. He instead replaced that accepted idea with the radical notion of an international family of citizens of God's kingdom that would voluntarily share, forgive, live simply, seek reconciliation, and give one's entire self to God and the ways of God. Jesus wanted to bring about a radical restructuring of Jewish life by replacing the old system of Jewish dominance of the region with a system built on love, compassion, and mercy. Jesus was also a radical in his private life in that he befriended sinners and social outcasts. He also brought groups together that traditionally hadn't been brought together (tax collectors, prostitutes, church leaders). This didn't sit well with some of the Jewish and civic leaders, putting him on the road to a horrific death on a cross.

To Love Is to Live

We came from Love and we will find fulfillment when we return to and embrace Love. Love is manifested when we welcome others—the stranger, the weak and hurting, and even our enemies—and we work for their well-being in our everyday lives. If this happens on a mass scale, the world will be transformed by Love. At the core of our problems is the reality that we have strayed far from Love and genuine concern for others. To love is to live.

In the beginning, Christianity was a very radical expression of peace and love. It preached nonviolence and compassion. Early Christians were joyful in the midst of suffering and persecution. They were alive to Love in a new, dynamic way that made them different from their surrounding society. This is no longer the case. For the most part, Christians today are indistinguishable from the rest of our fragmented, divisive, competitive, "me first" society.

American Religious Landscape

> *"Power always protects the good of some at the expense of all others.*
> *Only love can attain and preserve the good of all."*
>
> —THOMAS MERTON, DISPUTED QUESTIONS[60]

In 1986, *America* literary editor Patrick Samway S.J. interviewed Andre Dubus for the November 15, 1986, edition of the magazine. In his blunt manner, the acclaimed short-story writer had some tough words for the American religious landscape. Dubus told Father Samway:

> I've seen the whole of my fictive world through the eyes of someone who believes the main problem in the United States is that we have lost all spiritual values and not replaced them with anything that is comparable. We just pretend all this. We never have been a Christian country.
>
> As a matter of fact, there never has been a Christian country. Has there ever been a country that didn't kill its enemies, oppress the poor and bring the strong and the rich to power? Well, it saddens me and angers me. Maybe that's why I'm fascinated by the mystics, those who transcend all that drowns me. The mystics remain in harmony with the earth and their fellow human beings and, yet, are above it all as they enjoy union with God.

Dubus was spot on his assessment of the state of Christianity. It should sadden and anger us . . . and lead us to a more mystical expression of our faith. Years later, Henri Nouwen had a gentler view: "I am less and less clear what is good or bad religion, what is regressive or progressive, but I am more and more convinced how important it is to respond to real needs and to prevent ourselves from narrowing God to one or two images."[61]

Sometimes, probably often, our bad thinking become habits of the heart. A deceased friend, who was a Jesuit priest, once said to me, "Mini-prejudices and knee-jerk judgments can produce a mood of undeclared war."

A Question

The radical message for which Christ died is dramatically opposed to our culture of selfish individualism and unchecked consumerism. Should not our Christian faith compel us, by means of our transformed hearts, to live differently from the rest of our culture, whose values are rooted in the material realm and are far from the teachings of Christ?

We have reduced Christ to a sublime abstraction,
making it possible to ignore the very truth of Christ.

Accepting Surrender

The cost of following Jesus is nothing less than everything: one must abandon self in order to imitate the self-transcendence of the Cross and Resurrection. The Cross symbolizes the extremity of helplessness more than the extremity of suffering. The Cross rejects power and accepts surrender. When we have little or no worldly power to rely on, we are able to offer unambiguous love and service.

God is not asking us to become perfect;
God is asking us to surrender everything.

Love Is the Key

Jesus asks us to love as God loves—without counting the cost or holding anything back. Love gives all away. Love frees us to act for the good of another rather than for ourselves. God's love is unbiased and all-embracing. It doesn't ask who we are or how successful we are at what we do.

To give freely what we have freely received—namely, God's love—is the purest form of evangelization. Following the example of Christ will lead us to go poor among the poor, without power, without purse, and without provisions, but with charity and respect for those we encounter. If our efforts at sharing God's love are warmly received, fine; if not, we should move on. Our lives are our sermons, and our preaching should be benign and gentle, spoken with meekness and humility. We must seek peace above all else and then do good at every opportunity. Being an instrument of peace requires us to love our neighbor and to embrace the enemy in pardon.

In his book, *Zen Gifts to Christians*, Robert Kennedy, who is a Jesuit priest and Zen teacher, writes: "My neighbor is my very self; my compassionate service to my neighbor cannot be contrived. It must be as natural and as spontaneous as my breathing in and out."[62] The nineteenth-century Lithuanian Rabbi Yisrael Salanter, who often quoted by the eminent Jewish theologian and philosopher Emmanuel Levinas, said, "The material needs of my neighbor are my spiritual needs." Robert Kennedy wrote, "To seek direct contact with God is for Levinas to cultivate madness because we can only go to God through our neighbor."[63] My experience in Haiti helps me see the wisdom in the importance of my neighbor in my personal salvation.

Who Is Not My Neighbor?

For some reason, yesterday (July 10, 2016) during a period of quiet time, my mind drifted to the Parable of the Good Samaritan. The story begins with a religious leader, either a lawyer or a scholar, testing Jesus with this question: "What must I do to inherit eternal life?" Jesus asks him what the law says. The man gave a pretty straight-forward answer about loving God with all his heart, soul, mind, and strength, and loving "your neighbor as yourself." Jesus told him he had answered correctly. But the man pressed Jesus by asking, "Who is my neighbor?"

Jesus replies with story of the Good Samaritan. A man is beaten, stripped, robbed, and left for dead on the side of the road. Two religious people, a priest and a Levite, happen to come across the victim struggling for life. (A Levite was an important official at the Temple.) To avoid the wounded man, both the priest and the Levite cross the street and continue on their way. Then along comes a Samaritan. The people hearing Jesus tell this parable understood that Samaritans were despised people, outcasts shunned by society. The Jews hated Samaritans, whom they marginalized and subjected to extreme forms of prejudice.

Instead of crossing the street, the Samaritan approaches the wounded man, bends down, and anoints and bandages his wounds. He then lifts the man up and hoists him onto his donkey and transports him to the nearest inn, where he continued to treat the man. The next day, he gave the innkeeper some money and told him to give the man whatever he needed, and if he spends more than he was given, the Samaritan said he would pay him back on his return trip.

Jesus then asks the lawyer testing him, "Which of these three, do you think, was a neighbor to the man who fell into the hands of a robber?" The man gave the only answer he could, "The one who showed mercy." Jesus said to him, "Go and do likewise."

This parable emerges from the contemplative heart of Jesus. It calls Christians to "put on the mind of Christ" and to give ourselves away in compassionate love. Easier said than done. The radical message of Jesus essentially says that true freedom and real joy come from self-emptying love and loving the other. Of course, this is a very difficult task. Jesus was crucified for extending mercy and compassion far beyond the accepted limits of his society. It's an enormous risk to love people living on the peripheries of society—the homeless, the migrant, the refugee, the chronically poor who are living in massive slums surrounded by garbage, rotting waste, and perpetual violence. Jesus, of course, didn't avoid the risk; he paid the price for following his heart with his life. The Parable of the Good Samaritan challenges us to live the Gospel with radical compassion. The parable makes the primacy of the other abundantly clear. It is all about putting others first.

Our neighbor is not simply the person living next door to us. Nor is our neighbor the people we work with or happen to bump into as we go about our day. Our neighbor is not simply the people living in our town, city, state, or country. In the parable, Jesus is saying that our neighbor is the person we not only don't avoid but also seek out in order to help them. The priest and the Levite aren't diverted from their journey. When they see the wounded man, they simply circumnavigate around him and continue on their way without pausing. Jesus is saying that the Samaritan, by changing his own plans and stopping to help the wounded man, actually became a neighbor even though the wounded man was far outside the Samaritan's orbit of friends. The Good Samaritan, out of a spirit of pity and compassion, changed the course of his day. He took an unexpected action, drawing near the wounded man and helping him recover. He shared in the suffering of "the other." Perhaps he did so because he knew what it was like to be a victim, to have been wounded by prejudice, and so he could feel sympathy for the victim of the robbery.

In my life, I've often crossed to the other side of the street to avoid someone in pain. Jesus is telling us that we need to be open to changing our plans when we are presented with the possibility of tending to the needs of a wounded neighbor. Jesus wants us to move toward a person whom others ignore. By tending to the wounds of another, we are tending to the wounds of Christ. The Parable of the Good Samaritan calls us to leave our comfort zone and move toward our wounded neighbors. On March 27, 2013, Pope Francis said: "Following Jesus means learning to come out of ourselves . . . to go to the outskirts of existence, ourselves taking the first step towards our brothers and sisters, especially those farthest away, those who are forgotten, those most in need of understanding, consolation, help . . . ." The Pope went on to say:

> God thinks like the Samaritan who does not pass near the victim, feeling sorry
> for him, or looking the other way, but coming to his aid without asking anything
> in return; without asking whether he is a Jew, or a pagan, or a Samaritan, if he is
> rich, if he is poor: he doesn't ask anything. He comes to his aid: this is God . . .
> who moves toward us, without calculating, without measure. God is like this; God
> always takes the first step.

Jesus is always ready to bend down and help us; he wants to enter our lives, wash our feet, and give us hope. Jesus rushes into wounded hearts. He isn't afraid to be wounded by love. God is the Good Samaritan wanting to pour oil and wine on our wounds, wanting to bandage us and make us whole again.

Maybe the real question is not "Who is my neighbor?" but "Who is *not* my neighbor?" Jesus would answer that more poignant question with two words: *no one.*

I'll meet many of my "neighbors" at the airport this afternoon and on the flight to Haiti.

This evening I'll be very happy to see all the kids. They are my family. It hasn't been easy to tend to their many different emotional and physical wounds. But the struggle is teaching me more than I can describe. The kids are changing me. Slowly I'm learning to operate on a radical trust that God will provide us with what we need for this mission. I take strength in knowing so many of my journal readers stand in solidarity with Santa Chiara. Whenever I get concerned about the future or worry about the ballooning amount of money it takes to keep the operation afloat or where we are going to live at the end of the year, I close my eyes and think about all the miracles that happened to get us to this point.

Note: Living the lofty thoughts of Jesus in a dysfunctional and violent place like Haiti is not easy. To read and contemplate these lofty thoughts in Haiti is jarring. Even in such a safe haven as Santa Chiara, there are people on my staff who are vengeful, envious, dishonest, and thieves. Before I got a safe, I was robbed twice because I left my desk drawer unlocked, the thieves running off with more than $5,000. During my four-month stay in Haiti, someone stole a female staff member's cellphone. There is a constant flow of mean-spirited gossip. Contradictions abound. I find I'm continually wounded by love. Yesterday, I locked the door to my office and spent the day in solitude and silence. I could hear staff members talking very loudly, arguing about God knows what.

In Haiti, the response to violence is often more violence. Mercy never enters the equation. In his book Gandhi on Non-Violence, *Thomas Merton wrote: "Only the admission of defect and fallibility in oneself makes it possible for one to become merciful to others."*[64]

A Steep Climb

During a pilgrimage in 2000 to all the locations in Italy where Saint Francis spent time, I visited the small, remote village of Poggio Bustone, which is located about 16 kilometers from the city of Rieti. Just outside the village is the Convento di San Giacomo, which is believed to have been founded by Saint Francis in 1217. It sits in a high, rugged, and remote area that provided Francis ample solitude. Francis first came to Poggio Bustone in 1209. Down a flight of stairs from the friary is a small hermitage where Francis planted a cross to remind him of his redemption.

After a liturgy in the simple, little Church of Saint James the Great, built near the end of the fifteenth century, I climbed the mountain to soak in the spirit of solitude that permeates the shrine. The steep climb to the peak took me past six tiny chapels. The exhaustion I felt upon reaching the summit was a small price to pay for the chance to sit in the Grotto of Revelation, which is built of stone right into the side of the mountain. As an added bonus, the summit offers a spectacular view of the valley below. On this mountain, Francis tasted the mercy of God.

Poggio Bustone was a place of pardon for Saint Francis of Assisi. One day, Francis found a place for solitary prayer and stayed there for a long time. He was concerned about the future of his little band of friars and was praying for some sense of direction. While praying, his mind became preoccupied with the sins of his past. Francis's compunction over his sins was not a simple matter of feeling sorrow about wrong actions. It was a sincere attempt to separate himself from those things within him that were harmful to his relationship with God. He no longer wanted any behavior from his past to have any power over his present, which was consumed by a love of God and a desire to grow closer to God. He began to repeat over and over again the words, "O Lord, have mercy on me a sinner." Eventually the repetition of his plea gave way to a great joy. The depths of his heart were washed in a soothing sweetness. His spirit danced in the certainty that all his sins had been forgiven and his soul was filled with an abundance of fresh grace.

> *When you give God your heart,*
> *God gives you new eyes*
> *so you may begin to see things*
> *the way God sees them—*
> *through the eyes of love, mercy, and compassion.*

For me, Poggio Bustone symbolized the need we all have to taste the mercy of God. To feel mercy, you need to be merciful. The more merciful you are, the more mercy you will feel. But to truly feel God's unlimited mercy, you need to incorporate into your day moments of stillness, moments where you can climb to the inner summit of your life and see the vast horizon of God's love. In Haiti, I too easily get stuck in the mud of problems and the muck of negativity from some of the staff who traffic in gossip and complaining. Often it is in the face of a child that I see the face of God and a smile crosses my face and my heart is encouraged.

> *"It was because the saints were absorbed in God that they were*
> *truly capable of seeing and appreciating created things and it was*
> *because they loved Him alone that they alone loved everybody."*
> —Thomas Merton, *New Seeds of Contemplation*[65]

We need a sense of balance between our intimate relationship with God, which is nurtured in contemplation and our communal relationships with our families, communities, and coworkers. But our drive for usefulness, for action, seems to far outweigh our desire to be still. We want to just plunge immediately into deep contemplation, but it doesn't happen. It takes a lot of time to still the restless movement within us. We are doers, performers who always have an itch to be acting. It is hard for us to simply sit before God and listen. But how can we speak about God or share God's love when we haven't fully experienced it ourselves?

CHAPTER 6

We Are Thirsty

*"Compassion, loving kindness, altruism, and a sense
of brotherhood and sisterhood are the keys to human
development, not only in future but in the present as well."*

—His Holiness the Dalai Lama,
The World of Tibetan Buddhism[66]

A Larger Cosmic Good

One of the books I have with me in Haiti is an oversized, beautiful photo/essay book titled, *The Tibetans* by Art Perry. His black-and-white photographs are exquisite, dramatically capturing the heart and soul of the people, their ancient culture, and mystical way of life, as well as the rugged beauty of the highest plateau on earth. Perry's writing is insightful and compelling. I was drawn to the book by the photography, but reading the text in Haiti has been enlightening. In the midst of such violence and chaos, where cheating, lying, stealing, and bullying is commonplace, reading about the harmony and balance within the Tibetan culture is mind-boggling. Here are just a few sentences that give you an idea of what I'm getting at:

> This expansive, all-inclusive thinking is really at the core of Tibetan Buddhism. Nothing in Tibet is unrelated to everything else. Whatever action, thought, or simple gesture a Tibetan may initiate, the result must be for a larger cosmic good. The smallest act of selfishness or evil can start a karmic ripple that will swell into a tidal wave of suffering and tragedy beyond itself. For this reason, Tibetans have long been ecologically attuned to the well-being of all sentient beings on this planet.[67]

There is much to learn from cultures different from our own.

The Randomness of Life and Death

> *"A person on the way to God cannot expect continual progress or unwavering determination. We wobble along the journey, stumble off the path, find ourselves attracted to other directions, stand still, even regress. This is almost universal experience. What is significant is the strength of the reflex that keeps us bouncing back. There is something we keep returning to: a vision, a dream, a hope. Something gives us the courage to get up after each fall and resume the journey. This is concrete evidence of the Spirit's work, far more potent than any spiritual euphoria."*
>
> —Michael Casey, OCSO, *Toward God*[68]

A renewal is basically a matter of starting over again. Jesus suggested we needed to be born again . . . and again and again. That is, we constantly need to start over again. Jesus knows how easy it is for us to let God slip away from our consciousness, which we do whenever we begin to think we are in control of our lives and it is not necessary to trust in God for everything. To be born again, to start over again, means we return to a place where we are confident in God's love. In the beginning was the Word . . . which means God was with us in the beginning, that our very being at birth was united with God. But gradually we become separated from God, become our own distinct individuals. Without daily contact with God through prayer where we are nurtured by God's love, we slowly become more and more self-sufficient, trying to save ourselves from a host of problems life throws at us. As anxiety and worry worm their way into our lives, we try harder to control our lives instead of placing ourselves in the tender hands of God's loving care. Seeing the patterns of my life, I realize I'm in need of ongoing rebirth; I need to be continually renewed along the journey by the One who knows the way, or I'll wander off into cul-de-sacs of confusion and deadly addictions.

I need to be more aware that God is always offering me the grace to start over whenever I drift too far away from God. Forgetting God is easy because we live in a world of distractions, a world of endless diversions; moreover, the pressures of modern life, with its incessant demands, exhaust virtually all our energy. We are overwhelmed by tragic headlines from around the world, where so many people die from hunger or wars waged by tyrannical dictators . . . and from gun violence here in America where a madman with an assault rifle can walk into a movie theater or grammar school or church and wipe out dozens of lives in a matter of minutes.

Can we make any sense of the randomness of life and death? No, we can't. It is all a mystery. Yet we are surrounded by people who are not comfortable with living in a mystery . . . they want to live with religious certainty, want to have answers. But there really are no answers . . . except love. So many people from a wide range of faiths really don't put their trust in love. They believe they possess the truth, which they will defend by any means necessary, including violence and war. (As I pen these words, militant, extremist Muslims in northern Iraq are killing Christians who refuse to convert to Islam.) They want the rest of the world to live by their moral rules and precepts. Religious fanatics blow up abortion clinics, burn the Koran, harass gays, suppress women, excommunicate heretics, deny evolution, and resort to terrorism . . . all in the name of a loving God. It is no wonder atheism is on the rise . . . and no wonder our need for renewal is ongoing.

God is always offering us the grace of renewal, always inviting us to come home, to feel the embrace of divine love and forgiveness. Moments of grace pass by in a heartbeat. An attentive heart is essential.

> *God's love and mercy are far greater*
> *than my countless infidelities*
> *and my inability to*
> *totally surrender my will.*
> *Thank God.*

Note: *The above was written long before the Covid-19 magnified the randomness of life and death. Someone standing next to you coughs. You touch something they had touched. Within fourteen days you're in a hospital struggling to breathe. Perhaps before you became sick, you inadvertently infected others.*

As the death toll mounted, people were saying things such as: "Kinda feeling like the Earth just sent us all to our rooms to think about what we've done." Americans were frightened and feeling very uncertain. The notion of certainty and order, which are merely illusions, had been wiped away in a matter of months. All the things people cherish—job security, a solid economic system, a dependable healthcare system, a functioning government, great educational opportunities—all vanished in a wink, leaving us feeling vulnerable and disorientated.

Strong and Steadfast

God's mercy is always there to pick us up and dust us off. God pours his self-emptying love into unlimited acts of mercy wherein He eagerly shares in our sufferings. God's mercy heals and renews us, gives us new life. God's mercy is strong and steadfast in its embrace of sinners, absorbing our suffering and helping us carry the weight of our misdeeds.

Without God's mercy, I'd quickly wither and die. If I don't share God's mercy with those around me, with all those in need of mercy and forgiveness, then I'm guilty of hoarding the transforming power of mercy for myself. Divine mercy must flow through one human toward other humans. The more of God's merciful love we receive, the more compelled we are to extend an offering of mercy to others.

The gift of mercy must be shared.

Living Water

One day, near the end of a long, dusty journey, Jesus was tired and thirsty when he spotted a well. At the well, he asked a Samaritan woman for a cup of water. The woman was surprised by the request because a Jew would never speak to a Samaritan. She was also tormented by her past. She had five failed marriages and was currently living in shame with a man. She was truly marginalized and disorientated. She had come to the well at noon because she knew few people would be there during the hottest time of the day. She was so embarrassed by her messed up life, she wanted to avoid meeting anyone. But Jesus met her where she was. Jesus didn't judge her or reject her. After asking her for a drink of water, he offered her the living water that would renew her by the power of grace from above. She was born again, renewed in spirit in order to live a new life in God.

This is such a beautiful story illustrating that divine assistance is always trying to break through our pain and discouragement. Jesus was thirsty, not just for water, but for peace for the woman. He approached her and began a conversation. We are thirsty, and Jesus comes to give us a drink, because God thirsts for us and wants to give us hope and strength. Astonishing.

We're always "movin' on up." Our goal is upward mobility. We're in a hot pursuit of everything bigger and better. We hunger for a prestigious job, a higher salary, more power and influence. Yet, Jesus symbolizes a downward movement. We like the Jesus who produces miracles. The Jesus who bends down to help the lowly and hungry has less appeal to us. Sure, we can admire his compassion and tenderness, but we're not too quick to follow his example if it disrupts our lives. Jesus embodied the power of God, yet he elected to become powerless. He freely entered into wherever there was suffering in order to heal it. Jesus became one with the marginalized, not the powerful.

The Incarnation was downward mobility at its zenith. God became the child of a refugee couple forced to give birth in a barn surrounded by animals. Christ was born in a world where there was no room for him. His parents were homeless and powerless. Christ belonged to people who did not belong. And so, with people for whom there is no room in our world, Christ is present. Christ calls us to make our home among them, to be one with them, to love them as he does. Not all of us literally need to make our home among the rejected, but all of us need "to be at home" with them, that is to be comfortable among them, to spend time with them, to laugh with them, to cry with them, to embrace them, to be bound in fraternity with them, to have them present within us, always mindful of their needs. To be one with God is to be one with all. We are called to realize the unity of creation.

Everything is related to everything else.

CHAPTER 7

Uniquely Different Voices

A True Brotherhood

Years ago, long after I had lost my faith, I read about the Crusades in detail for the first time. I was horrified by the brutality employed by the Church and sickened by the political corruption that had infected the Church. My reading helped reinforce my belief that God did not exist. For a long time, religious intolerance was, for me, a stumbling block to God. It seemed that people of faith were more prone to hate than love, more prone to violence than peace. I made a rather fundamental mistake: I viewed religious fundamentalists as if they possessed the real truth of whatever religion to which they belonged.

Today, many people see bad priests, phony televangelists, and Christians killing each other in some parts of the world and reach the conclusion that Christianity is full of hot air and empty promises. Likewise, even more people, especially in the West, see Islamic terrorists flying planes into buildings in America and becoming suicide bombers in Iraq and Israel and believe all Muslims are dangerous and Islam is an inferior religion. In these tumultuous and terrifying times in which terrorism, war, genocide, and chronic, debilitating poverty engulf the entire globe, religion seems incapable of creating a community of peace, a climate of brotherhood. In the last few years, alleged Christians wave the Confederate flag, which has become a symbol of division and hatred.

Saint Francis's spirituality grew out of the tumultuous times in which he lived; it was an age of tremendous social change and horrific violence. Francis read the Gospels as a man of his times, a man who felt within himself the enraged passions of his age and who was swept along by the social currents of his society. He had all the aspirations of the people of his time. But reading the Gospel made it possible for him to liberate those aspirations from their limitations, and to make them blossom forth into a more complete vision of humanity and human destiny. The Gospel rubbed up against the turmoil within him, and in the depths of his heart, he encountered a peace beyond all understanding, a living peace that made the labor of transformation the only job he wanted. In God's humility and humanity, Francis saw a way to rebuild society. He knew the accepted form of society, with lords and subjects, no longer worked and new Gospel-inspired community of interdependent, mutually respectful people was essential for survival.

The ideal of a true community of all people, excluding no one, is still, eight centuries later, a long, long way from being realized. The blueprint Francis discovered in his time in the Gospel and which the Sultan found in the Koran is there for us to discover. Our survival depends upon it. We need to talk to each other, listen to each other, learn from each other . . . and grow in love and compassion together.

Different Tongues

> *"You can safely assume you've created God in your own image*
> *when it turns out that God hates all the same people you do."*
>
> —ANNE LAMOTT, TRAVELING MERCIES[69]

Interfaith dialogue requires that people of differing faiths avoid dogmatic assertions when speaking with each other. Theological arrogance and rigidity stifle any authentic exchange. Nor will dialogue succeed if our aim is selling our theological perspective. True dialogue requires an honest mutual exploration of our respective theologies and felt experiences of God; it a journey toward understanding, not convincing.

The world's faiths speak in uniquely different tongues of a transcendent reality common to them all. The path of peace is dialogue. Dialogue transforms a stranger into a friend. Perhaps people of differing faiths can each grow closer to God by drawing closer to each other. Friends can unite in the struggle against poverty and evil.

The following is from a letter Thomas Merton wrote to his dear friend Abdul Aziz, a Pakistani Sufi.

> Personally, in matters where dogmatic beliefs differ, I think that controversy is of little value because it takes us away from the spiritual realities into the realm of words and ideas. In the realm of realities we may have a great deal in common, whereas in words there are apt to be infinite complexities and subtleties which are beyond resolution. It is, however, important, I think, to try to understand the beliefs of other religions. But much more important is the sharing of the experience of divine light, and first of all the light that God gives us even as the Creator and Ruler of the Universe. It is here that the area of fruitful dialogue exists between Christianity and Islam. I love the passages of the Quran which speak of the manifestations of the Creator in His Creation.[70]

Thomas Merton harbored no illusions about the manifold differences across religious and cultural boundaries or the difficulty of dialogue across deep and often painful historical and conceptual divides. Nevertheless, it was his intuition that authentic dialogue is not only possible but gives access to a deep communication that is not merely communication, but communion. During an informal talk in Calcutta in October 1968, just over a month before his death, Merton described the character of such a communion across seemingly impenetrable boundaries:

> It is wordless. It is beyond words, and it is beyond speech, and it is beyond concept. Not that we discover a new unity. We discover an older unity. My dear brothers, we are already one. But we imagine that we are not. And what we have to recover is our original unity. What we have to be is what we are.[71]

As a Byzantine Catholic and Franciscan Christian, my understanding of the world has a distinctly Christocentric character. For me, personal communion with Christ is at the center and heart of all reality. I believe Christ is the Wisdom of God, the "unknown and unseen" Sophia, in whom the cosmos is created and sustained. But that belief should not hinder me (but it often does) from affirming the other *as other*, from saying yes to the other, from saying yes to everyone. Merton put it best:

> The more I am able to affirm others, to say 'yes' to them in myself, by discovering them in myself and myself in them, the more real I am. I am fully real if my heart says yes to everyone.[72]

This isn't easy. Authentic dialogue isn't easy. It isn't easy to hold on to the core of your beliefs without denigrating conflicting beliefs held by people of different faiths. But we must.

> *Diversity is not the cause of disunity.*
> *A garden consists of many plants but is still one garden.*

In a landmark work in Christology (which was attacked by the Vatican), Jesuit scholar Roger Haight lays down a serious challenge to the patristic hermeneutic:

> The world is pluralistic and polycentric in its horizons of interpretation. It is impossible in postmodern culture to think that one group of people is a chosen people. Or that one religion can claim to inhabit the center into which all others are to be drawn. These myths or meta-narratives are simply gone.[73]

Can my inner and cosmic Trinitarian narrative withstand the skepticism of historical consciousness? Like most people, I'm not a systematic theologian and so I'm not preoccupied with formulas. We all need to find the common thread, to reveal the hidden wholeness, to see the inscape of the soul. We must do more than preach tolerance at a comfortable distance, without listening, without relationship, without growth. We must open ourselves to one another. We must risk learning something new and essential on the path to God, and thus risk altering the presumptions that have shaped our respective faiths. Perhaps our faiths need to be more lyrical and less dogmatic.

Our modus operandi should be: *more poetry and less prose.* Prose flattens the world, sees it as unchangeable, accepts unthinkingly the status quo, perpetuates the royal consciousness, and causes numbness and conformity. Poetry bursts forth with new life, upsets comfortable conformity, imagines new realities, resists the predominate consciousness, sees the world from an alternative perspective to the mind-numbing prose.

Pope John XXIII's prophetic, universal, and all-inclusive vision for the Second Vatican Council in 1962 helped ignite a worldwide ecumenical dialogue. One of the council documents clearly states:

> The Catholic Church rejects nothing that is true and holy in these religions. She regards with sincere reverence those ways of conduct and of life, those precepts and teaching which, though differing in many aspects from the ones she holds and sets forth, nonetheless reflect a ray of Truth which enlightens all people .... The Church, therefore, exhorts her children, that through dialogue and collaboration with the followers of other religions, carried out with prudence and love and in witness to the Christian faith and life, they recognize, preserve and promote good things, spiritual and moral, as well as socio-cultural values found among these people."[74]

The following quotation is from an insightful essay by Thomas Cahill titled "The Peaceful Crusader" that appeared in the Op-Ed pages of *The New York Times* on December 25, 2006.

> Francis was not impressed by the Crusaders, whose sacrilegious brutality horrified him. They were entirely too fond of taunting and abusing their prisoners of war, who were often returned to their families minus nose, lips, ears or eyes. In Francis' view, judgment was the exclusive province of the all-merciful God; it was none of a Christian's concern. True Christians were to befriend all yet condemn no one.

Francis and Buddha

Note: The following reflection was written in 1999 for my book The Sun & Moon Over Assisi. *It might be hard to believe that anything was dropped from that 614-page book, but this essay was.*

One afternoon, during a break from writing *The Sun & Moon Over Assisi*, I took a leisurely stroll through a bookstore. A small book with a deep red cover caught my eye. Simple, yet crisp gold lettering declared the title: *Living Buddha, Living Christ.* I was intrigued; Buddhism has always attracted me. I removed the book from the shelf. As I noticed the author's name—Thich Nhat Hanh—I felt a sense of resistance rise within me. I was tempted to return the book to the shelf without ever opening it. Did the author's unpronounceable name form a mental roadblock that prevented me from entering the book? The unfamiliar, the foreign or unknown often frighten us; we fear what we don't understand.

In the past, my fledgling interest in Buddhism was usually curtailed by . . . *vocabulary*. The literature, written by masters with names like Sogyal Rinpoche and Trungpa Chögyam, was laced with difficult words like *anatman, anitya, Avalokitesvara, anapanasati, bodhisattva, Dharmakaya, karuna, Sambhogakaya,* and *śūnyatā,* and perplexing concepts like nonduality and reincarnation; adding to the difficulty are the numerous divisions and schools within Buddhism. Or did the weakness of my faith in Christ cause me to be concerned about being exposed to ideas that might raise conflicts or doubts in my mind? Buddhists don't think of Buddha as a God. In fact, for Buddhists, God, either as an individual or a concept, doesn't exist. Buddhism feeds the spiritual hunger of our confused world by offering a religion without a God. In Buddhism, as I understand it, God is a presence (or energy) that is in everything; God (or God consciousness) is realized only when a person has managed, through the strict and lengthy practice of meditation and mindfulness, to eliminate all desires, illusions, and ideas.

I flipped the book over to read the back of the dust jacket. I immediately spotted Thomas Merton's friendly and familiar name. Merton is quoted as saying: "Thich Nhat Hanh is more my brother than many who are nearer to me in race and nationality, because he and I see things in exactly the same way." With Merton's helping hand, I made my way past my mental roadblock and opened the book.

The first paragraph of the foreword made me smile, for it contained another friendly and familiar name: St. Francis of Assisi. Moreover, the foreword was written by Brother David Steindl-Rast, OSB, a Benedictine monk whose writings I knew and admired. Here is the first paragraph of his foreword:

> Twice in this book Thich Nhat Hanh puts before us a powerful image of Christian legend: In midwinter, St. Francis is calling out to an almond tree, "Speak to me of God!" and the almond tree breaks into bloom. It comes alive. There is no other way of witnessing to God but by aliveness. With a fine instinct, Thich Nhat Hanh traces genuine aliveness to its source. He recognizes that this is what the biblical tradition calls the Holy Spirit. After all, the very word "spirit" means "breath," and to breathe means to live. The Holy Spirit is the breath of divine life.[75]

I bought the book. And read it with great interest. Thich Nhat Hanh is a Vietnamese monk and Zen master; he is both a mystic and an activist for peace. The book examines the compassion and holiness that is at the core of the two vastly different traditions of Christianity and Buddhism, and in doing so, it fosters a healthy understanding of and dialogue between the practitioners of each of these noble spiritual paths without threatening or compromising the tenets of either.

Surveying contemporary life, Thich Nhat Hanh writes:

There is a deep malaise in society. We can send e-mail and faxes anywhere in the world, we have pagers and cellular telephones, and yet in our families and neighborhoods we do not speak to each other. There is a kind of vacuum inside us, and we attempt to fill it by eating, reading, talking, smoking, drinking, watching TV, going to the movies, and even overworking. We absorb so much violence and insecurity each day that we are like time bombs ready to explode. We need to find a cure for our illness.[76]

Thich Nhat Hanh suggests that the cure may be right before us, and all we need to do is take another (and closer) look at the precepts found in Buddhism and Christianity, precepts he calls "jewels that we need to study and practice." He then outlines the five main precepts of Buddhism—reverence for life, generosity, responsible sexual behavior, speaking and listening deeply, and ingesting only wholesome substances—and offers commentary on each one. Prior to each commentary, the monk rephrased the principles so they would address the problems of our times.

What I want to share are those Buddhist principles, written in the form of vows, which I believe would make a great guideline for all Christians to follow—especially me. Thich Nhat Hanh writes:

1. Aware of the suffering caused by the destruction of life, I vow to cultivate compassion and learn ways to protect the lives of people, animals, plants, and minerals. I am determined not to kill, not to let others kill, and not to condone any act of killing in the world, in my thinking and in my way of life.[77]

2. Aware of suffering caused by exploitation, social injustice, stealing, and oppression, I vow to cultivate loving-kindness and learn ways to work for the well-being of people, animals, plants, and minerals. I vow to practice generosity by sharing my time, energy, and material resources with those who are in real need. I am determined not to steal and not to possess anything that should belong to others. I will respect the property of others, but I will prevent others from profiting from human suffering or the suffering of other species on Earth.[78]

3. Aware of the suffering caused by sexual misconduct, I vow to cultivate responsibility and learn ways to protect the safety and integrity of individuals, couples, families, and society. I am determined not to engage in sexual relations without love and long-term commitment. To preserve the happiness of myself and others, I am determined to respect my commitments and the commitments of others. I will do everything in my power to protect children from sexual abuse and to prevent couples and families from being broken by sexual misconduct.[79]

4. Aware of the suffering caused by unmindful speech and the inability to listen to others, I vow to cultivate loving speech and deep listening in order to bring joy and happiness to others and relieve others of their suffering. Knowing that words can create happiness or suffering, I vow to learn to speak truthfully, with words

that inspire self-confidence, joy, and hope. I am determined not to spread news that I do not know to be certain and not to criticize or condemn things of which I am not sure. I will refrain from uttering words that can cause division or discord, or that can cause the family or the community to break. I will make all efforts to reconcile and resolve all conflicts, however small.[80]

5. Aware of the suffering caused by unmindful consumption, I vow to cultivate good health, both physical and mental, for myself, my family, and my society by practicing mindful eating, drinking, and consuming. I vow to ingest only items that preserve peace, well-being, and joy in my body, in my consciousness, and in the collective body and consciousness of my family and society. I am determined not to use alcohol or any other intoxicant or to ingest foods or other items that contain toxins, such as certain TV programs, magazines, books, films, and conversations. I am aware that to damage my body or my consciousness with these poisons is to betray my ancestors, my parents, my society, and future generations. I will work to transform violence, fear, anger, and confusion in myself and in society by practicing a diet for myself and for society. I understand that a proper diet is crucial for self-transformation and for the transformation of society.[81]

Just as Francis considered the Sultan to be his brother, I consider Thich Nhat Hanh to be my brother . . . even though I still enjoy a nice glass of chianti and can't imagine wanting to abstain from wine.

Note: Postscript from Haiti, penned on May 2, 2020: I did fairly well when it came to keeping three of those vows. On two of the vows, I failed miserably. Two years later in 2022, on the cusp of delivery this book to the designer, I came across something from an eminent British historian who stated that without the third-century BCE Indian emperor Ashoka, Buddhism would probably have died out or remained a smallish sect in northern India instead of having a huge religious and cultural impact across most of Asia. Imagine, thousands of years of human history essentially hinging on the presence of one person. Thich Nhat Hanh died on January 22, 2022 in Vietnam at the age of 95.

The Cradle of Civilization

Back in late May 2006, I was invited by a famous Franciscan brother who is a world-renowned artist and iconographer to accompany him to Istanbul for a twelve-day pilgrimage through Islamic Turkey. The trip was sponsored by Sufi Muslims with the express purpose of sparking interest in interfaith dialogue.

It was twelve remarkable days crisscrossing Turkey with Br. Robert Lentz, OFM, and five wonderful Muslims, two of whom—Gökhan and Akif—I'm still friends with. (Akif offered to help me during my recovery from Covid-19.) The pilgrimage included some remarkable people from the fields of academia and communications. I marveled at the sights and sounds of Turkey, an eclectic mix of cosmopolitan Istanbul to the more traditional cities of Konya, Antalya, Sanliurfa, and Ephesus. After my extensive travels, I found Istanbul to be the most beautiful city I have ever seen. Straddling two continents (Asia and Europe), Istanbul, which is often called the cradle of civilizations, is surrounded by three seas and dotted with splendid architecture from the Ottoman Empire. When you travel through Turkey, you travel through time, seeing traces of the Crusaders, Greeks, Romans, Phoenicians, Persians, the Byzantine Empire, and other civilizations everywhere.

I was captivated by the beauty and history of Turkey. I marveled at the lives of my new Turkish and American friends. I was grateful for encountering the lives of ordinary citizens, such as the welder and the coppersmith we spent time with in Istanbul. The highlight of my pilgrimage to Turkey, besides visiting the town that claims to be the birthplace of baklava, was our visit to Rumi's tomb in Konya. Before even traveling to Turkey, it was Rumi who opened the door to Islam for me.

A mosque in Istanbul. The friar in the photo is a famous icon painter, Brother Robert Lenz; *Photo by Gerry Straub*

The best of those friendships formed on the Turkey trip was with an artist who at the time had been a student of Robert Lentz, OFM, since 1999. His name is Lewis Williams. He painted an icon for a wall of Santa Chiara soon after it opened.

In the depths of my Covid-19 illness, many people were concerned about my survival. Chief among them was my friend Jonathan, who was so worried about me that he arranged for a private jet to evacuate me to Florida. As mentioned earlier, I was too sick to travel, even in a private jet. Even if I got well enough to travel, I was concerned about what would happen when we landed. I'd be on my own, still weak, and still in need of oxygen and perhaps even hospitalization. I wondered if I could even drive . . . or shop for needed supplies. I wrote about this in my *Haiti Journal*. It was during this uncertain time that I received the most amazing e-mail from a guy I had not seen since 2006 . . . Lewis Williams:

> Gerry, if you make it to Florida, by jet blue or private jet, I want you to know I'm available. I'm a CNA, certified nursing assistant, experienced with the elderly (that's you), a good cook and professional driver. I'm on unemployment and getting good support, so I'm free. Let me know if you're in need of any support. I'd love to help. Could even return to Haiti with you WHEN you get better. Lewis

Describing the Indescribable

Around the world and in countless languages, he is simply known as Rumi. He is regarded as the greatest mystical poet on Islam. His poems are still widely read and loved today. In his native Persian, his full name is Jalāl ad-Dīn Muḥammad Rūmī. In English publications, he is mostly referred to as Jelaluddin Rumi or as Mevlânâ Jelaluddin Rumi (Mevlânâ is a title or epithet meaning "Our Master").

Rumi was born in 1207 in Balkh, which is in present-day Afghanistan. Early on in life, he knew what it was like to be uprooted and displaced. When he was still a child, his family fled Balkh because of the dangers of the invading Mongols and settled in Konya, Turkey. His father, Bahauddin, was a great religious teacher who made sure his son received the best religious education possible. After his father's death, a close friend of his father's continued to provide spiritual training for Rumi. Over the years, Rumi grew in wisdom and awareness of God. Eventually he was widely recognized for his sanctity.

Besides being a Sufi mystic and masterful poet, Rumi was also a jurist, an Islamic scholar, and a theologian. His poetry transcends national borders and ethnic divisions. Muslims of all stripes throughout the Middle East and Asia have greatly appreciated his spiritual legacy for the past seven centuries. I recently read that in the United States, he is considered to be the nation's most popular poet. His poems have been translated into most of the world's languages.

Rumi is an icon for interfaith dialogue. Here a few lines from Rumi that could serve as an inspirational cornerstone to interfaith dialogue:

> *Out beyond ideas of wrongdoing*
> *and rightdoing there is a field.*
> *I'll meet you there.*
> *When the soul lies down in that grass*
> *the world is too full to talk about.*

Wouldn't it be wonderful if we could find that field and all sit down together and discover the goodness within each of us and all of creation? Rumi spoke of the divine in a way that truly resonated with me. He had the uncommon ability to describe the indescribable God—without getting bogged down in dogmatic assertions. He spoke of God in a beautifully inclusive manner. In Rumi's poetry, all the manifestations of God sprang from one source: Love. A major theme in all his writing was submission . . . losing yourself and submitting to God. Without a determined, sustained submission to God, the false self is enslaved to the ego and lives in a state of internal conflict due to contradictory impulses of the ego, and so our true self, our God-centered self, never emerges.

He wrote: "Your task is not to seek for love, but merely to seek and find all the barriers within yourself that you have built against it." The spiritual wisdom of those words is in perfect harmony with all the Christian mystics, from Saint Francis of Assisi to Saint John of the Cross to Thomas Merton. Rumi was one of the most passionate and profound poets in history, and his influence is still being strongly felt by people of diverse beliefs throughout the world.

It should come as no surprise that Merton thought highly of Rumi. In a letter dated November 17, 1960, to his Muslim friend Abdul Aziz from whom he learned much about Sufism, Merton wrote: "I'm also well acquainted with Jalalu'l Din Rumi who is to my mind one of the greatest poets and mystics and I find his words inspiring and filled with the fire of divine love."[82]

Heart-Sight

The thing that touched me the most on the trip to Turkey was the prayerfulness of our Muslim guides and the many Muslims we met as we traveled. During the trip, we visited many Muslims' homes, sharing fine food and rich conversation. Everyone we met took prayer very seriously, stopping whatever they were doing at the appointed time, slipping away to a private space and bringing the focus of their attention back to God. Prayer was never skipped or rushed or ignored. You could devote all the time you had to studying Islam, digging deeply into its dogmas and practices; you could evaluate Islam from every angle imaginable, comparing it to other faiths, assessing its strengths and weaknesses, and yet never really see the beauty of Islam. Antoine de Saint-Exupéry astutely observed, "It is only with the heart that one can see rightly."[83] As I traveled with my new Muslim friends, I began to see with my heart. Before meeting Akif and Gökhan, I viewed Islam through the lens of my intellect, which blinded me to the beauty of the faith of these devout men. Their faith compels them to live humble lives of prayer and service to others. I was judging their faith instead of their lives.

My ministry has been devoted to the poor. To learn about the poor, I had to live among the poor. As the famed liberation theologian Gustavo Gutiérrez, a Dominican priest from

Peru, has suggested, in order to understand the poor, you need to be one with the poor, sharing in their suffering. Spending time among the poor, I was able to see—with my heart—their humanity and dignity, and better understand the circumstances that forced them to live in a prison of suffering and overwhelming want. In the same way, by being with real, everyday Muslims who are sincerely trying to live their faith in truth and openness, I was able to restore my heart-sight.

This is what excited me then and still does: real people of different faiths traveling together in a journey in which they saw with their hearts the love of God within each other's hearts. Along the path of interfaith dialogue, we found common ground, places of deep agreement. When we learn how to accept our differences in theology, our differences in the way we understand and respond to God will be minimized.

One night during our memorable trip to Turkey, we were all traveling together on a long bus ride from one city to another. Gökhan and I were seated together. While most of the others had fallen asleep after an exhausting day of sightseeing, Gökhan leaned toward me and quietly said he loved me. It was an astounding moment. He meant those life-giving words . . . they were not casually spoken: they were sincere, coming from his heart. The trip changed in a flash. Each step along the way, we were being transformed from acquaintances, to friends, to brothers. That is the journey we all must make, a journey that will bridge our differences and lead to true peace.

Real people from very different cultures and religions can come together in peace and harmony, learning to understand each other, accepting each other, caring for each other, and, yes, maybe even loving each other. The only antidote to the growing division, hatred, and violence we see here in America and around the world is love borne from mutual understanding and a deep concern for the common good. The first step is humility.

Christian de Chergé was the prior of the Cistercian community at Tibhirine, Algeria, which was a Muslim stronghold. He was assassinated with six of his fellow Trappist monks in 1996. He and his brother shared their lives with Muslim friends and neighbors. He was a witness to the value of interreligious dialogue. He wrote:

> Every dialogue between believers of good faith should always begin with a joint recognition that God is calling us to humility. This means, it follows logically, that we renounce any claim to be better or superior; it means we are striving for a form of personal authenticity without which we could not even dream of laying claim to the Truth.[84]

The God-inspired dream is that all people can one day be gathered around the same table, sharing the same wine and bread.

The Light of Buddhism

In a talk Merton gave in Calcutta shortly before his death, he said:

> I think that we have now reached a stage of religious maturity at which it may
> be possible for someone to remain perfectly faithful to a Christian and Western
> monastic commitment and yet learn, in depth, from a Hindu or Buddhist disci-
> pline or experience. Some of us need to do this in order to improve the quality of
> our own monastic life.[85]

While in Asia, Merton told Brother David Steinal-Rast: "I do not believe that I could
understand our Christian faith the way I understand it if it were not for the light of
Buddhism."

While on his fateful trip to Asia, Merton visited Bangkok, India, and Sri Lanka. He
spent three successive days in conversation with the Dalai Lama. Merton believed the Dalai
Lama and Thich Nhat Hanh could help him drink from the ancient Buddhist teachings
and remain a faithful Catholic monk. Merton's last journal, *The Asian Journal of Thomas
Merton*, recounts in detail his sense that the dialogue with Buddhism was not to become
some "facile syncretism"—that is, a fusion of the two very different religions—and did
involve a conscientious respect for their important and significant differences.

Especially in *Zen and the Birds of Appetite*, Thomas Merton taught me that I could
learn from different religions how to enhance and deepen my Christian faith tradition of
prayer and service, meditation, and compassion. I found that to be very true during my trip
to Turkey. In *Zen and the Birds of Appetite*, Merton explored the explicit focus of the will in
reaching out to God, which amounted to the practice of prayer without God. For Merton,
this resembled a Buddhist-like emptying of knowledge, an almost total of abandonment of
what can be known. The concept of "no self" in both Christianity and Zen Buddhism leads
to compassion for others and an intimacy with all things.

Merton believed that many of our social concerns could be resolved if people became
less violent and less selfish. In *Zen and the Birds of Appetite*, he wrote that Buddhism is not
"a doctrine but a way of being in the world . . . not a set of beliefs but an opening to love."[86]
In Haiti, I try to instill in the kids an appreciation of nonviolence and the beauty of caring
for others as a way to live in greater peace.

In her collection of Merton's writings on Nature titled *When the Trees Say Nothing*,
Kathleen Deignan writes: "Merton found in the teachings of Buddhism a direct method
for dismantling the false, addictive self that is the source of all personal, social, and even
ecological suffering."[87]

Ecological destruction is on full display in Haiti. The trees have all been chopped
down; burning garbage, along with exhaust from old cars and trucks, pollutes the air. On
my island home off the east coast of Central Florida, the beauty and awe of creation is
equally on full display. Without my week spent every month in beauty of the island on

which I live in Florida, I could not withstand the suffering and heartache I see during the other three weeks in Haiti.

Thomas Merton and Thich Nhat Hanh, May 26, 1966

In a letter to Thich Nhat Hanh, dated June 29, 1966, Merton wrote:

> I suppose you are probably back in Vietnam by now. I thought of you today because I finished your excellent little book on Buddhism today. It is a really good book, and I especially like the chapters about contact with reality and on the way to live the inner life.[88]

Echoes of Merton

Merton speaks to the universal within all of us. I often find echoes of Merton's words in the more mystical traditions of other religions. For instance, in *New Seeds of Contemplation*, Merton wrote: "For me to be a saint means to be myself."[89] Martin Buber wrote in *The Way of Man: According to the Teaching of Hasidism*: "Rabbi Zusya . . . said, a short while before his death: 'In the world to come I shall not be asked: "Why were you not Moses?" I shall be asked: "Why were you not Zusya?"'"[90]

There is no point pretending to be who we are not. Who we truly are is revealed when we recognize ourselves in God. And then you begin to let go of those things and tendencies in your life that are not of God.

> *"Mystics have always recognized that to come deeper into the divine presence within you, you need to practice detachment. When you begin to let go, it is amazing how enriched your life becomes. False things, which you have desperately held on to, move away quickly from you. Then what is real, what you love deeply, and what truly belongs to you comes deeper to you. Now no one can ever take them away from you."*
>
> —John O'Donohue, *Anam Cara: A Book of Celtic Wisdom*[91]

CHAPTER 8

The Common Good

The Mystical Flame

We often talk about our sinfulness in terms of blindness and our redemption in terms of seeing. We are blind to the needs of the poor; we don't want to see their plight. We turn away from the sight of those who endure the pain of living without the basic necessities of life. No one wants to see what I filmed in slums of Haiti or in the refugee camps in Kenya. I don't want to see it. Because in seeing it, I can't forget it, and I must do something about it. But in the very doing of something for others, I begin to discover myself and liberate my false self from the unseen prison of my own ego. This is the great lesson that Saint Francis teaches.

The crisis of belonging that haunts so many people has given rise to a widespread spiritual hunger, a search for the mystical flame that long ago had been consumed by darkness and doubt and materialism. For me, poverty road was the road back to God. I firmly believe that being with the poor and with the saintly people who live their lives in service to the poor can rekindle the flame of faith, and an ember of faith fanned by the holy breath of God can turn into a blazing fire of love.

Christ always approached people in a gentle, humble manner, seeking only to refresh them with a tender touch, a kind word. He always personified the love to which he called others. He gave himself fully to everyone. He saw everyone as a brother and sister, a child of God. He broke down the walls that separate humans from each other. If we are to be the incarnate body of Christ, we too must love, must give ourselves away, and must be with the poor. Our individual welfare cannot be separated from the welfare of those around us. So much of what passes for compassion these days is little more than condescending piety. Such demeaning compassion often comes dressed as pity, which only shames rather than restores. True compassion stems from fellowship and interdependence. We need to recognize our common humanity and realize God sets a banquet before all of us.

The drawback to all our technological advances is that much of humanity is attempting to gain absolute control over nature and all the functions of human society. In the process, we have become trapped in a system that requires evermore extremes of control. Rather than cooperating with the tendencies of the natural world and going with the flow, we use technical force to overcome nature. Thus, we are uncomfortable with mystery and surprise, preferring the way of power rather than the way of wisdom. If you did actually manage the impossible and acquire complete control of everything in your life, you would be condemning yourself to a life of eternal boredom. In contrast, the natural universe employs an infinite number of variables interacting simultaneously in a fashion whose outcome is unpredictable, amazingly intricate, and beautiful.

> *The common good,*
> *which is the breath of freedom*
> *and the social bond between people,*
> *is being choked by*
> *the iron fist of individualism.*

A Hidden Reality

Friday, June 30, 2000, 8:10 am: A thick blanket of fog is covering Assisi, which hides the sun from us. The innermost essence of God is hidden from us, totally separated from the created world.

We can see hints of God's love, which is enduring and incomprehensible. God is utterly transcendent and lovingly immanent.

The call to holiness is an invitation to enter fully into a committed relationship with God. As we respond, God graciously nurtures growth in the relationship by using events, circumstances, and people in our lives as instruments to hasten a contemplative outlook on life. Prayer becomes a vital part of our day, and, in prayer, we encounter more fully the Author of our life. This personal encounter with the Creator slowly transforms us into a divine likeness, as it gently erases all traces of the ungodlike stuff within us. In prayer, we unlock the vault to our deepest self and allow light to shine on God, who is already abiding at the very core of our being, hidden from us yet patiently waiting for us.

Note: It is stunning for me to realize that I wrote that more than twenty years ago. Years later, I used it my book The Loneliness and Longing of Saint Francis. *I love the first two sentences. Yet two decades later, prayer for me is haphazard at best and holiness is far, far beyond my grasp.*

A Divided Heart

Note: The following was written years ago when I was in the midst of my ministry of putting the power of film at the service of the poor and was either constantly on the road filming in some slum or speaking at churches and schools across America.

Within his heart, Saint Francis could feel the beating of contradictory impulses. He felt a call to prayer and a call to service. Contradiction is a part of life. I'm often pulled in two—or more—directions at the same time. It causes me to feel fragmented and disoriented. When the psalmist spoke of a divided heart, I know what he was talking about. When what I feel and what I do are in conflict, it leaves me paralyzed. Both Saint Francis and Thomas Merton felt contrary forces tugging at them, causing them to endure periods of confusion and unrest.

Some days I want to chuck everything, shut down my (film) ministry and move to Assisi. Some days the urge to write is so overwhelming, I become truly frustrated that I don't have the time to give it the focused attention it needs. The crazy urge to make poverty films that will inspire people to help the poor seems perfectly sane, though I'm becoming increasingly weary of begging for the funds needed to make a film and the constant complaints about the length of the films. In the Abbey of Gethsemani, I saw more clearly my need to find equilibrium, a sense of unity within myself. Eventually the saint and the monk found a way to have the contradictory forces battling within them to join together, enabling the tensions to become life-giving.

I need to find balance in my life. I need to find time to work and time to pray and time to play. I need time with my family and friends. I've yet to discover the true rhythm of my life, a life nurtured by the natural contradiction of growth and decline, of light and dark, of dying and rebirth. I need to find myself in those contradictions, for they are me, and they are able to reveal my hidden wholeness.

The contradictions, inconsistencies, and incompatibilities of life
do not have to be explained or denied;
they must simply be understood and transformed.

Note: *Now, in Haiti, the same frustrations still exist—only on steroids. The noise and demands of so many children, the frequent trips to hospitals, the relentless shopping for food, diapers, toilet paper, soap, toothpaste, and an array of cleaning supplies is so exhausting it leaves little time or energy for the very thing that nourishes me—writing, even if no one reads what I write. Not writing is like not having water. The writing itself is my salvation. Yet, so are the kids.*

A Dizzying Merry-Go-Round

Modern life has become a dizzying merry-go-round of nonstop activity where it seems most of us are doing a thousand things all at once, where people are working longer hours and whose lives are more and more fragmented by an endless array of demands, where multitasking and instant messaging are the norm in the consumer-crazed, computer-driven, smartphone crazy world of ours that has virtually no room for stillness and silence.

We each need to create our own sacred space, a space outside the rat race, an oasis of silence, a space dedicated to inwardness, a simple space of sanity and sanctity. We can turn any space into a sacred space. A bedroom corner can be a basilica, a portal into the mystery and meaning of life.

I missed yesterday. I was too busy to see it.

Busyness Gone Crazy

For a long time, in both my writing and speaking, I've connected the plight of the poor with our unbridled worship of capitalism and its harmful and rarely recognized downside. But our blind pursuit of money also has a negative impact on our spiritual life. To earn the exorbitant amounts of money we need to sustain our ever-increasing standards of living requires an extraordinary amount of time—as well as high levels of energy, dedication, and commitment. We seem hell-bent on working until we drop. Thanks to modern electronic means of communications, we take our office home with us. If we make time to take an actual vacation, we take the office along with us. We are rarely, if ever, unplugged. Even if we are not busy doing something, we feel the need to at least look busy. We live in fast-forward, and pressing the pause button is the one sin we cannot commit. To rest is to fall behind, and we can't let that happen. We think of ourselves as too important to take the time to simply do nothing.

We are drowning in a sea of noise. Silence is unheard of, unthinkable. Even during a walk in the woods (if you can find the time . . . and a forest), we are unable to hear the sounds of nature because we have little buds in our ears so we can hear the sounds of music. Empty rooms often have TVs playing. The sounds of silence have been muted.

In 2009, after eight years of extremely active ministry, without a single vacation, I had pushed myself to the point of exhaustion. I began to make stupid mistakes at work and at home, mistakes that caused me a lot of grief. Without adequate rest, I lost my way and drifted into unhealthy behavior. By early 2010, I was toast; I had lost everything. Without the rhythm of rest, life dies. That simple fact can be clearly seen in nature, if you take the time to look. Every living organism needs the nourishment of rest. I'd metaphorically waved my finger at those who felt enough was never enough and wanted more of everything: money, recognition, power, security, possessions, and love. Getting more of everything required frenetic activity and constant productivity. Even though I was busy helping others, I too became a victim of far too much activity. The world has gone crazy with busyness and its deadening effect: stress.

The Person in the Mirror

Who I am on the surface is not the true me. I'm not whom I appear to be. My exterior is only the person I think I am and the guy I put on display for others to see. The real me is buried deep within—unknown to even me, unknown to all but God. I must cast off this projected exterior image, my false self, and discover my true self, the person I was created to be. That process of losing and finding is the stuff of sainthood. I'm living in a dense forest of unreality. Finding my way out is a difficult, confusing, scary task.

The key to finding myself is finding God.

I'm transformed into my true self only through the power of the One hidden in me. There is nothing I can do on my own. Even stripping myself of all that is not God will not bring me any closer to the reality of God. The one thing I can do is to respond to God's call to enter into union with God. I created my external self, not God. Out of the clay of my own egocentric desires, my own selfish, sinful actions, I molded the person I see in the mirror, the person who, for many years, loved to flee reality. In the mirror, I see a lonely guy who for years sought comfort in the pernicious trap of pornography. I was too weak to break its vise grip. The real me, my true self, slept silently in the depths of my being, undisturbed by all my surface activity, waiting, patiently, to be awakened by God. My true self was created by God, made for God. I cannot be my true self without knowing God. I am hidden in God. And God is hidden in me.

On my own I can learn something about God through reason and reading, but, as Merton writes in *Seeds of Contemplation*: "There is no human and rational way in which I can arrive at that contact, that possession of Him which will be the discovery of Who He really is and Who I am in Him." Merton goes on to say: "The only One Who can teach me to find God is God, Himself, Alone."[92]

For most of my life, I've been moving away from God, carried along on the tide I created. All along I've been fighting a wind that had been trying to force me to turn in the opposite direction. My initial movement away from God was propelled by the influence of sin and was powered by my ego and illusions. The habits acquired while traveling in the wrong direction are extremely hard to reverse . . . ask any alcoholic or drug addict. Habits easily morph into addictions. Breaking addictions is like breaking out of a high-security prison. But we must break out. Merton felt the door to contemplation would be closed if we hang on to "transient and unimportant things of the world."[93]

The superficial, fictional me I see in the mirror is far from the reality of God. The guy in the mirror is incapable of transcendent experiences. Only my openness to God's call can put me on the path to become more receptive to the mystical dimension hidden within me.

This stuff doesn't come quickly or easily, which is why we don't bother with it. I devoted a few pages of *The Sun & Moon Over Assisi* to explaining Merton's ideas on the true and false self. Mostly I quoted sources who understood. Back then, I had deceived myself into thinking I understood. In truth, my mind sort of got it—but it was just another theory neatly tucked away in a dingy corner of my brain. Slowly, I'm beginning to "see" it with different eyes.

Thomas Merton wrote so clearly about deep spiritual things that we think we get it. The fact is, his understanding was hidden in his words, which only point the way, showing us the right direction. But we must walk alone. Only God can teach me how to find God. This is why so many true contemplatives are so reluctant to talk about their inner life. They cannot teach us anything—aside from a few techniques to help us get started. But even those, with God's help, you can figure out on your own.

Find a quiet place.

Sit.

Be still, mentally and physically.

And listen.

Easy? No. It's the most difficult thing in the world. Nothing seems to be happening. Results take a lifetime. Maybe even longer.

We're so far from God that it is beyond our ability to measure. Merton knew this, even after a quarter of a century as a monk. He knew he was far from his goal and had miles to go. Perhaps he came close in Asia before his death. Perhaps not. Only God knows.

Exterior of Merton's Hermitage, December 2000; *Photo by Gerry Straub*

"Everything in modern city life is calculated to keep man from entering into himself and thinking about spiritual things."
—THOMAS MERTON, *NO MAN IS AN ISLAND*[94]

CHAPTER 9

Assimilating God's Words

A Vigil of Listening

The riveting voice we hear in Merton's journals has a more broken and uncertain modulation to it, which for me is helpful in confronting my own inner brokenness. His time in the hermitage humbled him. In the hermitage, his back was to the wall and he had to face his own failures. Merton's grace was to doubt himself and do what Saint Benedict advised his monks to do: "Listen, listen very carefully, child, to the words of the Master."

What voices am I listening to? For too many years, I listened to all the wrong voices. A few years ago, during the aforementioned shattering crisis in my life, I spent nearly nine months on a forced sabbatical of silence, sitting alone in my home. My back "was to the wall," and I had to face the huge gap between what I claimed to be and who I actually was. I had to face my own sinfulness, my own failure to love. I had to shut out all the voices, but the voice of the Master. Real listening, deep listening, is very hard. In the stillness and silence, I faintly heard that I was loved, unconditionally. In my bones I felt the reality that no amount of good I did could cause God to love me more, and no amount of bad I did could cause God to love me less. God's love is very, very different from fickle human love.

Jonathan reminded me how Merton's monastic life was a vigil of listening, a continual striving for a state of mindfulness. He listened, first and foremost, to the voices of the Old and New Testament, as well as Buddhist, Islamic, and Hindu voices, which could pull him out of his chronic self-analysis to a more inclusive, other-oriented appreciation of God's presence on every level of his experience.

Note: In the middle of November 2020, as I sat in the stillness and silence that graces the hours before sunrise in Haiti reviewing the manuscript for this book before timidly submitting it to a publisher, this reflection spoke loudly to me. In Haiti, I have not adequately realized the impact exhaustion was having on me. I had ignored warnings from friends that I was on the precipice of burnout. The stress of an insufficient amount of funds and staff needed to properly care for the kids, as well the staff agitation caused by divisive gossip, pushed me into explosions of anger. My frustration level was off the charts. The noontime devil of doubt was whispering to me to give up. I urgently need to find time in Haiti for rest and listening to the affirming voice of the Spirit wanting to refresh and renew me.

It is now the end of May 2022. The sun is rising in Florida. I had just spent two days still reviewing the manuscript for this book. I was exhausted from the tension and stress of the quickly deteriorating conditions in Haiti. I only had four days in the tranquility of my island home before returning to the insanity of Haiti. In the summer of 2021, the president of Haiti was brutally assassinated in his own bed. In the vacuum of leadership that followed, the many gangs took control of the periphery of Port-au-Prince and life spiraled downward into a state of anarchy. Protesters burned down businesses. Key intersections were blocked by burning tires, bringing movement about the city to a standstill. Kidnappings and murders increased. People feared leaving their homes. Schools, banks, and businesses were forced to closed for weeks. Priests, nuns, doctors, diplomats, and kids were routinely kidnapped; many died in captivity.

Early in 2022, the situation went from unimaginably bad to insanely bad. The gangs began decapitating people and leaving the heads of their victims on the streets to further terrorize the citizens. In large sections of one slum, the homes (which were little more than shacks) were burned to the ground, forcing thousands of people to flee. People were shot and killed as they fled their homes. The gangs also blocked the main roads from the port, which meant that fuel and cargo trucks could not reach the city. This resulted in a severe gas shortage. In March, my JetBlue flight to Fort Lauderdale was forced to fly to the Dominican Republic for jet fuel. Food and vital supplies were not reaching stores. The price of virtually everything skyrocketed. Haitians are desperately trying to escape from Haiti; many have died in capsized, overcrowded rickety boats headed for Puerto Rico or the Florida Keys. I still had to leave Santa Chiara to try to find essential supplies. I often traveled with an armed security guard. Whenever I drove out of Santa Chiara, I wondered if I would return.

When most of this book was written, things in Haiti were certainly bad, but now life in Haiti is nerve-rackingly difficult. The tragic war in Ukraine was still on the horizon. As I pen these words in the stillness, silence, and beauty of Hutchinson Island, there is a ferocious debate in America over the sale of semiautomatic assault rifles in the wake of yet another mass killing of innocent children, this time in Uvalde, Texas, in which an eighteen-year-old boy slaughtered nineteen elementary students and two teachers. Just days before, another eighteen-year-old armed gunman entered a grocery store in Buffalo, New York, and intentionally targeted Black people, killing twelve. Most of victims had not yet been buried when the kids in Uvalde were slaughtered. In most states, an eighteen-year-old kid can't buy a beer but can easily and legally buy an assault weapon designed for combat. The scourge of White supremacy is on the rise; laws are being passed in some states designed to make it harder for Blacks to vote. Books are banned in Florida. The Sunshine State is making life darker for gays. Around the world, humanity is experiencing a deepening sense of dislocation, alienation, and tension.

The world seems to becoming unhinged. God seems to have left the stage. We are scared.

Is God hiding or are we simply evading God?

There are no easy answers to the complex problems we face. Merton said: "The answer is not found in words, but by living on a certain level of consciousness."[95] We need to wake up, to see beyond our own limits, and not take ourselves so seriously. In Haiti, I dropped my need for answers, for certitude. In becoming a marginalized person, I began to see things in a new light. The road to sanctity was not paved with dogma and ritual, but in being fully alive to the suffering of others. In Haiti, trials are always accompanied by the grace to defeat them. If my eyes are open.

> *"The more I am able to affirm other, to say 'yes' to them in myself,*
> *by discovering them in myself and myself in them, the more real*
> *I am. I am fully real if my own heart says yes to everyone."*
>
> —THOMAS MERTON, CONJECTURES OF A GUILTY BYSTANDER[96]

A School of Life

At Gethsemani, especially in his hermitage, Thomas Merton struggled with the angels who bore him messages from God. As Merton himself wrote, here he forged his inner experience of continuity "between the natural and the supernatural, between the sacred and the profane." Merton's journals were media for becoming a man of prayer, a man who listened, deeply. He wrote of his encounters with people and books and "the wind through the pine trees" as a form of prayer that gave him access to a heart-place where he could, as he penned, "enter the school of life."

For Merton, one way of praying was to engage in a continual process of "assimilating God's words," offered in books, in the teaching afforded by spiritual directors, and, most important, in finding God's "words" mediated by "experience" itself. He wrote: "We cannot be true monks if we do not assimilate and make our own the teaching given us from morning to night by God."

It is no different for all of us who live outside monastery walls. God's wisdom is most clearly seen and felt when I become aware of the many occasions of God's mercy that have been manifested in my life. When I take the time to look, I see evidence of God's protection and infinite concern for my well-being. Merton emphasized how meditation enables us to "enter deeply in the school of life itself." Merton said a monk's whole life should be "a meditation, a learning from God, a school of wisdom." Merton believed meditation should not just be praying with ideas but fed by the realities of our lives. While briefly living in a slum in Haiti in 2010, I wrote:

> Haiti and her suffering people taught me how to live, how to love, how to be whole. Haiti taught me about faith, hope, and patience. Haiti taught me about death and resurrection. Welcome to Haiti . . . a school of life.

Wherever you are, be it in a monastery or a slum, in a city or a small town, whether you are a farmer or corporate executive, God wants your life to be your own private school where you learn about love, mercy, kindness, and compassion . . . in essence, where you learn about God.

Merton understood that most people have a faulty image of God and see God mostly as a harshly stern judge who needs to be feared or manipulated. Jesus wanted to correct that fatal misunderstanding by showing us that an honest, loving relationship with God was possible. In fact, such an unthinkable relationship was already planted in our human consciousness and was just waiting to be discovered by us.

Meditation, for Merton, was a tool to discovering a God who is not to be feared, but a God who is, as American theologian Walter Brueggemann lists in his "credo of five adjectives," consistently *"merciful, gracious, faithful, forgiving, and steadfast in love."*[97] Merton knew this truth, which is why he, like countless others, sincerely continued to seek, pray, and, often, suffer. The school of life does not offer any puff classes.

We experience God's love in proportion to our
experience of our own weakness.

Homeward Bound

Merton's distinctive Trappist habit hid the poor and fragile man wearing it. Merton had a pilgrim's restless, searching heart. He understood that we are all homeless until we find our home in God. Maybe that's why he was attracted to Saint Benedict Joseph Labre, the homeless saint who wandered the streets of Rome begging. In his private journals, Merton frankly admits he was always in the dark, always on the road, and always in need of God's mercy to him in all things. In his journals, he deliberately sets out to debunk his status as a spiritual guru or master, a deadly honor his readers bestowed upon him.

Merton scholar Anthony T. Padovano said, "He writes in his journals about his pettiness, his envy, his sexual temptations, his doubts. He wanted everyone to know that the mystical journey was profoundly human. That it wasn't exotic. It wasn't artificial."[98]

Over the last sixty-five years or so, Merton was and is symbolic of many lost souls, lonely, isolated people looking for something they can't describe, can't put their finger on, looking for meaning, looking for redemption or recovery . . . basically, looking for God. Somehow, through his elegant words on a page he connects with our everyday, muddled lives of flesh. In him we find a common ground where people from around the world can see, respect, and even embrace each other. In his very real shortcomings and struggles, we see our own . . . and realize it is OK.

Jonathan points out that in his journals, Merton removes his Trappist habit so we can see his self-deceits, his struggles with competing and conflicting desires, and the darkness of his heart. In the pages of his journals, we see a real flesh and blood human being striving to enter the heart of God, striving to go Home. In his failures, problems, struggles, and disappointments, we see ourselves and know we are not alone . . . and that even "Saint" Thomas Merton wore pants just like us. No matter what inner difficulties he faced, Merton always moved forward in hope of discovering his true self . . . and therein was his salvation.

We find salvation by returning to the unity in which we were created. Salvation consists of the restoration of unity with God and all of creation, a unity that has been fractured by sin, ruptured by our living out of our inner brokenness, which causes deeper disunity.

I'm not sure I'm ready to remove my outer habit, that of a globe-trotting, crusading filmmaker striving to be a prophetic voice for the poor while often either hiding or ignoring his own inner spiritual poverty, his own sinfulness, his secretly clinging to things he knows are blocking him from entering a fuller, deeper relationship with God.

Note: That last paragraph was written before I put down my cameras and essentially moved to Haiti to care for abandoned kids. The experience is having a great impact on me. During the four months I was virtually quarantined in Haiti and Covid-19 nearly stole my life, I truly addressed some inner issues that needed correction. "Addressed" . . . not resolved.

CHAPTER 10

The Divine Flow of Life

Sharing and Serving

We need each other to become whole. Human convergence comes through love. Love unites what has become fragmented and isolated. In our unity, we still keep our individuality, with each gift of life creating a beautiful particle that helps form the whole of life, the full body of Christ. God is unity. God pulls us out of our isolation by showering us with the grace to see that our lives and gifts must be put to the service of others and all of creation. Through acts of sharing and serving, we shall move toward union. In reaching out to others, we are reaching out to God.

We haven't yet begun to tap the powerful and sacred energies of love, as Christ asks us to do, even to the point of loving our enemies. Through love we shall evolve to what we were created to be . . . fully realized children of God and heirs of heaven, which can be materialized right here on earth.

The Fount of Life

For most of my life, I felt life was a meandering stream, seemingly without design or purpose. I failed to see the divine flow of life and how I play a tiny part in directing that flow. Slowly, I've come to see that our lives are a distant echo of the life of God. God's face is my face, your face, all faces. The face of love is the face of the other. My energy, your energy, all energy is but a share of God's unlimited energy. We try to create our self-design, rather than submit to the divine design at the foundation of our being. Living out of our own self-design, own being, rather than assuming (or submitting to) the divine design, is to have the flow of our life go nowhere. Authentic, fruitful living flows out of the fount of Life.

> *You created every part of me,*
> *knitting me in my mother's womb.*
> *You saw my body grow*
> *according to your design.*
>
> (Psalm 139: 13, 16)

A Thousand Things

Saint Francis of Assisi said, "The truly clean of heart are those who look down upon earthly things, seek those of heaven, and, with a clean heart and spirit, never cease adoring and seeing the Lord God living and true."

> *My heart is not clean. It is sullied by a thousand things, none dirty unto themselves. It is sullied by my unhealthy desire for a thousand things that are merely distractions from the true longings of my soul. I see and seek the things but not the Spring that animates everything. I often clutch what is not mine, what belongs to everyone. I often long for earthly things more than heavenly things. The time I spend adoring God are weak, skimpy, fleeting episodes. Praising God is a low priority, usually left to the hands of fickle whim. It is no wonder I don't often see the wonder of the living and true God. My heart is busy, occupied with a thousand things.*
> *My heart is not clean. Lord, have mercy.*

My own sinfulness and lack of any kind of "progress" along the spiritual road often left me feeling discouraged. But a heart that is not clean is not cause for despair. For its very uncleanliness prompts a tidal wave of grace. Where sin abounds, grace is even more bountiful. Access to that overflowing grace requires an honest effort to look down upon earthly things and seek those of heaven. The essence of what Merton said over and over again in countless different ways is this: the treasure we seek is not here or there but within our hearts. Our treasure is God, and God alone.

God grant me the grace to truly feel my intrinsic poverty.

Note: *I wrote those words a dozen years ago. They appear in my book* The Sunrise of the Soul. *I'm repeating them because I still need to hear them, still need to be reminded that the spiritual life is a continual pruning, a constant renewal. The promised land is always a distant land.*

Walking Toward the Light

I am a sinner not immune to temptation. I stumble often, frequently succumbing to the deception of my ego. My heart is fickle; my faith is weak. Holiness seems far beyond my reach. Yet, each day, like Merton, I must pick myself up and keep walking toward the Light, toward the day when I've finally emptied myself of all that is not God. Unity with God does not happen in a flash; it is not won by a lottery ticket, instantly bestowing the riches of heaven upon you. Unity with God takes time, as day by day, month by month, year by year we slowly and deliberately let go of more stuff cluttering our tiny hearts to make room for the infinite source of love and life.

As a cloistered monk, Merton faced the tremendously difficult task of ridding himself of the three great temptations we each face: the temptation to be successful, to be right, and to be powerful. Jesus, with much effort, rejected these very same devilish, egocentric temptations in the wilderness. Before 1995, those "temptations" were my goals.

Trials and temptations are God's way of showing
us the broken nature of humanity.

Inner Disunity

Even my sin cannot separate me from God, because there is no separation between ourselves and God. Sin is our attempt to grab something we feel we lack. Lust seeks a forceful union with another to compensate for the inner disunity we feel.

God accepts our humanity—why can't we? God does not dole out punishment. We do.

God is aware of the hurt we feel before we sin, the hurt that caused us to sin. God does not wish to heap more hurt on top of that hurt by punishing us. We are doing a fine job all by ourselves. When we sin, we are trying to bury ourselves because we do not like who we are. God saves sinners. Punishment is not part of the equation. The devil is the manifestation of our temptation toward self-destruction.

CHAPTER 11

The Reality of Uncertainty

Messy Moments

Darkness, at times, surrounds all of us. It's impossible to calculate the amount of mental and physical suffering that is endured each day. So often, everything seems hopeless. Despair often shadows our days. We cling to a hope that things will change, that we'll catch a break.

To look deeply into the darkness of your own imperfect life is the surest way to be transformed by the hopeful light that springs forth from the mercy of God.

God is not hiding in the corner of an empty church. God is hidden in the endless stream of busy, messy, mundane moments of everyday life. Moreover, God is also hidden in the many tragedies that dot the vast landscape of humanity. God is not beyond the clouds; God is on the ground, down in the gutter with us.

At the heart of every life, there is a deep, mysterious pain. No one can avoid it or cure it. The lived experience of my faith informs me that, despite my imperfections, faults, and failures, God loves me beyond measure, beyond what I can imagine. The awesomeness of God is incomprehensible from the gutter of our lives, from the dark basement of despair.

What can I give to God?
Nothing . . . absolutely nothing
Except for my trust and total self-surrender.

I would never deliberately choose self over God—except that I do so in countless little ways every day without realizing it.

In *The Asian Journal*, Merton wrote: "Faith means doubt. Faith is not the suppression of doubt. It is the over-coming of doubt, and you overcome doubt by going through it. The man of faith who has never experienced doubt is not a man of faith."[99]

Don't Know

There are days when my uncertainties almost overwhelm me . . . and I doubt almost everything. But I take comfort that being uncertain is, oddly enough, an act of faith. Conversely, certainty is not a true sign of faith. To question spiritual truths does not mean your faith is weak. To be uncertain means to walk in vulnerability, trusting God in all your steps, both the steady and the unsteady steps. Like Christ, we need to carry our cross; we don't need to conquer our crosses.

Pema Chödrön, a popular and respected Buddhist nun and author, claims that anxiety doesn't come from lack of certainty, but from the false assumption that there are certainties. The truth is that not every question has an answer, nor does every problem have a solution.

Everyone can, at times, identify with Thomas, that most human of apostles, who doubted the resurrection of Jesus without being able to put his finger in the wound on Jesus's side. I'm a "doubting Thomas" at least a few times a month. That particular story from the Gospel of John makes you wonder if any of the other apostles had similar doubts but were simply afraid to voice them.

Pope Francis understands the reality of uncertainty. In a wide-ranging interview with Italian Jesuit and journalist Antonio Spadaro, the Pope was asked to comment about certitude and mistakes. He said:

> In this quest to seek and find God in all things there is still an area of uncertainty. There must be. If a person says that he met God with total certainty and is not touched by a margin of uncertainty, then this is not good. For me, this is an important key. If one has the answers to all the questions—that is the proof that God is not with him. It means that he is a false prophet using religion for himself. The great leaders of the people of God, like Moses, have always left room for doubt. You must leave room for the Lord, not for our certainties; we must be humble. Uncertainty is part of every true discernment that is open to finding confirmation in spiritual consolation.[100]

> *"Faith is the substance of things to be hoped for and these*
> *things are not manifest to the intellect, even though its consent*
> *to them is firm and certain. If they were manifest, there*
> *would be no faith. For though faith brings certitude to the*
> *intellect, it does not produce clarity, but only darkness."*
>
> —SAINT JOHN OF THE CROSS, *ASCENT OF MOUNT CARMEL*[101]

Sparks of Light

All of us have struggles with questions of doubt and faith. I have many days of doubt, days of feelings of abandonment by God. Endless are the days when I see no trace, no evidence of a loving God. While there is nothing normal about me, this struggle with doubt is normal.

Mystics of all faiths tell us our faith needs to be wide enough, deep enough, to embrace the days of doubt and finds sparks of light within them. For me, that happens when I see the smile of an abandoned kid or a beautiful bird eating the seeds I put out for the birds.

In This Darkness

We are lost. All is hopeless. Look around, the evidence is clear. War, hatred, violence, lying, cheating, stealing, and corruption abound. Greed and lust have all but become virtues. There can be no doubt: we are lost, all is hopeless. We are powerless to change anything.

But in this darkness, God sheds a light. What was impossible for us to see—love, mercy, compassion, kindness, hope—is possible with God. God has the infinite power to change everything. But we have the on/off switch to that unlimited power. That on/off switch is surrender and obedience. To have access to God's power, we must first surrender our own will and then submit to the will of God. The switch is right before our eyes, but we choose not to see. We mask our blindness and hopelessness with an array of illusions and deceptions. So, the darkness remains because without God we are lost and all is hopeless.

"What do I want?" is the question we strive to answer. Jesus would have us ask a different question: "What can I give?"

Note: I wrote that many years ago, yet the question is still being asked. In early May 2020, before contracting Covid-19, I was in Haiti, unable to leave because all flights to Haiti from the States were banned because of the pandemic. The future the Santa Chiara Children's Center was in grave doubt due to a lack of sufficient funding. I had enough funds to possibly make it to the end of July. I was forced to face the reality that I'd have to radically downsize to survive. I'd have to move perhaps twenty children to another home and dismiss about twenty staff members. I couldn't see any light in the darkness. I'd been stranded in Haiti since February 29, and I desperately wanted to have a little time in Florida. I longed for a hot shower and air-conditioning. I felt my emotional and spiritual tanks were empty.

Yet, it seemed God was asking me to give more. I struggled with the feeling I had no more to give. I found myself realizing I had to dig deeper. I resurrected an old practice of repeating the Jesus Prayer. One night, I watched my film Silenzio. The film was shot on location in Franciscan Italy. It is a film without words. It is a visual feast that celebrates the resplendent countryside and medieval towns Saint Francis loved. The images are accompanied by soaring, soothing, inspirational music. Along the way, the film visits many exquisitely beautiful churches whose walls are covered with magnificent, centuries-old art. As I watched, I could feel the stress and tension fading away. For two hours, I left the chaos of Haiti and entered the peaceful world of Assisi.

Sometimes in the midst of the present moment, we feel estranged from God. It is easier to see God's gentle guiding hand when we look back at our personal journey. As I watched the film, I understood how Saint Francis and Assisi put me on the road to poverty and many encounters with the suffering of the poor. I sensed how God's grace helped me make so many films with funding that seemed to come from nowhere. As I breathed in the name Jesus and exhaled the unspoken words "have mercy on me a sinner," I grew in the trust that things will work out for the benefit of all at Santa Chiara. I had been doubting my need to stay here. I felt a pull to retire to the tranquility of my island home in Fort Pierce, Florida. The feeling that I had given enough and wanted to permanently leave Haiti began to dissolve. While I wanted to go, I knew I couldn't leave, couldn't abandon the kids.

The last two years at Santa Chiara had been a daily grind. I felt as if I was in a perpetual state of crisis management. I wondered how I wound up in Haiti. I thought about all that I experienced in making my poverty films in far-flung slums around the world. I thought about the process of writing the books I was lucky enough to get published. I thought about all the presentations I gave at churches and schools. I wanted to know the deeper meaning of my very unusual journey. It wasn't until I was late into the writing of this book that I realized that the book had been, inadvertently, a means of seeing all my varied experiences as a unified whole, each step leading to the next, each step taking me deeper into the heart of reality.

I'm in the autumn of my life. Autumn is a time of harvest. In writing this book, it seems like a season to gather together lost moments and experiences, bring them together, and hold them as one. The late Irish writer John O'Donohue called this stage of life the "harvest of the soul."

Always Knocking

Faith is evolutionary; it is always changing and growing. A static faith is a dead faith. My faith moves forward, and then slips back. It is never steady. The forward movement of faith embraces the divine traits of mercy and forgiveness. When I become petty and unloving, my faith has stumbled and fallen backward a bit. This is normal . . . even for saints. God is always knocking. Some days we hear and respond. Some days we ignore or pretend not to hear the knocking. The point of faith, on our good days and on our bad days, is to strive to move forward.

Saints don't have to be perfect,
but they have to bear witness to a larger reality.

Errors and Failures

The following is from an essay by Jonathan Montaldo titled "Merton's 'Voice' in His Journals: Opening the Heart's Inner Ear":

> The deep significance for us of Merton's witness may consist in his errors and in his acknowledged failures. He incarnates in his journals his quintessentially human fate to stand with his feet straddling a divide between what he longed to be and what he actually was. Merton's limitations illuminate. His more than occasional ability to transcend them, by moments of insight which recall him to his vocation to move forward in spite of himself toward God, both motivates and encourages.

Readers misunderstand the false steps, the back sliding, the being caught in the same old compulsive thinking that Merton regularly discloses in his journals if they fail to understand his persistent dedication to the evangelical task of being "pure of heart." Merton's personal integrity in his later journals is missionary: "I am thrown into contradiction," he wrote from his hermitage in 1966. "I am thrown into contradiction: to realize it is mercy, to accept it is love, to help others do the same is compassion."[102]

As Merton elaborates the paradox of his desiring purity of heart, while witnessing in himself the ability to evade the humility and self-disregard necessary for its procurement, he places before the eyes of his readers their own struggle with conflicting desires which attends their own spiritual journeying.

Merton focuses his reader on the inadequacy of confining religious experience to the esthetic or only to the intellectual and academic. Writing to Etienne Gilson he had begged:

Please pray for me to Our Lord that instead of merely writing something I may be something, and indeed that I may so fully be what I ought to be that there may be no further necessity for me to write, since the mere fact of being what I ought to be would be more eloquent than many books.[103]

Feeling the Light

I love the following quote. I think the poet got it exactly right. Faith is this simple, yet this complex.

> *"Faith is the bird who feels the light*
> *and sings when the dawn is still dark"*
>
> —RABINDRANATH TAGORE, *FIREFLIES*[104]

For Love to Give Love

How sad, how tragically sad, that we allow ourselves to be ruled and controlled by our illusions and fears. Regrettably, we live much of our lives in a prison of falsity. This isn't God's plan for any of us. God wants us to know true peace and freedom.

We were created in the image of God, which is to say we were created to mirror the love of the Trinity by giving ourselves away, for life to give life, for mercy to give mercy, for compassion to give compassion, for peace to give peace, for love to give love.

Because we do not know our real self, our true nature, we live in darkness and doubt. Conflicts haunt us. We feel threatened. And so, we build walls around ourselves for protection. In the depths of our being, we feel isolated, alone, naked. Joy is fleeting. Bitterness grows in our uncultivated garden starving for sunlight. The goodness and creativity of God is unknown, hidden, in part, by our own brokenness, our own weakness.

Fear is the root of all violence.

A Quantum Leap of Faith

In a surprising twist, science, especially quantum physics, is expanding faith in the Trinity as it shows us that relationships are all there is in the universe. I confess to having a hard time understanding the quantum theory in physics. But the quantum principle of a complementarity that tolerates ambiguity, approximation, probability, and paradox greatly appeals to me. Inflexible certitudes turn me off. Any religion that has been reduced to mere performance of certain rituals, affirming certain "truths," adhering to certain moral principles, and being part of a special group is useless. Religion is about participation, not merely following. Authentic religion helps the believer to fully enter into the divine flow of life, which for Christians means actively participating in the mystery of the Trinity. Christianity is more than going to church on Sunday and trying to be good the rest of the week. Christ calls us to something much deeper.

God's Plan

In his 750-page book, *The Promised Land*, President Barack Obama says he didn't view his political path as a call from God. He writes, "I suspect that God's plan, whatever it is, works on a scale too large to admit our mortal tribulations; that in a single lifetime, accidents and happenstance determine more than we care to admit . . . and that the best we can do is to try to align ourselves with what we feel is right and construct some meaning out of our confusion, and with grace and nerve play at each moment the hand that we're dealt."[105] Sounds right and reasonable to me.

Is it God's will that I am in Haiti? I don't know. It just feels right for me to there in the midst of the suffering. In *No Man Is an Island*, Merton advised: "Let us not be too glib in our statements about the will of God. God's will is a profound and holy mystery, and the fact that we live out everyday life engulfed in this mystery should not lead us to underestimate it holiness."[106]

Clean and Whole

In God, there is no trace of vengeance, not even for a split second. Wrath and vengeance are human traits. God knows nothing of wrath because wrath is a turning away from peace and love. Wrath is born from a failure of wisdom and goodness on our part. God is the goodness that cannot be wrathful. Fourteenth-century English mystic Julian of Norwich said, "If God were vengeful for even a moment we would never have life, place or being. In God is endless friendship, space, life and being." The Church was dreadfully wrong to say that sinners are sometimes worthy of blame and wrath. God neither shames nor blames us; God only loves us and always sees us as clean and whole. No matter how hard we resist it, God constantly showers us with the grace to see ourselves as God sees us. It is in our capacity to forgive that is a true sign of our holiness. When we forgive others, we are overcoming our own imperfection, selfishness, smallness, and spiritual ignorance and becoming more aligned with God's love.

> *"Not forgiving is like drinking rat poison and*
> *then waiting around for the rat to die."*
>
> —ANNE LAMOTT, *TRAVELING MERCIES*[107]

Far from Perfect

Each of us is ordinary in our own ordinary way. We don't do perfect very well. We are all flawed. We are all in conflict with ourselves. We are all unfinished. But in our flaws and conflicts, grace abounds. Grace teaches us to trust in life, trust in God . . . a God who isn't bent out of shape by our imperfection. So much of our lives are lived in shadows, and at times, we experience utter darkness. It is in the shadows and darkness that we can catch a glimpse of the Light. We see our hurts, our faults. We embrace them, heal them. We are not called to be perfect like Jesus was. We are simply asked to do as Jesus did: to strive to be holy.

We are all ordinary, in extraordinarily different ways. Each of us is complex and complicated in our own unique way. I am a bundle of eccentricities. I am a sinner who struggles with a host of weaknesses and unholy proclivities. I am not perfect, nor will I ever be perfect. If I thought I had to reach perfection, I would give up instantly. I simply acknowledge that I am on the road toward perfection and that by God's grace I will make strides toward an ever-deepening holiness. If I became overly scrupulous about failure to love as Jesus would have me love, I would drive myself crazy. My faults bother me, but they do not distress me. Day by day, and by God's unmerited grace, I will chip away at them.

Letting Go of Everything

Saint Francis was a mystic. Many people don't understand mystics. They are puzzled by them, and perhaps a bit apprehensive or fearful of them. Mystics are often perceived as extremists or far too rigorous in the practice of their faith. Such spiritual phenomena as levitation and the stigmata are viewed with skepticism. We can't comprehend a direct experience of God, whether in visions or messages. My hunch is that Saint Francis had fallen in love with God in such a deep, profound way, and that made him a mystic. He experienced the presence of God everywhere and within everyone. Francis was totally submersed in God and God alone. Nothing else mattered. He let go of everything else.

In my previous books on Saint Francis, I presented myself as walking in the footsteps of the saint or walking in the shadow of him. Clearly that was metaphorical language. In reality, I held on to lots of things that were far less than godly. While I longed for God, I did so without the passion and persistence of Francis. Still no matter how hard any of us try, God is light-years beyond our comprehension.

A mystic does not have a new vision of God; a mystic has a new way of relating to all people and all of creation.

CHAPTER 12

Hidden in the Insignificant

A Broken Heart

The Hasidic Jewish tradition suggests that only someone with a broken heart is a whole person. Some interpret that to mean that when a person has a broken heart, the presence of God rushes in to heal and love the broken heart. While I believe that to be true, I think there is more to it. When my heart is broken by the sight and reality of the desperately poor in Uganda, I'm taken out of myself and am made whole by virtue of my realization that I'm connected not only to these people but to all of creation. I'm whole when I realize I'm part of the whole creation of God. In the wholeness of my humanity, I can see more clearly the huge gap between human misery and human compassion.

The people in the slums and camps where I've filmed have only one agenda: survival. Seeing so many people nearly half dead from hunger filled me with sadness. I was distressed and ashamed. Yet for most of my life I too was half dead from my own hunger . . . hunger for power, status, and money. I was half dead to the suffering world around me. In reference to the Civil Rights Movement and the war in Vietnam, Rabbi Abraham Joshua Heschel never tired of saying: "In a free society, some are guilty, but all are responsible."[108] (I should note that Merton and Heschel were friends; they considered each other kindred spirits. They exchanged frequent letters. They were both distressed over the loss of holiness in modern life. They both believed in the essential unity of all humanity.)

There are no easy answers to the endless questions that arose from what I saw in Uganda. There are no quick fixes, no good theological excuses either. Answers and solutions will only come from a broken heart. We need our hearts broken in order for us to truly step outside of our own ego, to strip ourselves of our own need for comfort and security and enter fully into the pain and suffering of our African sisters and brothers and to walk in solidarity with them, demanding that they be set free from poverty, hunger, and disease and be allowed to live in peace, simplicity, and dignity. As they walk with all their fears and hopes, the people of Uganda breathlessly await our response to their unjust plight.

Our greatest violation of poverty is to hold the
good God gives—goodness has to flow.

"In the economy of divine charity we have only as much as we give. But we are called upon to give as much as we have, and more: as much as we are. So the measure of our love is theoretically without limit. The more we desire to give ourselves in charity, the more charity we will have to give. And the more we give the more truly we shall be. For the Lord endows us with a being proportionate to the giving for which we are destined."

—Thomas Merton, *No Man Is an Island*[109]

A Climate of Desperation

Poverty isn't just a matter of not having sufficient income to live. Poverty isn't just living with hunger. The poor also experience a total lack of a sense of well-being and peace of mind which so many of us take for granted. Poverty isn't about the lack of food, shelter, and security; poverty is the rage one feels when you can't do anything about it. Poverty creates a climate of desperation. Poverty is the sense of hopelessness that kills the spirit.

"Christ does not provide his followers with a set of wings to flee into heaven, but with a weight to drag them into the deepest corners of the earth."

—Madeleine Delbrêl, *We, the Ordinary People of the Streets*[110]

In the Dark Corners

Before I began making films on global poverty, my knowledge of economics could've fit in a thimble. But seeing up close the impact of insensitive economic policies forced me to begin thinking deeply about the impact of economic strategies. The emerging global economy has a strong tendency to foster soulless consumerism and mindless worship of technology, and it often tramples the rights of workers and the poor. We need to be attentive to the human consequences and social impact of globalization.

Poverty will not be reduced until we address the extraordinary growth of the inequality of income and wealth that has been fueled by American-style, no-holds-barred capitalism. *Selfishness* became the watchword of capitalism. Unfettered free markets and financial systems perpetuate structural injustice and social sin that often keep people trapped in poverty. Merton would've had a field day with this stuff.

> *As long as I enjoy comfort and require security,*
> *I will have a hard time feeling*
> *true compassion for the poor and the weak.*

If you're looking for Jesus, you'll find him in the midst of those who are being crucified, rejected, alienated, and oppressed. He is in the dark corners of your neighborhood, waiting for you to help him. Unless we stand shoulder to shoulder with the poorest of the poor, we will not find the crucified Christ, nor experience the richness of his resurrection.

Giving a few dollars to the poor is not the same as being one with the poor, which is what Christ requires.

> *"We live is a globally interconnected world, and the destruction of the*
> *web of life in one part of the planet or in one urban neighborhood will*
> *have dramatic consequences for all of us in the not-too-long run."*

> —Rabbi Michael Lerner, The Politics of Meaning[111]

An Internally Displaced Person

I'm a very different man than the one who came to Gethsemani in 2000 for a hermitage adventure. Back then, after five years of near total emersion in the life of Saint Francis as I wrote my first book about the saint from Assisi who took poverty as his bride, I came seeking a deeper experience of God. In the twenty years since then, I've encountered a great deal of suffering and death in some of the most horrific slums on earth and that experience has changed me . . . transformed me. I look at everything differently now.

The two places that had the most significant impact on me were Uganda and, of course, Haiti.

In Uganda, besides spending time in the massive, dehumanizing slums of Kampala, sprawling cesspools of hopelessness, I visited a few IDP camps in the north, in a lawless area that had been decimated by a twenty-yearlong, brutally violent civil war in which children were forced to be soldiers . . . it was kill or be kill.

IDP means internally displaced persons. In an IDP camp, all the people forced from their homes in a particular country are huddled together in a camp inside that same country. A refugee camp is inhabited by people fleeing violence or hunger in another country. It is a distinction without much of a difference when it comes to harsh living conditions. The sight of so many kids with bloated bellies in the IDP camps in Uganda was terribly distressing. Images of them that I captured on film still haunt and disturb me.

In a way, I'm also internally displaced person, forced from my safe, comfortable inner ideas about God.

I hear far too often how people see the tsunami of suffering that washes over humanity every day as a legitimate reason for doubting the existence of a benevolent, merciful, and loving God. Yet, I also was truly inspired by the faith of the people I filmed, people who somehow had the faith and inner sources to not only endure unimaginable suffering but also manage to smile and harbor the hope that things would get better.

On a deeper level, the brokenness of the people I filmed put me in touch with my own brokenness and the realization that we are all wounded in some way, that we're all in need of the boundless mercy, tenderness, and forgiveness of God.

Spiritually we are all "internally displaced persons." We are in exile from our truer selves because we live out of parts of our souls in imposed isolation for self-protection but where we can never be comforted. There are days when I truly feel the inner experience of spiritual poverty. There was a time when this distressed me and threw me into a pit of doubt. But now I see these dry spells as occasions of grace prompting me to turn more fully to God, to surrender more of my false self into the loving hands of God. It is all about letting go . . . and acknowledging our dependence upon God and our neighbors. This is tough, especially in our culture that promotes personal strength and independence.

When we embark on an inward journey, we eventually arrive at a place of keen awareness of our own powerlessness and hopelessness, and, like Christ, must yield to the mercy of God.

I've come to believe that the way to God, for me at least, was through the misery and nothingness of my false self. It was in these slums I saw more clearly my true self and my complete dependence upon God. It was in these slums that I felt more tangibly God's love. Love is a mystical force that pushes open the door to forgiveness and mercy. Each film I made took me deeper into the heart of God, even though the journey is painful.

The pain of physical poverty I've witnessed all over the world along with my own spiritual poverty has taught me a great lesson: only when I have nothing left but my own inner suffering and I can recognize and accept that I am an internally displaced person does the encounter with Christ in every other internally displaced person, a real tangible relationship with all who suffer, become manifest and even fruitful. Jonathan reminds us that in Sorrow's face, epiphanies of our human kindness can be seen and understood.

On June 8, 1965, Merton wrote in his journal: "The great joy of the solitary life is not found simply in quiet, in the beauty and peace of nature, song of birds . . . nor in the peace of one's own heart, but in the awakening and attuning of the heart to the voice of God—to the inexplicable, quiet, definite inner certitude of one's call to obey Him, to hear Him, to worship Him here, now, today, in silence and alone, and that this is the whole reason for one's existence, this makes one's existence fruitful and gives fruitfulness to all one's other (good) acts . . . ."[112]

I need to find my hermitage space to better attune my heart to the voice of God.

> *God's love manifested itself in Christ's poverty and humility.*
> *God became like us so we could become like God.*
> *Happy are those who know the need for God.*
> *All good must be given back to God.*

Dozing Disciples

The late theologian from Great Britain Nicholas Lash said, "Faith in God, and God alone, is inherently iconoclastic." That is to say that faith in God is a radical idea. Atheism today is based on an idolatrous impression of God, a God who has been reduced to a wellspring of easy self-consolation and security in times of trouble. Lash dashed the cultural assumption that "God's word is spoken for comfort rather than truth."

In an essay on the life of Nicholas Lash that appeared in the July 18, 2020, edition of *The Tablet*, which is published in Great Britain, John McDade wrote:

> Knowledge of God, he [Lash] said was "knowledge of him whose presence is felt in absence; whose touch is perceived in torture; whose approach is experienced less as the rising of light than as the gathering darkness of our dying." Think seriously, he said, about Rahner's words that when we gaze upon the crucified Jesus, we should realise that we are spared nothing. "Why on earth," Nicholas wrote, "should we, disciples dozing in the garden of Gethsemani, expect it to be otherwise."

As you will read later in Part Five, five years before reading McDade's essay, I wrote in my *Haiti Journal* in May 2015 that in Haiti I felt that the presence of God took on the form of absence. Stay tuned.

A Chance to Grow

In the familiar parable of the mustard seed found in Mark's Gospel, Chapter 4, Jesus compares the kingdom of God to "the smallest of all the seeds on earth," yet the insignificant mustard seed grows into "the largest of plants," whose branches attract all manner of birds and provide shade for all. The lowly mustard seed is very easy to overlook, yet it is filled with life-giving potential. In Haiti, mustard seeds abound, in the form of neglected and abandoned people who are being swept away by the ill winds of severe poverty. But each person, Jesus tells us, contains possibility and purpose. I can't help thinking of all the small kids in Haiti who are not given a chance to grow into the person God created them to become. The Santa Chiara Children's Center is a place where some of those who are small and forgotten are given a chance to grow.

Conventional Wisdom

You can meet the spirit of the broken Christ in the harsh, barren landscape of unjust poverty, in dark places where Christ still has no home. Jesus lives outside the city of conventional thought, beyond the bounds of conventional wisdom.

We do not see or respond to the unjust suffering of the poor because we're distracted by a torrent of trivialities. Our lives are swept up in a perpetual hustle and bustle as we hurry here and there, striving to make progress in our endless quest for more and more.

Perhaps the discontent I feel almost constantly results from wasting most of my life pursuing trivialities, chasing illusions, and not truly and honestly digging deeply into the meaning of life until my life was nearly over. Now it is too late for a do-over.

In one miniscule way, I'm like Merton. He wrote, "Well, I am very slow to learn what is useless in my life!"[113]

CHAPTER 13

Making Sausage

The Voice of the Shepherd

John's unique Gospel says the voice of the shepherd calls us and that the followers of the shepherd know the voice of the shepherd. The mystical voice of the shepherd calls us home, home to the experience of shelter and peace. We often lose touch with this voice because of the many distractions of life.

At times, we are driven to ask big, life-altering questions, such as what is the meaning of my life or did I make a huge mistake making a promise or vow that I feel I can no longer keep or do I have some deep unhealed wounds? These big, unanswered questions often follow some tragedy or nagging difficulty in our lives. But the voice calls us from this place of inner conflict and tells us to come home to a place of harmony.

For too long I listened to the voice of the world, for too long I lived by false assumptions about life, for too long I was too busy to listen to the inner, mystical voice of the shepherd calling me home. I knew the words of Psalm 23—*the Lord is my shepherd*—but I didn't know the voice of the shepherd. I was lost.

Even after my conversion, I became so busy with my ministry, the voice of the shepherd became muted. A few years ago, I realized I needed to find a place of silence in order to hear more clearly the voice of the shepherd. Slowly I began to hear, albeit faintly, an inner voice in my own life calling me home to a deeper mystical experience. But as I resumed filming and speaking, I found myself once again becoming too busy to hear the gentle voice of the shepherd.

I need to listen more intently for the voice of the shepherd. I need to be more diligent in creating space of silence. My time in Merton's hermitage taught me that I needed to create my own Gethsemani hermitage within the walls of my busy life. I still haven't fully put that lesson into practice.

And the Spirit Said

Note: Many fleeting thoughts that drift through our minds each day actually have the potential to improve our spiritual lives, but they go unnoticed because they are lost in the clutter and busyness of our days. Over the years, I've tried to overcome this reality by jotting down in a small notebook the thoughts that come to me during the day and during my brief times of stillness and silence. Here is a sampling of my daily encounters with the silent voice of the Spirit.

The gentle, silent voice of the Spirit said: "You have always been a scared little boy."

I'm afraid of the truth about myself, afraid to speak what I really think or believe.

I no longer want to live in fear.

I can fit in anywhere, but I don't fit in anywhere.

To walk on the path God wishes us to take requires a paradigm shift in which worry becomes trust, doubt becomes faith, despair becomes hope, sadness becomes joy, unwelcomed becomes embraced, ugliness becomes beauty, Good Friday becomes Easter Sunday.

Every person is a mystery to even his or her closest friends.

Words have no meaning unless accompanied by action.

If you stop talking, your hearing will improve.

I know what I want to do. I know what I should do. What I want to do is not what I should do.

You are who you are when you are alone. Who you are with others is mostly fiction.

We pay a high price for fidelity to our illusions.

Without silence, stress increases.

Find the eternal space within your soul that neither time nor flesh can touch.

Solitude gives me the space and opportunity to be alone with God.

Hidden from the sight and influence of others, in solitude we are able to encounter our true selves.

My poverty exists in my weakness to resist certain temptations, even though after continually succumbing to temptations I feel dreadful and loathsome.

Detachment from things not of God leads to a greater attachment to God.

Give up something of no real or lasting value to gain something priceless and eternal.

You will not experience peace of mind if there is hatred in your heart. Hating just one person destroys your peace.

Every day, God comes to us in human form—and we turn our back.

God is not interested in rules and regulations; God is interested in love and communion.

Note: At this moment it is May 30, 2022; it is Memorial Day. I'm in my fourth full day in Florida, with just six days left before returning to Haiti. About half of my time so far on the trip has been devoted to fine-tuning the manuscript for this book. The time spent in these pages have been like being on a private retreat. The above passage really impacted me as I sipped my Rebo coffee. Every one of those "thoughts" ring very true.

I realize that my monthly ten-day break in Florida is much less about handling the nettlesome administrative chores for the orphanage, much less about my desire for hot water and air-conditioning, and is more about the regenerative nature of silence. Yesterday, I was "working" on this book from before sunrise until well after sunset. During the day I mentioned to a friend during a phone call that it had been the happiest day I've had in a long time. I felt wave after wave of peace wash over me. I was doing what I truly needed to do . . . not just for the sake of a book few people will read, but for my inner healing.

Climbing the Mystical Ladder

Only God knows who I am, originally, essentially. The Good News is God wants to tell me who I am and what I can be. Right now, God is busy trying to teach me how to listen. Truly listen.

Asceticism plays a part in the spiritual life just as discomfort plays a part in the natural life. We do what we need to do in order to fight cold and heat; so also, we need to fight sin and weakness. But compulsive asceticism is of no use. At the very least, asceticism can be an effective self-management tool. God knows I can use a tool like that. When asceticism and mysticism wed, the saints tell us they give birth to a luminous creation . . . as long as both are hidden with Christ in God. Some degree of mysticism is within the reach of everyone, and all Christians should aspire to climb as high as they can on the mystical ladder.

> *"All our salvation begins on the level of the common and ordinary things. . . . And so it was with me. Books and ideas and poems and stories, pictures and music, cities, places, philosophies were to be the materials on which grace would work."*
>
> —Thomas Merton, *The Literary Essays of Thomas Merton*[114]

Brother Hollywood

In the mid-1980s, I lived in the little town of Cambridge in Upstate New York. I had left Hollywood and my television career and had secluded myself in a quiet corner not far from the Vermont border. I lived in a one-room apartment above an antique store for about six months. During the dead of the winter, I did little more than read philosophy and history books. I was on a search to discover if there was any meaning to life. My friends thought I had lost my mind.

Just outside the town, atop a mountain, there was an Orthodox monastery. Even though at the time I considered myself an atheist, the monastery became my refuge. The monks called me Brother Hollywood. Among other ways of earning their daily bread, the monks made sausages and delivered them to stores throughout a wide region. I worked in the kitchen and often accompanied Brother Stavaros when he made deliveries. The conversations were always stimulating. It was one of the best times of my life. I went from *General Hospital* and "Luke & Laura" on the run to making sausages with Orthodox monks. I considered it a promotion. Living in such a small town dramatically slowed down the pace of my life.

One monk, Brother James, became a priest and eventually left the monastery to pastor a small Orthodox mission in Georgia. We remained close friends, exchanging lots of emails and phone calls until he retired in 2018 and moved to Hawaii, where his brother and mother lived, and he cut off all communication with everyone. Fr. James called me "The Jerk." I was friends with two other monks. One was Brother John. Sometime in the 1990s I returned to Cambridge, New York, to visit the monks. Brother John's welcome was deeply heartfelt. I was saddened to learn of his death in January 2020. What follows is something Br. John wrote with the request that Br. David read it at his funeral:

> Why, O Lord, is it so hard for me to keep my heart directed toward you? Why do the many little things I want to do, and the many people I know, keep crowding my mind, even during the hours that I am totally free to be with you and you alone? Why does my mind wander off in so many directions, and why does my heart desire the things that lead me astray? Are you not enough for me? Do I keep doubting your love and care, your mercy and grace? Do I keep wondering, in the center of my being, whether you will give me all I need if I just keep my eyes on you?
>
> Please accept my distractions, my fatigue, my irritations, and my faithless wanderings. You know me more deeply and fully than I know myself. You love me more deeply and fully than I can love myself. You even offer me more than I can desire. Look at me, see me in all my misery and inner confusion, and let me sense your presence in the midst of my turmoil. All I can do is show myself to you. Yet, I am afraid to do so. I am afraid that you will reject me. But I know—with the knowledge of faith—that you desire to give me your love. The only thing you ask of me is not to hide from you, not to run away in despair, not to act as if you were a relentless despot.
>
> Take my tired body, my confused mind, and my restless soul into your arms and give me rest, simple quiet rest.

Brother John was a monk at New Skete Monastery for at least forty years. Yet, he still harbored all the doubts and confusions as the rest of us . . . especially me.

Note: It is still Memorial Day; the sun is now slowly lifting its head over the island. In the complete silence of my home (without noisy chickens, goats, and barking wild dogs below my window), I read Brother John's deathbed words aloud. I read them very slowly. They really spoke to me. Like all of life, monastic life is a daily struggle. Merton's life surely illustrated his struggle and confusions, his doubts and secret aspirations. He would passionately write something and within pages or weeks or months and sometimes years, he would contradict himself. His early spiritual writings were very dogmatic. His initial writings on the Eucharist and Mary the mother of Jesus were very stringent. But in his Asian Journal, written in the last months of his life, we see a much different Merton. He no longer brims with certitude. He has become marginalized. He had embraced the poverty of the Gospel and the simplicity of Zen; he held on to his Marian devotions while treasuring Buddhist meditation.

My inner monk needed to hear the honest voice of Brother John as he was about to be embraced by Sister Death. I too asked God to please accept my distractions, my fatigue, my irritations, and my faithless wanderings. I realized I could no longer beat myself up for my failures and faithlessness. God does not do so. God only and always comes with a gentle touch, a healing balm. The still, small, silent Voice always says, "It's OK. Pick yourself up, dust yourself off, love yourself, and strive to do better. You have the amazing gift of today."

For the Life of the World

In September 2000, I attended the Divine Liturgy at St. Nicholas (Orthodox) Cathedral in Downtown Los Angeles. Afterward, I was browsing in the bookstore when I spotted a book by Fr. Alexander Schmemann. The back cover of the book featured an endorsement blurb from Thomas Merton. Merton said *For the Life of the World* was "a powerful, articulate, and indeed creative essay in sacramental theology. . . . Schmemann can allow himself to go to the very root of the subject without having to apologize for his forthrightness or his lack of interest in trivialities."

I bought the book—and many other books by Fr. Schmemann over the coming years. Simultaneous with my interest in contemplative prayer and my fascination with monasticism, I was at the time feeling a pull toward the Orthodox Church. I had no idea where those dual interests were leading me. Twenty years ago, I could never have imagined that my faith journey would take me to Haiti. While I never made the move toward the Orthodox Church, I do attend a Byzantine Catholic Church in Florida because I am drawn to a more Eastern expression of Christianity. I love icons; they are the best sermons.

Monasticism

A few hours before his accidental death in Bangkok, Thomas Merton said: "The monk is essentially someone who takes a critical attitude toward the contemporary world and its structure."[115] What an interesting statement; it implies that each of us who look seriously at life are in some degree monks seeking a monastic and even mystical dimension that is missing in organized religion. It also means that when we believe society and the Church are headed in the wrong direction, we have an obligation to speak up, to dissent from the accepted norm. Merton noted in his *Asian Journal,* which was his last book: "It is the peculiar office of the monk in the modern world to keep alive the contemplative experience and to keep the way open for modern technological man to recover the integrity of his own inner depths." This became truth for me, a modern technological dummy. I think we can all live a better life if we became more monk-like, more open to the contemplative and mystical traditions within our faith. We can't become complacent.

The Peril of Stagnation

The great Jewish rabbi and influential theologian Abraham Joshua Heschel, whom Merton greatly admired and corresponded with, understood that self-critical thinking and dissent were central to Judaism and to all vibrant and healthy religion. In *A New Hasidism: Roots,* he wrote:

> Inherent to all traditional religion is the peril of stagnation. What becomes settled and established may easily turn foul. Insight is replaced by clichés, elasticity by obstinacy, spontaneity by habit. Acts of dissent prove to be acts of renewal.
> It is therefore of vital importance for religious people to voice and to appreciate dissent. And dissent implies self-examination, critique, discontent.
>
> Dissent is indigenous to Judaism. The prophets of ancient Israel who rebelled against a religion that would merely serve the self-interest or survival of the people continue to stand out as inspiration and example of dissent to this very day.
>
> An outstanding feature dominating all Jewish books composed during the first five hundred years of our era is the fact that together with the normative view a dissenting view is nearly always offered, whether in theology or in law. Dissent continued during the finest periods of Jewish history: great scholars sharply disagreed with Maimonides; Hasidism, which brought so much illumination and inspiration into Jewish life, was a movement of dissent. . . . Creative dissent comes out of love and faith, offering positive alternatives, a vision.[116]

CHAPTER 14

Through the Eyes of Faith

Montaldo Study Note Number 4

Seeing It Clear through Dark Times—
Thomas Merton's Contemplative & Eschatological Faith

During Lent, 2020 the Church of Corpus Christi in Manhattan invited me to give a short "sermon" on the topic of "faith" during one of their four Sunday Lenten Vespers Services. What follows are my remarks, the most personal I have voiced in public, but it was the right moment in the right place with the right audience. To share my words in Gerry's book is similarly most appropriate:

If it were on an exam, I couldn't answer the question from the Gospel of Luke, "When the Son of Man comes, will he find faith on the earth?" In my youth. I could've written a paragraph on these big questions, but I can no longer memorize and parrot textbook answers. I no longer have answers is not false humility, but statement of fact. Soon to end my seventy-fifth year, I also cannot often rise above the ground floor of my society's "easy questions."

I *am* woke enough to believe Siberia is burning. I can smell bad trouble with CNN's breaking news. Leonard Cohen's "I've seen the future and it's murder" raises no argument in me. I am aware enough to be rereading Albert Camus's *The Plague*. Not yet cursing the day I was born, I can empathize with a frog content in warm water, not realizing he is dying forward to a rolling boil.

Humphrey Trevelyan, British author and diplomat, wrote that artists must experience despair: "Artists must be shaken by naked truths that will not be comforted. This divine discontent, this disequilibrium, this state of inner tension, is the source of their artistic activity." A rough beauty comes when "faith" in the good, true, and beautiful fails a Leonard Cohen or an Albert Camus.

Congressman John Lewis from Atlanta will be remembered by those in his lineage for his admonition that they "Keep the faith." But what is the quality of faith he prays they keep? Thomas Merton provides a useful although too broad distinction on what the act of "keeping faith" might mean. The monk distinguished between what he called a Christian's "eschatological faith" and a "contemplative faith." His two adjectives for faith are at opposite ends on a spectrum of Christian faith experience.

A Christian whose faith is purely "eschatological" believes most human experience is irredeemably unsaved from being a hot mess. We who are purely eschatological believe nothing can be done to improve the human condition. These pure only-at-the-end-of-this-world types hide in safe, padded cells of conscience until death blessedly directs them to stand at Christ's right hand.

At the opposite end of faith's spectrum, one whose Christian faith is purely "contemplative" believes only "love will keep us together." "Eat His body, drink His blood, and will all join hands and sing, 'Alleluia.'" Jesus's radical call is to enjoy our human nature just as it is. There is enough wheat to go around no matter how tall the encroaching tares.

These extremes of faith between the eschatological and the contemplative are non-existent perfect types. Our individual and collective faiths are actually always a mixed bag. We find something sweet in every bitter meal.

I tasted a sweetness that came after total despair two years ago in just this time of year. In the summer of 2017, I attended the death of my brother, which made me my intimate family's last one standing. His wife, neglecting her own health, had cared for him through a long illness. Two weeks after my brother's death, she was diagnosed as having stage-four lung cancer. I flew back to Louisiana to accompany her through her agony for her last two months. My best angels rose to this terrible occasion; I entertained my better angels; I did the death-packing and the final cleaning of their home; I comforted their neighbors and cooked a celebratory meal to honor these two lives lost; and I buried and honored their ashes in my family's New Orleans tomb. In brief, I was the good soldier until the following winter when I was picking out the belt in my closet tough and long enough to hang me. After heroics, I became suicidal.

I spent hours in bed or chair dazed and unresponsive. I planned my death over and over, possibly in the next hour. Only when I finally went to the Veterans Administration for help, only when I stopped self-medicating with alcohol, only when I openly admitted to friends the hidden fissures of my character that I calmly confessed with the aid of 40 mg of Prozac, did I begin an uncertain climb forward toward a light. For a year and a half now, I have never been more content and felt more blessed. Through the kindness of friends and my own desperate prayers, I am making my own Thomas Merton's declaration in his journals after his own hard times, "Suspended by God's mercy I am content for anything to happen."

As my sister-in-law Donna was dying, she gave me my brother's wedding ring. When I returned to New Jersey, I put it in my safe. One night, as my mental health improved, I had a dream: my father and mother, my two sisters, Janet and Charlotte, and my brother Charles and I were holding hands in a tight circle and dancing. We wore golden crowns. Seeing our festivities as if from above, our dysfunctional relations reconciled, I was aghast and unbelieving, but, as I awoke, I went to the safe and put my brother's golden ring on my wedding finger. By this act, I agreed to marry my crazy family.

In our family's life together, I learned the role of the "good boy" and group enabler, while setting myself apart from soap-opera lives. I thought myself the "golden boy," appearing inexplicably in a collection of tarnished brass. I assured they would know my assistance descended on them from great heights. I knew God loved me only if I proved I was good. I harbored these delusions until the day I sat on a porch with my brother Charles, everyone now dead but us. Charles confronted me: "I want you to know how much you've hurt everyone in our family. You always had your head in a book and you did some good, but you never loved me. You thought you loved God while hating us. Does the first epistle of Saint John mean anything to you?"

I wear my brother's wedding ring now to honor him while remembering his harsh but true judgments. I now realize that my family loved me in spite of myself, that they loved me in my false heroics in spite of themselves. After my dream of our dancing with golden crowns, I wrote a poem:

All I Once Held Dear

The muddy, bitter waters I swam in as a boy

become clear and now splash sweet upon my lips.

What I long despised, I accept most precious.

What I hated in myself, I love.

The mistranslations of my life's essays untangle.

My sentences are simple. What I buried, I dig up to the sun.

Out of the dark rooms this year with all of you,

my family, friends, lovers, you intimate strangers

whose dark faces I feared, I now see you in the bright.

I know, I know: no one more surprised than I.

No one more astonished in this moment rescued

by hidden saviors, finding me when lost.

Blessings on these who cut the locks on my doors,

who stripped me of straight jackets,

who led me out of jails.

You are my salvation and divine. You, God's grace.

Accept my grateful kiss, you, each every one, God's holy face.

We live in the mysteries that the one chance others will ever have to see God's face, while they wait for the Son of Man to come again, is seeing the face of God shining from our own. When Lazarus came out from the tomb, did he first look for Jesus or did his eyes focus upon his beloved sisters, Martha and Mary? Jesus quickly dried his own tears and left to be about His Father's business, but Martha and Mary peeled away their brother's burial shroud and made him supper. Until the Lord comes again, we are left in each other's hands to receive the nourishment we need, not only just to live, but to taste a portion of that Love that just might one coming day raise us together from the dead.

Read Thomas Merton's solemn declaration of his Christian contemplative faith:

This is our glory and our hope, we are the Body of Christ. Christ loves us and espouses us as His own flesh. Isn't that enough for us? No it isn't. We do not really believe it. Be content. Be content. We are the Body of Christ. We have found Him. He has found us. We are in Him. He is in us. There is nothing further to look for except the deepening of this life we already possess. Be content.[117]

Here is Merton's text on contemplative and eschatological faith upon which I based my words at Corpus Christi:

If it were a matter of choosing between "contemplation" and "eschatology," there is no question that I am, and would always be, committed entirely to the latter. Here in the hermitage, returning necessarily to beginnings, I know where my beginning was: having the Name and Godhead of Christ preached in Corpus Christi Church. I heard and believed. I believe that He has called me freely, out of pure mercy, to His love and salvation, and that at the end (to which all is directed by Him) I shall see Him after I have put off my body in death and have risen together with Him. That at the last day "all flesh shall truly see the salvation of God." What this means is that my faith is an eschatological faith, not merely a means of penetrating the mystery of the divine presence and resting in Him now. Yet because my faith is eschatological it is also contemplative, for I am even now in the Kingdom and I can even now "see" something of the glory of the Kingdom and praise Him who is King. I would be foolish then if I lived blindly, putting all "seeing" off until some imagined fulfillment, for my present seeing is the beginning of a real and unimaginable fulfillment! Thus, contemplation and eschatology are one in Christian faith and in surrender to Christ. They complete each other and intensify each other. It is by contemplation and love that I can best prepare myself for the eschatological vision—and best help the Church and all men to journey toward it.

> The union of contemplation and eschatology is clear in the gift of the Holy Spirit. In Him we are awakened to know the Father because in Him we are refashioned in the likeness of the Son. It is in this likeness that the Spirit will bring us at last to the clear vision of the invisible Father in the Son's glory which will also be our glory. Meanwhile it is the Spirit who awakens in our heart the faith and hope in which we cry for the eschatological fulfillment and vision. In this hope there is already a beginning, a "promise" of fulfillment. This is our contemplation: the realization and "experience" of the life-giving Spirit in Whom the Father is present to us through the Son, our way, truth, and life. The realization that we are on our way, that because we are on our way, we are in that Truth which is the end and by which we are already fully and eternally alive. Contemplation is the loving sense of this life and this presence and this eternity.[118]

In My Brokenness

Perseverance in prayer grows out of a spirit of humility. I pray because I know I'm powerless without God. Faith is always accompanied by humility. There was a time in my life, back in my thirties, when I was always on the verge of despondency, because, I see now, the folly of my pride made me think my own counsel contained all the answers.

It's in the recognition of our true powerlessness and vulnerability that the seeds of faith are planted. Faith grows out of a profound loneliness and desperate longing. Through the eyes of faith, we see the emptiness of our perishable lives and see how we were created for union and communion, with God, our true selves and each other. Faith is an endless exodus to the heart . . . our own heart and the heart of God. God is an artist of exodus.

Faith is more than clinging to a belief or a dogma or merely obeying God. Faith is approaching God and getting to know God and giving yourself to God. And that takes time. And prayer. Faith is an ever-deepening desire to taste God more fully . . . which primarily happens in the stillness and silence of prayer. Unfortunately, our frenetic busyness deadens our capacity for contemplation.

Faith moves us beyond the superficial and trivial. Faith gives us the eyes to see the beauty and interconnectedness of all creation.

My faith tells me that God loves me in my brokenness. God loves me fully and unconditionally, without a hint of reservation, even in my darkest, most sinful, most unloving moments. God does not demand perfection; God gives love. The essence of faith is trust . . . trusting in God's undivided, unmerited love. Sadly, life today tends to teach us not to trust anyone.

*"We should never delude ourselves into thinking that the things we do
in private, including very small acts of infidelity, of self-indulgence, of
bigotry, of jealousy, or of slander, are of no consequence since no one
knows about them. Inside the mystery of our interconnectedness as a
human family and as a family of faith and trust, even our most private
actions, good or bad, like invisible bacteria inside the blood stream,
affect the whole. Everything is known, felt, in one way or another."*

—RONALD ROLHEISER, OMI[119]

A Sweet Communion

*"The real voyage of discovery consists not in seeking
new lands, but in seeing with new eyes."*

—MARCEL PROUST

While I stood humbled in the massive Basilica of St. Peter's and was overwhelmed by its size and spectacular array of statues and art, it was too noisy, too busy for me to feel anything other than chaos. Until I saw a simple act of faith. I was walking down the right side of the church, past all the side altars, including one housing the magnificent Pietà by Michelangelo. About halfway to the main altar, there is a small chapel reserved for quiet prayer and meditation. Inside the chapel, the Blessed Sacrament was exposed. I went in and sat down for a few minutes, but my mind was too jittery to enter into any kind of contemplation or worship.

As I left the chapel and became engulfed in the sea of people working their way either up or down the crowded aisle, some with video cameras pointing to the elaborately decorated ceiling, I spotted a young, beautiful nun dressed in a full, traditional habit, including the headdress. She looked peaceful, calm, unhurried. As she walked past the chapel where the Blessed Sacrament was exposed, she paused, turned toward the chapel, knelt down, and prostrated herself so her veiled head almost touched the marble floor. She remained in that position for about ten seconds. She then stood up, turned toward the front of the church, and continued walking. Her silent, devout act of reverence at merely passing the chapel caused me to cry. I returned to the chapel, knelt down, and prayed. It was a time of sweet communion. We seek to make connections. God calls us into communion.

Later in the day, I saw the same sister in the piazza in front of the basilica. I went up to her and told her the impact she had on me. She said, "With any experience of tears, God is trying to get in touch with us." We hugged. After she urged me to pray the rosary each day, we parted—her memory firmly emblazoned on my mind.

Jesus was present outside the little chapel and alive in the humble nun. Humility is the first fruit of honesty with oneself. True humility plunges one into adoration of God.

"My soul glorifies the Lord, and my spirit rejoices
in God my savior . . ." (Luke 1:46)

Humble Eyes

In the slums of the world, I saw more clearly my own weaknesses, and subsequently I slowly began to see the importance of humility. Only through humble eyes can God be seen. I am nothing; God is everything. But in my nothingness, God gives me everything. Humility helps shatter illusions. Humility is the truest form of honesty. It sees our weaknesses and vulnerabilities. Humility allows God to transform our weaknesses into strengths.

Humility is a pathway to prayer. Prayer is the doorway to the heart, the center of our being, the place where we can let go, let go of pretense, pride, ego, and a host of things blocking us from the true source of life, the true source of love, God.

In the innermost chamber of the heart, we see the dissonance between the Spirit of God and our spirit; it's here we struggle to dissolve that difference. In the safety of the heart, we can let go of fear and we can risk change. In the heart, conflict gives way to harmony. In the heart, what's mine becomes God's. In the heart, humility becomes holiness.

God wants us to see each other as tabernacles,
as secret hiding places for the divine.

Note: *In the predawn darkness of April 30, 2020, I came across this reflection as I reviewed the manuscript for* The Sunrise of the Soul *one last time before the publisher sent it to the typesetter. The thought that we need to see each other as tabernacles housing God seems unreasonable. Yes, I wrote it—some years ago—and I still believe it to be true, yet my behavior rarely reflects that belief. Sometimes as I'm driving around Port-au-Prince and spot a pathetically sad looking person dressed in rags and sitting on the ground, I feel a deep sense of empathy and want to stop the car and offer them something. I keep driving. Seconds later, a street kid or young male adult aggressively tries to clean my windshield with a dirty rag, begging me for a few pennies for his cleaning efforts. They often touch their stomach to communicate to me they are hungry. I don't think for second that they are a tabernacle of the divine. Rather, I get angry at their aggressiveness and their failure to not respond to my waving them off.*

Inside of Santa Chiara, there are some staff members who really annoy me. They would annoy me far less if I thought for even a split second that God was within them. It is easy to write poetically about the spiritual life and how it should inform our actions, but moving from the pristine whiteness of a printed page to the gritty reality of daily life is a huge struggle. I'm not sure if Merton pulled it off. I certainly haven't.

Addendum: It is now September 6, 2022. I smiled when I read the above note. A few months ago, on a back road leading up to supermarket Pétionville, I spotted an old homeless woman dressed in rags surrounded by bags of her stuff. She was cooking on some burning twigs. She looked lost and lonely. While shopping, I purchased a small pizza for her. On the way back, I stopped the car where she was camped. I lowered the passenger window and called her. She looked stunned and confused. She slowly made her way to the car. I handed her the pizza. She looked bewildered before she smiled and took the pizza. Every time I go to the market, I see her. I always bring her something to eat . . . a Jamaican patty, a chicken wrap, or a pizza. She knows me now. Sometimes I give her a little money. When I stopped to give her something a few days ago, I saw a well-dressed Haitian man who was watching from across the street. As I drove away, he smiled and gave me a thumbs-up. Maybe he will also give her some food . . . and the goodness spreads.

A Broken World

Tuesday, April 21, 2020, Port-au-Prince, Haiti. Sigmund Freud said we understand things best when they are broken. We find our giftedness in our brokenness. We are in a broken world right now. Our lives are heavily burdened. The pandemic is a time when we learn about ourselves, we learn about our depths, we learn about our faith, our need for God, and we learn about the call of the Spirit to pray. It is a time when we appreciate the kind word, the blessing, the caring, the gratitude we have for all the first responders who risk their lives to help others, the understanding we have for those who are struggling in life, the empathy we have for those who feel they are misunderstood. These are the moments when we learn about ourselves. In these moments, we discover our own emptiness, our own poverty—a poverty we all share. It is when we are broken and struggling, we learn who really loves us. Be grateful for the people in your life who love you, who forgive you, who show up for you, who stand up for you.

Note: On the night of April 27, 2020, at about 9:30 pm, there was an exchange of gunfire that lasted for nearly a minute. I kept typing. A kid crying would have made me get up. Still, the sound of gunfire is unsettling. All the while, loud music was playing. There is no silence in Haiti.

The Silent Life

I have a first hardcover edition of Merton's book *The Silent Life.* I love the cover. Later paperback versions all had different covers, mostly featuring images from nature. In the middle of the original hardback, there were seven pages of images from Trappist monasteries throughout Europe. The monastic life depicted in the seventeen photographs had captured no longer exists. Monks are now seen as unessential; their solitary life of prayer and work are considered irrelevant. For many people today, monks are just overly pious guys fleeing the struggles of life. The cover photo that I loved featuring hooded monks quietly sitting side by side in prayer did not appeal to many people. Publishers of later versions knew this and opted for a more appealing images of silent, peaceful nature.

Today, the silent life no longer exists. We live inside a noise-making machine. The inner silent life is unknow to most of us as we have become addicted to externals, to a frantic quest for affluence. Our idols are money and power. We strive for self-sufficiency while the saints acknowledge their insufficiency and saw the interconnectedness of all living beings. In his book *Thoughts in Solitude,* Merton wrote: "The value of our weakness and of our poverty is that they are the earth in which God sows the seed of desire [for God alone]."[120] Sit in solitude and welcome silence at least for a short time once a week. My small apartment in Fort Pierce has become my solitary monastery, which is essential for me to continue my community work in Haiti.

First hardcover edition of Merton's book *The Silent Life*

CHAPTER 15

Our Cluttered Hearts

Shop Till You Drop

We live in an age where modern transportation allows us to go anywhere we want; ironically, we also live in an age where many have lost their sense of direction. The late Monsignor William Shannon, the great Merton scholar whom I had the honor of spending time with shortly before his death in 2012, said, "Physically we can go anywhere we want to, even to the moon and probably to Mars, but spiritually many among us have no notion of where we really want to go." Our society gives priority to material progress over moral growth and to the efficiency of getting things done over social responsibility. Our entire economy is based on greed. We worship money and property. Our growing affluence has diminished our sense of gratitude and dependence upon God. We have fallen far from God. Jesus said we should resist the temptation of self-preservation and privilege; he made it perfectly clear that those who seek self-preservation are lost. Jesus gave up everything and became nothing; he held nothing back for himself.

Monsignor Shannon said, "We cannot ignore the fact that we live in a cultural milieu that constantly ignores the needs of the spirit." Thomas Merton felt that the sickness of our mass society was that it had forfeited its sense of solitude and its capacity for contemplation. Imagine what he would think of our 24/7 society of perpetual consumption, a society in which we live to achieve, accomplish, perform, and possess. We want more, own more, use more, eat more, and drink more. Merton scholar Anthony Padovano bluntly and correctly stated, "Consumption and contemplation are not harmonious."[121] We want to add more.

Only solitude can save people from the slavery of unthinking conformity to the accepted norms of our consumerist culture that denies the inner realities of the human spirit. Our natural capacity for contemplation has been virtually snuffed out by meaningless distractions and diversions that are manufactured by the titans of corporate greed. "Shop till you drop" needs to be replaced by "stop until you're healed."

A Place of Self-Emptying

> *"The truest solitude is not something outside you, not an absence of men or of sound around you; it is an abyss opening up in the center of your soul."*
>
> —Thomas Merton, Seeds of Contemplation[122]

Solitude isn't the same as withdrawal, which has negative connotations. Solitude has positive qualities. During those periods of extended solitude in my life, infrequent as they were, I stopped running from myself and became friends with myself; solitude gave me space to enjoy my own company. In solitude, I learned that I'm not alone; moreover, it taught me there is no such thing as aloneness. Spiritual growth, for most of us, doesn't come from fleeing the world, but from entering into it fully. However, for the sake of our spiritual health, we each need periods of solitude. We also need to develop an inner solitude that can be entered no matter where we are.

As Merton pointed out, entering into solitude with the idea of affirming ourselves, separating oneself from others, even interiorly, in order to be different, or by intensifying one's individual self-awareness is not in harmony with the purity required for spiritual growth. For the Christian, pure solitude is a place of self-emptying in order to experience union with Christ; in the interior abyss, we become detached from our petty false self and open ourselves up to the vastness of the Infinite Presence.

> *Our hearts are a tangle of contradictions,*
> *fragmented and overwhelmed by*
> *disappointments, struggles, worries, and doubts;*
> *in the noise and chaos of our cluttered hearts,*
> *we cannot hear God, cannot know God, cannot feel God's love.*

This beachfront is a two-minute walk from my apartment in Fort Pierce. It is here that my inner conflicts are washed away and my sense of tranquility is restored. I am grateful for this space that gifts me with monthly stillness, silence, and solitude.

The Creative Power of Silence

"The door to solitude opens only from the inside."

—Thomas Merton, *Disputed Questions*[123]

Merton's monastic life offered him the kind of high-octane silence few of us can experience. Still, whatever degree and frequency of silence we can find will greatly enhance the quality of our lives. Merton writes:

> Not only does silence give us a chance to understand ourselves better, to get a truer and more balance perspective on our own lives in relation to the lives of others: silence makes us whole if we let it. Silence helps to draw together the scattered and dissipated energies of our existence. It helps us to concentrate on a purpose that really corresponds not only to the deeper needs of our own being but also to God's intentions for us.
>
> This is a really important point. When we live superficially, when we are always outside ourselves, never quite "with" ourselves, always divided and pulled in many directions by conflicting plans and projects we find ourselves doing many things we do no really want to do, saying things we do not really mean, needing things we do not really need, exhausting ourselves for what we secretly realize to be worthless and without meaning to our lives: "Why spend your money on what is not food and your earnings on what never satisfies?" (Isaiah 55:2).[124]

Without the silence, meager as it is, that I experience in my island home in Florida, I would never have survived seven years in Haiti. It resets my inner compass, shows me where I've strayed, shows me my uncorrected faults, and pulls me back to the true center of reality. Without silence, I'd be toast. An appreciation of silence was Merton's gift to me . . . and you.

Note: As I read the above early on the morning of October 28, 2022 while in Florida, I made a huge decision. For the last two years, as the turbulence grew in Haiti, I dreamed of going to Rome and Assisi one last time. I wanted to reconnect to the time and place where 28 years earlier my life dramatically changed in a flash of insight. The Franciscan friar in charge of Sant' Isidoro's in Rome is a friend of mine and he will be returning to Ireland in June 2023 and once he is gone, I would no longer be permitted to stay at the friary. I felt an urgency to go to Italy one more time, and began making plans to go in March 2023. But then doubts began to creep in. I needed a period of extended silence more than a nostalgic trip that would be exhausting and include two long days of travel. Suddenly, this thought hit me: "A person in need of stillness and silence would not go to a busy big city and a medieval town crowded with tourists. They would go to a monastery." I decided to spend ten days next March in a Trappist monastery in South Carolina.

CHAPTER 16

Our Existential Hunger

Putting God in a Box

Out of the vestiges of God we happen to detect, we create concepts of God and ideas about God that have little or nothing to do with God because we simply do not know God. Until God intervenes, all we can do is stumble along in the direction of God. But God is far-off, and so we make do, coping as best we can, struggling as we walk. Because we think we are in control, we feel a measure of peace. However, to find God, we must lose control, drop our need for security—and this is the last thing we want to do, so we really don't look . . . we just pretend we're looking. We put God in a box and are happy . . . which is, ironically, the source of our unhappiness.

We were all made for love, caring, and compassion . . . to be expressed in an infinite variety of ways. Love doesn't take time to think things over, to calculate or measure the cost. It simply acts, often in an unreasonable manner and never with moderation. To think of God is to think of abundance. To think of Jesus is to think of emptiness. This is the mystery, beauty, and wonder of the Incarnation: God who is full became empty. The One who is rich beyond measure became poor by taking on the limitations of human flesh. The miracle of Christmas is that the divine spirit took on bodily form. By sharing in the poverty of our humanity, God gave us the gift of being able to share in the richness and fullness of God to the extent of our willingness to follow Jesus's example of self-emptying love, a love that requires us to turn away from every instinct toward selfishness. God gave God away. Do I give myself away? Christmas should not be about acquiring; Christmas should be about surrendering.

Our existential hunger to love and be loved is fixed on acquiring material goods. While we fill ourselves with things, we are starving our souls. We don't need to reject the things of the world; we simply need to spend more time cultivating our interior life and less time consuming more and more stuff. A simple life is the surest path to a life of genuine depth and meaning. Simplicity helps us remove the clutter from our lives, which creates an environment for the inner freedom required for a more mystical life and a deeper communion with the ultimate mystery. Simplicity of life helps us to avoid wasting time and energy on trivial distractions.

Love, detachment, and humility form a triptych of the holy life.

The more we surrender our lives to Christ, the more we're able to let go of status, privilege, power, and wealth. In time, our lives become more focused and simpler, as we more fully realize that only a few things really matter. At the core of Jesus's social justice teaching is to live simply. You can see simple living manifested in the lives of all the mystics and saints. When he was first elected, Pope Francis impressed the world by his simple lifestyle in Brazil and how he shunned all the privileges accorded to the Vicar of Christ.

Note: As I read this in the Spring of 2022 in the peacefulness of my island home, I was tempted to delete it. Not because I did not like it. I like it very much. I believe every word of it. Yet, I know it sounds truly crazy, cutting against all the norms of life in America. When I talk about the sentiments expressed in the above passage, Haitians look at me as if I were nuts. They live in overwhelming need; every day is struggle. They have nothing material to surrender, and there is little time or quiet to contemplate what inner tendencies they need to renounce. But now things are getting materially more difficult for many Americans. Inflation and rising prices, especially for gasoline, as a result of America's support of Ukraine as they heroically resist the unwarranted invasion from Russia as well as a stumbling economy in the wake of our long battle against the global pandemic, has left many American families in financial trouble; they are struggling to keep their homes and feed their kids. Many Americans are now working two jobs to stay afloat. Some are on the verge of giving up, which is very different than surrendering to Christ. Any realistic look at our lives reveals we have much we can do without. Moreover, the false self must vacate its throne. For that to happen, we must recognize the dark forces and unhealthy compulsions that bind us.

A More Delicate Language

"When people lack a language for depth, life remains trivial."

—DOROTHEE SÖLLE

My friend Michael Paul Gallagher, the late Irish Jesuit professor of theology at the Pontifical Gregorian University in Rome, wrote in his final book, *Into Extra Time: Living Through the Final Stages of Cancer and Jottings Along the Way*:

> Escape from the cult of clarity that pretends to be the full story of truth. The opposite of faith is not doubt but a wrong kind of certainty. Blaise Pascal called it the spirit of geometry against the spirit of finesse. Where can we find a more delicate language in ourselves? When we have an attack of wonder. It can happen through anything that arouses the imagination of newness—drama, poetry, beauty, affection, even trouble or the needs of others. All these can open towards another self-listening and towards the possibility of prayer.[125]

For me, reading Merton in places of extreme poverty opened me up to new ways of seeing and thinking and gently pushed me toward a new way of praying. Prayers of petition became for me a thing of the past, except for one elementary petition: give me a pinch of wisdom and a particle of wonder. *Help me, God, to see the invisible in the visible.*

The Detached Heart

Thomas Merton wrote, "According to the Christian mystical tradition, one cannot find one's inner center and know God there as long as one is involved in the preoccupations and desires of the outward self."[126] It seems to me that the single-minded pursuit of profit has led the world economic system down a catastrophic blind alley. I wonder if capitalism is even conducive to integral human development.

Our capitalist worldview is imbued with the mistaken idea that more is better, when in fact all great spirituality teaches that we need to let go. German mystic Meister Eckhart said, "The spiritual life has much more to do with subtraction than it does with addition." If having more stuff made us happy, most of us would've been happy long ago. Sadly, most of society seems driven to higher levels of doing and acquiring, which only increases spiritual blindness.

In his book *Ascent of Mount Carmel*, Saint John of the Cross said: "To come to possess all, desire the possession of nothing." His startling words stand in direct opposition to our American ambition for power, money, pleasure, glamour, security, and an ever-increasing standard of living. The saint came to realize that an unrestrained appetite for these things fragments the soul, causing our lives to be too divided and cluttered to find the true peace and joy that can only be found in loving and serving God above all else.

On the cross, through grace, reconciliation and union with God became possible. Saint John of the Cross asks us to live the Paschal Mystery, to enter the living death of the cross. In *The Ascent of Mount Carmel*, he says, "The soul must empty itself of all that is not God in order to go to God." The detached heart knows the fullness of peace, joy, and freedom, and sees the face of God illuminated in all of creation. To be holy is to be whole.

Those who struggle for their daily bread can offer great insight to those of us who struggle to go deeper into our spiritual lives. The road to mystical consciousness is paved with an acceptance of our natural state of exodus, acceptance of the reality of human misery, acceptance of our limitations and fragility. The poor know about these things. The humanity of Christ illuminated the vulnerable character of human nature.

Jesus is the humility and humanity of God.

As I made my film *Endless Exodus*, which explored the plight of undocumented migrants, I came to see that an awareness of oppression and a struggle for justice are integral to genuine mysticism. The all-embracing Christ invites us to be with Him, so that He, through us, can be with all people. We are all migrants. As people of faith, we are migrants going from sin to grace, from earth to heaven, from death to life. Our migration is grounded in our belief that God first migrated to us in the person of Jesus and through him we are called to migrate to God. If migration worked itself into the self-definition of all human beings, we would not be as threatened by migrants as we often are; instead, we would see in them not only a reflection of ourselves but Christ who loves us.

Action is as important as prayer; each of us must take responsibility for meeting the world's need, for we are the accomplices of evil if we do nothing to prevent it.

As soon as you open your heart to God,
you are in the mystical world.

A Homeless God

"The shadows fall. The stars appear. The birds begin to sleep. Night embraces the silent half of the earth. A vagrant, a destitute wanderer with dusty feet, finds his way down a new road. A homeless God, lost in the night, without papers, without identification, without even a number, a fragile expendable exile lies down in desolation under the sweet stars of the world and he entrusts Himself to sleep."

—THOMAS MERTON, FROM THE PROSE POEM "HAGIA SOPHIA"[127]

Being Fully Present

In *Gravity and Grace*, Simone Weil flatly states, "Attachment is a manufacturer of illusions and whoever wants reality ought to be detached." In *New Seeds of Contemplation*, Thomas Merton writes, "We do not detach ourselves from things in order to attach ourselves to God, but rather we become detached *from ourselves* in order to see and use all things in and for God."[128] In her book *Ascent to Love: The Spiritual Teaching of St. John of the Cross*, Ruth Burrows reminds us of this truth: "The detached heart has a far greater joy and comfort in created realities, for to treat them possessively is to lose all joy in them."[129]

Our spiritual heritage is brimming with reminders of the importance of detachment. Each day of my Franciscan life reminds me that I must guard against the onslaught of distractions our culture hurls at me each day. I need to incorporate structured time for spiritual reading and reflection. I need to create time for stillness, carving places in my daily schedule for contemplation, meditation, or prayer. I need to be less concerned with doing so many things, and instead develop my innate capacity for simply being   being fully present to the integrity and capacity of each moment. Knowing these things and doing them are two different things.

More often than not, I seem to be far from God. But in those moments, frequent as they are, God is near. So near, I don't have to struggle to find God, for God is already seeking me, rushing to embrace me. It is only in stillness that I can sense God's movement. Whether I'm aware of it or not, God's love is continually coursing through my very veins. For me, meditative walks and listening to sacred music are excellent ways to help me cultivate the inner stillness and silence needed to recognize the reality of God within me.

In *New Seeds of Contemplation*, Merton writes:

> Contemplation is always beyond our own knowledge, beyond our own light, beyond systems, beyond explanations, beyond discourse, beyond dialogue, beyond our own self. To enter into the realm of contemplation *one must in a certain sense die*: but this death is in fact the entrance into a higher life. *It is a death for the sake of life*, which leaves behind all that we can know or treasure as life, as thought, as experience, as joy, as being.[130]

But contemplation doesn't smooth your journey. Merton warns: "Let no one hope to find in contemplation and escape from conflict, from anguish or from doubt."[131] Moreover, Merton says:

> Contemplation is no pain-killer. What a holocaust takes place in this steady burning to ashes of old worn-out words, clichés, slogans, rationalizations! The worst of it is even apparently holy conceptions are consumed along with the rest. It is a terrible breaking and burning of idols, a purification of the sanctuary, so that no graven thing may occupy the place God has commanded to be left empty: the center, the existential altar which simply "is."[132]

Merton believed that the true self is discovered through contemplation—a process whereby one no longer finds identity in doing, but in *being*. There is a tremendous tension between the false and true selves because accepting the reality that human existence is of infinite worth is difficult to accept. To accept it would mean treating everyone differently than we do.

Our Limitations

It is within the space of our limitations that God shows us more of God's love. Until we see, understand, and admit our limitations, the noise of our desires and wishes keeps us focused on ourselves and our needs. Our lives become centered on our achievements, reputations, and winning respect and approval from others. It is in our limitations, our weaknesses, our flaws and failures that God unexpectedly emerges with an unabashed, loving hug.

Within the walls of Santa Chiara my vulnerability became more visible to me, and I saw my own need for healing and further transformation. God the Creator came in his love to embrace each of us in our most vulnerable moments. Our limitations, finitude, suffering, shortcomings, weakness, disability, and frailty can be gifts if our hearts are open to the transformative love of God. These unwelcomed conditions do not rob of us of our humanity; instead, they give us an opportunity to confer dignity on someone else through self-emptying acts of mercy and compassion. No matter our own inadequacies and defects, we are all called to be angels of compassion.

Too Much Talk of Silence

Until this and the last chapter, I was feeling good about this book as I read it for the last time before it goes to the typesetter and book designer. It is September 6, 2022, a sizzling hot day in Haiti. In the alley below me, an old truck is delivering water for bathing and cleaning to a neighbor. The truck is making so much noise I can't think.

What I was thinking was that these last two chapters might detract from the book as they sound impossible for most people to implement. Too much talk of silence and solitude. Yet they are the foundation of Merton's life, and some measure of silence and solitude should be part of a Christian's life, even if only for short periods of time

Moreover, most people are too busy to simplify their lives. Kids today in America expect and demand far more material things than I ever hoped for as a child and teenager. Every member of the family now needs their own private entertainment center. Life without a cell phone is impossible even for teenagers. Everyone is busy taking selfies for Facebook. My kids have no access to cell phones or any electronic devices. It is amazing to see them make up games and play for endless hours, just having fun together. They are happy to line up for one cookie or an apple.

I hope you keep reading . . . there is lots of good stuff ahead.

CHAPTER 17

Hungry and Naked

The Broken in Body and Spirit

Note: On January 18, 2013, while working on a film for Catholic Charities of Los Angeles titled The Wings of Love, *I encountered a homeless man. Later that night I jotted down these thoughts:*

Today I walked a mile with a homeless Hispanic man named Antonio to his "home" under a freeway overpass. I would guess he was in his late fifties, but it is hard to say as homelessness is such a tough life it ages a person rather rapidly. Antonio has lived in the dead-end space for two years. I was amazed at the creative way he managed to transform the harsh, dirt space into something that actually resembled a home.

He had an area where he could cook and heat water for a shower. He actually constructed from scrap wood a shower stall that provides him with a degree of privacy. He had a table and a chair. In one corner he constructed a platform for a bed. He decorated his "home" with an assortment of discarded trinkets and toys. There were statues of saints and animals, and pictures of Christ and the Blessed Mother. There were lots of candles. Because it was a hidden, dead-end space, he goes virtually unseen. He had a number of shopping carts filled with things he has pulled from the garbage. Catholic Charities had given him a bag of food, two warm blankets, and some fresh lemons.

I don't think Antonio's homelessness was linked to drugs or alcohol. His must be an intensely lonely life, especially at night when I'm sure he must have to cope with hungry rats wanting to feast on his food. Yet he is still able to smile . . . and express genuine gratitude for the help he gets from Catholic Charities.

As we walked under the overpass on the way to Antonio's place, we walked past four or five tents. Seated on the ground outside the tents were six or seven younger men and women. One guy was playing a guitar. They warmly greeted Antonio but looked a bit puzzled by my presence. I said I would respect their privacy and not film them. They said they appreciated that. On my way out, I passed one of the women defecating in the dirt. After she pulled up her pants, she wobbled in such a way as she returned to the tents that made it abundantly clear she was totally stoned on drugs. It was really a hard thing to see . . . and filled me with sadness.

We have no concept of just how insidious drugs are. It is like having a monster on your back, and the monster needs to be continually fed . . . and you will do anything to feed it. I have no idea of the woman's story, what hardships she encountered in life that pushed her to drugs for some relief from the misery. The young people living a stone's throw from Antonio's imaginative "home" are truly lost and forgotten. Yet God has not forgotten them and cries out to us to do something for them, something that shows them the love and mercy of God.

The Gospels make it abundantly clear that God is on the side of the poor, the broken in body and spirit, and the outcasts of society, the lepers, the prostitutes, the orphans . . . and today, we must add the addicted. We've become so separated from the poor and the suffering that we've lost the chance to find true fulfillment by giving of ourselves. Exposure to those saddled with dire poverty uncovers our clinging selfishness. We must all work to help create a society that is founded on welcome and respect, embracing the most vulnerable amongst us.

To walk with the poor is to walk with God.

A Christmas Story

In the middle of writing my first book on Saint Francis of Assisi, I was struggling with the saint's love of poverty and his desire to live among the poor. Voluntarily entering into poverty seemed a bit crazy. We need money. Nobody wants to be poor, or even be with poor people. As I was trying to understand this as I wrote in the comfort of my home, I received an invitation to make a film at the St. Francis Inn, located in a dreadfully poor section of Philadelphia.

The St. Francis Inn is only a few miles from the Liberty Bell and Independence Hall. The distance between center city and Kensington may be geographically short but it's worlds apart socially and structurally. The Kensington section of Philadelphia is known as the Badlands . . . the place hardly calls to mind the spirit of brotherly love to which Philadelphia lays a special claim. Kensington is a place of drugs, despondency, and death. The mean streets are littered with throwaway people, people who are marginalized, ignored, and forgotten, people whose lives are lived in fear, in overwhelming want, and without hope.

It was at the St. Francis Inn back in winter of 1997 that I began my ongoing education about poverty, about prayer, and learned what it means to be totally dependent upon God for everything. Making my humble little film, titled *We Have a Table for Four Ready*, about the Inn changed my life. The film aired on many PBS stations, and as a result, the film generated enough funds to build a larger kitchen and add a little chapel on the second floor where the homeless could have a peaceful space for silence and prayer. That experience led me to dedicate my life to putting the power of film at the service of the poor. The Inn taught me about poverty and prayer.

At the end of 2005, I returned to Philadelphia to see what else the St. Francis Inn had to teach me as I made a second film about The Inn, which was titled *Room at the Inn*. Even after spending most of the previous five years living among the poor around the world and with those truly wonderful men and women who have dedicated their lives to serving the poorest of the poor, I still struggled mightily with the subject of poverty, both material and spiritual, and its meaning for my life. I went back to Philadelphia because I still had much to learn. I arrived just a few weeks before Christmas, a time when we celebrate the incarnation of God, a God who chose to be born into poverty. It was a good time to be among the poor, to come to a place where Jesus in the form of a homeless person can find room at the inn.

As was my habit, I kept a diary as I filmed. Here are two short entries:

Sunday, December 4th—9:35 pm, Philadelphia: It's been a long, cold day and I'm tired. But I'm thrilled to be here . . . in fact, there is no other place on earth I would rather be . . . with the exception of Assisi. On Sunday, the main meal is served from 11:30 am to 1:00 pm. The people on the long line waiting for a table endured the bitter cold as the temperature never rose beyond the mid-thirties. Close to 300 people entered the Inn for lunch. Infants, kids, adults and the very old were all bundled up, many with woolen hats and hooded coats.

After the meal, I filmed some of the abandoned buildings in the blocks surrounding the Inn. Some streets look like war zones. Later in the afternoon, I went to Center City to grab a few shots of Independence Hall and the Liberty Bell.

Friday, December 9th—6:05 am, Philadelphia: This morning, I woke up at 5:15 am. I looked out the window and was greeted by a winter wonderland. It was snowing like crazy. While the coffee was brewing, I stepped outside the front door in order to see how much snow had fallen overnight. All dressed in white, Hagert Street never looked so beautiful. The street was silent and empty . . . except for one solitary figure standing on the corner, his back leaning against the wall of the Inn. For me, a man standing alone on a corner at 5:15 am during a snow storm symbolized the loneliness we all know. The infancy story of Christ tells us we can have hope and joy, can overcome our immense loneliness and can find unity, integration, solidarity and reconciliation of all with all.

At night, I often scribbled notes and ideas for the filmscript.

As the guests enter the dining room you can clearly see how destitution grinds people down. Sadly, we tend to think of the homeless as social nuisances. Jesus had a different point of view and suggested that the poor are portals to God.

The Inn is theologically situated in the biblical conviction of the poor being a profound, redeeming revelation of God's presence and grace. But our culture tends to separate us from the poor who live out of sight in hidden pockets of despair and want. We are blinded to the needs of the poor by our own desire for property, comfort and acquiring more material goods for ourselves. At its root, there is only one reason for the existence of poverty: selfishness, which is a manifestation of a lack of authentic love.

Peter Maurin, co-founder with Dorothy Day of the Catholic Worker, said: "On the Cross of Calvary Christ gave His life to redeem the world. The life of Christ was a life of sacrifice. We cannot imitate the sacrifice of Christ on Calvary by trying to get all we can. We can only imitate the sacrifice of Christ on Calvary by trying to give all we can. What we give to the poor for Christ's sake is what we carry with us when we die."[133]

*"Anyone who has really understood that God became human
can never speak and act in an inhuman way."*

—Karl Barth

A person who enters the Inn is greeted as a guest. The team never refers to them as a client or a case, because to do so would imply an objectification of that person and create a position of power and supposed expertise over them. People who enter the Inn for food are treated as a brother or sister, a cherished member of God's family. The Inn is cluttered with the wreckage of lives that have been victimized by the tyranny of addiction and unjust social and economic structures. Yet amid the carnage there is hope . . . and even joy. The hope and joy that comes from an awareness that we are all children of a loving God.

Many Christians still wonder why we should help a homeless alcoholic, suggesting that they have done nothing to merit our help. This attitude betrays a fundamental lack of understanding of the magnitude of God's love for us, which is lavished upon us despite the fact that our sinfulness renders us unmeritorious of God's help. We have done nothing to merit God's self-emptying love, yet God never turns away from us, is always looking to lend us a hand. The fact that a homeless alcoholic has done nothing to merit our help is irrelevant.

While making *We Have a Table for Four Ready,* I slowly realized that every conception I had about the homeless and the addicted turned out to be a misconception. I met real people, people just like me in so many ways. It's easy to label a homeless person as lazy or mentally ill or an alcoholic or drug addict as weak. The labels removed my obligation to do anything . . . it's their fault they are homeless; it's their fault they are addicted. Christ didn't label people or judge people . . . he reached out to them, he excluded no one. According to Christ, we have a responsibility to help everyone who is in need.

In my first visit to the St. Francis Inn I met a woman who was, I would guess, in her mid-twenties. But she looked far, far older. She was a prostitute. And a drug addict. She looked strung out, worn out, beaten down by the pain of her life. Her face was gaunt and unwashed. Her coarse hands were filthy; caked dirt had collected under her fingernails. She wore a tattered old sweater. It would have been so very easy to have judged her, even blithely dismiss her as useless, not worthy of our attention. But when you hear her story, judgment is suspended, and compassion takes its place. When she was an infant, her drug-addicted parents put alcohol in her baby bottle to keep her from crying. By the time the little girl, a precious child of God, was five years old, she was already an alcoholic. By the time she was fourteen, she was walking the streets of Kensington, turning tricks to earn money to feed her drug habit. For this poor soul, drugs were a way to deaden the pain of her life. She died of a drug overdose a few years after I met her. I have a photo of her in my home library. I never want to forget her . . . or forget that I must help people like her, people whom God loves but whom we ignore.

> *"If God is our treasure, then we must be dominated by the thought*
> *that God's endless wealth is found in his self-giving and self-emptying,*
> *that is, in the very opposite of the wish to have everything."*
>
> —HANS URS VAN BALTHASAR, *LIGHT OF THE WORLD*[134]

The streets of Kensington are littered with lost souls, a fact that seems more poignant at Christmas. At Christmas, we tell our kids that Santa is going to bring a gift to every boy and girl. No one stops to think how crazy that sounds or ask, "Who is this Santa Claus guy who does something so outrageously generous as to give a gift to every child?" Santa is kept alive in our hearts, even when we grow up, because the unfathomable generosity that Santa embodies is planted deep within the hearts and souls of all human beings.

Jesus illustrated the same irrational, Santa Claus kind of generosity when he told the parable of the shepherd who cared so much about one lost sheep, he abandoned everything to go look for it. In Kensington, you see many lost sheep that have strayed. And at the St. Francis Inn you see many people who have abandoned everything to look for them . . . to be present when a lost sheep wanders into their courtyard so that they can give them the greatest gift of all . . . the gift of love.

One night, during a swirling snowstorm, I filmed a recovering addict named Doug and he told me how the people at the St. Francis Inn loved him until he could love himself. In terms of economics, the St. Francis Inn hasn't done much to alleviate the poverty in Kensington. Their love and compassion generate a spiritual power that cannot be measured in terms of dollars and cents, a power that can change lives.

In a talk given hours before his death in Bangkok, Thomas Merton said, "The whole idea of compassion is based on a keen awareness of the interdependence of all these living beings, which are all part of one another and all involved in one another."[135]

The enemy in our battle to overcome chronic, unjust poverty is our misguided spirit of individualism . . . our snobbery, apathy, prejudice, and blind unreason. Though we are many, we are one body in the eyes of God, all animated by one Spirit. As members of one body, we each have a responsibility for one another.

We cannot separate justice and charity . . . they must go together, hand in hand, in order to solve the problem created by chronic poverty.

Radical Dependency

It took more than six months to edit *Room at the Inn* and a few months to complete the sound mix and the authoring and manufacturing of the DVDs. While I loved the film (in fact, I considered it the best thing I had ever done up to that point), I was concerned about the film's length. At two and a half hours, many people felt it was too long and that thirty minutes needed to be trimmed from the film. I tormented over this issue, but, in the end, I elected not to cut anything.

On Saturday, November 4, 2006, at five in the afternoon, we had a fundraising screening of *Room at the Inn* at Fuller Theological Seminary in Pasadena, California. About seventy-five people attended the event. There was a reception featuring wine and cheese prior to the actual screening. Excluding the cost of the food and drinks, which were provided by local Board members, the event cost about $1,000 to mount (rental of the theater, parking, printing, and mailing invitations). We raised about $800 in donations and sales of the films. I was not too concerned by the fact that we "lost" about $200 on the evening because I felt a number of people were really touched by the film. But the event sparked a heated debate over the length of the films produced by my ministry. The debate was sparked by a note sent to me by Chair of the Board, who was seasoned TV producer, in which he expressed his concern about the length of *Room at the Inn* and his strong conviction that the length of our films jeopardizes the fulfillment of our mission to the poor.

The note was short and concise, with just four paragraphs. One paragraph discussed the length. Another the structure of the film. The third suggested the film was too personal. I responded with a nine-page letter. As a result, the board chair resigned.

A good friend of mine who was very familiar with my long struggles over the lengths of my books and films—*Sun & Moon*, for instance, tops 600 pages, and *The Fragrant Spirit of Life* (set in Uganda) was over three hours long—wrote to me saying that my determination not to buckle under the pressure to shorten *Room at the Inn* reminded him of a passage from my book *The Sun & Moon Over Assisi*:

> Over and over again in the life of Saint Francis, in book after book, we read of the saint's determination not only to follow but also imitate the life of Christ. Especially in poverty. There is no doubt that Christ was poor. He worked for his daily bread as a carpenter in a small, impoverished village. Lacking money or possessions was not what made Christ poor. Besides, he was far from destitute. He was poor—absolutely and totally poor—because no thing possessed him. He

belonged completely to God, and whatever things Christ has he used as a visible manifestation of God's love. Following the example of Christ, Francis was poor in order that his inner emptiness could become a womb containing the fullness of God.[136]

To be honest, I did not see the connection between that passage and my struggles over length. In a follow-up e-mail my friend said: "Christ's poverty, his not being possessed by *any thing*, made him free. The same for Francis, whose total detachment made him utterly free to follow wherever God led him. My point is that you do not allow yourself to be possessed (that is, held in the grasp of) a static rule or opinion that dictates how long a piece of work should be. You are free to follow where the Spirit takes you. No question your films could be shorter. But as an artist who paints on a large canvas, I believe your subject dictates the length for you, not the accepted norm."

That response surprised me . . . but I think there might be a grain of truth in it. I am not imprisoned by society's demand that everything be reduced to a bumper sticker. I had devoted fifteen years of my life to making films on poverty, while at the same time trying to understand Saint Francis's ideal of poverty. Every film explored the same thing. Every film addressed the idea of radical dependency upon God.

Sometime in 2005, the *National Catholic Reporter* (NCR) did a big cover story on my film work; Tom Roberts, the editor of NCR at the time, opens his editorial on my first film ministry with these words: "If you talk to Gerry Straub long enough, even in casual conversation, the phrase 'radical dependency on God' will come up. If you dare ask him what it means to him, he'll tell you that it means, for instance, having a certain confidence that an extra $15,000 will show up each month to make up the difference between what's pledged and what it takes to do his work." Tom goes on to say, "'Radical dependency' for me is a frightening prospect." *Me too.*

Physical poverty and poverty of spirit are both frightening. I still do not know exactly how to follow Saint Francis or Christ. My films and books are journeys into understanding the boundless mystery of God, a God whose mercy, compassion, and love are without limits. I may have been tormented over the length of my films (and this book), but I have been comforted by God's love and compelled to extend that love to those whose lives are tormented by poverty.

Running the Santa Chiara Children's Center takes a whole lot more money than making a documentary film. For the first five years, I would guess that virtually every month began without the funds needed to make it to the end of the year. It has been a wild, scary *radical dependency* ride. It never gets easy or less nerve-racking.

Note: In the last two years, Santa Chiara has moved from a month-to-month operation to a quarter-to-quarter operation. My worry factor has decreased from twelve times a year to four times a year.

An Epic Love Poem

Note: On May 23, 2022, I was in Haiti. The night before I was up from midnight to well after 3:30 in the morning battling a severe case of diarrhea. I thought about a little girl in Haiti who just weeks before died from diarrhea. Hours later, I was awake and moving slowly. I was searching for something on my computer when I came across a file labeled "An Epic Love Poem." I opened it.

It was not about a love lost or found; it was about how lost I was while trying to make a film about a mission serving the poor in the Skid Row, Downtown Los Angeles. Skid Row was a fifty-block area where thousands of long-term homeless slept on the streets in tents or cardboard boxes. The year was 2003. The film was titled Rescue Me. *The epic poem was not really a poem. Nor was it about homelessness. It was about filming the homeless. It was never intended for publication; it was simply an expression of my internal struggle to understand what I saw and felt as I filmed, which I had recorded in my private journal. It was my attempt to understand my inner artist. As I read it, in a flash I understood why I abandoned my lucrative career as a Hollywood television producer. I was searching for something I could not define and could never find in Hollywood.*

While editing *Rescue Me*, I watched the footage for endless hours. There were over 125 hours of material. I knew every inch of footage by heart. Yet, for a long time, I had no idea how to organize the material into a story. Now, after watching the finished film four or five times, I am trying to understand how the film came to be the film it is. It never started out to be so long, so deep, so emotionally and spiritually charged. How did it happen?

First and foremost, the Union Rescue Mission gave me the creative freedom and space to discover the hidden beauty of the URM and the people they serve. Not a soul asked me what I was doing or when it would be done. I just showed up, day in and day out for nine months, filming whatever caught my attention. I was given the gift of time . . . enough time to fall in love with the mission, the staff, and the street people.

The mammoth physical size of the URM, the broad range of services they offer, and the complexity and severity of the problem of homelessness left me feeling so overwhelmed I almost walked away from the project after only one week in Skid Row. About a month into production, I was still totally befuddled as to how to proceed. The following entry from my journal gives a hint of my frustration:

> The film will feature a mixture of digital video, 8mm B&W film and still B&W photography. So far, I have shot about 15 rolls of photographs, a little over 500 images. While working on *When Did I See You Hungry?* each roll of 36 photographs yielded at least a dozen quality images. In *Skid Row,* I am lucky if I capture 2 or 3 good images per roll. I know the reason why the yield is so low.
>
> As I traveled around the world for the global poverty book, I was able to spend time with my subjects. I talked with them, even laughed with them. More

important, I listened to them. We established some kind of relationship, albeit brief or fleeting. I blended in and I took in what I saw. It all just happened. Down on Skid Row, I am hunting for pictures. The people resent me and have no interest in talking with me. They are suspicious and angry. They see me as intrusive and are unable to accept the purity of my motives. As a result, the photos are rushed. Worse, some are simply stolen moments. There is no intercourse, no exchange of civility. As I traveled the world for *When Did I See You Hungry?*, I was able to embrace the people and therefore able to capture their humanity and dignity. I am desperately trying to become one with the people of Skid Row, spending more and more time on the streets, trying to gain their confidence and respect.

By the time filming was completed, I did gain the friendship and confidence of many of the street people, most notably a woman named Loretta, who is featured near the end of Part One.

My existential awareness of the mystery of evil was pulled more clearly into focus on the mean streets of Skid Row. The things I saw distressed me, and I did not know how I personally should respond to the suffering I saw. Skid Row forced me to ask myself some troubling questions about the relevance of traditional Christianity in our society, which is deeply divided by social injustice.

Thomas Merton wrote: "A poem is for me the expression of an inner experience, and what matters is the experience, more than the poem itself." Merton saw the life of an artist as sharing himself with others. The year I spent in Skid Row was the most illuminating, most transformative experience of my life. The film is merely a reflection of my inner, spiritual experience. The people of Skid Row unmasked my own poverty. As all of us do, I deny my poverty, but the poor gave me the hope and courage to face it.

Skid Row actually taught me something about filmmaking also. When you are standing in the middle of Skid Row with a camera in your hands, surrounded by suffering and chaos, the creative moment goes by in a flash. You must be extremely aware and unobtrusive at the same time, staying open to some compelling, ephemeral collision of event and artist. Your entire being must interact with the people. Skid Row forced me to look beyond labels and concepts in order to discover the remarkable world before my eyes. The art of photography and documentary filmmaking is really the art of mindfulness.

As I made the film, I abandoned myself to my first impressions. If something I saw deeply touched me, I knew the image I captured would convey to others the sincerity of my emotions. In Zen, they speak about the "beginner's mind," which essentially is an empty mind—"empty" in the sense that it is free of preconceived ideas or answers, free from limiting self-centered thoughts. A "beginner's" mind is ready for anything, open to countless possibilities, while the expert's mind is closed to all but a few choices. Being empty and open is the essence of mindfulness. In Skid Row, I learned how to be empty and open.

As I approached the completion of the film, I worried a lot about the length, that it was far too long for people to sit through, too long to make it attractive to potential distributors, so long as to mitigate any chance it could find a TV broadcast slot. I worried also that my reflections (the interludes I called "Snapshots from the Streets") were too deep, too spiritual . . . in short, too hard and demanding for most viewers. Thomas Merton would have told me not to worry about anyone not willing to make the effort to discover the truth I discovered in Skid Row.

Thomas Merton insisted that the artist should never preach, but he did believe the artist had a prophetic role to play in society. He insisted that art should not be contaminated by dogma. He felt the artist should work on the margins of society, distancing himself or herself from "the officially subsidized culture." In Skid Row, the "officially subsidized culture" says the homeless are lazy and they need to be pushed out of our sight. In centuries gone by, a monk would have made a film on homelessness . . . if film had been invented. A monk would have said such dire poverty is an injustice, a betrayal of the ideals of Christ, a crime against God.

Even if he or she had no ties to conventional religion, Merton believed the artist was essentially a spiritual person. For Merton, the artist was a hermit, a pilgrim, a priest, and a prophet all rolled into one. The artist is a unifier, showing how everything connects. In Skid Row, everything does connect . . . it is just very hard to see amongst the thicket of misconceptions and judgmental attitudes and the towering primacy of real estate values. On Skid Row, life is raw and real.

Here is another entry from my journal; this one penned near the end of the editing process, some fifteen months after the project began.

> Making the film *Rescue Me* was a titanic struggle, a struggle which involved far more than trying to make sense of the plight of the poor of Skid Row and how best to tell the complex story of the Union Rescue Mission, but also just how to make a significant film on an insignificant budget. The creative challenges were enormous, finding a point of view and an authentic voice took a great deal of time. And time is money, and money was in very short supply. I was constantly confronted with the administrative reality that I had to be efficient, make the absolute most of my time and videotape. But I intuitively knew that I had to just hang out (with the camera rolling) in order to find out what was before my eyes. In the end, I ended up with around 125 hours of footage, far more than needed for a two-hour film. And as the footage piled up, the cost and complexity of viewing, transferring, logging, selecting, and editing the material also swelled.

> The administrative need for efficiency conflicted with creative need for inefficiency, the need for spontaneous encounters, the need to catch some fleeting, haphazard moment that spoke the truth. For me, the pen and the camera are instruments of exploration, ways to get at and understand some aspect of life which befuddles me—such as 10,000 homeless people in a fifty-block area of downtown Los Angeles who sleep in cardboard boxes or in overcrowded missions.

For the artist, efficiency is a problem because it denies complexity. In the real world, simple and efficient do not exist. Life is filled with chaos and confusion, littered with accidents; in life, errors abound and failures are always around the next bend in the road. Life is rife with unresolved problems and riddled with nagging doubts and uncertainties. Life is blurry; art tries to bring it into focus. But it cannot succeed if the artist tries to simplify his or her craft in order to comply with an increasingly efficient, brand name art peddled by Hollywood and the commercial art world.

I am still very conflicted over the film's long length—three hours and twenty-four minutes (mercifully divided into two parts, each running a tad over one hour and forty minutes). There are days I feel as if the length is perfect, that the film is as long as it needs to be to tell the full story of the URM and provide a theological perspective that will compel the viewer to reach out to the poor. I take comfort in the fact that I was willing to cut more than an hour from the film, but the URM insisted that nothing be cut. Initially, all the Mission wanted was a simple thirty-minute promotional film. They ended up with a never-ending saga. I frequently find myself becoming either defensive or apologetic about the length. The faces of my TV friends register their skepticism when I tell them how long the film is. In the end, it is as it is, and I cannot second-guess myself to death. *Rescue Me* is an epic love poem to the URM staff and the people they so nobly serve.

Many of the URM staff who viewed the film told me that they saw the mission in a way they had not seen it before. Those comments reminded me of an incident in Thomas Merton's life. In 1960, Merton worked with a photographer on a pictorial study of the Abbey of Gethsemani. When the book was published, the abbey that was captured on film surprised Merton, because on the pages of the book, the abbey looked far different than the one Merton held in his mind. He wrote:

> And now a man, an artist, comes along with a camera and shows us, beyond a doubt, that the real monastery, the one that is so obvious that we no longer see it, the one that has become so familiar that we have not even looked at it for years, is not only beautiful, but romantically beautiful. It is romantic even in the ordinariness, the banality that we ourselves tend to reject.[137]

I think most of the URM staff could relate to Merton's experience. As with Merton and the monastery, the URM had become all too familiar to the people working there. They more easily saw the problems and imperfections than the promise and beauty. We cease to see what we are familiar with; art refreshes our perception. Art is about seeing, about attentiveness, about mindfulness. Art transforms something ordinary and familiar into something wonderful. For Thomas Merton, the artist had the potential to portray the latent beauty and perfection of things. The artist strives to get to the core, to reach the intimate source of life and making it accessible through the symbolism of his or her art.

Thomas Merton believed the artist should stand before the work before him in complete humility, stilling the classifying habit of his mind, embracing spontaneity, staying open to the kind of ecstasy experienced by "mystics, children, lovers." Merton once suggested that 75 percent of the creative process was unconscious. "To be an artist," Merton wrote, "you have to be constantly ready to mean more than you realize. If your work corresponds only to the present level of your thought—and to the 'meaning' accessible to your environment, you are not yet an artist."[138] Skid Row took me deep beneath my conscious (and judging) mind. Things drew together and connections were made in mysterious ways. The film emerged from the crucible of experience, which transformed my fledgling understanding of liberation theology into a deeply rooted conviction. Being one with the poor is not merely an ideal; it is an essential part of the Christian faith. For months on end, I stood silently and humbly before the people of Skid Row. Developed in the womb of silence, the film became a synthesis of prayer and poetry. The two primary interests in my life—art and contemplation—joined hands on this film. At the end of the film I say, "I too was rescued at the Union Rescue Mission." Those words pulsate with multiple levels of meaning for me. Art is the basis of healing . . . for me. As an artist, I can be vulnerable.

A URM staff member, who was featured in the film, said, "I was on the streets for years. And I have worked here for years. I have seen it all, which makes it hard for me to understand how the film manages to make me cry as if I had never seen this stuff before." He asked me how this could happen. My answer was simple: "That is the power of film. More than any other medium, film can powerfully convey emotion."

PS. Putting the power of film to the service of the poor was my sole mission for fifteen years; then I put down my cameras and began directly serving the poor in Haiti. After toiling for twenty-two years in the field of chronic poverty, this is what I've come to believe: It truly cannot be God's will for so many of our brothers and sisters to suffer and die from the cruel effects of chronic poverty. God wills the fullness of life and love for everyone, not just a select few. Jesus came to give good news to the poor. God wants our help in creating social and economic justice, insuring food, shelter, jobs, and humane living conditions for all. Of course, no one wants to hear this and very few believe it.

Note: Seeing as Merton was mentioned so much in this reflection, I feel I should mention that Thomas Merton loved to photograph his surroundings. In the fields and forests surrounding his hermitage, he looked through the lens of his camera and saw the hand of God in creation. His camera became an instrument of contemplation.

The Human Face of Jesus

As I made my films on global and domestic poverty, I slowly learned to see the poor and the marginalized, the alcoholic and the drug addict, the mentally ill and the homeless not as objects of pity and charity but as brothers and sisters with whom I'm intimately related. The longer I walk with the poor—and with Jesus—the more I see the need to put to death the idea of my own self-sufficiency. To think of myself as separate from God and all of creation, including the poor, is an illusion.

Saint Francis understood we all are the human face of Jesus; he knew that all of humanity comprises the divine face. God assumed flesh and was born into a world of oppression and persecution. Can we ever grasp the reality of the divine presence dwelling in a depraved humanity and that subsequently every man, woman, and child is uniquely precious, equal, and blessed, all brothers and sisters?

The poor, the weak, and the hurting are God in skin.

Jesus is hungry and naked. Yet we build and decorate elaborate churches in His name, but do not feed or clothe Him. Every day, God comes to us in a distressing disguise, clothed in the rags of a tormented and neglected poor person, in hopes that the encounter will provide a place for healing and hurt to meet, for grace to embrace sin, for beauty to be restored. However, as my Irish friend and author Father Daniel O'Leary writes: "It takes a great love, and many deaths, to transform the eyes of our souls so as to see God's face in every face. Inevitably, inexorably, this love, this hope, will lead to a crucifixion."

To turn your back on the poor is to turn your back on Jesus.

Relinquishing Everything

Matthew's Gospel reminds us that to serve Christ is to serve the least of our sisters and brothers. But Jesus is not merely suggesting that we be charitable. Hardly. Jesus is asking us to abandon our love of self and to embrace our own weakness and vulnerability. Jesus is saying we cannot enter into the universe of God without relinquishing everything that binds us to the false security of our own imagined self-sufficiency. God desires (and maybe even requires) absolute allegiance. Jesus is asking us to give ourselves entirely over to him every day of our lives. And this we find terrifying.

The Mystery of Life and Death

When I look into the sad face of a starving child living in a slum, I find myself looking into the very mystery of life. Chronic poverty with its desperate and endless struggle for survival fills me with grief. Yet these dreadful and hopeless slums can be sacraments of transcendence that can unlock our unconsciousness and lead us to a place of solidarity with the poor. The mystery of poverty and pain, the very mystery of life and death, is too deep, too sensitive, and too fragile to be understood or solved by one person, one church, one religion, or one system of thought. But in these places of desperation, I often catch fleeting glimpses of hope and the feeling that life is truly magnificent and precious. The cross is clearly visible in these nightmarish slums, but so is the joy of Easter.

For me, seeing so much suffering in the massive slums of the world forced me to forget myself, my own limitations, and hear the silent voice of God calling me to respond, not only to the shameful injustice, but also to God's infinite mercy and love. In seeing so many starving kids with bloated bellies, I became less concerned with my own subjective needs and harmful compulsions, and more aware of the self-emptying love of Christ, which I needed to imitate to the best of my ability, puny as it is. But the noise of life sometimes distracted me and rendered me deaf to God and capable of hearing only my own confused and rambling voice. Without solitude and silence, I easily lose my self. And God.

The pandemic of consumerism and busyness deadens our capacity for contemplation and causes a deterioration of our interior lives. Without the stillness and silence of solitude, we easily slip back into the mediocrity of a comfortable Christianity, which is no match for the gun-toting, despairing nihilism of postmodern life where everything is reduced to a commodity for sale, where unbridled greed has caused a catastrophic global economic recession, where materialism without qualification and sex without love are affirmed and championed, where mainstream corporations distribute pornography without shame or reproach, where dialogue has given way to vitriolic hate speech, where alleged Christians threaten to burn Muslim scriptures, where conflicts are settled by violence, where barbarous acts of terrorism threaten all, where loneliness has reached epidemic proportions, where blind religious fundamentalism passes for true faith, where drug addiction and alcoholism are rampant, where thousands of kids die every day from hunger, and where selfishness and individualism have created prisons of poverty and are destroying the earth. In stillness and silence, we are able to catch a glimmer of the interconnectivity of all life, to see the sun as our brother and the moon as our sister, to see all of humanity and all of creation as part of our family.

Even in solitude I'm powerless to create (or even merit) the desire of my heart, the desire to see the face of God. It is only by grace that God gives us eyes to see, ears to hear, and a heart to understand. The lived reality of God's grace and presence leads us, in our own fragility, to greater and greater heights of compassion for others.

In the Gospel of Matthew, Jesus says, "Come to me, all you that are weary and are carrying heavy burdens and I will give you rest." In solitude, I want to bring all the stuff I've been shouldering for years and place it at the feet of Jesus. In a spirit of genuine friendship, Jesus is inviting me, through the unplanned circumstances of my life, into a time and place of solitude so I can learn from him who is gentle and humble of heart and who sincerely wishes that my soul finds the rest and peace it so desperately needs. Jesus, who ate and drank with prostitutes and had the most disreputable of friends, accepts me just as I am, just where I am on my wandering journey through life, during which I've often been troubled and sidetracked by the paradoxes and enigmas of Christianity. Though vested in divinity, Jesus took on human flesh. Though possessing all power, Jesus entered into our weakness and became powerless for us. Jesus entered into our nothingness so we could be filled with everything, with eternity. He entered into our frailty and futility, our sin-filled humanity and blessed us with countless hidden graces to help lead us to our true home with God. But, for the most part, we look away, and go our own way, just pretending to be a friend of Jesus.

Since before my teenage years, I've been strongly attracted to Jesus. But as a teenager growing up in New York City, I looked at life in my little slice of the Big Apple, which at the time was slowly and reluctantly becoming racially integrated, and saw that most Christians did not really take Jesus seriously, did not act according to his way of life. The same lips that proclaimed Jesus was Lord also uttered disgraceful racial epithets. My entire adult life confirmed the truth I saw then, that we don't really take Jesus seriously. We more readily embrace war, embrace works of death, than we do peace, works of life. Why? Because the Gospel has not become flesh within us. We have not incarnated God's word. We trust in the ways of the world, not in the ways of the Word.

Merton truly understood that solitude gives us the time and space for the difficult and ongoing work of self-examination. In solitude, we have the chance to reflect on just how far we have strayed from the Way. Jesus asks us to empty ourselves of everything, but we seem to only want to acquire more and more. Jesus was and is a truly countercultural figure. Christ is not asking us to be successful or productive. Christ is looking for us to be present . . . present to God in prayer and present to each other in acts of love and mercy, especially present to the poor and the suffering.

The seduction of property blinds us to the needs of the poor.

Los Angeles, CA, circa 2003, from *Rescue Me; Photo by Gerard Straub*

"True solitude is deeply aware of the world's needs.
It does not hold the world at arm's length."

—Thomas Merton, Conjectures of a Guilty Bystander[139]

CHAPTER 18

The Emptiness of the Desert

Addicted

As victims of overstimulation, we are becoming addicted to anything loud and fast. Sadly, our lives are increasingly marked by a hunger to grab all we can. Saint Francis of Assisi believed the essential ingredient of Gospel poverty was "living without grasping." Wholeness is attained when we achieve freedom from the greedy tendencies of the ego and its insatiable hunger for possessions. A person becomes whole when the self learns how to be empty, willing to lose itself in order to enter into a deep and rich communion with others. Through charity, God lives in us and we live in God.

Charity is love animated.

The Still Point

We are being engulfed by the noise of too much talk. Opinions and ideologies are hurled at us from all directions. Voices shouting "Buy me" or "Believe this" are incessant. We need a worldwide week of total silence, a week where everyone on the planet shuts up, completely refrains from all speaking, unless compelled by a true emergency or to cry out for help.

The super-excited, overstimulated pace of life today is way out of sync with the way God operates. God works without rush or noise in stillness and silence. Christ invites us to "come apart and rest awhile." We need to stop running and find the still point where God waits to embrace us.

Note: Of course, the deadly coronavirus forced much of America and the world into isolation. But few were actually still. Television viewing went through the roof. People were clamoring for the return of sports and their active social lives.

You're Movin' Too Fast

I think perhaps the first step in becoming more serious about our prayer life is a need to slow down. We've become addicted to speed. We drive fast cars and eat fast food. I can hear the words from the Simon & Garfunkel song titled "The 59th Street Bridge Song (Feelin' Groovy)" echoing in my head: "Slow down, you're movin' too fast, ya gotta make the morning last, just kicking down the cobblestones and feelin' groovy."

We live life in fast-forward. Efficiency is our top priority. We feel compelled to squeeze the most out of every hour. The cult of speed has pushed us to the breaking point. The pace of life is spinning out of control, leaving us feeling more and more exhausted from the nonstop rush. We need to rethink our relationship with time and how we use our time. Long ago, in a much slower age, Gandhi, a man Merton greatly admired, said: "There is more to life than increasing its speed." I remember taking twenty to thirty minutes every night to read a bedtime story to my daughter. When I read a bedtime story to her three kids when they were little, they could barely sit still for fifteen minutes. In fact, the marketplace has tapped into our need for speed by creating one-minute bedtime stories. How insane is that? Family meals are a thing of the past. We eat separately, often in front of our own personal entertainment centers. Our fast-food diets are killing us.

Within all of society there is a growing need to save time and maximize efficiency. We've become incapable of doing nothing. We've gone from the survival of the fittest to the survival of the fastest. Our love affair with capitalism is generating extraordinary wealth (for some) while gobbling up natural resources faster than Mother Nature can replenish them. We are working longer hours and, in the process, becoming less happy and more sickly. Stress-related illnesses such as insomnia and migraines are on the rise. We have no time for sleep, no time for exercise. People are becoming fearful of taking a vacation, and if we do go on vacation, we take our work with us thanks to an array of portable electronic devices that keep us plugged in and up to speed. The lack of sleep, exercise, and relaxation gives rise to even more illnesses, such as diabetes, heart disease, indigestion, and depression. Inevitably, life in a hurry becomes an unlived, superficial life . . . that is over all too fast. Milan Kundera, a Czech writer who went into exile in France in 1975, said his novella *Slowness* that there is wisdom in slowness: "When things happen too fast, nobody can be certain of anything, about anything at all, not even about himself."[140]

When it comes to doing things too fast, I'm as guilty as anyone else. I enter a supermarket with this thought in mind: how fast can I get out of here? I become impatient with people moving too slowly with their carts and blocking my rush down the aisle. I reach a boiling point over long checkout lines. Then I get mad when I get home and realize I didn't get all that I needed to get because my primary goal had become getting the hell out of the store. A long line is an opportune time to pray, perhaps simply repeating a mantra such as the name of Jesus. When I remember to do that, I'm always surprised how quickly I calm down and become present to the moment at hand, which might include an otherwise unseen person in need of the blessing of a smile.

Thomas Merton has much to teach us about the importance of slowing down our lives, of making time for the most essential thing in life: discovering ourselves and uniting with God. If our lives are too busy to make time for God, our lives are far, far too busy.

Note: Shortly after I wrote this piece (back in 2014), I sent it to Jonathan, telling him I wrote it quickly, in under twenty minutes. He responded with this:

> *When I was director of the Merton Center at Bellarmine, I invited a Cambodian monk, Henepola Gutaratana, who had written a book on meditation and started a "monastery" in West Virginia, to give an all-day conference on meditation. He came into the Merton Center in his robes for a visit and a personal tour by me. When I took him into the tower-shaped room and pointed out to him that here were Thomas Merton's books in all their editions and translations, his eyes got very wide and he looked directly at me and asked, "But when did he pray?"*
>
> *Merton wanted to slow down his writing and flee the business of being a writer, but he could not. He worked "full tilt." He escaped into writing like I escape into books: reading Stephen Batchelor's books on Buddhism or reading the food magazine Saveur—they provide escape so that I don't have to sit in my room in silence.*

When I read this in Haiti on March 25, 2020, just days before my seventy-third birthday, it stopped me in my tracks. I couldn't leave Haiti as the virus was beginning to take root in the poverty-stricken nation where the poor had no access to the kinds of sanitary conditions needed to halt the spread of the virus. I was working 24/7 and squeezing in two hours a day in the predawn darkness between 4:00 am and 6:00 am to work on this book. When was I praying? Not often. That is an insane thing to admit while one is writing about Merton's prayer life.

I should mention that after recovering from the virus and being on oxygen for over a week, I set aside more time to pray . . . and to just lie on the couch and listen. But that quiet couch time was short lived. There were things to do.

Doing Nothing

A Zen poem says:

> *Sitting quietly, doing nothing*
> *Spring comes, and the grass grows by itself.*

Most of us think that not much happens on its own, that movement of any kind requires a push from us. I know I have a tendency to think I need to make things happen. Yet, in retrospect, I see all the best things in my life sprang from unplanned moments, when something wonderful happened by itself. All that was required of me was seeing it.

The Wings of a Hummingbird

One of the lessons I've learned over the past few years is that carving out space for silence and stillness, no matter how fleeting it may be, is essential to spiritual equilibrium and growth. I've discovered simple things I can do to find slices of silence. While driving, I turn off the radio, even if only for a few minutes. No matter how busy I am, my day usually presents ample opportunities to simply close my eyes and breathe deeply for two minutes. The most relaxing and peaceful thing I used do when I lived in California was spending a few minutes in the early morning watching a hummingbird dancing on the water of my fountain. In Haiti, I stand on the balcony and watch the sunrise. The gratuitous mystery of the mundane can inspire a vivid awareness of the wonder of God's gift of creation. In my film *Holy Pictures*, I say, "On the wings of a hummingbird, my spirit soars to an awareness of the sacred." Pausing to watch the sunrise or sunset also produces a peace-filled moment of wonder. But silence and solitude do not make all my problems go away. They are simply good friends who help me simplify my life.

Note: I made Holy Pictures *seventeen years ago. As I reflect on my own spiritual journey as I write this book, I'm astounded by how often I failed to follow my own advice in the books I've written. I seemed to have captured the essence of a great Truth, but then pretty much acted as if I had never even heard the Truth. The difference between knowing and doing is frightening. All we can do is keep moving forward, no matter how slow our progress.*

I love it when I see a hummingbird in the tree outside my office window in Haiti. The hummingbird is an amazing creature. It remains still while its tiny wings are moving so quickly that they become nearly invisible. They seem so delicate, yet they must have amazing strength to be able to hover over a flower for so long, and once it has had its fill of sweet nectar from a plant, it darts off in a burst of speed that would make Superman envious. Perhaps the hummingbird would make a good symbol for the importance of stillness within movement in the spiritual life.

A Listening Heart

Our real pilgrimage is into the depths of silence . . . and leads to a true light. The quest for God is a journey, a pilgrimage to the depths of the soul. The quest requires a listening heart, an ear quickened to the silent voice of God, and a vigilant spirit actively waiting and watching. To be a pilgrim is to live on life's threshold, walking on the edge of reality, striving for what lies beyond the reality we see with our flawed human eyes.

Jesus often sought the emptiness of the desert to experience a fuller union with God. God never shouts to be heard over our noise. Only silence gives God a chance to speak. To effectively listen to God—or even to another human being—one needs to be silent and attentive. If we are truly listening to God or another, truly paying attention, there will be no hint of self-reflective consciousness—there will only be silent receptivity. To listen is to be silent. We need to empty our hearts, to sit in stillness. Silence allows us to live within, helps us to concentrate on the serious, profound inner mysteries of life. Noise takes us out of ourselves and distracts and scatters our thoughts.

Silence is not simply a wordless state; it is an attentive waiting. Deep, spiritually active silence allows us to hear the unity of life. Silence stills the intellect and opens the portal of the heart. Holy silence takes our humble prayers to new and exalted heights of contemplation. Be still, and hear the voice of God. It is in stillness that we find our emptiness, the emptiness that can only be filled by welcoming God into our hearts. Seeing my own emptiness and impermanence prompted me to fall to my knees and pray.

My poverty is a cry to God.

*"Man needs to enclose himself in the inner closet of his heart
more often than he needs to go to church: and collecting all his
thoughts there, he must place his mind before God, praying to
Him in secret with all the warmth of spirit and with living faith.
At the same time, he must also learn to turn his thoughts to God
in such a manner as to be able to grow into a perfect man."*

—Saint Dimitri of Rostov, *The Art of Prayer:
An Orthodox Anthology*[111]

Make Room Inside

If most of us had to spend any length of time living in Merton's hermitage, one of the first things we would do is measure the walls to see where we would put a gigantic, flat screen TV. In the week I spent in his hermitage in 2000, I didn't even have a radio. It was total silence . . . and it was deafening. The silence spoke louder than any TV. Near the end of the week, I jotted the following down in my journal:

> **Friday, December 8, 2000.** This morning I awoke to the chant of birds. In this ragged meadow of solitude, I'm learning about the world and relationships. After five days of solitude, my thoughts have become far less clamorous. The excess of the world which I lugged here within me has slowly been discarded. I don't miss the demands of the phone and e-mail, always shouting, "Answer me."
>
> Out of the quiet, simplicity is emerging, speaking forcefully to me. "Make room inside," it says, repeatedly. I'm being introduced to my hurt and my dreams. And my failure to love. I'm being introduced to myself. What a gift!
>
> In the sleep of winter, life renews itself.

Experience since then tells me that we need frequent periods of silent renewal as we work our way through life . . . perhaps at least once a year. But the thought of making time to do nothing but sit in silence seems absurd. From childhood, our culture programs us to ignore contemplation. Before television and the ascendancy of mass advertising, kids formed their understanding of life and the world, their personal cosmology of the world's meaning, in their homes, from their parents and older relatives. Today, before a child enters the first grade or has any serious exposure to religious ceremonies, he or she has already absorbed about 30,000 advertisements—they will spend less time in high school.

Whatever spiritual and moral truths a parent tries to transmit to their child cannot possibly compete with the onslaught of sophisticated advertisements. The impact of the nonstop advertisement blitzkrieg aimed at the young all day, all week long, along all forms of media cannot be undone in an hour at church on Sunday. Corporations pay big bucks to attract the brightest, cleverest people to create their dazzlingly deceptive ad campaigns, employing every artistic and psychological trick in the bag. No kid can withstand the onslaught. Sadly, grownups increasingly seem to be unable to resist the hard sell. As a result, consumerism has become the dominant faith in America . . . and Christmas is its major feast day. On the day we celebrate God entering our poverty, we equate desire and delight with shiny things we find in a mall. Jesus asked us to give everything away to the poor and follow him. But we give each other iPads and rush back to the mall for after Christmas sales.

In *No Man Is an Island*, Merton bluntly says:

> Half the civilized world makes a living telling lies. Advertising, propaganda, and all other forms of publicity that have taken the place of truth have taught men to take it for granted that they can tell other people whatever they like provided that it sounds plausible and evokes some kind of shallow response. [**Note:** *Can you image the monk's reaction to the shamefully deceptive negative political ads we must endure every two years?*]
>
> Americans have always felt that they were protected against the advertising business by their own sophistication. If we only knew how naïve our sophistication really is! It protects us against nothing. We love the things we pretend to laugh at. We would rather buy a bad toothpaste that is well advertised than a good one that is not advertised at all. Most Americans wouldn't be seen dead in a car their neighbors had never heard of.[142]

Merton's humble hermitage is a sign pointing a way to a different way, a healthier, more fulfilling way. Our mostly unrecognized need to experience union with God is the cause of the deep anguish in the human heart. Contemplation is a path to that healing union . . . or more accurately, healing reunion. Humanity's alienation from God began when we lost our appetite for contemplation and hungered for things beyond God. For Merton, contemplation was not a solution to anything; it was much deeper than that . . . it was a way of life.

We say, "My life or yours." Jesus says, "My life for yours."

We speak out of human aggression. Jesus speaks out of divine surrender.

The more you dig into the life of Jesus, the more the life of Jesus digs into you.

*"To the extent that we are far from Jesus, we are the source of
our own greatest burdens: without him as Lord, we are in thrall
to the tyranny of our passions and, therefore, susceptible to the
world's manipulation and the influence of the Evil One."*

—ERASMO LEIVA-MERIKAKIS[143]

What We Are

The more we worship God, the more we grow in humility. The more we grow in humility, the gentler we become. The gentler we are, the less aggressive we become. Stripped of aggression, the purer we are. As we grow in purity, the more receptive we are to the gift of God's spirit. The more filled we are with God's spirit, the more loving and compassionate we become.

*Nothing can separate us from love
if love is not what we have
but what we are.*

Saint Teresa of Ávila said, "Humility is walking in truth." Progress along the mystical path will be stalled without humility. Without humility, we lose our sense of balance and fall far from the "meek and mild" attitude exemplified by Jesus.

And the Dragons Come

It was late at night. About 10:30 pm on April 7, 2020, the Tuesday of Holy Week. I'd been in Haiti for about forty days, unable to leave because the pandemic was ravaging America. My mind was abuzz with crazy ideas. Something happened earlier in the day that opened some very deep emotional wounds. The pain was real. The day was an endless parade of problems and a constant demand on my time and attention. I was truly exhausted and dealing with some mysterious pain in my left leg. Layered on top of all this was the concern about the spreading coronavirus in the States. By April 8, 14,721 Americans had lost their lives at the hands of the virus. Fr. Rick Frechette, a Passionist priest and doctor who runs two hospitals in Port-au-Prince, told me that he had ten patients in his hospital who were infected with the virus.

At 10:30 pm, I was on my way to bed, after consuming a bit too much brandy, when something stupid happened downstairs in connection with the diesel generator. I exploded. I screamed at some of the staff. In a fit of rage, I put on my pants, stormed downstairs, and yelled into the night air, "I'm outta here! I can't take it anymore!" I got into my car and attempted to drive away. A woman staff member forcibly tried to stop me. The guys wouldn't open the gate. The woman pleaded with me to get out of the car, saying there was a curfew in effect and the police would shoot me for being out at night. I said I didn't care. I played some jazz music very loudly. Eventually, I got out of the car. The way I walked to the back steps showed everyone I was drunk.

The next day, I wrote Jonathan. I mentioned a bit of what had happened the night before, how I lost my mind. Within minutes, Jonathan wrote back, saying:

> These nights happen and keep us on our knees. We are brothers in going wild from some grief. It happens to everyone.
>
> In Merton's journals there is a night in June when he alludes to having beer in his hermitage refrigerator. It's a hot night. As he writes, one can detect the alcohol affecting his brain. Then he writes the best lines for me in all his journals:
>
> "But where will I be when it's dark, and the dragons come, and there is no more beer?"
>
> Stay humble. No other way forward.

Many nights during my long pandemic-forced imprisonment in Haiti, the dragons would come, besieging me with a startling array of wild thoughts, debilitating doubts, questioning absolutely everything. I tamed the dragon with French brandy. Of course, prayer would've been better, but I often took the easiest way to tame the dragon.

Later in the day, I had to go out and buy a bigger, better diesel generator. I put the $15,000 cost on my ministry credit card, pushing me deeper into debt. The dragon often came in the form of wanting to give up, to get on a plane to anywhere. But there were no planes flying. There was only brandy.

A few days later, on Holy Thursday (April 9, 2020), I was invited to attend a special afternoon liturgy at the Missionaries of Charity. Because of the coronavirus (which had claimed its first two deaths in Haiti), the public was banned from any of the sister's liturgical celebrations—except for me. I guess after giving the sisters two retreats, I was an honorary member of the community. The celebrant was a wonderful Passionist priest from Mexico who had once celebrated the Eucharist at Santa Chiara. He also was at my side when I was hospitalized with the MRSA virus and had to have the infection lanced without any anesthesia. My takeaway from his often-humorous homily was this: the Eucharist is the washing of the feet. We need to ask ourselves this question: What is the quality of my heart in the service of others? I know somedays when I'm helping some sick kid or staff member that my heart is not in it. Somedays, I get so exhausted I feel as if I'm grudgingly offering a hand of help.

Note: *After my recovery from Covid, I decided, after more than two weeks without wine or brandy, to give up both. When the dragons come, I'll pray. (A month later, I felt a glass of wine at night was OK, but I have not had brandy again.)*

Washing the Feet of Another

In Father Daniel O'Leary's last book, *Horizons of Hope*, published after his death from cancer in January 2019, he wrote movingly about the ceremony of washing feet on Holy Thursday. Here is part of what he said:

> In his washing of the disciples' feet Jesus was offering an unmistakable paradigm shift away from the pomp, finery, and clerical show that was alive then, as it is now. His action warns of a kind of boundary-crossing in the Church's self-perception, when values are reversed and the last will be first—anawim becomes elite. It is a moment when the whole notion of authority is turned on its head.[144]

Later he writes:

> Given our propensity for greed and power, the sacramentality of foot-washing will always be relevant, and even urgent.[145]

A Place of Forgiveness, Pain, and Conflict

Back in June 2018 when I began attending daily Mass at the Missionaries of Charity, part of my motivation for getting out of the house at six in the morning every day was that I was seeking a sense of fellowship. But I've come to see it was more than that. I wanted to be part of their community. I wanted Santa Chiara to be a family, which is the most elemental form of community. It's disappointing that Santa Chiara, despite my wishes and efforts, never really became either a family or a community. It's a collection of individual adults, all with different dreams and goals. The common thread among them is poverty (and, for most of the staff, a lack of education). It is also a collection of "cliques," each with negative assessments of the other cliques and the people who comprise them. Instead of the pulling together for the common good, they spread nasty gossip about each other.

Community is a place where we learn to care for each other, which makes community a place of forgiveness. Community is a place where the ego dies, which makes community a place of pain. Because each of us carries our own inner conflicts into community, community becomes a place of conflict. The values of the world are in conflict with the values of community. In community, we learn to move from independence to togetherness. In community, we give others the space to grow into what they were created to be.

I've spent enough time inside religious communities in the States and in Italy to know how community is supposed to work. It doesn't always work thanks to human weakness.

I'm on a solitary journey amidst lots of people who see me as an important figure in their survival. They depend on me. I'm far from the experience of community, which I desired. At the moment, I feel isolated and very alone. I have one female friend who is a lifeline from complete lonesomeness. She keeps me in touch with real humanity.

Note: The divisive nature of the nonstop gossiping threatens the future of Santa Chiara. Sadly, the staff is not pulling together as a team. Longtime staff members are sowing seeds of disunity because they hold old grudges or perceived slights. In October 2020, two staff members were shouting at each other. The commotion was over one person taking another person's juice. The argument ended with one of the two throwing the juice at the other. The adults often act worse than the kids. Later in the afternoon, there was another loud, angry exchange between two staffers. It took some time to get to the bottom of the problem. One staffer simply did not want to do what she was told to do, namely clean the toddler's bathroom after another staffer had given the youngest kids a bath. For me, the fracas was discouraging. Finding funding is hard enough; squelching squabbles is draining. What is not draining are the kids. Sure, they can be tiring, but they are the hope.

By June 2022, we were actually becoming a family. Most of the uneducated staff had been terminated and replaced by nurses and teachers for whom there was no work as Haiti's poor economy had imploded due to the increase in brutal violence and staggering inflation.

Instruments of Incarnation

Every moment is a moment of grace . . . if my eyes and heart are open. No moment is insignificant. Incarnation may break through at any time. Every event of our lives is open to God; prayer reveals how. I need to handle all life, and every moment of my life, with care, respect, and love.

All creation is in the state of evolution, in the process of becoming. Incarnation transforms us by grace, changing us into what we were made to be: love. We are instruments of incarnation, calling forth a new creation. We are mothers of incarnation by giving birth to the word of God by the way we live and work. The incarnation, life, and death of Christ teaches not to place any limits on forgiveness and sharing. The mystery of the incarnation deals with the stuff of life—and the choices we make. God is with us . . . every moment of every day. If we forget that, we are doomed. Only in silence can you hear the vast, boundless depths of the Spirit speaking more and more clearly about the unlimited love and mercy of God. Be still. Be quiet. Be.

Truth and serenity lie sleeping in silence and solitude.

The Beauty of Creation

Saint Francis of Assisi thought the entire world was a sacrament revealing the presence of God. The beauty of creation—the fields and vineyards, rocks and woods, flowing springs and blooming gardens—drew Francis into a deeper love of God and a growing desire to serve God by loving and serving others. In their book *Care for Creation: A Franciscan Spirituality of the Earth*, Ilia Delio, Keith Douglas Warner, and Pamela Wood write:

Do we really believe that God dwells with us, in our lives and in the natural world of creation? Does the Body of Christ move us to contemplate God in creation? If so, then how can we say "Amen" to receiving the Body of Christ and perpetrate destruction of the environment? There is a disconnect between what we claim to be or rather what we claim to see and what we actually do. It is an alienation of heart and mind that has rendered a desecration of the environment, as if we take the host, the Body of Christ, and continually stomp on it while saying, "yes, so be it!"[146]

In his book *Walking with Francis of Assisi: From Privilege to Activism*, Bruce Epperly writes:

I believe that Francis's message is even more important in light of this most recent pandemic. Francis—and his spiritual sister, Clare—remind us we are all connected. The paths of greed, consumerism, individualism, and nationalism endanger the planet and its peoples. In the spirit of Francis, we need to break down barriers of friend and stranger, citizen and immigrant, rich and poor, if we are to survive in this increasingly interdependent world. Nations need to see patriotism in terms of world loyalty as well as self-affirmation. We need the Franciscan vision of all creation singing praises to the Creator if we are to flourish in the years and centuries to come. Like Francis and Clare, we need to become earth-loving saints, committed to our planet and its peoples—in our time and our children's and grandchildren's time.

As I walked the streets of Assisi, I realized I needed the wisdom of this saint who sought to reform the church based on his experience of the Living God. I recognized that the church always needs reformation, but this reformation needs to be grounded in inner spiritual experience. . . .

Francis discovered that, despite being a military prisoner recovering from the trauma of battle, the everyday world whose values he took for granted was not his only option. His life could be different. The world could be a very different place than he had imagined. It dawned on him that his destiny might involve becoming one of God's messengers, midwifing in time and space the Reality that beckoned him. He realized he had the freedom to become a citizen of a world not yet born, living by a different set of values than his parents and peers, and inviting them to see life from a new perspective: God's vision rather [than] thirteenth-century consumerism, parochialism, and status-seeking.

Francis was on the edge of an adventure in spiritual transformation that would take him from privilege to prayer and from self-interest to world loyalty. His journey would inspire future adventurers to follow the path of spiritual activism, imagining a transformed church responding to a transformed world. . . .

God calls us to mystical activism, a deep-rooted spirituality inspired by our encounters with God and commitment to our spiritual practices, to bring beauty and healing to the world. Walking in the footsteps of Francis and Clare, we are called to be mystics of the here and now, not some distant age. . . . Within the concrete limitations of our life, our gifts are lived out and expand as we devote ourselves to prayerful activism.[147]

Letting Go of Everything

Saint Francis was a mystic. Many people don't understand mystics. They are puzzled by them and perhaps a bit apprehensive or fearful of them. Mystics are often perceived as extremists or far too rigorous in the practice of their faith. Such spiritual phenomena as levitation and the stigmata are viewed with skepticism. We can't comprehend a direct experience of God, whether in visions or messages. My hunch is that Saint Francis had fallen in love with God in such a deep, profound way, and that made him a mystic. He experienced the presence of everywhere and within everyone. Francis was totally submersed in God and God alone. Nothing else mattered. He let go of everything else.

In my previous books on Saint Francis, I presented myself as walking in the footsteps of the saint or walking in the shadow of him. Clearly that was metaphorical language. In reality, I held on to lots of things that were far less than godly. While I longed for God, I did so without the passion and persistence of Francis. Still, no matter how hard any of us try, God is light years beyond our comprehension.

A mystic does not have a new vision of God; a mystic has a new way of relating to all people and all of creation.

> *"Mystics see through a lens of paradox: dazzling darkness,*
> *beautiful wound, the longing that is the remedy for longing.*
> *Paradox points beyond itself to a truth that both transcends and*
> *includes logic, a truth that is alive, generative, and whole."*
>
> —Mirabai Starr, "Dazzling Darkness"[148]

> *"Faith…is always contradicting itself, because everything we say about*
> *God is so inadequate that it always runs us head first into a paradox."*
>
> —Thomas Merton, Run to the Mountain[149]

CHAPTER 19

Full of Wonder and Grace

The Morning Dew

"The dawn is by its very nature a peaceful, mysterious time of day—a
time when one naturally pauses and looks with awe at the eastern sky. It is
a time of new life, new beginning and therefore important to the spiritual
life: for the spiritual life is nothing but a perpetual interior renewal."

—Thomas Merton, *The Inner Experience*[150]

sitting in silence
I hear nothing
and everything

dawn is nice
but too early
to enjoy

the sun rises slowly
and sets too quickly
leaving me in the dark

five birds swaying
on the telephone line
enjoying the breeze

gentle and loving Mary
full of wonder and grace
gives birth to possibility

July 18, 2010, 7:22 am: I just penned those simple lines. At this moment, I'm seated at my desk and looking out at my garden where the birds are gobbling up the seeds I had spread out for them before dawn. The angel on the birdbath and the statue of Saint Francis watch in silence. The grass glistens with the morning dew as a blue bird dances about. It is peaceful and calm. It is now and now is all there is. The calmness and beauty of this moment can easily be lost by useless worry about the future or regrets about the past. The darkness of the past few months is slowly lifting. I needed this time of silence and solitude. Our senses have become dulled to the wonder of creation, which it takes for granted.

Jewish Morning Prayer

I am grateful to you, God of life, for remembering me again. Your grace has awakened my body and my soul. For this gift, I thank you.

We need to be astonished by life, rather than try to explain it or its meaning.

My God, the soul you have placed within me is pure. You created it; you fashioned it; you breathed it into me; you safeguard it within me.

Think about it: according to Jewish tradition, we have the divine breathe within us.

May our handiwork reflect our connection to the divine.

School of Wisdom

When I came across this piece penned by Jonathan Montaldo in which he explores Merton's ideas about contemplation and relationships I asked him if I could include it in the book. From my earliest days in Haiti, I saw the impoverished nation as a school of my life.

In all his writing Merton characterizes the contemplative life as a life of relationships informed by love in search of freedom. We are the primary actors in the formation of our own identities. We create networks of nurturing interrelationships with our fellow human beings. We affect and are affected by the matrix of nature's evolution within which we move and have our being. Through this trinity of relationships, we experience communion with the Source that underwrites our being in time, the Logos that energizes our becoming "one with everything in that hidden ground of love for which there can be no explanations." Contemplation is a deepening awareness of and attention to all our relationships; it is the deciphering in real time of the essential unity of all beings; it is an active consciousness that knows with certitude that the world is ours and that we are God's. "The world dictates no terms to us. We and our world interpenetrate. If anything, the world exists for us, and we exist for ourselves. It is only in assuming full responsibility for our world, for our lives and for ourselves, that we can be said to live really for God."

Merton taught that contemplation is for everyone and that the context for seeking God's presence is always our everyday lives. In unpublished notes for a conference he had prepared for his monastic novices on "prayer," Merton urged them to meditate by entering "the school of their lives," to meditate upon the events of their lives as a "school of wisdom" in which they were being taught to become their truest selves. He reminded his students that contemplation is "a response to a call: a call from God Who has no voice, and yet Who speaks in everything that is, and Who, most of all, speaks in the depths of our own being: for we ourselves are words of God." Thus, contemplation was attentiveness to the "words" God was always speaking through their most personal experiences.

An Orthodox monk friend of mine told me, "God is always speaking in the ordinariness of our days, with all of its humdrum tasks needing to be done. We keep thinking that encountering God will be some ethereal, cloud-based event, when it actually is within the ordinariness of our day's demands. God is so totally 'other' that he is able to be present in our ordinariness without, in any way, being diminished by being so ordinarily present."

It is in dealing calmly and correctly with every day's realities . . . instead of running away from them, which is a form of refusal . . . that we stand the chance to meet, face to face, the God who breathes silently behind and within those realities. If we deal correctly with each day we will not go to heaven; rather, we will discover that we are already in it. That is what happens for me in Haiti . . . when I let it.

Every day God asks the same question:
Are you willing?

The Unifying Force

Behind Merton's instruction on meditation to the novice monks was the premise that God was teaching us something from morning to night. Meditation, according to Merton, was where we "digest the nourishment" we've been given by God throughout the day, whether within liturgical settings, during formal times of prayer or periods of work, or even during the most mundane moments of our day. Meditation was also where we assimilate God's word through the experiences of the day and begin to make them our own. In meditation, we begin to "penetrate the inner meaning of things" and "plunge into the depths to find the wisdom of God in everything." By exploring their own lives, experiences, failures, and blessings in meditation, Merton believed the young monks would come to know the meaning of their own lives. The same is true for all of us who live outside of monasteries.

When I was a teenager, I thought I caught a glimpse of what I perceived the meaning of my life was supposed to be: a missionary priest in China. I even entered a Vincentian minor seminary. I was too young, too sensitive, too serious, and had too many doubts, and so I didn't last too long. The pain of leaving is still with me. I look back at my life now, sixty years later, and I believe God was speaking to me when I left home and entered the seminary; moreover, I think most of the real problems I've had in life stemmed from a deep-seated need to compensate for a lost vocation. But even with three failed marriages behind me, I have, by God's grace, resurrected that vocation in a unique manner. I may have given up, but God did not.

Through meditation Merton hoped young monks would awaken to God's divine action in his life, and through compunction and self-knowledge, the monk would be better able to cooperate with God's action in his life. The monk's whole life would become a meditation, a continual learning from God, and a wise and humble cooperation with divine Wisdom and Providence. A monk's life would become a ceaseless prayer, and every grace would be seen and seized. Merton believed God's love permeated our days, and true peace resided in trying to respond faithfully. For Merton, meditation should be the unifying force in our lives. Our life should be a continuous, simple meditation in which everything has meaning. Moreover, the lessons of meditation need to flow out into action that is "impregnated with love and realism."

Note: Of course, Merton lived in a world that did not have twenty-four-hour-a-day cable news to distract and absorb his attention. On my last week in Florida in June 2022, my cable service went out. I thought it was a storm-related outage so I never called the cable company. By the end of the day, service had not yet been restored. I suddenly realized that I had actually enjoyed the complete silence, even though I normally have the TV on but muted. The next day, there was still no service. I decided not to inquire about the problem. For four straight days, there was no cable TV, no distraction, no nonstop chattering noise. I heard no upsetting news. I felt as if I had been on a replenishing silent retreat. Why is that I don't have the wisdom or courage to unplug everything once in a while?

Through the faithful practice of meditation, in time, one's life will become more realistic, concrete, and simple. You will no longer be encumbered by unwieldy thought structures and patterns. Lofty and abstract thinking will be rendered mute. There will no longer be a preoccupation with the self. Life will be more peaceful and simpler under the watchful and loving eye of God.

Because meditation is built into the structure of a monk's life, Merton spoke to the novice monks about how meditative prayer can, at rare times, become mystical prayer in which a person loses themselves entirely and experiences "a divine enlightenment which gives us a momentary taste of what is really real, beyond and above the illusory 'reality' which we perceive through the mist of everyday experience—a reality that does not belong to this world but to the world to come." But Merton cautioned the young monk's not to "waste time thinking about our 'degrees of prayer.' Those who have really advanced in prayer are aware of having no particular well-defined 'degree' of prayer. They generally don't know where they are, and don't try to find out. They leave that to God."[151]

The mystical is what lies just below the surface.

Note: *In June 2022, I made one last pass over this manuscript, essentially just to clean up any sloppy mistakes. When I began the task, the manuscript contained about 112,000 words. I had hoped the book would be under 100,000 words. By the time I was halfway through this review, I had added another 11,000 words. Merton whispered to me: "Don't worry about it." Or was that the devil speaking? The answer won't be revealed in known number of books sold, but in the hidden number of lives changed.*

The Table of Eternity

I need transformation rather than answers. I lament all the time I wasted searching for answers in an endless river of spiritual books, when the experience I was seeking was within me, buried under my feverish reading and doing all manner of unimportant, frivolous things. I really wish I had back all the hours I spent looking at pornographic material that offered me fleeting pleasure, which always left me feeling empty and down. Serving the poor, sheltering a woman with kids, or feeding a hungry child always left me feeling full and up. When I draw my last breath, it is those positive things that will comfort me as I transition to whatever is next. I have no idea what is next. It really doesn't matter. The little humanitarian good that I did was not done to get a better seat at the table of eternity; it was done to bring eternity into the present moment, to reveal God's eternal love to one desperate adult or child.

CHAPTER 20

A Whirling Dervish

Pay Attention

*"The enlightened attention rejects nothing nor welcomes
anything—like a mirror it responds equally to all."*

—Chuang Tzu (Zhuangzi)

Merton would strongly suggest that the health of our interior life rests upon our attentiveness. We need to be able to truly pay attention to hear the wordless voice of God that is continually drawing us into Oneness. To be attentive, we need to be awake and alert to the boundless grace of the present moment. Our lives have become so splintered, divided among so many responsibilities, so many demands upon our time, that most of us feel frazzled and fatigued. So much of modern technology, designed to make things easier for us, has in fact increased the things that tug for our attention. The internet, cell phones, laptop computers, social media, streaming videos, and the ever-expanding world of cable television all squeeze every ounce of stillness and silence out of life. Life has become a blur, a whirling dervish of enticements and anxieties. Entering into our interior life, where we can encounter the love and mercy of God, is becoming increasingly difficult.

For me, writing has become an avenue into that interior empty space where the fullness of God resides. The very act of writing demands attentiveness. Simone Weil, the French mystic, social philosopher, and activist in the French Resistance during World War II, claimed that all study and serious reading, with its required concentrated focus, was in essence an excellent preparation for prayer. When I'm concentrating on my photography or writing, I'm in a more prayerful mode, more open to the movement of the Spirit. With a pen or a camera in my hand, I'm far less easily distracted by nonsense.

The Buddhist road to enlightenment is paved with attentiveness. Thomas Merton's dance with Buddhism helped him embrace a freer, more experimental form of writing. His thoughts flowed out onto the page in clear, simple words that expressed the openness of his heart and spirit. It also helped him see the entire world in a more positive light. Buddhist meditation practices drew him into a deeper silence, which helped him to be more aware of his true self. Merton's interior journey helped him affirm and deepen his

Christian understanding that (as he wrote), "Christ alone is the way." And the way of Christ is all-embracing love and peace.

The human heart is drawn to God. The language of the heart is love. Not soft, wimpy, fleeting Hollywood-style love, but a bold, deep, penetrating love that requires openness and transformation, a love that perpetually gives itself away. We live in a world of hearts. Sadly, most hearts are broken, unloved, and unable to love. God wants to give us new hearts, mystical hearts throbbing to love and to be loved. If you can imagine a world of divinely transformed hearts, you will see a world at peace, a world of plenty where no one goes hungry. Such a world begins within each of us, if we are able to shake off the countless distractions of modern life and pay attention to the silent voice of God.

The less you have, the less you have to distract you from God.

Peanut Butter and Cat Food

After spending much of my adult life inside the television industry as a network executive and producer, I feel qualified to pass this judgment on the industry that once sustained my life: it is a deeply flawed medium. Instead of being a powerful tool for education or human betterment or cultural enrichment, it has been kidnapped by Madison Avenue and transformed into just another advertising tool that delivers boorish and puerile amusement.

Back in the early eighties, a vice president of programing at NBC in New York called me into his office. At the time, I was the executive producer of one of the network's soap operas, featuring a young actor named Alec Baldwin; I had been hired to improve that show's sagging ratings. His words were blunt and to the point: "Do you know what your problem is? Let me tell you: you think you are an artist. And you are, don't get me wrong. But that's the problem. We don't want art. We only want filler, something to keep the commercials from bumping into each other."

Of course, he did not want art. He wanted something titillating, something that would attract more viewers—such as "a hot babe in a hot tub," which I was forced to do. The executive worshipped at the altar of ratings. I quickly learned that television was the starter in the engine of the nation's economy, a tool to sell more peanut butter and cat food, more aspirins and fabric softener. The commercial advertisements that fuel television deliver one common message: do not be satisfied with what you have—only more "stuff" can make you happy.

With few exceptions, mostly found on PBS and in a few quality dramas on the networks, most television fare offers little more than mean-spirited comedy and excessive violence. Plus, a heavy dose of sex, because Madison Avenue knows that sex sells.

The vast majority of television programming has a negative impact on life. Yet no one seems able to live without its endless images. They are now in every room of most homes. I wish I had the courage to unplug mine . . . permanently.

> *Weary are my days when I crave God*
> *and resist God at the same time . . .*
> *which I do nearly every day.*

Note: *The growth in cable television, satellite television, distribution networks such as Netflix, live-streaming, and YouTube have super-saturated us with nonstop, around-the-clock access to boundless entertainment of every flavor. We now watch movies and videos on our cell phone, which become larger and capable of making more videos to share on Facebook or Twitter. Dancing cats abound on Facebook. In Haiti, once the kids are all asleep, the staff passes the night watching videos on their cell phones.*

Kierkegaard's Television

> *"The present state of the world and the whole of life is diseased. If I were a doctor and were asked for my advice, I should reply: Create silence! Bring men to silence. The Word of God cannot be heard in the noisy world of today. And even if it were blazoned forth in the midst of all the other noise, then it would no longer be the Word of God. Therefore create silence."*
>
> —Søren Kierkegaard[152]

The Danish philosopher Søren Kierkegaard died in 1855. If he had had a radio and TV, imagine what he might have said.

CHAPTER 21

The Sleepy Consensus of the Multitude

My Noisy Ways

In *The Sayings of the Desert Fathers*, Saint Anthony says: "Let your heart be silent, then God will speak." I read that a long time ago. I firmly believe it is true. But I can't remember the last time I truly allowed my heart to be silent, really silent. When a drug addict or an alcoholic tries to stop his or her destructive behavior, they usually fail, relapsing four or five times before they finally—if they are lucky and have lots of support—kick the habit. Human nature is weak. I cannot tell you how many times I've tried to carve out time in my day for silence and solitude. Yet I relapse into my old noisy ways. Sitting still seems like a waste of time . . . even though I know it is not. You must just do it. I don't, at least not on a consistent basis.

As I worked on this book, Thomas Merton forced me to address my lack of persistence when it comes to making silence and stillness and solitude an integral part of my day. I'll have to change . . . and like every other human being, I really don't want to change. I'm fine the way I am. OK, shine me up a bit, polish me, spruce me up, but don't do anything to fundamentally alter my ways. They are, after all, my ways. We like holding on to stuff . . . even bad stuff, like drugs and alcohol, and our own pet sins that follow us everywhere. But this time, I feel my determination to incorporate more silence into my day will stick. When I was deathly sick with Covid, I was in a cocoon of silence. I was aware of every heartbeat, every labored breath. When I was able to be detached from the big oxygen tanks, I stood silently on the balcony each morning before sunrise; I could really feel the gentle breeze and thanked God for it. In stillness and silence, more things become visible.

Note: I need to escape from the distorting influences of society by checkering my life with periodic periods of solitude. Only solitude allows me to reconnect with the truth of my own nature and my relationship with God.

I was reading this in predawn darkness of December 20, 2020, when I received a WhatsApp message from Orlane, my "adopted" twenty-year-old daughter, who lives in an apartment adjacent to Santa Chiara. She said her refrigerator was empty. "Dad, I need some bread, juice, macaroni, burger meat, and chicken to cook." It was a Sunday morning. I had planned to sit alone most of the day and work on completing this book. It had been a stressful week. The violence and killing had accelerated. Our generator and my car both needed repairs. I needed a day apart. A day to be silent. Suddenly, I had to squeeze in a shopping trip, which would eat up about three hours.

Note: *On October 29, 2022, I was reviewing the typeset interior design of this book. I had spent three of my nine days in Florida reading this book one more time. I had made perhaps three dozen minor corrections. Reading it was a challenge because I felt no one would read it. I wondered why I was spending so much time and energy making insignificant changes in a book no one was going to read. I was tempted to just let it go and stop reviewing the balance of the book.*

It was a few minutes before I read the previous note that I had placed a call to Orlane. I first met her when she was ten, during one of my visits to Haiti documenting the aftermath of the earthquake. She has been calling me "dad" since then. Her nickname was Baby; it still is. No one calls her Orlane; to one an all she is simply Baby, even though she is now 22. She is the primary reason for the existence of the Santa Chiara Children's Center. In 2014, she was very sick with some mysterious illness. She had been taken to many clinics and no one could diagnose the problem. I returned to Haiti and took her to a string of clinics. Being inside the clinics shocked me, as the conditions and level of care were abysmal. Through a recommendation of a priest who was a medical doctor in Haiti, I found a top-notch physician who uncovered the problem. She needed immediate surgery to remove a large kidney stone. The doctor was amazed at the size of the stone he removed and found it hard to believe the child could live with the enormous pain it caused for so long. It is a long story…but within a short time, I found a small apartment in a small slum for Baby…which became the first home of Santa Chiara. Baby was the first and only child. The apartment was in Peguyville, which is adjacent to Pétionville.

Back to the phone call. The day before Baby felt very weak and dizzy. She had been coughing to two weeks. She took herself to a hospital about 20 minutes from Santa Chiara. Tap-taps were not running because of the gas shortage, so Baby took a motorcycle taxi. They hospital ordered six or seven tests. Baby had enough money to pay for two of them. The doctor gave her prescription and she went home. When I am in Florida, Baby writes me at least once a day. She wrote saying she was sick. I had only returned to Florida a few days earlier. Before leaving I heard a coughing a little, but it did not alarm me. She said she did not want to tell me that she had a bad cough for two weeks because she saw how many problems I was handling and did not want to bother me. I told her she was my daughter and she is never a problem. I had someone give her the money for the remaining tests the next. A staffer drove her to the hospital. I had told her to keep my informed. She sent me a few photos of the tests but by four in the afternoon I had not heard from her so I sent her a text message asking how she was doing. She replied with one word: weak. I asked where she was. Another one-word response: home.

I made a WhatsApp video call to her. She looked and sounded dreadful. She was constantly coughing. The coughs themselves sounded painful. She had left the hospital at noon and took a motorcycle taxi home. She had to return to the hospital the next day for some additional tests. She will know the results in three days. The medical staff at Santa Chiara feared she had covid or tuberculosis. The video call was deeply disturbing. I was to upset to return to work on this book. Last Spring, I was proud to attend her graduation from high school. Before I met her, she had never been to school. I called the doctor at Santa Chiara and she said she felt the illness was serious. She really needed to be hospitalized. But that was not possible in Haiti. Later in this book, I share some journals I wrote in Haiti; Baby was frequently mentioned. I love her. After she turned 19, I got her a little apartment near Santa Chiara. She has been part of the staff for three years. The kids all love her as she was once one of them. Baby still calls me daddy. People often ask me why I stay in Haiti in the face of all the violence. I stay because of Baby. I should be in Haiti caring for my daughter instead of working in this damn book in Florida.

Here are three sentences from the many letters Baby has written to me:

"The most important thing I have is your love."

"I can see what no one can see in you: your sadness in front of your joy."

"Thank you so much, Dad, to accept me in your life. You are all to me."

Baby, taken on the day she graduated from high school.

Voluntary Poverty

Dorothy Day often spoke of the importance of voluntary poverty, which was at the heart of her worship and the life of the Catholic Worker movement she cofounded. She was not endorsing misery or squalor. In the introduction to his book of the selected writings of Dorothy Day, Robert Ellsberg writes:

> The poverty she espoused meant reducing the area given to self-interest, learning to locate the ultimate source of security elsewhere than in material values. To become poor was to become dependent on God and available to others, and to withdraw from the spoils of exploitation, for, as the Church Fathers had frequently taught, all that we owned beyond our needs was stolen from those who were hungry.[153]

> *Voluntary physical poverty is a means to a healthy spiritual poverty.*

Stumbling Blocks

The Camaldolese Benedictine monk Bruno Barnhart wrote:

> He [Merton] was continually occupied with the quest for contemplation, for that deepening of consciousness that is an experience of union with God. And yet at the same time we observe in him—more and more clearly as he finds himself—a restless, creative spirit, an impatience with outworn ways and entrenched structures and the sleepy consensus of the multitude.[154]

Today the "sleepy consensus" of the multitude (multitasking at the multiplex) would say that there is nothing wrong with materialism and consumerism. Merton would strongly disagree.

Materialism and consumerism are stumbling blocks to entering fully into the transcendent faith to which Christ calls us. Our society glorifies the amassing of individual wealth and an ever-growing greater accumulation of goods. Anything that furthers our goal of individual material prosperity is good, and anything that hinders it is bad. Ethics and morality are not part of the equation. Economic individualism and free competition without reference to the common good go against the spirit of the Gospels.

The best way to preach the Gospel is with one's life. Every act of love, compassion, and sacrifice transforms our world in which hatred, cruelty, and avarice reign into a new world in which the kingdom of God blossoms.

We prefer the reality of this world to the mystery of the next world, and so we value what is expedient and useful instead of what is holy and creative. We erect visible idols to replace the invisible spirit of God. Our lives are consumed by competition, and our work is dedicated to producing a commercial commodity. As a result, our spiritual fire has been all but snuffed out. By serving the poor we are not only practicing Christian charity, we are also reforming ourselves.

Jesus took on the role of servant . . . should we not do likewise?

Silence Speaks

Thomas Merton spoke often about the "false self" and the "true self." Father Bruno Barnhart—a former Prior of the New Camaldolese Monastery in Big Sur, California, as well a highly regarded spiritual writer who was mentioned in Merton's journals and who died in 2015—never used those terms. Instead, he referred to them as the "superficial self" and the "deep self." I like that. Here are two passages from Barnhart's insightful writing that emerged from his deep appreciation of silence.

> This Jesus whom we encounter is a light at the center of the world, a fire at the world's edge. He moves beneath the images of himself as an ultimate center of energy. I am always losing him and finding him again, migrating from one image, one station, to another on the journey. He awakens that which lies at the core of my being; the series of Jesus' healings in the gospels are the story of the gradual raising of this nascent person that I am to life and consciousness, to freedom and fullness. The knowledge of Jesus Christ is a unitive knowledge: it is the luminosity of my own true and eternal being. . . . In him I possess the secret knowledge of this unity and of this dynamism, which is history. I cannot capture in words the gravitational pull of this solar Christ, moving in the depths of my being.[155]
>
> When I discover myself as a unitive energy, welling forth from the darkness of the ground, I have found myself, I am at home.[156]

Our Major Task

When you read monks such as Barnhart and Merton, or writers on the contemplative life, such as Richard Rohr and Cynthia Bourgeault, you can't help but see that the contemplative life is really an ongoing pilgrimage to the depths of your being. The further we travel, the more we evolve. Jim Forest, who was a longtime pen pal of mine and who had a long friendship with Merton, wrote in his Preface to Rowan Williams's book *A Silent Action: Engagements with Thomas Merton*, that:

> One of the major tasks of the contemplative life is the ongoing search for the actual self, the unmasked self, a self that is not merely the stage clothes and scripted sentences that we assemble and dutifully exhibit each day to appear to be someone, but the self that exists purely because it exists in God. Rowan notes how often Merton is drawn to a "delusory self image" but then quickly abandons each self-image as a ridiculous deception.[157]

Epiphanies of Human Kindness

Montaldo Study Note Number 5

The Epiphany of Our Kindness in Sorrow's Face

Back in 1958, in Louisville, Kentucky, on the downtown corner of Fourth and Walnut Streets, after visiting his doctor, the Trappist monk Thomas Merton stepped out onto the busy sidewalk and found himself suddenly in deep communion with the human beings he saw there. In that moment of sunlit clarity, the haze of his monastic separation burned off from his eyes, and Merton discovered kinship with everyone on the street.

"Thank God," he wrote later in his journals about the event, "I'm a member of the human race just like everyone else. I was suddenly overwhelmed with the realization that I loved all those people, that they were mine and I theirs, that we could not be alien to one another even though we were total strangers. . . . A member of the human race! To think that such a commonplace realization should suddenly seem like news that one holds the winning ticket in a cosmic sweepstake. . . . I have the immense joy of being a member of the human race: if only everybody could realize this! There is no way of telling people that they are all walking around shining like the sun."[158]

This paragraph from Merton's journals is famous, but there is another that follows shortly after that is another powerful revelation of a deep truth about us human beings. On that same afternoon trip in Louisville, Merton had bought for fifty cents a book of photographs from *Life Magazine* called *The Family of Man. The Family of Man* had photographs of ordinary folk at weddings and funerals, in bars and churches, children at play and elders at rest. Merton reacted powerfully to this book:

All those fabulous pictures. How scandalized some would be if I said that the whole book is to me a picture of God's face and yet that is the Truth. There, there is God in my own Kind, my own Kind—"Kind" which means "likeness" and which means "love" and which means "child." Human kind. Like one another, the dear "Kind" of sinners united and embraced in only one heart, in only one Kindness, which is the Heart and Kindness of God. I do not look for sin in you, Humankind. I do not see sin in you anymore today (though we are all sinners). There is something too real to allow sin any longer to seem important, to seem to exist, for it has been swallowed up, sin has been destroyed, and there is only the great secret between us that we are all one kind. God is seen and reveals God's self as human, that is, in us and there is no other hope of finding wisdom than in God-humanhood: our own humanity transformed in God.[159]

My sister Janet died in 2000, it seems like yesterday, a very young sixty-seven-year-old. Two years before she had discovered a small lump on her left breast. The doctors removed it. Doctors treated her with chemotherapy and radium, and pronounced her clear of cancer. A year passed and she became sick again. Doctors told her cancer was now everywhere in her lungs, her liver, and her bone system. She lived for seven more months and lived more beautifully than I had ever experienced her living before. It was as if she had surrendered to her life's end every mask she had worn to protect herself and became the person we had seen before only in glimpses. She reconciled enmities, she drew her children to herself, and she healed long-standing open wounds. We were awed by her kindness to us and by her appreciation of every kindness we were moved to show her, she being so kind. I spoke to her every day for seven months and every day she ended our conversation by telling me she loved me, a mantra ensuring I would not forget. She lost consciousness only four days before she died. Her body cremated, this beautiful human being whose depths of kindness I had only just begun to appreciate became fire and disappeared.

Without the graces of palliative medicine, my sister would have been unable so strongly to show her true face as she departed from us. But it was more than medicinal herbs that robbed her death of its sting. It was the epiphany of kindness in the face of sorrow, it was her revelation of kindness in the middle of everything that was failing her, that made her dying a final act of compassion for the life she had loved living.

At the banquet of human existence to which we have been invited, the menu is both sour and sweet. We eat our bread together sometimes celebrating, sometimes in tears. Just as weeds flourish with the wheat, evil in our lives nestles close in the heart of what is good. The climate of our lives is always changing. We are hot, then cold. Now we are happy this month, depressed in the next. This year we are famous, next year, disgraced. In the morning, we are kissing our children a good day as we leave for work, and, by the afternoon, we are incinerated, disappearing like incense into a blue sky. We are all kin as we suffer the curved streets of this life that every one of us travels.

But being kindred, why are we so unkind to one another? Why are we blind to each other's dilemmas as being identical to our own? Why do we so unrelentingly accept unkindness as the order o relations among us when it is our kindness that binds us all together? To be unkind is to be unnatural.

How do we relearn kindness in an unkind world? Humility is the mother of kindness. Humility prevents our taking first places at life's banquet; humility prevents our hogging resources while sisters on other continents or just down the street cannot feed their children. Humility helps us step down from the pedestal of individual, unkind destinies to share life with the crowd of us. Humility helps us see how easy it is to lose everything we hold dear in an instant: our houses, our status, our families, our very selves lost in the distractions of the ten thousand things that keep us from realizing our kindness with one another.

For the health of our collective souls, we must uncage our kindness from the narrow cells of our immediate family and friends. We must go off the restricted reservations of our corporate interest groups. We must leap over the wall of the gated communities of our minds that divide our world into the precious few who are saved, while the rest of them, not our kind at all, go unwashed in the Lamb's blood. Who will deliver us from these narrow-minded perspectives every one of us easily adopts that divide our one humankind into the family and the strangers, into the haves and have-nots, into tribes of Abel and tribes of Cain, into the descendants of Sarah and the offspring of Hagar?

This virus of irresponsibility for other human beings, our own kind, infects our relationship with all of nature upon which the health of all creation depends. The circumference of our enacting kindness must, therefore, as Albert Einstein wrote, be as large as planet Earth's. We must repair our kindness to all beings. We should convert ourselves to fostering ecologies of kindness in all our relationships as a daily spiritual practice.

Now has always been the acceptable time to be kin to one another, not next week, not in our next reincarnation, not in heavens that are elsewhere than where we all are now. This great work of our becoming epiphanies of human kindness in our relationships is the personal inner work that we each must take up more deeply.

I love this poem written in South America by the great Palestinian-American poet Naomi Shihab Nye:

Kindness

Before you know what kindness really is
you must lose things,
feel the future dissolve in a moment
like salt in a weakened broth.
What you held in your hand,
what you counted and carefully saved,
all this must go so you know
how desolate the landscape can be
between the regions of kindness.

How you ride and ride
thinking the bus will never stop,
the passengers eating maize and chicken
will stare out the window forever.

Before you learn the tender gravity of kindness,
you must travel where the Indian in a white poncho
lies dead by the side of the road.
You must see how this could be you,
how he too was someone
who journeyed through the night with plans
and the simple breath that kept him alive.

Before you know kindness as the deepest thing
inside,
you must know sorrow as the other deepest thing.
You must wake up with sorrow.
You must speak to it till your voice
catches the thread of all sorrows
and you see the size of the cloth.

Then it is only kindness that makes sense anymore,
only kindness that ties your shoes
and sends you out into the day to mail letters and
purchase bread,
only kindness that raises its head
from the crowd of the world to say
It is I you have been looking for,
and then goes with you everywhere
like a shadow or a friend.[160]

My mothers and fathers, my sisters and brothers, dear cousins, we are all one kind: we must recognize ourselves as kin or not be well. Kindness is our only cure. Kindness is the medicine prescribed to be taken every day until its light burns off the cataracts on our eyes and everywhere we look we shall see kin, everyone our own kind everywhere. Even in the middle of all that fails us and in full view of Sorrow's face, may we realize the epiphany of our hidden kindness revealed at last.

The More You See, the More You Love

The wars and acts of violence that have plagued our world over the centuries, especially in the last one, have almost always been the result of a lack of understanding, a failure to see the other person (or the other race, religion, or country) as one filled with the same spark as myself.

By looking deeply at the suffering and oppression of others, we begin to see the blindness of our own deception and self-centeredness, and we can then begin to have the courage to look suffering in the face in order to befriend it, to listen to it, and to learn from it. Saint Catherine of Siena urges us to: "Rouse yourself; open the eye of your understanding and look into the depth within the well of divine charity. For unless you see, you cannot love. The more you see, the more you love."[161]

The simple fact that we choose to look at others with understanding and compassion is a first step toward our own healing. Yet it is so easy to close our eyes. Our culture and the entertainment industry encourage us to close our eyes, to not see the suffering, to not feel the suffering, to not respond to the suffering. (Hollywood produces escapist entertainment that distracts us from the realities of life. If we saw the suffering, we would have to change the way we live, we would have to reject the idea of unbridled consumerism, endless growth, and the destructive spirit of individualism; as a result, we would see the unity of all life and we would want to live more simply so others could simply live.) We cannot detach ourselves from suffering; we need to transform the suffering. Compassion is love that is willing to run the risk of suffering with the victims of poverty, violence, and war. Thich Nhat Hanh suggests:

> Love cannot exist without suffering. In fact, suffering is the ground on which love is born. If you have not suffered, if you don't see the suffering of people or other living beings, you would not have love in you nor would you understand what it is to love. Without suffering, compassion, loving-kindness, tolerance, and understanding would not arise. Do you want to live in a place where there is no suffering? If you live in such a place, you will not be able to know what love is. Love is born from suffering. . . . We need to touch suffering in order for our compassion to be born and to be nourished.[162]

Blessed are those who can venture into the heart of suffering and learn that life is beautiful. We may not be able to take away someone's pain, but we can be with them in their suffering. The willingness to be in communion with another's suffering is the surest way to lose one's separate self. German Lutheran pastor, theologian, and anti-Nazi dissident Dietrich Bonhoeffer went so far to say: "Suffering and God are not contradictions, but rather a necessary unity."[163]

Shortly before he was murdered in 1980, Archbishop Romero received an honorary doctorate degree from the Catholic University of Louvain in Leuven, Belgium. In his acceptance speech, Romero raised a number of questions: What does the incarnation of the Son of God say to our world of suffering? What does it mean to serve the Word "made flesh"? Does commitment to those who suffer provide a privileged way to appreciate the incarnation? Since his martyrdom, violence, injustice, and seemingly meaningless suffering continue on a massive scale . . . begging each of us to answer the lingering question: how do we respond to the hidden presence of the Son of God incarnated into our universal world of suffering?

No Escape

It is pain and suffering that truly shapes our lives. No one can escape pain and suffering. It can either crush us or help us grow. Suffering either strengthens or kills. It is through suffering that we really get to know ourselves. But we need to do more than just endure the suffering that visits us. We need to reflect on it and allow it to enlighten and transform us.

We can't escape conflict in our lives. Conflicts are a part of life. But we do have a choice in how we respond to a conflict. Fighting is always a bad choice.

An Act of Kindness

Note: The following is from a journal of a trip to see Jonathan.

May 5, 2000, O'Hare Airport, Gate 12B. The flight to Louisville is delayed by an hour, which offers me the chance to get a latte at Starbucks. Most of the people waiting to board the flight are going to the Kentucky Derby. I was going to Gethsemani Abbey with Jonathan. The actor Hal Holbrook was among those going to the derby. He was very neatly dressed, and looked terrific for his age, which I figure is hovering on the far side of seventy. He was sitting reading a paper when a black woman wheeled her mentally disabled daughter into the lounge, and parked the wheelchair near the actor. The girl, who was about 20 years old, was severely retarded. She made loud noises and wild gestures. She began poking Mr. Holbrook. He turned to her and smiled. Within seconds, he was playfully interacting with her. She tugged at his neatly pressed jacket. He let her. The mother recognized the actor, and asked for his autograph. He graciously obliged. I was delighted by the actor's kind response. He was very at ease with the girl who made most people uncomfortable.

The girl opened a floodgate of memories from the time I spent making a documentary film on the L'Arche community in Tacoma, Washington. My time in L'Arche taught me about the value of littleness and listening. Society teaches a very different lesson: we need to be strong and we need to be heard. It is only when I see and appreciate my own littleness, my own limitations that I can encounter the enormity of God, a God without any limitations. If I think I am God, I will not search for God. I recall the insightful words of Jean Vanier: "When I walk with Jesus, He always leads me to the poorest, the lowliest and the lost, so that I may open my heart to them."

> *If you are poor or needy,*
> *if you are despised by all,*
> *if you are a sinner,*
> *then Christ considers you*
> *to be his friend*
> *and he welcomes you*
> *to his banquet table.*

Note: When I wrote this, Jean Vanier was my inspiration; I read all his books He was considered by all to be a living saint before we sadly learned that he had engaged in lots of unsaintly, sinful, and disgraceful behavior with multiple women over a lengthy period of time. Within a year of his death in May 2019 at the age of ninety, it was revealed that Vanier had coercive sexual relationships with six women between 1970 and 2005. The women needed psychological therapy for years in order to recover from the emotional abuse. Shockingly, Vanier initiated the sexual relationships under the context of his giving them spiritual guidance and accompaniment. I was devasted by the revelation. Now I don't know what to do with all his books that I own. His message was powerful enough to change lives . . . but not his own hidden behavior, his own unfulfilled need for intimacy. Jesus was not enough for Vanier. Or most of us. Or me.

Jean Vanier was my hero. Jesus is the only hero we need. He never disappoints.

How do we reconcile all the good Vanier accomplished through L'Arche, the international community of homes that is loving, supporting, and caring for adults with intellectual disabilities, with his dreadful mistreatment of women? My time in a L'Arche community had a tremendous impact on life. When I was speaking with members of the core community of disabled people, I realized I had to really listen to them, to be fully attentive to them, in order to understand what they were saying. I then understood I really wasn't listening to my own family and friends. I remember one young man named Mark who asked me every day how I got to Tacoma. I always answered that I flew . . . "and boy are my arms tired." He always laughed. Laughter is the best medicine.

The Saint's Vision

We have a tendency to make some living people saints. I know an American doctor in Peru whom I think of as a saint. There is a priest/doctor here in Haiti who I truly believe is a saint. Paul Evdokimov was a Russian born theologian who died in 1970 and was the subject of some of Merton's writing. In Evdokimov's writing about the "saints" in Dostoevsky's novels he said:

The saint is an "icon" not merely in the sense that he [or she] "stands for" or "witnesses to" the divine order, but because he [or she] is truly the channel through which God's energies enter into the human world. The saint's vision of the world is God's vision of the world, because the saint is "transparent" to God: in the person of the saint contemplating God, God contemplates the world.[164]

That is a very high standard for anyone to meet.

CHAPTER 23

A Hidden Wholeness

Unreasonable

In the *First Life of Saint Francis,* Thomas of Celano wrote: "Whenever he [Francis] found an abundance of flowers, he used to preach to them and invite them to praise the Lord, just as if they were endowed with reason."[165]

Our reason can only lead us to knowledge about God, not to God. Dependence on reason is unreasonable. We need to stop brooding over the incomprehensible, which is beyond the power of understanding.

> *O most pure Theotokos, teach me childlike*
> *humility of heart and purity of spirit.*

Elimination and Restoration

"When I was in sin . . ." That's the way Saint Francis described himself before his conversion, before he "put on the mind of Christ" and began to live his life through Christ in the Spirit and slowly started to die to his self. We don't much like the word "sin." I don't, even though I'm acutely aware that I am a sinner. Despite my progress in curtailing sin, I still sin a lot. Sin, the way I understand it, is a failure to love. I fail often. I fail when I put myself first. (**Note:** *I put myself first three or four times yesterday . . . and once already today.*)

Conversion involves a "metanoia," a turning away from sin and becoming a "new creation." In that sense, Francis didn't restore himself because restoration implies a return to an original condition. According to Christian theology, we were born in sin. In other words, thanks to original sin, sin has always been a part of our nature. In that light, Francis wasn't engaged in a process of restoration but one of elimination. (I find this theological statement to be false and very damaging. We were, I believe, in a state of Original Goodness when we were born.)

Eliminating sin in my life has proven to be an extremely difficult chore. I can't seem to get out of my own way, and my own way sometimes reverts to a self-seeking persona that is not in harmony with the life of Christ. Francis let go of his own way, let go of everything he knew and loved, and, leaving all behind, jumped into the unknown abyss of God, where he became so united with God that he became a new person, a new creation. The old man had died; Adam no longer lived within him. Adam is still alive and kicking within me. Sin keeps me alienated from the fullness of God.

Original sin didn't eclipse original goodness. Original sin damaged and diminished original goodness. Deep inside us there is goodness that has been tarnished by selfishness. Original goodness contains a trace of sacredness that cannot be erased.

For repentance to be real and true, it must be more than a fleeting twinge of remorse. Genuine repentance must lead to a transformation of our lives. Repentance involves two steps. Stop doing something bad. Start doing something good. (**Note:** *Or perhaps, it is the other way around; that is, start doing something good and stop doing something bad.*) Contrition should evolve into acts of goodness.

Thomas Merton saw sin as a symbol of our state of alienation from God . . . and our true selves. Our identity hinges on the realization that we are, at our deepest core, one with God. I am not just me and me alone. I am me and God. In other words, if I view myself as just me, I'm divided from God . . . and from everything. If I see myself as being united with God at the core of my being, then I am whole. On the way to God, our false self—that is, the self that is divided from God—begins to dissolve and eventually disappear, until we are, as Merton put it, "no one." To be "no one" is to be our true self, one who is united with God. (**Note:** *This makes so much sense to me, yet I am far from being "no one" and still very far from the wholeness to which I aspire. Reading these words afresh today, August 9, 2014, is helping me see more clearly where I am on my journey.*)

The self that disappears along the way is our false self, the descendant of mythical Adam's disobedience, an egocentric act that caused our spiritual death by destroying our relationship with God. The resurrected Jesus restores that relationship and allows us a way to once again become grounded in God, to become who we were meant to be.

Over and over again in the New Testament we read that we are supposed to actively participate in the life of Christ . . . to die with Christ by dying to sin in order that we may rise with Christ. The journey of conversion begins with a death to self so we can "put on the mind of Christ" and live our lives in unison with Christ through the power of the Holy Spirit. Living a "life in Christ" is something that does not just happen; it's not like putting on a new coat. It is a process, a long arduous struggle. Why? Because we stand in our own way . . . our false self resists and rebels every step of the way, fighting for its own way, the way of sin, the way of self-seeking pleasures.

To live a life in Christ means we must die to this false self. For Christ to flourish, our false self must vanish. Ditching a lifetime's worth of false understandings is not an easy task as we desperately want to hold on to what we think is the truth about ourselves and the world around us. We don't want to really believe that sin slowly destroys our intrinsic relationship with God, even though God never stops loving us. We think sin is simply a matter of morality, when in fact it is really a manifestation of our false self. Sadly, the false self wants to listen to the serpent's song of lies and illusions instead of God's song of true harmony. We may say otherwise, but we seem to like stumbling around in the dark rather than being bathed in the Light of God.

The first time I read about the concept of a *false self* and a *true self*, my intellect understood the theological principles underpinning it, but the idea didn't resonate in my heart. But gradually I began to see that the inner struggle going on inside of me really was a matter of my old self, my false self, resisting my efforts to live a life in Christ. Prayer was not easy. Often it was dry, arid. It was difficult to see God in the daily, mundane events of my life; God still seemed distant, beyond my reach. Years of unbelief and skepticism caused me to often question the merit of trying to live a more God-centered life, trying to live a life in Christ.

Note: Reading this in light of working on this Merton book is truly reinforcing my need to make contemplation a more important part of my day. I can no longer merely just squeeze it into some early morning moments or leave it to chance. Even more important, I can't call writing contemplation, even if I'm writing about Merton and his love of contemplation.

Sometimes during Mass, my mind would wander and entertain the thought that my attendance is a waste of time, that the Mass is nothing more than an antiquated, lifeless ritual or that the concept of transubstantiation was nothing more than theological mumbo jumbo and that the consecrated host is merely a symbol and not the body of Christ, so there is really no need to eat a symbol. The false self has a very active mind, continually questioning, doubting, and constantly trying to restore itself to the throne of my life, trying to force God to abdicate. I'm also troubled by my frequent inability to resist the temptation to sin, which in some cases had become rather habitual. Yes, I had professed Christ with my lips and in my heart, yet my false self shouted back, "No . . . you alone are all you need! Jesus is a fairy-tale messiah and God does not care. Wake up. Live for yourself. You are your own ultimate fulfillment."

In the twenty-five years since my rebirth in Christ, I've slipped and betrayed him often. But grace and mercy help me to get back up and try again to live a life in Christ. Day by day, little by little, the false self dies. I've no idea how long it will take for the rebellious Adam who lives within me to vanish. (**Note:** *At my age it is unlikely I have enough time left to complete the task. But rather than be discouraged by that, I need to just try harder.*)

In his book *Merton's Palace of Nowhere: A Search for God Through Awareness of the True Self,* James Finley writes:

> Adam is not seen as some historical figure who committed a particular act that brought about a kind of ontological birth defect that is handed down from child to child. Rather, Adam is now. Adam is ourselves in disobedience to God. The garden of Eden prior to the fall is just as much in the future as it is in the past. Both heaven and hell live not only beyond us but also within us, and it is through the door of ourselves that we enter both.[166]

The false self makes life hell. I know, I've been there. Dr. Finley correctly points out:

> The serpent's lie is a dark and twisted echo of God's creative act in which he made us sharers of his own divine life. Indeed, for us to want to be like God is simply for us to want to be who God created us to be in his own image and likeness. The spiritual life for Merton is a journey in which we discover ourselves in discovering God, and discover God in discovering our true self hidden in God.[167]

Saint Francis made that journey. It was a long, hard trip, and he suffered greatly along the way. He discovered what Thomas Merton expressed centuries later: "The secret of my identity is hidden in the love and mercy of God." Merton went on to say: "There is only one problem on which all my existence, my peace and my happiness depend: to discover myself in discovering God. If I find Him I will find myself and if I find my true self I will find Him."[168]

Saint Francis, the helper and the hermit, discovered his *true self* and God through his selfless service to others and in the inner desert of prayer and contemplation. In the process, he removed the shackles of sin and the mask of illusion and was able to have a face-to-face relationship with God. I can't help but think of the way Francis described himself before his dramatic encounter with the leper: "I was in sin." Thomas Merton identifies sin with the illusions of the false self, which hinders us from recognizing Christ. He writes:

> Every one of us is shadowed by an illusory person: a false self. This is the man I want myself to be but who cannot exist, because God does not know anything about him. And to be unknown of God is altogether too much privacy. My false self and private self is the one who wants to exist outside the reach of God's will and God's love—outside of reality and outside of life. And such a self cannot help but be an illusion. We are not very good at recognizing illusions, least of all the ones we cherish about ourselves—the ones we are born with and which feed the roots of sin. For most people in the world, there is no greater subjective reality than this false self of theirs, which cannot exist. A life devoted to the cult of this shadow is what is called a life of sin.[169]

During my 1997 pilgrimage, I composed this prayer for myself:

> *Saint Francis, help me to walk out of the shadow of sin and into the glorious sunshine of God's presence. Help me liberate myself from anxiety and fear and inordinate desire. Help me keep the flame that was rekindled two years ago burning and don't let the winds of doubt and skepticism blow it out. Help me cherish all you have given me. Help me surrender all that is unloving in my life. Help me be guided by God's holy will, not by my unhealthy desires and whims."*

I was frustrated by my failure to fully live a life in Christ. I've come to see that the transition from the *false self* and a life of sin to the *true self* living in oneness with God is a very slow and long process. (Amen.) That doesn't mean I'm satisfied with the pace of my progress; it only means I won't become depressed or distressed by my inability to instantly and completely make my false self vanish. He's been around for a long time, and he's a stubborn cuss. (**Note:** *I give thanks to God, whose mercy has allowed me to make whatever progress I've made since I penned that prayer in Assisi, and I pray for the grace to go much further. I need to do better. I must do better.*)

The spiritual life is a journey . . . a journey of elimination and restoration.

Merton believed that from the moment of our conceptions, we have received a sacred mission to awaken fully to the infinitely rich and inexhaustibly interesting journey of being alive. Merton taught his readers that true religion should always make them personally and communally free.

"Solitude is necessary for spiritual freedom. But once that freedom is acquired, it demands to be put to work in the service of love in which there is no longer subjection or slavery. Mere withdrawal, without the return to freedom in action, would lead to a static death-like inertia of the spirit in which the inner self would not awaken at all."

—Thomas Merton, The Inner Experience[170]

Original Sin v. Original Goodness

Note: *On the last day of June 2022, I read the previous section and the words "original sin" jumped out at me. Before I began to think for myself about spiritual matters, I had blindly accepted the idea I was born in sin. I never realized just how unhealthy that concept was. I remember years ago, in the mid-1970s, before I became an atheist, I briefly studied to be a permanent deacon. Most of my classmates were much older than I was. They envisioned being parish administrators. I wanted to preach. My favorite course was homiletics. I actually delivered a sermon at my home parish in Little Falls, New Jersey.*

I vividly remember a professor who was a scripture scholar say that Adam and Eve were mythological figures, not actual human beings. The story of Adam and Eve was just a fictional story employed to explain a theological truth. I was delighted, even excited, to hear his lecture. It was to me, a breath of fresh air that freed me from a ridiculous story whose sole message was that I was born with the sin I had inherited from Adam. However, I was carpooling with an older coworker from CBS. He was at least twenty years my senior. On the drive home, it became very clear he was deeply upset by hearing that Adam and Eve were not actual people. He kept shaking his head in disbelief. I wanted to sell him a deed to the Brooklyn Bridge. All of this suddenly flooded my mind on that last day of June. And I wrote the following:

I have come to believe that the Christian doctrine of original sin is misguided. It is harmful and divides us into categories of good and bad. The Book of Genesis begins with the story of creation. Actually, it begins with two vastly different stories of creation. Each story reflects the mindset of the Jewish people at different times in their faith journey. The Torah was simply a collection of stories. They weren't even numbered. The first story is filled with the goodness. After the first five days of creation, God looked at his handi-work—light, water, vegetation, all manner of living creatures, first fish and birds then cattle and reptiles—and "God saw that it was good."

At the end of the sixth day, after creating man and woman, God said all that he had made, including the seed-bearing plants and the foliage of plants to eat, "was very good." God rested on the seventh day, which is something I need to try to do.

All of us, all of creation, is fundamentally good. Not evil. We weren't, according to the first story, born in sin. A day in the story is not an actual day, but a period of time, perhaps a million years or even a billion years. In his book *Messengers of God*, Elie Wiesel said, "The concept of original sin is alien to Jewish tradition."[171] In fact, the doctrine of original sin is not found in the Old Testament. Jesus, of course, was a Jew. He taught Jewish ideas—love, kindness, mercy, forgiveness, and peace. Jesus was the embodiment of goodness.

The main characteristic of the first story is the affirmation of goodness. The story needed to end there. But many, many centuries later, the ruling elite who governed an area, all men, took everything and enslaved others. Those under the ruler were seen as less worthy. It was a patriarchal system of rules and justice, but not concerned with social issues such as caring for poor. The second story of creation introduced dichotomy into life, that things are good or bad. Out of this came a pessimistic worldview of the domination of power over others, which is reflected in the nonsensical second creation story of Adam and Eve in the garden of paradise, both naked and happy, until the devil in the form of serpent talks Eve into eating an apple from the one tree God told Adam (not Eve) not to eat the fruit from.

After Eve's fateful bite of an apple, the blame game begins, and we were on the road to a world of good and evil. Eventually the idea that Adam's decedents are automatically sinners because of the sin of their ancestor was born. But the concept was not only foreign to Holy Scripture but also very destructive. Yes, we are all born into a dysfunctional world, but we do not enter with some stain on our soul. Birth is a joyous occasion. A baby is not born a sinner. As she or he grows, they undoubtedly will become sinners because of their own human frailty and inept actions they take. Often the bad actions are the result of selfishness, of putting their needs ahead of everyone else's needs as they climb up the social ladder, acquiring more and more shiny items—big houses, fancy cars—on their way to the top. The world became more and more divided. More cold. More heartless. Goodness declined. Sin increased. We need to recapture our original goodness, a goodness that was affirmed by God. The force of goodness is a force of oneness.

We still live in a class-dominated society, where most people seek power and domination over others. If you chose a life of service to others instead of accumulating the stuff of a good life, you will be seen as odd or a bit crazy.

There has always been a struggle between these two worldviews. One said we were born into a world of a loving God who wants us to be filled with love, kindness, and generosity. The other radiates with fear as it says we were born into a world in which the rich, powerful, and elite dominate the poor and the weak. If you were not born into an elite family, you were a sinner in need of salvation.

The truth is simple: we were created by love, born in love, and exist through love. Love is a unifying force. You were born into a world created by a loving God who wishes you would live a loving life of caring for others. It is only through love that the existing violence and division that plagues humanity today will be healed and we will be made whole. Ilia Delio, a Franciscan sister, scholar, and author, writes, "We belong to one another because we belong to an Infinite heart of love. God Is love and continues to love the world Into a unity of mind and heart. Heaven Is where God's life and our life become so Intertwined that divine and created life are dynamically entangled In everlasting love."[172]

When you fall in love with God, you fall in love with all of creation . . . and see with loving eyes that it is all good. But it won't be easy, won't be filled with flowers and bird song. Just as it is when we love another human, it means a certain amount of self-emptying as you put the person you love ahead of yourself.

Flowers and Bird Songs

An encounter with God, as the mystics have claimed, is not a gentle affair, filled with pretty flowers and chirping birds . . . and all the right words. An encounter with God is like being wakened by an earthquake . . . it shakes us to the very core of our being, crushes our false self. To confront the transcendental is to lose control and be filled with trepidation and awe. Nothing is the same . . . everything changes after an earthquake. God topples the false temples of our lives, and when the dust settles, God gives us the grace to rebuild on a firmer foundation. Yes, there are flowers, but thorns also. A genuine encounter with God is ineffable, beyond concepts, images, and words. Infinity and eternity take on clearer meaning, seem more real. Dualistic discourse becomes a thing of the past, replaced by mystical nonduality. All is One.

We really don't want an earthquake and a new reality. We want flowers and bird songs. We want our own secure, stable way.

> *"There is in all visible things an invisible fecundity,*
> *a dimmed light, a meek namelessness, a hidden wholeness."*

—THOMAS MERTON, FROM THE PROSE POEM "HAGIA SOPHIA"[173]

An Explosion of Love

Because of sin we got Christ. Thank God for sin. But Jesus was not about sin or judgment or power. Jesus had a new level of awareness of the reality of God's love and the unity of all of life. He sensed God's presence in everything. He was fully integrated with God.

Jesus was about wholeness, about evolving toward a new consciousness. Merton said Jesus was the "fully integrated one." He had a new heart, a new mind. Jesus had entered into the evolutionary flow of God, giving us a new direction aimed toward the future, not the past. In Jesus, God was breaking through to humanity.

Jesus belonged to the whole, which is why he could reach out the woman at the well, to the leper, to the blind man, to all those living on periphery of life. There was no separation between him and others.

Jesus went from an individual Jew faithful to the law to a person with unbounded energy not defined by his culture. "I am, may you be." Jesus was creating a new way life, a life of forgiveness, mercy, compassion, and love. Each of us needs to be recreated, evolving into a new understanding and embodiment of love, a new wholistic way of living, loving, and embracing all of creation.

Jesus's death and resurrection were an explosion of love in which the power of God invades the present and birthing something new. Our hearts are evolving into new hearts centered in God that creates a new consciousness in which, as Merton said, "we contain all divided worlds within ourselves and we transcend them in Christ." This gives birth to an understanding that we are all brothers and sisters. Christ was transcultural.

All of life is moving toward oneness.

Windows of Wonder

Daniel O'Leary was an Irish priest who spent his entire adult life ministering in England. He was a famous author in England and a columnist for the great independent Catholic magazine *The Tablet*, which is published in Great Britain. We had been pen pals for many years before his death in January 2019. I saved every email he sent to me, as each was a gem of inspiration and hope. He was kind enough to gift me with a subscription to *The Tablet*. He also wrote a blurb for one of my books.

In one of his magazine columns, titled "Windows of Wonder," which was published in *The Tablet* on May 17, 2008, Fr. Daniel offered some insight into the life of Thomas Merton:

One morning the mystic, monk and poet Thomas Merton realised to his surprise, that contemplation is not about the acquisition of a consciousness emptied of everything except thoughts of God. It was the opposite—not a movement towards a distant God but a sinking into a deeper awareness of one's own life and to find God already there. Contemplation, he surmised, was not a different state to our usual way of being. There is only one reality. Our hours and our days are divided not between time spent with God or with the world but between those occasions when we are more, or less, aware of God's presence in our experiences—when we are more, or less, distracted from that presence by the heartaches of our work.

"It is enough, to be in an ordinary human mode, with one's hunger and sleep, one's cold and warmth, rising and going to bed, putting on blankets and taking them off, making coffee and then drinking it," Merton wrote. "Also defrosting the refrigerator, reading, meditating . . . contemplation is a way of being really inside our daily experiences. We are in contemplation when we perform the routine task of our lives so as to perceive in them that our lives are not little, anonymous or not important any more, but that what's timeless, eternal, is in the ordinariness of things."

The story of God's inner being is written everywhere, strewn around us like pearls in a parking lot, like love letters in a tip, like treasures hidden in every field. All we ask for is the grace to notice and believe in this extravagance, to identify the grace place. This is the work of contemplation.

> ***Every Drop of Rain***
> *Oh God, you are*
> *in the breeze*
> *You are*
> *in the trees.*
> *Oh God, you bring me*
> *to my knees.*
>
> *You are everywhere.*
> *You are in everything.*
>
> *You are in the crying child*
> *You are in the kids running wild.*
> *You are within every tender embrace.*
> *You are with us as we run the daily race.*
>
> *You are in the morning coffee.*
> *You are in the sting of bee.*
> *You are our delight*
> *in the middle of a dark night.*

You are in the sunrise.
You are a constant surprise.
You are in every drop of rain.
You hold us when we are in pain.

"Our goal should be to live life in radical amazement . . . [to] get up
in the morning and look at the world in a way that takes nothing
for granted. Everything is phenomenal; everything is incredible;
never treat life casually. To be spiritual is to be amazed."
—ABRAHAM JOSHUA HESCHEL[174]

CHAPTER 24

An Act of Self-Examination

Montaldo Study Note Number 6

Thomas Merton's Public Exposition of Our Deceitful Hearts

I admire him (Thomas Merton) but cannot imagine him my "spiritual master." He long ago set me free from hero worship. He wrote beautifully about spirituality while proving he couldn't easily live a spiritual life. He confessed himself to be fallible and thoroughly human. He possessed a literary gift for artful self-disclosure. He judged his best writing was autobiographical, marked by "confession and witness."

His autobiography, *The Seven Storey Mountain*, is a romantic document, a self-idealizing confession of a floundering young rouge's having found a monastery as the perfect life raft on his youth's angry sea. Readers still find his story capable of changing their own lives. But after its publication and status of best-seller since 1948, he wrote out loud that he had distorted his true self by the story's presentation of him as a Christian monastic hero on a marble stairway to paradise.

Writing journals after the publication of his autobiography, Thomas Merton conscientiously refocused himself and disclosed to his journals' future readers the more visceral truths about his struggling monastic practice. Writing journals began to function as a discipline of honesty with regard to the crooked road his life had taken by his split-hearted pursuit of both monastic vows and the exigencies of a literary and public career. His journals became, as he himself characterized them, "part of a documentation that is demanded of me—still demanded, I think—by the Holy Ghost."[175] And what Merton documented carefully were the states of mind he could easily have hidden, which, once being disclosed to journals, could and do damage his publicly professed religious life.

Merton knew he had placed himself in the occasions of sin endured by many a spiritual writer who, having publicly brought attention to themselves as spiritual seekers and having reached their goal—perhaps unconsciously—of being sought after as "sages," experience pride to be as debilitating a sin in their spiritual lives as unchecked lust. Their self-righteous criticism of others tempts them to sin against their communion with the saints. Their excessive self-concern and self-analysis become for them a form of unbelief in the forgiveness of sins. Ambition in "spiritual masters" poisons everything they once achieved with good will. The Chinese Taoist Chuang Tzu warned those who came to believe their own press that public good works placed them above other human beings: "Achievement is the beginning of failure. Fame is the beginning of disgrace."[176]

There are few journal entries that so transparently document Merton's understanding that his spiritual life and his monastic vocation were being compromised by the temptations of his literary success as that for January 19, 1961:

> Someone accused me of being a "high priest" of creativity. Or at least of allowing people to regard me as one. This is perhaps true. . . . [T]he sin of wanting to be a pontiff, of wanting to be heard, of wanting converts, disciples. Being in a cloister, I thought I did not want this. Of course I did and everyone knows it.
>
> . . . [S]t William, says tonight's breviary, when death approached, took off his pontifical vestments (what he was doing with them on in bed I can't imagine) and by his own efforts got to the floor and died. So I am like him, in bed with a miter on. What am I going to do about it? I have got to face the fact that there is in me a desire for survival as pontiff, prophet and writer, and this has to be renounced before I can be myself at last.[177]

All his false steps, his continual backsliding, his being caught in the same old compulsive thinking that Merton regularly confesses to readers of his journals should be placed in the context of his authentic and dedicated pursuit of the evangelical monastic goal of attaining purity of heart. Merton's personal integrity, especially in his later journals, is missionary. "I am thrown into contradiction," he wrote in his journal at his hermitage in 1966, a year that found him at fifty-one in love with a student nurse of twenty-four. "I am thrown into contradiction: to realize it is mercy, to accept it is love, to help others do the same is compassion."[178]

As Merton elaborates the paradox of his seeking purity of heart, while witnessing in himself the ability to evade the self-disregard necessary for its procurement, he places before the eyes of his readers their own struggle with conflicting desires that attends their own inner and public work.

By writing journals, Merton discloses first for himself the deep layers of his heart's deceits so that he might assume and incorporate them. His practice of writing journals is thus akin to the ancient asceticism of rigorous self-disclosure practiced in the Egyptian desert by early Christian monks and reported to the West by the fourth-century writer John Cassian. Of the need for constant self-examination and self-disclosure to an elder in monastic practice, Cassian passed on this word of advice from the desert that Merton heeded well: "He who manifests his thoughts is soon healed; he who hides them makes himself sick."[179]

Professor Edward Kaplan of Brandeis University wrote an article about a seminar he offered at Brandeis utilizing the writings of Thomas Merton and Abraham Joshua Heschel. He entitled his article "To Keep the Pain Awake: Learning About Faith."[180] Among his seminar's methodologies, he presents neither himself nor the authors as magisterially having all the answers to questions to be raised in the class. He emphasizes instead the importance of the depth and quality of the questions we ask on the religious journey, questions that arise out of foundational human discontents that never allow us to settle without deep anxiety for easy, unexamined answers.

Kaplan reports that his students hate this aspect of his methodology. Like all of us, his students want answers in black and white transmitted by a professional expert; they insist the heroes and villains be clearly delineated, that the right and the wrong ways to approach religious questions be clearly exposed. But insecurity is the guardian angel at the continuing presence of mysteries that attend our experience of being alive. These foundational mysteries, to paraphrase French philosopher Gabriel Marcel, can never be reduced into solvable problems. They remain painful despite any efforts to anesthetize our seemingly primal mental wounds.

Anyone who takes up serious inner work to discover the truth about themselves and their predicament, anyone who struggles to accept that they share these same painful predicaments with all their neighbors, anyone who strives for a modicum of human integrity will always find their experience as having an edge of being in exile from any sup- posedly settled questions (traditionally defended by corporate entities for whom settled questions preserve their own power), especially when they learn through experience that these settled questions systemically continue to reproduce evil effects.

In his letter to a "southern churchman" in his book *Faith and Violence*, Merton eschewed he had answers to the problem of human evil:

> I mistrust an obsession with declarations and pronouncements. While silence can constitute guilt and complicity, once one has taken a stand he is not necessarily obliged to come out with a new answer and a new solution to insoluble problems every third day.
>
> After all, was it not [Dietrich] Bonhoeffer who said it was an 'Anglo-Saxon failing' to imagine that the Church was supposed to have a ready answer for every social problem?
>
> When one has too many answers, and when one joins a chorus of others chant- ing the same slogans, there is, it seems to me, a danger that one is trying to evade the loneliness of a conscience that realizes itself to be in an inescapably evil situation. We are all under judgment. None of us is free from contamination. Our choice is not that of being pure and whole at the mere cost of formulating a just and honest opinion. Mere commitment to a decent program of action does not constitute the

cure. Our real choice is between being like Job, who knew he was stricken, and Job's friends who did not know they were stricken, too. (So they had answers!)

If we know that we are all under judgment, we will cease to make the obvious wickedness of "the others" a fulcrum for our own supposed righteousness to exert itself upon the world. On the contrary, we will be willing to admit that we are 'right-wised' not by condemning others according to our law or ethical idea, but by seeing that the real sinner whom we find abominable and frightening (because he threatens our very life) still has in himself the ground of God's love [. . .] that ground is the sinful heart of sinful human beings just as they really are—as we really are, you, and I, and our disconcerting neighbor.[181]

An Undivided Heart

"Do not give your heart to that which does not satisfy your heart."

—SAINT ABBA POEMEN[182]

When it comes to following Christ without reservation, I know exactly what to do. What I lack is the courage to do it. By recognizing my weakness, I become strong. I need to stand before God in a stance of constant conversion. Humility is the heart of Christianity and the gateway to prayer. The acknowledgment of our own weakness is the first step toward an acknowledgment of Christ's strength. God reveals my sinfulness to me, not to make me feel guilty but to offer me forgiveness and freedom from the bondage of sin. God is humble. God lives in our poverty and weakness. God alone calms and satisfies all our desire.

Passion is an expression of love or hunger. Only the pure of heart see God in everything. A pure heart is an undivided heart. I need to remind myself daily to walk humbly behind Christ. My anguish, my fear, my temptations can become a path to God if I acknowledge my littleness, my weakness and transform them into a trust that God alone can bring light into my darkness if I abandon myself completely and take refuge in God's love. The Rule of Saint Benedict reminds us: "Never despair of the mercy of God."

> *"Like the deer that yearns*
> *for running streams,*
> *so my soul is yearning*
> *for you, my God."*
> —Psalm 41 (42)

Note: April 17, 2020, Port-au-Prince, Haiti: *Such beautiful, truthful, sincere, and inspiring thoughts. It is disheartening to know that twenty years after they were written, they remain just* *thoughts. My weaknesses are more clearly evident to me now than then. My heart is still divided. Yet I believe God's mercy has no bounds.*

At times my heart is filled with a love of God. At other times, I'm close to despair, unable to think clearly or make a firm decision about my life. Should I live alone or should I commit to share my life with a young Haitian woman who has captured my heart? I suppose everything I want is on the other side of fear. Mixed in with my own personal confusion and doubt is the reality of the pandemic, which will inexorably alter life as we have known it, and the looming financial crisis at Santa Chiara, which threatens our existence.

What follows is a reflection titled "New Ardor," which I wrote yesterday and sent today to the 177 people who subscribe to my daily Haiti Journal, *which I condensed a bit.*

> *"He who desires to make any progress in the service of God must*
> *begin every day of his life with new ardor, must keep himself*
> *in the presence of God as much as possible, and must have no*
> *other view or end in his actions but the divine honor."*
>
> —Saint Charles Borromeo

Yesterday, I woke up exhausted. The day before, my sciatica was causing me great discomfort. Walking was painful. Sitting was even more painful. Many of the Santa Chiara staff were balking at some of the necessary changes that had to be made. Some of the kids, including my adopted daughter, Bency, were not doing what they were told to do and openly showing signs of disrespect to the staff. The kids had become so unruly, that for the prior two weeks, I had to go downstairs at 8:00 pm to make sure all the kids were silent and in the bed. The night before, two older girls were sleeping in the same bed. I separated them. Ten minutes later, a staffer told me that in all likelihood, within minutes of my leaving the room, they would be back together in the same bed. I did not believe it. They said, "Go look." I did. They were in the same bed. I made them sleep on the floor in the vestibule outside the supervisor's office. I was told that one staffer said, "He is really serious." The staff applauded the disciplinary action. I don't like being the disciplinarian. I like the two girls, both about nine years old, so punishing them was distasteful.

About three hours before the bed check, I had received a summary of our bank accounts from our bookkeeper in Florida. I knew the situation was bad and that we might run out of money by the end of June. But the report was so alarming it felt like a slap in the face. The previous week saw extraordinary expenses (nearly $22,000) to repair and upgrade our power system. As I sat pondering the bleak numbers, I was feeling more and more desperate about our financial situation. We were on the brink of extinction.

Most of America, most of the world, is experiencing a financial collapse and bracing for a coming recession. The death toll from the Covid-19 in the Unites States had topped 32,000 people. In the past month, 22 million Americans had filed for unemployment. The stock market lost 35 percent of its value. Many people feared dying of hunger more than they feared dying of the virus. Keeping my little home of hope and healing opened was incredibly insignificant in light of the global suffering the virus has unleashed. I was not concerned about myself. Presumably, in a few months, I would be able to return to Florida. But I was intensely concerned about the well-being of my kids and the staff.

So, it was in this exhausted and deeply concerned state, I happened to come across the quote from St. Charles Borromeo saying I needed to start this new day with "new ardor." Ardor was in short supply. I wanted to flee. The relentless problems have overwhelmed me. The kids never tire of watching the film *Annie*. "The sun will come up tomorrow . . ." goes the song they all know by heart. I wanted to sing, "The sun will *not* come up tomorrow . . . you will all die." But the saint was telling me I needed more passion, more love, more enthusiasm, more zeal, more devotion. I wasn't sure I had the energy to do any more of anything.

In the morning (April 16), someone came into my office and said there was a little girl that had a terrible eye infection and needed to be taken to the hospital. The little girl came to us about a month ago, along with her twin sister. The girls were the younger sisters of one of our long-time employees. The girls lived in Cité Soleil, and at the time, there was a very high level of gang violence. Gunfire could be heard at all hours of the day. Many people had been killed. The staff member begged me to allow her little eight-year-old twin sisters to stay at Santa Chiara until the violence subsided. The thought was the girls could stay for a week. I had not realized they had not left.

Note: I'll never forget my first visit to Cité Soleil, the worst slum in Port-au-Prince. The devastation, the tin shacks, the rotting trash, the spewing sewage, a little girl urinating in the garbage, a woman defecating in the open, naked kids with bloated bellies running barefoot through pig-infested mud and rubbish . . . it was all too much to take in. And then there was the fetid and nauseating stench from rotting garbage that was intensified by the blistering heat. The nightmarish slum literally assaulted my senses, left me feeling helpless and emotionally wrought.

We were about to take the girl to the infectious disease and skin hospital, which would cost about fifty bucks and tie two staff members up for most of the day, when Nurse Rose told us not to take her, as our doctor would be at Santa Chiara soon and he would examine her. I had the staff isolate the little girl. I bought the little girl some special cookies. I sent a message to the staff member and told her the girls could no longer stay at Santa Chiara and she had to remove the one twin right away and the other one could stay until the doctor checked her out. That was a difficult message to send. But for the survival of Santa Chiara, I must begin downsizing.

Saying "no" to people in such dire circumstances is hard.

Later in the morning, I had to zip to a local supermarket for some school supplies. I saw the Missionaries of Charity van in the parking lot. I could see that three sisters were in the van. I walked up to the vehicle, and they all waved. They opened the back door, and we chatted for a few minutes. Inside, I saw two of the sisters by the ice cream section. I knew one very well, as she attended one of the retreats I gave the sisters. I was wearing my mask. They were not. I said to my friend, "Where is your mask?" She pointed to her cloth bag. I said, "A lot of good it's doing in there." She laughed. We had a nice chat. She asked if I was OK. I told her that I only had the funds for another month. She told me not to worry, to trust in God. She said, "God gave you this work and God will provide what you need to do the work. Pray and let the worry go." They were looking for sugar-free ice cream as one of the sisters is diabetic. I was very happy to see them. They told me that a priest would say Mass at 3 o'clock that afternoon. I said I'd be there. One sister said, "We'll be waiting for you." I was happy for the hour of quiet and prayer. After communion, I felt a deep sense of peace.

Later that evening, peace had vanished. I was yelling at kids and arguing with some of the staff. I wanted to be anywhere other than Haiti. After forty-nine days in Haiti, I'm a lost soul, and in many ways, I'm poorer than poor people I'm struggling to help. I feel alone and isolated.

The next day (4/17), I opened the Liturgy of the Hours for the first time in over a year. It was Friday within the Octave of Easter. The Daytime Prayer opened with Psalm 199, verse 25:

> *My soul lies in dust;*
> *by your word revive me.*

I felt I was dust. I was depressed. Everything seemed wrong. Everything seemed hopeless. In this parched, dry space, I was pulled to a book I had not opened in years: *The Gospel in Parable* by John R. Donahue, S.J., a professor of New Testament at the Jesuit School of Theology. The first highlighted section presented a series of provocative questions along with alternative answers, the first being:

"Who are the poor?" Are they the economic poor, or is it a metaphor for powerlessness and vulnerability?

The second highlighted passage was longer and intriguing.

Luke portrays Jesus himself as one who "hears" and "does." Like Jesus, the disciple is to live in the presence of God and manifest this presence to others.

Luke thus constructs a solemn introduction to the whole travel narrative. The way to eternal life leads through imitation of Jesus, the one who lived in the presence of God and came to seek and to save the lost (Luke 19:10). Following Jesus on the way involves compassion for the suffering neighbor and attention to the word of God. In choosing "outsiders" to illustrate true discipleship, Luke suggests that those most busy with religion are often the least able to embody its true value. Perhaps one of the reasons that generations of Christians have found the parable of the Good Samaritan so consoling to narrate and so impossible to imitate is that *they are too busy being Samaritans to listen to the word with silent attentiveness* [italics added]; nor do they experience that freedom possessed by the outsider who has so little to lose that only eternal life can be found.[183]

The phrase I italicized really hit me. I'm so busy bandaging the wounded, feeding the hungry, transporting the sick, hugging the lonely and abused, that I don't take the time for extended periods of stillness and silence and so I'm not being nurtured, consoled, and sustained by the loving embrace that I really need.

But the real message for me wasn't what was written in the book, but what was in the book: namely, two pieces of paper. The first was a receipt from a Cuban-American bakery called Porto's in Burbank, California. The receipt was dated October 16, 2016. At the time I was commuting between California and Haiti every month. I don't miss those grueling trips. When I was in California, it was my habit to have breakfast at Porto's. That morning I had a cheese omelet on a croissant . . . and a latte with an extra shot of espresso. The receipt brought back sweet memories of my life in California. I liked the life very much. Yet, I know I could never go back to it.

It was the second piece of paper that was most important, even though it dredged up painful memories. It was a copy of a letter dated May 16, 2010, which happened to be Ascension Sunday, that I sent to Monsignor Clem Connolly, who was the pastor of Holy Family Church in South Pasadena, California. In the letter I wrote: "I think perhaps you are the one person who can help me navigate my own *Long Day's Journey into the Night* as false charges based on rumor, gossip, inuendo, and idle speculation are threatening to destroy my ministry and ruin my life." In the letter I was crying out for help. Those days when the letter was written were the darkest days of my life. Life had lost all meaning. My desire to live was fading. Yet I survived. I also wrote: "Eight years of nonstop work in the worst slums on earth and speaking at churches and schools across the country have necessitated that I postpone my deep desire to write a book based on my personal journey and search for God. I was also unable to finish a book on Thomas Merton which was based on my experience of living in his hermitage for a week, a grace which Brother Patrick Hart allowed me to have after he contacted me after reading my book on St. Francis of Assisi, *The Sun & Moon Over Assisi*." The letter ended with: "I think I need to let go of my [film] work with the poor and focus my attention on book writing and dealing with my own weaknesses, if I can find a way to support myself."

Reading the full letter exactly ten years and one day after it had been written had a powerful impact on me. It reminded me not only of my darkness, but also of my survival. It also made clear to me how easily I can slip into depression, the feeling that all is lost, that life has no meaning.

In our obsession with happiness, we easily forget that depression is part of the human condition and that all sorrow need not be numbed with antidepressants such as Prozac. No pill can get to the root of the multidimensional causes of depression. The loud drumbeat of fear and anxiety can be quieted by contemplation.

It was stunning to read what I wrote about my deep desire to write a book about Thomas Merton that I couldn't finish due to my extensive film work and packed calendar of speaking events. The letter hinted that I wanted to stop making films in order to write books. Ten years later, my mission to the kids in Haiti comes at the expense of not being able to write full time. Some days I think it is too great a price to pay. But of course, I can't stop my work at Santa Chiara. Instead, I must find ways to carve out more time from each day that I'm in Haiti and add a few days to each time I'm in Florida each month . . . assuming the global pandemic ends and I'm still standing and airline travel resumes. (**Note:** *Of course, as you've read, just over a month later, I was knocked down by Covid-19.*)

Thomas Merton's writing was an act of self-examination. It's poetic. It's prophetic. It's beautiful. My writing about Merton's writing was an act of *my* self-examination, albeit not prophetic or beautiful. It is all part of the mystery of God. In the economy of Divine Providence, nothing is ever lost. Even the worst experience of my life had in time a hidden benefit and helped me become the person I am.

A Wounded Healer

When I read that long, rambling journal entry sent on April 17, 2020, just over two years later, on the morning of May 31, 2022, I was shocked that I remembered every single detail of that one single day of my life at Santa Chiara. Over the last seven years, there have been countless days like that and even much worse—days filled with nonstop struggle, tension, and worry. Yet, I saw afresh that with the struggle of caring for so many abandoned and often abused children and an uneducated and often belligerent staff, I was also coping with my own deficiencies, weaknesses, and failures. For most of those years, I was lost and lonely . . . and starving for real love. Yet somehow, I was so driven, even obsessed, with caring for the kids that I pushed aside all the barricades blocking my creating a real home for them. Why or how am I still standing?

In this book, I've repeatedly used the word "grace." I really don't know how to define grace . . . or even understand it. Yet, as I read this passage from two years ago, I see grace in operation. Despite my overall impurity of thought and action, my false motives, and my stumbles, my desire to care for the kids was pure and real. They had melted my heart. I felt that caring for them was the reason I was alive; it was the task I was supposed to do. It was not really a matter of spirituality or theology or even faith. It was simply an awareness of our broken humanity in dire need of healing. I was, to use Dutch priest and popular author Henri Nouwen's phrase, a wounded healer.

Note: It was for me inspiring to read that passage on October 29, 2022 as this book was on the cusp of being printed and released. In our daily conversations these days we hardly talk about transcendence; we mostly speak a transactional language. When it comes to the mysterious dimensions of life, we are mostly mute. The idea of grace has no relevance for most of us. But grace is important; without the blessings of grace, Santa Chiara would have closed long ago. This may sound corny or delusional or just downright too pious, but I feel grace working within me. There is no other viable explanation for my still being in Haiti and still making a little difference in the lives of a few kids. While I am increasingly dubious about Catholicism, I think it got right about grace. Grace is operational in my life; look to see if it is also working in your life . . . my hunch is that it is. Grace is operational everywhere and within everyone. What is missing is awareness.

City of the Sun

The name sounds enchanting . . . Cité Soleil. The name means "City of the Sun." But even under the stunningly bright Caribbean sun, Cité Soleil is a dark and dangerous place, a slum so wretched few outsiders enter it. More than a quarter million people are crammed in the three dense square miles that make up Cité Soleil, the largest and oldest slum in the sprawling capital city of Port-au-Prince.

They live in rusting peak-roofed tin shacks. Open sewers and the stench of rotting garbage intensify the brutally ugly reality. Kids run around naked or in tattered clothes, and many of them have never been to school. With the rat population outnumbering people ten to one, the nights bring on even more horrors. Children must find sticks and beat away the diseased rodents throughout the night to keep from being bit as they try to sleep.

People are so hungry they eat "cakes" made of clay, dirt, spices, sugar . . . and filthy, contaminated water. Pigs rummage alongside kids in search of food buried in the dense rubbish. People are sometimes forced to give up their kids to servitude because they can't afford to feed them. There is virtually no electrical power. Nights are spent in nearly total darkness. When it rains at night, the rain seeps into the shacks and the poor sleep in the mud. Fetid canals thick with noxious garbage run through Cité Soleil.

Women and children squat in the rancid, insect-infested rubbish to defecate and urinate without the dignity of privacy. Many children have intestinal worms, which eat up to 20 percent of a child's nutritional intake every day. Haitians are among the poorest-fed children in the world, and no child there can afford to lose 20 percent of his or her food. The effects of such losses are anemia, vitamin deficiencies, a weakened immune system, lethargy, and poor cognitive development. Intestinal worms magnify the impact of chronic diarrhea from bad water, common in all parts of Port-au-Prince. Half the newborn children in Cité Soleil will die before they reach the age of five.

If all of that is not bad enough, Cité Soleil is riddled with unbridled violence. There is little police presence and reformers are routinely assassinated. Guns and gangs rule the slums. People are decapitated or burned alive for opposing the neighborhood gang leader. Murder, rape, kidnapping, looting, and shootings are common, as every few blocks are controlled by one of more than thirty armed factions. Lawlessness was so pervasive it wasn't even uncommon for UN peacekeepers to be killed in Cité Soleil. Few residents live past the age of fifty; they die from disease, including AIDS, or violence. Death is in the air.

The residents of Cité Soleil live in the shadows. There are no stores, no job opportunities, no social services. They live virtually in exile and at the mercy of gangs, local politicians, and global economic forces beyond their control. The grinding poverty and desperate daily search for food have left them literally numb to the normal aspects of life. Yet in the darkness, there are gentle rays of light. Every day in Cité Soleil, grace and violence, blessing and bloodshed, intermingle as the joy of the crib of Christ and the pain of the cross of Christ are both present.

Note: I wrote that about ten years ago while making my film Mud Pies & Kites, *which was set in Port-au-Prince and featured lots of footage shot in Cité Soleil. I could never have imagined that years later I'd enter the violent slum unescorted to bring food to a former employee who had just given birth to a child. Most of the kids at Santa Chiara came to us from Cité Soleil. Many of our staff still live there. In May 2022, we moved the grandmother of one of our children from the slum to a little place close to Santa Chiara. We paid her rent for one year. In June 2022, I read a fresh statistic that one in five children in Cité Soleil suffers from malnutrition. By then, it was far too dangerous for me to enter the slum, as residents of the slum were being murdered every day.*

The Heart of Darkness

I cannot learn about God. I can only unlearn the things that are keeping me from a full awareness of God. To find Christ, you must make a pilgrimage to the center of your being, to the place where the human and the divine meet. The key to being a pilgrim is to remain still interiorly as you journey—otherwise, you are just a wanderer. To pray is to embark on a journey without end—a journey deep into the heart of darkness, of paradox, of mystery. The journey to God is slow. Each day, we inch our way along a steep, winding road. The pace of spiritual transformation moves about as quickly as traffic in Los Angeles.

Spirituality is essentially a journey in which we move from what we are to what we will be; it is a journey to weakness. We truly learn to live when we begin to explore our weaknesses. Every experience of weakness is an opportunity for growth and renewed life. Weaknesses transformed by the reality of Christ become life-giving virtues.

The Margins of Society

*"Only through poverty of spirit do we draw close to God; only through
it does God draw near to us. Poverty of spirit is the meeting place of
heaven and earth, the mysterious place where God and we encounter
each other, the point where infinite mystery meets concrete existence."*

—Johannes Metz, *Poverty of Spirit*[184]

Saint Francis found God not in pomp and glory, but in infirmity and foolishness. He found
God in what we throw away. Francis found the God of endless light hiding in the shadows,
on the margins of society. I was looking in all the wrong places.

I believe God has drawn me to the margins of society; I pray someday soon I understand why. I only know I feel the reality of God more strongly in these horrible slums than
I do anywhere else. The spiritual lesson seems clear: to become poor is to know the richness
of God. Of course, that does not mean I'm endorsing poverty. Far from it. The kind of
physical poverty I've been witnessing is an injustice on a grand scale. It must be eliminated;
human dignity must be restored.

I need to become poor in spirit, to recognize my own limits and my own dependence
upon God for everything. The only thing I'm sure of is my own sinfulness and my profound
need of God's love and mercy. As that awareness grows, I in turn have no other choice but
to be more merciful and loving to all, especially those who live on the margins of society.

To forget the poor is to forget God.
To become poor in spirit
is to know the richness of God.

"The prophet's field of concern is not the mysteries of heaven, the glories
of heaven, but the blights of society, the affairs of the marketplace.
He addressed himself to those who trample upon the needy, who
increase the price of grain, use dishonest scales, and sell refuge corn."

—Abraham Joshua Heschel, *I Asked for Wonder*[185]

PART TWO

Out of Africa

Nairobi, Kenya, 2000; *Photo by Gerry Straub*

CHAPTER 25

A Life Wildly Out of Balance

Traveling Man

Between 2000 and 2012, I made five exhausting trips to Africa, visiting Kenya twice and Uganda three times. On my first trip to Nairobi, Kenya, I took nearly a thousand photographs in the Kibera slum, which is the largest slum in all of Africa. I made two feature-length films set in Eastern Africa. During those trips, I kept extensive journals, parts of which ended up in the screenplays. Over this and the next chapter, I'll share some of those journal entries. My African experiences had a profound impact on my life. As usual, Merton was my travel companion.

A Grueling Trip

Saturday, May 13, 2000, North Hollywood: I leave early tomorrow morning for Nairobi, Kenya. A taxi will be picking me up at 5:30 am. I have an 8:05 am flight to Minneapolis, arriving at 1:38 pm. At 3:10 pm, I'll catch a flight to Amsterdam, arriving at 6:10 am Monday morning. Four hours later, I'll board a flight to Nairobi; the flight is scheduled to land at 8:15 pm. This will be a grueling trip, with a total of twenty-three hours of flying time on the three flights.

Confession: I'm very nervous about this trip. Crime in Nairobi abounds, touching nearly everyone. Nearly half the population is unemployed. Government and police corruption are widespread. Power outages are commonplace. The infrastructure is crumbling. Illness from tainted food is a constant threat.

I'm tired before I even begin the trip, worn down by all my travel this year and emotionally drained from all the suffering I've seen, especially in India and the Philippines. I'm nervous about my own safety. I dread seeing the levels of poverty I'm sure to encounter in the slums I'll be visiting.

No one seems to understand what I am doing. At times, I don't understand it. Who wants to see pictures of slums? I don't know; I only know I feel compelled to take them and to try to understand what I have seen. God led Saint Francis into the arms of the poor, so he could be embraced by them and also embrace them.

I'm still trying to figure out Saint Francis's love of poverty, and why he opted to live and minister among the poor.

None of it makes any sense. This trip—the photo/essay book—is simply an exercise in faith.

Faith requires we surrender our wills.

Only Dangerous at Night

May 15, 2000, 11:35 pm, Nairobi, Kenya: I was greeted at the airport by Brother Frederick, a German friar whom I had met a few years back at Collegio Sant´Isidoro in Rome. As we drove along a darkened, lonely stretch of road after leaving the airport, Frederick told me a story that confirmed my fears about Nairobi. He said a few nights ago, some Missionary Sisters of Charity, dressed in the habits made famous by their founder, Mother Teresa, were driving to the airport. They were escorting a person who had been visiting them. Suddenly, their car was forced to stop due to two flat tires. When the sisters emerged from the car, they were forced to the ground by a gang of thugs, who robbed them and the person they were accompanying at gunpoint. The thugs had spread nails and other debris on the road, which punctured the tires of the sisters' car. If they could rob Sisters of Missionaries of Charity, what the heck would they do to me. Brother Frederick said the road is only dangerous at night. Hardly soothing news, seeing as it was night.

Nairobi, Kenya, 2000; *Photo by Gerry Straub*

Living Without

Fleeing poverty and starvation, forced migration has become a way of life. Extremes of famine, war, poverty, and drought uprooted thousands upon thousands of Africans. Most migrants end up living as squatters in massive slums in the largest cities, where they endure a life without running water, without toilets, without electricity, with nothing but misery and diseases such as malaria and tuberculosis. To be a migrant in Africa is to be a non-person, unwanted, and unneeded.

Turmoil and tragedy are commonplace in Africa. As I was filming, I came to understand that choice in Africa was often reduced to famine or flood, corruption or coup, cease-fire or peace pact. Africa was slipping out of the control of the leaders who claimed to govern it and beyond the reach of the international institutions and coalitions that sought to rescue it. Africa was and still is suffering from multiple crises: ecological, economic, and political. Roads were crumbling and health systems had failed. When I was there, the phones didn't work, and power outages were normal. Schoolchildren had neither books nor desks nor teachers. Fresh water and forests were under increasing and unprecedented stress. War and disease thwarted any effort to reduce the severe poverty. Real per capita income across the continent at the time was estimated to be under $500. More than 40 percent of Africa's population lived on less than a dollar a day. Two hundred million Africans lacked access to health facilities. Every year, 2 million African children die before they reach their fifth birthday. On top of this woe, AIDS was taking a terrible toil, infecting an estimated 23 million people. Spending time in Kenya was a shocking eye-opener. I doubt it has gotten much better.

I think of the words of Archbishop Óscar Romero: "It is not God's will for some to have everything and others to have nothing."

Out of Africa

> **Friday, May 19, 2000, 5:30 pm, Nairobi, Kenya:** I've decided to go home three days early. I was scheduled to return to LA next Tuesday, but I'll be leaving tomorrow instead. I've had enough.
>
> Kenya is emotionally and physically exhausting. Nothing works. Nairobi lacks enough water to power the generators that provide electricity, and so they are going to start rationing the electricity; starting this weekend, the electricity will be cut off for eight to ten hours a day. The phones don't work; I just spent nearly three hours trying to call the airline office. The friars will be busy this weekend, leaving me only Monday to see more slums, and to be honest, I've seen enough. I've already shot twenty-four rolls of film—nearly 900 photographs that graphically captured the harsh reality of life in Nairobi for the thousands upon thousands of people who live in the sprawling slums that dot the city, where open sewers and diseases such as malaria and tuberculosis make life a living hell.

After five full days of witnessing the misery of extreme poverty, famine, drought, hunger, illness, suffering, and death, I simply need to go home a few days early. During my time in Kenya, I did not see any wildlife. I have seen only life wildly out of balance, where poverty is crushing people to death in ways too cruel to imagine.

My mind is filled with scenes from the slums I've visited during my week in Africa. This is the last stop on my six-month tour of slums around the world. The places and faces have changed, but the common reality remained the same: unthinkable, unending misery.

"I am not alone in my tiredness or sickness or fears, but at one with millions of others from many centuries, and it is all part of life."

—Etty Hillesum, *An Interrupted Life and Letters from Westerbork*[186]

Note: During the trip to Nairobi, I was staying in the home of the friars. While the home was very modest, it was far removed from the debilitating conditions I encountered during the day. The home was located a safe distance from the Kibera slum. My first "home" in Haiti was in the middle of a small slum in the Peguyville section of Port-au-Prince. There was no separation between me and the kids I fed during the day. I recall how frightened I was during those early days in Haiti. Now, I've become part of the Haitian landscape, become one with the poor.

A Life of Fatigue and Long Journeys

In 2012, I watched some dreadful news reports on the massive refugee camps in Africa. It broke my heart and compelled me to contact a Jesuit priest I knew from my days of teaching at the Pontifical Gregorian University in Rome. In his eighties, he was living and teaching in Nairobi. I told him of my desire to film in a refugee camp. He connected me with the head of Jesuit Refugee Service in Eastern Africa. Within months, I was flying to Nairobi, Kenya, to make a film titled *We Anoint Their Wounds*.

Eastern Africa is a place of immense beauty and vitality. But it's also a place of immense agony and misery. In Eastern Africa, countless people are left outside the circle of life; they are marginalized, disempowered, ignored, and forgotten. They are refugees, desperate people fleeing hunger and violence in such drought-stricken and conflict-riddled nations as Somalia and South Sudan. They live in huge, isolated, overcrowded refugee camps.

On my ninth day in Kenya, I boarded a small plane for a flight to the northwest corner of the country. I wasn't too thrilled about getting on a plane with propellers. We landed in the desert. There was no airport—just a short runway for landing. But I was more worried about the drive from the airport to the massive Kakuma refugee camp, which is located in the midst of a very harsh desert area. Just before boarding the plane, I learned that the two-hour drive from the airfield to the camp is so dangerous we'll have armed guards with us to protect us from bandits who randomly terrorize and rob relief workers heading for the camps.

As we crossed the arid, barren desert, I felt the pace and panic of contemporary life that lives in the shadow of illusionary wealth melting under the hot sun and that I was I entering a new reality. In spiritual language, the desert is a place where humanity is handed over to God, a place where a person is totally submitted to an immense and intimate encounter. For the refugee, the desert is a place where they are stripped bare of their country, their fields, their friends, their family, their home. It is a place of total isolation and marginalization. It is hell.

In the Swahili language "kakuma" means "nowhere." An apt name as the camp is located literally in the middle of nowhere, about as isolated as you could get.

Under the burning heat in Kakuma, life is direct and raw. To be a refugee means to live on the edge of society, socially and politically ostracized. Around the world there are more than 50 million people who have been forcibly displaced, and 80 percent of them are women and children. I met many teenage kids who have spent their entire lives in the Kakuma refugee camp . . . and may never leave this awful place. Some of these kids know more about death than life.

The camp itself defied my expectations. I had envisioned a sea of white tents. But most of the Kakuma camp is so settled that the refugees have constructed more permanent homes. Many people have lived in the camp for more than twenty years, and over time the camp was transformed from the impermanence of tents to more stable and secure structures, including shops and businesses. The place actually felt more like a slum than a refugee camp. Nonetheless, there are still plenty of tents . . . which are occupied by newly arriving refugees.

Unlike refugees in urban settings, these refugees have nowhere to go, as they are surrounded by endless miles of desert in every direction. In the Kakuma camp, the refugees have settled in for the long haul. About 95,000 people call the Kakuma camp home. Each year, only about 2,000 refugees from the camp are fortunate enough to be resettled to other nations, including the United States, but sadly, each year another 5,000 new refugees enter the camp . . . and so the population is constantly growing.

The film also looked at the harsh, hidden, and lonely lives of refugees who fled the camps and are living in the shadows of Nairobi, the capital of Kenya. Many refugees lived in massive slums. In order to survive, some refugees have no other option than picking through the rotting waste of garbage dumps, desperately searching for food to eat and recyclable items to sell. I spent four difficult hours filming in a garbage dump. Refugees live a life of fatigue and long journeys. It's a draining, dreary life, filled with fear and anxiety. For many it can be a life of constant uncertainty and unbearable physical suffering. For the most part, it's a life of being ignored and scorned. Refugees are often greeted with deaf ears and hard hearts, forced to face a wall of indifference.

To be a refugee is to endure a life of mental anguish, a life of being unwanted and unloved. People who are starving, homeless, friendless so easily lose the sense of their human dignity. Jesuit Refugee Service (JRS) works to restore their self-worth, their human dignity, in such a way that their hope and trust in humanity are rekindled. JRS is a ministry *of being* with refugees rather than just *doing for* refugees. It is a lesson that served me well in Haiti . . . just being with the kids was as important as what I could do for them.

CHAPTER 26

Being Sick in Africa

The Promised Land

> *"A Church that does not unite itself to the poor in order to
> renounce—from the place of the poor—the injustice committed
> against them is not truly the Church of Jesus Christ."*
>
> —Archbishop Óscar Romero[187]

During the first trip of my three trips to Uganda in 2007 and 2008, I spent all of my time in Kampala, the capital of Uganda, a dreadfully sad, poor, war-torn nation that is nothing short of a nightmare. Once part of a prosperous ancient African kingdom, Uganda was then struggling back onto its feet after half a century of unimaginable violence, pain, and suffering. Half of Uganda's 31 million people didn't have access to clean, safe water, making them vulnerable to cholera and diarrhea. Respiratory illnesses were widespread. Less than 10 percent of the population had access to electricity. About 90 percent of Uganda's total energy requirements were met using firewood and charcoal.

The infant mortality rate and life expectancy were among the worst in the world. Only half the boys and about a quarter of the girls completed primary school. About 65 percent of the adults were illiterate. Sixty-five percent of Ugandans lived below the poverty line, on less than the equivalent of $15 a month. The mind glazes over those facts and statistics; they are so far beyond our comprehension that we cannot come close to grasping their reality or understanding the meaning they have on the people living in such an unimaginable reality such as Uganda. As the facts and statistics wash over us, we turn away. But to stand in the midst of such an overwhelming tragedy, to learn the name of just one person living in such a hell, changes everything and you can no longer turn away, no longer ignore their suffering.

The northern part of Uganda had been ravaged by a brutal civil war for more than twenty years. Few people in the West were aware of the horrifying wave of violence triggered by a rebellious guerilla group known as the Lord's Resistance Army (LRA). The LRA's tactics were beyond despicable. The LRA kidnapped children as young as seven years old and trained them to fight and kill in their army. While the captured boys were turned into killing machines, the captured young girls became sex slaves and were given to rebel commanders as trophies for military victories. For every ten girls who were lucky enough to escape from the LRA, nine had been infected with AIDS. An estimated 40,000 children were abducted, tortured, and forced to become child soldiers or "wives" in the LRA.

The war killed, maimed, raped, and displaced well over a million people. In order to survive, this displaced population was forced to live in internally displaced persons (IDP) camps. The displacement camps in Gulu and Lira were hell on earth. Some camps had as many as 60,000 people crammed into a small space, living in squalor and with an array of deadly diseases. They lived without electricity and access to clean water. Health care was virtually nonexistent. The morbidity rates in the fetid camps were horrifying; at its worst point, it was estimated that 1,000 people were dying each week. Girls and young women living in the camps routinely suffered sexual and physical abuse. Memories of my time in the camps, seeing so many naked, starving kids with bloated bellies still distresses me.

During the first trip, I spent a lot of time in the massive slums that blanket most of Kampala. The agony in these slums defies adequate description. The people in the slums of Kampala had no voice, no power, no rights . . . and no way to make their plight known. From a purely physical perspective, the slums in the south were worse than the camps in the north. In the slums, the people had the freedom to move about the city without fear of being kidnapped or murdered. They also had more access to food and assistance. But the conditions in the slums themselves were excruciatingly bad. The stench from human waste was unbearable. The dilapidated huts made of discarded scraps of metal and wood barely offered shelter from the weather. When it rained, many of the slums flooded, thereby intensifying the misery.

One day I had the foolish idea to film in one of the slums at night. The darkness made the dangerous and foreboding slums even more ominous. Illuminated only by candles, the shadowy figures on the narrow, muddy paths seemed both more threatening and more hopeless. The sound of babies crying and the elderly moaning intensified the horror. Even in the darkness, I could see clearly how truly uncomfortable everyone's existence was. The small dwellings had little furniture, no space to relax. It was a cramped life, where survival trumped all else. After leaving the slum, we stopped in a small, hole-in-the-wall bar for a beer. As we discussed what we had seen, I began to get a stomach cramp. I went to the bathroom. The bathroom was nothing more than a small concrete room, with a few holes at the base of one of the walls leading to the alley behind the building. You faced the wall and did what you had to do. The piss just flowed outside. There were no toilets, no sinks. It stunk. I knew it would only be a matter of time before I would need a toilet as the cramping became worse with each passing moment. I returned to the bar and asked the driver how long it would take to get back to St. Augustine's. Depending on traffic, the drive would take at least thirty minutes. I said we had to leave immediately.

Traffic was heavy and the drive was agony. Every pothole we hit, every delay we encountered pushed me further into the realization that we would not make it back in time. The pain in my stomach was intensifying more quickly than the van was moving. I desperately needed a toilet. But I knew, between wherever we were and where we were going, there were no toilets. I dreaded the thought that I would have to relieve myself in the street. I did all in my power to resist the inevitable.

The Jesuit compound, tucked safely behind a wall, was located smack in the middle of a very poor area. I was thrilled when we turned off the main street and headed for our destination. The last few miles were the worst. The dirt road was littered with deep potholes that slowed us down to nearly a crawl. I was so close, yet so painfully far. As we inched our way down the road, the headlights illuminating the steady stream of people walking in the shadows, I prayed I could hold on just a little longer. I also prayed that the old man who guarded the gate would be there and quickly open the gate for us.

Those prayers were answered. We arrived at the gate, beeped the horn, and within minutes, the steal gate slowly swung open. "Thank God," I thought as the driver drove the short distance to the flight of stairs leading to the main house. I got out of the car as gingerly and quickly as possible and began the long climb up the stairs, confident that in a matter of minutes I would be able to relieve the mounting pressure in my stomach. Before Uganda, it would have been hard to imagine how just seeing a toilet could make me so happy.

When I reached the top of the stairs, I was stunned to see the gate pulled closed and locked. Before that moment, I had never seen the gate closed or locked. I screamed for help. The old man had the key. As he slowly made his way up the stairs, I was beyond desperate. As he fumbled for the key, I tried to hide my anxiety and desperation so as not to make him nervous. At last, the gate was unlocked, and I scurried toward my room. The residential area was in the form of a cloister where all the rooms face a large garden. It is a classical quadrangle pattern that I loved. But not that night, for my room was at the furthermost distance from the entrance to the cloister. I turned left, walked to the end of the corridor, and then turned right. My room was the last room on the left at the end of a long corridor. As I made my way down the corridor, I began to relax because I knew I would make to the promised land . . . a bathroom with a toilet.

But I was wrong. Halfway down the corridor, my stomach exploded and I defecated all over myself. I stood there in a state of utter disbelief. I cried. I entered my room and stood there motionless for a few moments, not knowing how to even begin to clean myself up. It was a disgusting mess, and I hoped that the water was at least running. It was not. Worse, I was still sick, still needed to spend time on the toilet. It took me at least an hour to clean up and calm down. Besides being ridiculously upset, I was angry that I found myself in such a predicament, so hopeless. I was there to try to help, but that night I could not even help myself, could not even find a toilet in time. I wished I was not there, wished I had never come to such a dreadful place.

But the sun rose the next morning and chased away the darkness of the previous night. I attended morning Mass. After receiving the Eucharist, I sat silently in my seat. Suddenly I recalled a distant memory of a homeless man and was filled with an unimaginable peace. In 2003 I spent about six months in the Skid Row section of Los Angeles making a film about the heroic work a mission was doing in response to chronic homelessness and drug and alcohol addiction. One day, I spotted a man who was obviously experiencing the effects of a stomach cramp that resulted in an episode of involuntary diarrhea. As it dawned on him what had happened, he looked truly lost and not sure what to do. There he was . . . standing on the curb of a busy street having just defecated in his pants and not sure how to handle the degrading situation. It was an image I've never forgotten. The loneliness, isolation, and hopelessness of his sad situation were hauntingly palpable.

The sudden memory of that man made me realize that what had happened to me the night before was actually a moment of profound grace because it allowed me to feel, albeit only briefly, the complete powerlessness of the people I film. I now knew what it was like to have absolutely no ability to do something so simple as finding a toilet when I was in desperate need of one. In that moment, the homeless man in Skid Row and I became brothers in a very tangible way, because I felt his agony, knew his despair.

Every encounter is a Eucharistic encounter.

A Death Sentence

On my second trip to Uganda, I visited a hospital in the city of Soroti. It wasn't something I'd planned to do. The trip had been one of perpetual movement. We were constantly filming or spending endless hours traveling from one location to the next, over dreadfully poor roads. But, one day, we were forced to slow down because the van needed to be serviced. Soroti is a fairly large city located northeast of Kampala. As we strolled around the city, we passed the Soroti Hospital.

Laurie Kroll, a saintly American woman who cares for orphans in the area, told us about the dreadful conditions in the hospital. We decided to peek in and see for ourselves. Laurie told me the area has only one doctor for every 22,000 people, which sounded hard to believe. She said patients at the hospital are literally on their own. The hospital doesn't provide food. The grounds of the hospital were covered with families and friends cooking for the patients. If you have no one cooking for you, you don't eat. A patient's family and friends must also procure the medicines they need, including IV fluid. Before entering the hospital, I stopped to film a little boy, nearly naked, seated on the ground, urinating into the dirt; his head was bandaged, and he looked alone and lost—and certainly too sick to be sitting in the dirt where he had just peed.

Once inside the hospital, my film crew and I couldn't believe what we saw. You don't associate the word "hospital" with chaos and neglect. The place took us by surprise, did not feel like a place of healing. It felt like a place without hope. What we saw was shocking and upsetting. The place smelled like the inside of a hamster cage. The smell was nauseating and made me want to gag. As we walked through the various wards, we often stopped to talk with and film the patients, and their images are forever etched in my mind.

Hardest to see were the severely malnourished infants. I filmed one three-year-old boy who weighed about 13 pounds and had a liver disease. I spoke at length with the father of a young boy, perhaps ten years old, who had a liver infection that wasn't being treated because the father didn't have the money for the medicine. The medicine cost a mere $12. The father was about to return to his village, which was a two-day walk, and sell what he could, borrow what he could, and walk back to the hospital with the money. At best, the boy was five days away from getting the medicine he needed, during which time it was safe to assume his condition would only worsen. Twelve bucks—that's all he needed to help his son. I discreetly gave the father the money he needed. Moments later, we came across a teenage boy who had a severe liver disease. He was in great pain and discomfort from his extremely distended belly that prevented him from lying down. We were told he was unable to sleep and was forced to sit up all day long. Bed after bed had heartbreaking stories of suffering and neglect.

That night after dinner, we returned to the hospital to better document the nightmare. The place seemed worse at night. The sight of so many seriously ill and virtually neglected people sleeping on the floor and under beds made us sick. The sounds of moaning pierced the poorly lit wards. Many family members were sleeping on the floor in the halls. Very few beds had mosquito nets. The place was a hotbed for malaria and other infectious diseases. It was extremely difficult to take in all we witnessed. As we walked through the various wards, both during the day and at night, no one asked us what we were doing, no one asked us why we were filming. There really was no one in charge, no one to question or stop us. The sick too were virtually ignored. I prayed I did not get sick, would not end up in what was little more than a warehouse for the sick and dying.

But I did get sick. Very sick. It happened in Gulu, in the war-torn north of the country, less than a week after filming in the ghastly hospital in Soroti. Even though Gulu was definitely the most dangerous and perhaps the poorest part of Uganda, I was fortunate to be staying in the right place when I developed symptoms of malaria. Never before in my life had I felt so desperately sick. I was staying with Comboni Missionary Sisters from Italy. Most of the sisters had been in Africa for fifty years. The Congregation of the Comboni Missionary Sisters was founded by Bishop Daniel Comboni in Italy in 1872. He was can-onized a saint in 2003. His prophetic intuition saw the need to integrate the presence of women serving the poorest and most abandoned in Africa.

The sisters took very good care of me. My room in the convent was simple. But it did have one luxury. Adjoining the small, unadorned, cinder-block room was a private bath-room, for which I was extremely grateful. I was dreadfully sick with malaria for two days. I had a fever of nearly 104°F and was shaking uncontrollably—and if that wasn't bad enough,

I had simultaneous and frequent attacks of diarrhea and vomiting. I felt hot and cold at the same time. When the sisters said I needed to go to the hospital, I managed to joke: "I would prefer to go to Lourdes instead." The thought of going to a hospital petrified me.

But the sisters assured me I'd be going to a special private hospital, one that catered primarily to Western relief workers and Ugandans who could afford better medical treatment. I was examined and given an injection of some kind of new, super-effective medicine for malaria. The exam, the blood tests, the injection, and the prescribed pills cost less than $25. I returned to the convent, and after a few days of rest, I was able to resume filming, though with a lot less energy.

For me, malaria was an inconvenience. For the poor of Uganda, malaria is a death sentence. One old sister, while lamenting my sickness, said it was also good that I had malaria so I could better understand the plight of the poor, many of whom will die from the disease. Unless you experience their pain, you cannot help them relieve their own suffering.

The Cries of the Poor

The cries of the poor and the oppressed, the very stench of their unjust deaths, has been met by a heartless indifference that amounts to nothing less than cruel inhumanity. In a world of wealth, the poor live in an endless Shoah, living on pennies a day, dying hungry and alone at night. Forced displacement, unemployment, exclusion, isolation, rejection, starvation, no permanent home, no sewage, no access to clean water and medical care: these are the harsh, menacing realities faced by the acutely poor. Their corpses are piling high, thousands upon thousands a day, all victims of our insensitivity and apathy.

Where is the indignation? Where is the compassion? We've lost our sense of mercy, lost our sense of connectedness. It's easy to blame the corrupt governments that imprison the poor in massive slums; it's harder to raise our voices in protest, to cry out for the rights of the marginalized.

Whether implicitly or explicitly, we all seek security and consolation. Yet even when we find some level of security, some degree of consolation, it isn't enough. For many, security and consolation are beyond their reach. Far beyond. Jesus claimed that true security and consolation could only be found in God.

In Uganda, seeing so much intense, unfathomable suffering shook my notions of security and unmasked my true helplessness and inability to control anything in life. When you look, really look, at the suffering on full display in Uganda, you are forced to clearly see that life is unfair, often brutally unfair. In the midst of so much suffering, our flimsy ideas of God are blown to pieces. God's seeming silence in the face of such widespread suffering and violence is baffling.

Yet, as Saint Francis discovered, Jesus is found and encountered at the foot of the cross. The mystery of love and the mystery of the cross are one and the same. The inflowing of God's love purges and transforms . . . and it hurts. We must die to our self-centeredness, must divest our ego and put on the mind of Christ and grow in love for all of humanity and give our lives, as Jesus gave his life, so that others, even our enemies, may live.

Jesus wants to shatter our complacency toward the suffering poor, wants us to see and feel their suffering; he wants us to renounce our own security and share our love and material possessions with those who have nothing. When we let go of our own security and put our trust in God alone, the Kingdom of God shall expand and suffering shall decrease.

We live in a tempestuous, havoc-ridden world. As Christians, our lives need to be a healing balm that soothes the countless wounds and suffering that torments the lives of so many people. The violence of war and the violence of hunger and preventable diseases needs to be embraced by the peace of Christ. Within each of us a war rages. This is where the first negotiated peace plan must be implemented. Once compassion, mercy, peace, and love have been incorporated within ourselves, we will be able to reach out to the wounded of the world around us. The wounded abound in Uganda. In Uganda, you see a human landslide of misery, countless fragile lives tumbling into despair.

Uganda, 2009; *Photo by Gerry Straub*

The word "compassion" comes from two Latin words that together mean "to suffer with." To suffer with someone, you need to go where it hurts, to places of pain and brokenness, to places of anguish mend misery. To suffer with someone, you need to enter their weakness; you need to be vulnerable with the vulnerable, powerless with the powerless. We want to think of ourselves as compassionate, yet we want no part of suffering, want nothing to do with misery, want to avoid feeling weak and ineffective. We don't look to enter pain. We avoid pain at all costs. We have a ready supply of painkillers.

Our society is based on competition, not compassion. Yet Jesus tells us to be as compassionate as God. God is so compassionate that the divine entered into our humanity and shares in our weakness and suffering. God, the All-Compassionate, is with us . . . even in our misery and pain. And so, we too must enter into and be with those who are alone in the world, alone in their misery and pain, even if all we can offer is only our presence.

> *"The marginal person, the monk, the displaced person, the prisoner,*
> *all these people live in the presence of death, which calls into question*
> *the meaning of life. He struggles with the fact of death in himself,*
> *trying to seek something deeper than death; because there is something*
> *deeper than death, and the office of monk or the marginal person*
> *or the poet is to go beyond death even in this life, to go beyond the*
> *dichotomy of life and death and to be therefore, a witness to life."*
>
> —THOMAS MERTON, *ASIAN JOURNAL*[188]

Shrouded in Silence

Despite all our longing and talk, we don't see much love and peace today. Society is becoming increasingly fragmented and polarized, which poses a great danger. We are in desperate need of a spirit of communion and compassion to wash afresh over all of us. We need to resurrect the lost art of conversation in which we truly listen to and share with each other. Through authentic communion, compassion, and conversation, we can find our common ground and work together for the common good of all, while at the same time realizing that we are all fumbling around in the dark of an infinite mystery that is beyond words and understanding.

While God is beyond words and shrouded in silence, God nonetheless is in a perpetual conversation with each of us, even if most of us are rarely listening; our failure to recognize and appreciate this divine conversation has caused us to turn a deaf ear to the other, to anyone who does not believe as we do, which in turn stifles communion and compassion.

Looking Back

As I watched the sun rise over Haiti on the morning of June 14, 2020, and thought about those two dreadful stories from Uganda, it dawned on me that all the harsh experiences over the last twenty years slowly turned me into the person I am today. I couldn't be doing what I'm doing in Haiti if I hadn't made those trips to Kenya and Uganda, along with all the other dreadfully sad places I visited while making films. All the films are always playing in my head. I remember every person I photographed. They live inside me. I'm not sure why I went to all those places or how I found the strength and courage to go and endure all the bad things I saw. Someone once asked me how I do what I do. I said, without thinking, "If God gives you a job to do, God gives you the grace to do it." It is really that simple, that beautiful. It comes down to faith and trust.

At this moment, I'd love to be in a little café in Fort Pierce, Florida, sipping a double latte and eating a sinfully delicious pastry while reading *The New York Times*. Afterward, I'd take a stroll along Jetty Park and marvel at the pelicans. But given the choice to fly to Florida on the noon flight, I would not leave. The chaos and turmoil of Haiti is my salvation. The abandoned kids and my ragtag staff are my family. I recall one day back in early 2015 thinking that I needed to stop filming the poor and to go live among the poor. *Oh, God, please . . . filming the poor is hard enough, do I really have to live among the poor?* Yes. Besides, no one watched the films. They were too hard, too long, too demanding.

Thomas Merton was with me while filming and is with me while serving. More important, Christ was continually at my side. His angels guided and protected me. The Spirit inspired and moved me. When I was so dreadfully sick with Covid, I thought I was going to die. I wasn't nervous about dying. I didn't beg for a healing. I was OK with going if Sister Death beckoned me. I simply told God there was more for me to do, that I needed to better secure the future for my kids, God's kids, and would be happy to do so if it were God's will. I later learned that the kids prayed for me the entire time I was on oxygen. I vividly remember a few who managed to sneak into my office and the horror on their faces, the tears in their eyes, as they looked down at me as I struggled to breathe.

Aftermath of the earthquake, Port-au-Prince, Haiti, January 2010; *Photo by Gerry Straub*

In reading these stories of extreme poverty, please don't make the mistake of thinking I'm a saint. Far from it. I am a sinner. Period. I screw up every day. Every day of mine has some measure of ungodliness in it. I still have unholy habits I find impossible to break. I am a weak, deeply flawed man. In saying so, I'm not putting on a mantle of false humility. I'm telling the unvarnished truth. I'm riddled with doubts. Some days I even doubt the existence of God. Dark nights are very familiar to me. Yet something in me makes me pick myself up after each fall and drives me forward to a finish line I probably will never cross.

I live the Cross.

I carry the Cross.

I endure the Cross.

Roma v. Sluma

Note: In June 2000, I traveled to Italy to attend a month-long study pilgrimage to Assisi and other places that played a significant role in the life of Saint Francis.

June 7, 2000, Rome, Italy: During my annual visits to Rome since 1995 to teach my month-long film writing course at the Pontifical Gregorian University, the streets of this vibrant city never failed to excite me. I loved just walking around the city, taking in the sights and sounds. I loved Rome's style and grace . . . and its flair, which all too frequently bordered on excessive. During all those visits, I walked the streets for endless hours, always seeing more and more. The pulsating energy of the city energized me. The art, history, and beauty of the city inspired me. The people and fashions were an infinite source of fascination.

But none of the allure of any of these things interested me this time. I walked the streets for about four hours during each of the three full, free days I had before the pilgrimage began. I walked from Sant´Isidoro (a Franciscan friary where I lived) to the Vatican at least six times, always taking different routes, never retracing my steps. As I covered the familiar ground, an unfamiliar feeling shadowed my steps: apathy, detachment, dislike.

Today, as I walked down the Spanish Steps, stepping past hordes of tourists soaking in the sun and quickly licking giant scoops of delicious melting gelato, I asked myself why I was not feeling my usual sense of excitement over the visual feast spread before me. I didn't understand my lack of enthusiasm for a city that has never failed to inspire and invigorate me. Then it hit me: crazy as it might sound, I'd rather be walking in the slums of Nairobi or Manila or Calcutta.

After spending so much time in the slums of so many impoverished cities, I was able to see below the surface of the glamour and style of Rome. I also saw clearly the huge gap between the "haves" and the "have nots." The slums showed me the true face of humanity; Rome showed me the masks that cover our humanity. In the slums, I saw real life, laced with struggles and simple pleasures and extraordinary acts of kindness; in the slums, I felt the love and mercy of God. In their poverty I saw my poverty. In their need I saw my abundance. The poor showed me the beauty of simplicity and the power of love. They showed me what real courage and determination was.

In Rome, I saw how truly superficial life can be, people hurrying from here to there in hot pursuit of money, power, sex, fame, glamour, and personal gratification; store after store enticing you with things you really don't need in order to deaden the pain you are hardly aware exists because you are so busy. Cell phones, short skirts, silk ties, gold jewelry, diamond rings, leather purses, antique furniture, luxury cars, fine wines, gourmet delicacies . . . so many goodies on display, creating so many desires, so much anxiety. Life is blur, a merry-go-round of sights and sounds. I'll take the harsh reality of the slums.

Note: As I read those words on June 17, 2022, as the sun rose in Haiti, I wished I could be whisked off to Rome for just a week of indulging in gelato and pizza in between visits to a dizzying array of art-filled churches.

A Mountain of Garbage

July 11, 2000, Rome: Today's paper brought news of a tragedy in a faraway place that struck home for me. Yesterday, in the Philippines, on the outskirts of Manila, the city's largest garbage dump, which is literally a mountain, collapsed, killing at least seventy-one squatters who lived off the refuge of others. This place is difficult to imagine, difficult to picture, difficult to describe or comprehend or explain. In January of this year, I visited the Philippines to take pictures for my photo/essay book on poverty. I was there for ten days and was deeply troubled by what I saw. But in the darkness of despair, I was also inspired by the heroic work being done by the Salesians, Vincentians, and Franciscans who were walking hand in- hand with the poor, giving selflessly of themselves so others may experience the gentle embrace of God's love and mercy.

One evening I walked the mean streets of metro Manila with the Salesians, a religious order of priests and brothers founded by Saint John Bosco, as they ministered to the army of over 70,000 street kids whose pitiful lives have reduced them to roving packs of animals, living off the spoils of the streets, defecating in public, and sniffing glue to temporarily snuff out the pain of their lives. These kids know only rejection and violence. Love has no meaning. Survival is their only game. They huddle in dark corners of parks. They sleep behind bushes or in vacant lots and abandoned buildings. A bath is a luxury beyond their wildest imagination. They have lost all social skills; they are wild animals, fearing any kind of structure or discipline. These are lost lives.

Yet the Salesians can see past the filth, past the erratic and antisocial behavior, and see a child of God. They spend endless months trying to establish a relationship with the street kids, trying to build a bridge of trust between them. Night after night, they walk the streets, engaging the kids in conversation in hopes that eventually one will come home with them. "Home" is a shelter and school that offers them the chance to rebuild their young lives. They are given a shower, clean clothes, and a warm bed. And lots of love and understanding. Once a kid has begun to wean himself from the lure of the streets, with its freedom and excitement, they offer them an education, a chance to learn to read and write, and learn a practical trade, such as automotive repair.

The Franciscans took me on a tour of the slums, which took my breath away. Squatters living in tiny cardboard and wooden homes built alongside train tracks. Every week, a passing train hits some old person or some kid, maiming or killing them. I was shocked by the sight of so many naked kids being bathed in the streets and gutters because they live in "homes" that have no running water. I saw an encampment of families living under an overpass; they used draining water from the road above for cooking, washing dishes and clothes, and bathing. One massive slum, known as the Tondo, was located near the water's edge. It was a dark, dismal netherworld of makeshift homes built with pieces of scrap wood and metal. The muddied alleys formed a twisting labyrinth, strewn with rotting garbage. The stench from the open sewers was sickening.

The Payatas, January 2000; *Photo by Gerry Straub*

As bad as all of this was, it was in fact not as bad as what I had seen in India. Or so I thought until I visited the garbage dump in Payatas, the same dump that is in the news today. There I met a young Vincentian priest who would have made the Order's founder, Saint Vincent de Paul, proud. Thomas Merton once said that serving the needs of others is to do God's will. This young priest was definitely doing God's will; he was serving the needs of the poorest of the poor, scavengers who live off the waste of society. The priest showed me the dump, which is so massive it forms a "mountain" more than fifty feet high . . . over seven stories. The dump covers seventy-four acres. It is the main dump for the 10,000 tons of garbage produced in Manila every day.

What follows is the short reflection I wrote on January 14, 2000, on the flight home from the Philippines on the day after my experience at the garbage dump. The images of what I had seen were still haunting me . . . and they still are.

I'll Cry Tonight

It was the saddest, most inhumane place I have ever seen. What I saw, smelled, and felt was beyond imagination. The place is known as "Payatas." It is a giant garbage dump located on the outskirts of metropolitan Manila in the Philippines. Actually, Payatas is a mountain of garbage, stretching high into the sky. And the mountain is home to 75,000 people who live in and off the dump. The people of Payatas earn their living scavenging through the waste of others. Entire families, including children as young as four years old, spend long hours picking through the garbage, searching for scraps of recyclable and reusable material they can salvage and sell for a few pennies. For most of them, this is the only life they know: a garbage dump. Scavenging is an arduous and hazardous life. Disease, such as tuberculosis, is rampant. Many of the children are disabled; most suffer from malnutrition. Their tiny bodies are infested with intestinal worms and covered with wounds received from sharp objects hidden in the garbage.

All day long, day in and day out, a relentless chain of garbage trucks slowly made their way up the muddy road to the peak. As the trucks dump the garbage, people are anxiously waiting the chance to find something of worth, some discarded treasure in the garbage. The competition is fierce; fighting over the rubbish is common. Old women, young kids, stooped over feverishly using metal hooks to shift through the stinking, rotting debris. At the base of the mountain is a camp, a hellish hamlet of shacks where the garbage-pickers live. The place is a nightmare, a blight on society.

The Payatas scavengers are the lowliest of the urban poor. They truly are our anawim, the Old Testament term for the poorest of the poor, those completely overwhelmed by want, without voice or rights in their surrounding community. Scripture makes it abundantly clear that to forget the anawim is to forget God. Jesus made care for the anawim a litmus test for our love of God.

After spending so much time in the horrific slums of India and the Philippines, I thought nothing could shock me. But nothing could prepare a person for the horror of Payatas. After snapping a few rolls of film, I paused while reloading the camera. I turned to the Franciscan friar accompanying me and said, "I'll cry tonight." I kept taking pictures until I ran out of film and daylight. As I descended the mountain, my shoes and clothes muddied from the filth, I felt myself becoming sick from the smell. And from the reality that people are forced to live like this, like wild animals picking at the corpse of obsessive consumerism. The dreadful images I captured during my time in Manila's oldest and largest open pit dumpsite still haunt me. I pray I do not forget the people of Payatas or forget that I am part of the reason they are forced to live on a mountain of garbage.

Every day, the poor trek up the mountain to forage for used plastic containers, cardboard boxes, copper wire, aluminum, bottles, bits and pieces of machinery, broken toys, and appliances to sell to junk shops. It is raw capitalism. Some young boys actually leap onto the dump trucks as they make their way up the mountain so they can get first crack at the "gold"—perhaps a discarded watch—in the garbage. Most scavengers are poor farmers who moved to the city for survival. It is hard to imagine that life for the people of the Payatas garbage dump could get any worse.

The Philippines, 2000; *Photo by Gerry Straub*

But yesterday it did . . . with a deadly vengeance. For days the area had been pounded by wind and rain from typhoon Kai-tak. The mountain of garbage became loosened by the heavy rain, and it collapsed and burst into flames. An avalanche of mud and garbage poured down on the people. The thundering, tumbling debris flattened 100 of the squatters' shanties, crushing more than seventy people to death. Many of the dead were children. After the collapse, rescue workers and fire trucks could not reach the area because they could not get down the narrow, crowded alleys leading to the dump. Hoses had to be pulled from the main road, many blocks away. It took several hours to extinguish the blaze, which had been caused by toppled kerosene lanterns and stoves inside the homes and a live electrical cable that snapped and ignited trash and trapped methane gas. The rescuers removed the body of a young mother who was still clutching her infant son to her breast with both arms as though trying to shield him from harm. Terrified voices could be heard screaming from beneath the pile of debris. At least a hundred people were still missing and feared dead.

As I read the accounts of the disaster, memories of the place washed over me. Having been there, seen the people, I felt connected to their nightmare. Sadly, we have become disconnected from the poor . . . and have lost the chance to open our hearts to them, lost the chance to experience the grace of giving our lives to them.

> *"There is no charity without justice. Too often we think of charity as a kind of moral luxury, as something which we choose to practice, and which gives us merit in God's sight, at the same time satisfying a certain interior need to 'do good.' Such charity is immature and even in cases completely unreal. True charity is love, and love implies deep concern for the needs of another. It is not a moral self-indulgence, but a strict obligation. I am obliged by the law of Christ and of the Spirit to be concerned with my brother's need, above all with his greatest need, the need for love."*
>
> —THOMAS MERTON, LIFE AND HOLINESS[189]

A Piece of Broken Bread

> *The vision and message of Christ*
> *transcends geography, culture, and status—*
> *and even time . . . it includes everyone, everywhere,*
> *always and forever more.*

God hides in a piece of broken bread and in the broken life of a slum-dweller. The life of Christ makes it clear that God chooses humility over majesty, that infinity dwells in the finite. Jesus embraced simplicity, poverty, and humility. What do we embrace?

While God's love embraces all people, God has clearly demonstrated deep concern for the poor and the needy, the helpless and the oppressed. God demands that we side with the poor, the powerless and victims of injustice. To walk with the poor is to be in harmony with the will of God. Justice requires that all people have a place to sleep, enough food to eat, and work that makes them feel worthwhile.

The crucified and transfigured Christ's lesson of love compels us to judge no one, to exclude no one; moreover, it requires us to help others to carry their cross, fully sharing in their pain and suffering. The incarnation of Christ epitomizes God's passion for the poor and the disinherited.

In *Letters from the Desert*, Carlo Carretto said: "The Eucharist is the silence of God, the weakness of God."[190]

> *O sweet Lord*
> *I want so very much*
> *to avoid the bitter cross*
> *You ask me to carry,*
> *the cross of putting aside*
> *everything that is outside*
> *the realm of Your love.*
> *Actually, nothing is outside*
> *the realm of Your love,*
> *because You so long for us,*
> *so thirst for us,*
> *that You follow us*
> *into the darkest corners*
> *of our lives*
> *looking to embrace us*
> *with Your mercy and compassion.*
> *Yet I so often*
> *want to embrace things*
> *that You find*
> *unhealthy and unfitting*
> *for a seeker of God.*
> *O Lord help me see, feel and know*
> *that outside of You*
> *there is nothing of any worth,*
> *and that with You*
> *all is priceless.*
> *Help me nail to the cross*
> *the secret things in my heart*
> *that I must sacrifice*
> *in order to follow You*
> *more closely*
> *and love You*
> *more dearly.*

PART THREE

Lessons Learned along Poverty Road

Uganda, 2009; *Photo by Gerry Straub*

CHAPTER 27

The Harvest of the Soul

The Mysticism of Everyday Life

We live in a constant state of genesis, always changing, always evolving, always being born anew. Today we begin again. This very moment is pregnant with new possibilities for growing in God, with God, through God. Today is a new creation.

Each day brings its share of sweetness and bitterness, of joy and misery, of comfort and pain, of laughter and tears, of hopes and disappointments. Each day brings rejection and acceptance, loneliness and communion. Each day brings moments of fear and despair and courage and delight. Each day brings a flood of words and a desert of silence. Each day we have moments of transparency and deception, moments of faithfulness and infidelity, moments of strength and weakness, moments of purity and lust, moments of beauty and cruelty, moments of abundance and famine, moments of peace and turmoil.

Each day God is present in all these things, in all the ups and downs, in the heartache and elation, in the victories and the defeats. But God's presence is veiled and silent. It's only through faith we can see and hear God, even though our seeing and hearing are gravely impaired and far from perfect. We really don't know God, yet we do know God. In our not knowing is the beginning of our knowing. But the fullness of knowing will always be beyond us yet hidden within us.

To see God in all things each day is the mysticism of everyday life, the ordinary mysticism that sees the extraordinary work of God even in mundane events. With everyday mystical eyes we are able to see God in both the cries of the poor and the laughter of a child, in both a tender kiss and in a deadly disease.

In a Fog

There is nothing so steady and relentless, so committed and enduring, so firm and unwavering as God's love for us. Over and over again, in story after story, Jesus tells us that the defining characteristic of God is not anger but love. Yet we stumble around in a fog of misplaced guilt and wrong attachments. As children of God, we are called to be people of love, people who accept God's love and people who transmit God's love.

In his Gospel, Luke depicts Jesus as one who "hears" and "does." I wish my kids heard what I said and did what I asked them to do. Just as Jesus did, his followers need to live in the presence of God and then express this presence to others.

> *"Is our solidarity with the poorest and most abandoned (above and beyond anything we do for them) is a convincing witness to genuine freedom, overcoming of ethnic exclusion and nationalism, and a refusal to get sucked into the consumerism which surrounds us?"*
>
> —Giacomo Bini, OFM Former Minister General of the Order of Friars Minor

Giotto fresco of Saint Francis in prayer before the San Damiano crucifix

A Gift of Love

The end of isolation is found in prayer. Through prayer, we become aware that God is present. Through prayer, we become at home with the living presence with whom we can share everything. In the presence of God, we become aware of our complete dependence on the Creator. Prayer fosters within us a spirit of humility and the realization we cannot truly live without God.

Prayer is a gift of Love, and a means of living our whole life as a communion with the Lord, who through the Incarnation came to share in our human condition. As we encounter God in the depths of ourselves, we are no longer astonished by the darkness of God's mystery, but we merely accept it, living by faith. We no longer belong to ourselves but to Love, the giver of the gift. When we enter fully in the presence, we experience spontaneous joy . . . even during trials, hardships, and suffering. Even when we are weak, empty, and hurting, we know the Lord is present. Trusting in this presence we are compelled to accept everything as coming from God.

> *"The gift of prayer is inseparable from another grace:*
> *that of humility, which makes us realize that the very depths*
> *of our being and life are meaningful and real only in so far as*
> *they are oriented toward God as their source and their end."*
>
> —THOMAS MERTON, CONTEMPLATIVE PRAYER[191]

Contemplation and Action

> *"No one can be sent by Jesus to heal the world who has not first*
> *been called out of the world by Jesus to his side in solitude."*
>
> —ERASMO LEIVA-MERIKAKIS

Saint Francis of Assisi spent roughly half of his time in prayer and deep contemplation, often in far-off, remote mountaintop hermitages. It was during this time that the Lord spoke to him in the depths of his heart and he came to understand what course of action the Lord was asking him to undertake. The saint's quiet time gave direction to his outward ministry and gave him the strength and courage to complete it.

Christ certainly desires that those who follow him spend time in prayer, apart from the roar of the crowd in the silence of their most private space, communicating with the Father. But Christ also requires his followers to feed the hungry, to shelter the homeless, to visit the sick and imprisoned, to extend a helping hand to the poor, to embrace the leper. In fact, from Christ's perspective, how we care for the poor is the only authentic indicator of how much we love God. Both the New and the Old Testament reveal God's preferential love for those the world ignores and rejects. The essence of Christ's message is: make every stranger, no matter how poor or dirty, no matter how weak or unlovable, your neighbor.

Prayer and compassion are the wings of Christian life. Prayer prompts us to reach out in compassion to the suffering and weak, and helps us embrace all of humanity. In prayer, we learn what to do, how to respond to the poor, the persecuted and the suffering. And it's prayer that sustains and guides what we do for them. Action is as important as prayer; each of us must take responsibility for meeting the world's need, for we are the accomplices of evil if we do nothing to prevent it.

My time with the poor taught me a valuable lesson: we are all beggars. None of us is sufficient unto herself or himself. All of us are plagued by unending doubts and restless, unsatisfied hearts. By ourselves, we are incomplete. Our needs are always beyond our capacities; we only find ourselves when we lose ourselves. Prayer and contemplation free us from self-serving and prepare us to lead a life of service to others without unconsciously desiring our own success.

We live in a world of stark inequality and injustice. So did Jesus. Jesus had a deep concern for those who suffered and were marginalized. So should we. For the follower of Jesus, compassion is not an option; it's an obligation . . . and a sign our lives have been transformed into the healing presence of Christ.

CHAPTER 28

Gospel Values

Baby Steps

The Gospel presents us with profound social, economic, and political challenges. Issues of global poverty and hunger, corporate corruption, racism, and national policies of war and nuclear arms are Gospel concerns. The Gospel demands a response from us, which can be boiled down to three simple and clear things that we, as the body of Christ, cannot tolerate in our private and public lives: hunger, cheating, and violence. Moreover, we are compelled to treat all with dignity and equality, constantly on alert to extend mercy and compassion to all who are hurting.

The Gospel values of mercy, compassion, and love can be found in the core beliefs of all faiths. They are universal human values, and it is those virtues that can unite us as a human family and help us see and know that the chronically poor around the world are our brothers and sisters, and we must stand with them in fraternity and solidarity. We can begin to do this by taking at least baby steps toward defying political polarization, consumerism, and militarism and putting our full trust in God's abundance, mercy, and love.

State of Alert Stillness

Without solitude and silence, I easily lose my self. And God. Silence gives me space for receptivity; it allows me to hear the speechless language of God and to respond with my heart. Silence produces an inner restfulness that helps the soul to soar. The greatest malady of our time is the absence of stillness and silence. To become more and more silent, to enter deeply into creative silence, takes courage. The wordless is foreign to us. Yet God transcends language and intellect. Listen . . . don't think. Deep silence is profoundly liberating.

Prayerful silence is more than a lack of words; it is a state of alert stillness. The point is not to rest, but to concentrate and focus the heart and mind on God. Beneath the appearance of passivity is an active state of attentiveness. In deep silence, we are fully awake, fully open and one with God.

To enter the silence of meditation is to enter our own poverty as we renounce words and images, as we renounce thoughts and imagination, as we renounce our concepts and intellect and we sit alert, waiting to hear from God . . . even if we must wait a lifetime.

The Radiant Presence

To feel the Spirit, to feel the Radiant Presence, you need consistent, daily time for meditation, time to sit in stillness and silence. Yesterday, we had no internet service for more than eight hours. Without the internet, I had no access to my e-mail or to news reports. Without periods when we are disconnected from the noise of our lives, we will not have access to the divine spark that creates new life.

In Haiti, I've learned that during every day, in every moment, I must let go of what is inessential or an illusion so that I can be faithful to what is essential. That is the only way I can live a devoted life. The pandemic gave us a chance to be brutally honest with ourselves, to listen to the searing truth about the way we live.

Unchecked Human Exploitation

History teaches us that pandemics change the world. Covid-19 had a dramatic global impact. Seán McDonald, who is a Columban priest who works to raise awareness of the connection between justice and peace issues, environmental sustainability, and theology, wrote in the June 27, 2020, issue of *The Tablet*:

> People are shocked and traumatized by the pain and death of loved ones and the economic chaos that Covid-19 is causing. But the connection between the destruction of the natural world—which, in little more than two decades, has given us Covid-19, SARS, MERS, Ebola, HIV, Zika, and H1N1—and the pandemic, is often neglected. Large-scale deforestation, habitat degradation, intensive agriculture, illegal wildlife trade and climate change have all contributed to biodiversity loss and will make the rise of new pandemics more likely.
>
> For a long time, we have known that viruses and pathogens have leapt from other species to the human population. The destruction of biodiversity means that this happens more frequently now than in the past; worst still, unless we address the loss of biodiversity, pandemics will happen at an even greater rate in the future.

In discussing Covid-19 in an interview for *The Tablet*, Pope Francis mentioned the Spanish phrase, "God always forgives, we forgive but, sometimes, nature never forgives."

Everything is connected. Seán McDonald writes: " . . . the 'common home' humankind shares with the whole of creation faces a single and complex socio-environmental crisis, and requires a true ecological conversion."

What we do to the natural world will have consequences. We must change our ways of relating to the natural world.

*"Living our vocation to be protectors of God's handiwork
is essential to a life of virtue; it is not an optional or
secondary aspect of our Christian experience."*

—Pope Francis, *Laudato Si'*

A Broken Home

Each day we grow more disconnected from the earth. The ecological crisis we are experiencing is self-created. We have thoughtlessly and ruthlessly plumaged the planet we share, our common home. Carbon reduction and loss of biodiversity threaten us all, with the poor being hit the hardest. Greed and exploitation have the upper hand thanks to social media pumping out rivers of false stories and a steady diet of misinformation and baseless conspiracy theories. Elections in America are joining a host of endangered species. Lies are repeated ad nauseum until they become the truth while we are struggling to pay for the gas we need to get to work.

We are not separate beings. We are a diverse, multilayered family sharing a broken home. We need to downsize. Quickly. We can live and even thrive on much less.

*"The artificial separation between humans and cosmos is
at the root of our contemporary moral confusion."*

—Teilhard de Chardin[192]

One Central Point

Love is not something God does. Love is what God is. God showers love on each of us. The Gospels agree on one central point: Jesus calls us to love. Christ consistently dismantles the walls that divide us from each other. His love shimmers with words of affirmation, words of kindness. His love calls us into a life of service and sharing.

We more readily embrace war, embrace works of death, than we do peace, works of life. Why? Because the Gospel has not become flesh within us. We have not incarnated God's word. We trust in the ways of the world, not in the ways of the Word.

*"God who is infinitely rich became man in order to experience
the poverty and misery of fallen man, not because He needed this
experience but because we needed His example. Now that we have
seen His love, let us love one another as He loved us. Thus His
love will work in our hearts and transform us into Himself."*

—Thomas Merton, *No Man Is an Island*[193]

My Heart's Desire

What is my heart's desire? It seems to desire so many things, some good, some bad. How do I know the difference between a desire that is good and one that is bad? Maybe I should not think in terms of good and bad, but in terms of healthy and unhealthy. If the desire is self-centered, then it is unhealthy, because it deflects me from the self-emptying love that is the one and only path to God.

Sin is a failure to love; sin is wanting my own way instead of God's way. God's way is paved with humility. God gives God away.

A good and healthy desire is one that longs for God. When I desire God more than anything else, all my other desires will bow to that one true, most noble desire: a desire for God and God alone. A desire for God is nurtured in stillness and silence.

Note: Early in the morning of May 6, 2020, I read that passage just moments before sunrise in Haiti. My heart was cluttered with unhealthy desires. It was my sixty-eighth consecutive day in Haiti, courtesy of the travel restrictions imposed by the pandemic, which had by that date taken over 70,000 American lives. I was exhausted from the daily chaos and stress, going from one crisis to another. The kids and staff were getting on my nerves. I missed daily Mass at the Missionaries of Charity; there was no priest available. My office was beginning to feel like a prison. It was crystal clear to me that Santa Chiara would run out of funding by the end of July. I was tormented by the fact that before then I would have to move at least a dozen children to other homes; I would also have to furlough at least twenty members of the staff. The staff knew the situation was bleak, and they were very worried about losing their jobs. They barely survive on the meager salaries I'm able to give them. But they are fed each day, and they know that if they get sick, I'll cover their medical expenses. Our little compound is a safe haven for them.

In the face of all the woes and worries, instead of going deeper into prayer, I found myself wishing I was anywhere other than Haiti. I daydreamed about a simple life of retirement in Florida, envisioning visiting my eighty-two-year-old sister and her husband in Upstate New York. I also dreamed of visiting my daughter and three grandchildren in Arizona; I had not seen them in at least four years. Yet I knew deep down I could not abandon my kids in Haiti.

In short, I was in a state of confusion. My heart was empty and broken. The desires of my heart were conflicted. I didn't know what I wanted or what I didn't want. Yet, a child's smile or a child crying would temporarily erase the doubts.

Jesus, have mercy on me a sinner. I am spinning out of control.
Embrace me. Console me. Guide me.
Please, I beg you, let me feel your tender love, your firm hand of support.

Just over two years and a month later, on June 17, 2022, just before eight o'clock in the morning, I stood alone on the back porch of the second floor and watched the kids running around the yard below, screaming, playing, and having fun, and I felt a deep sense of peace, even though the situation in Haiti had grown more grave and hopeless. It was a new day . . . and the only day that mattered. The above prayer had been answered.

Loving Service

It is in stillness that we find our emptiness, the emptiness that can only be filled by welcoming God into our hearts. In the state of emptiness, we are better able to encounter the fullness of God. In stillness, we learn that no one is self-sufficient. We need others and the Other. Only when I am vulnerable is it possible for me to be broken and restored to the image of God. Leonardo Boff, the Brazilian theologian and author, said, "The roots of sanctity are planted in the depths of human frailty."[194]

Jesus came to liberate not oppress. Can I do anything other than what he did? Am I a sacrament of salvation for my neighbor? Christ's message can be reduced to this: make every stranger, no matter how poor or dirty, no matter how weak or unlovable, your neighbor. Tough message. Even tougher is the fact that Christ does not want you to defeat your enemies; he asks you to pray for them.

Grace is God's way of talking to us. We can best experience grace and therefore hear God more clearly when we stop living for ourselves and instead give ourselves in loving service to others.

It is easier to be self-centered than to be patient and loving.

Prayer stimulates a mindfulness of God, which in turn stimulates acts of love and mercy. Love is service. It is the emptying of self. It is losing in order to find. Acknowledging my own weakness increases my ability to be more merciful toward others. The Christian life can be reduced to this: live the beatitudes.

Note: *As I reviewed the manuscript for this book in late June 2022, I felt the entire book up to this point was a prelude to the last two parts . . . my diaries written in Merton's hermitage and my daily journals from Haiti. They are unfiltered, raw, breezy, sometimes funny, and yet really deep and confessional.*

"If we do not labor to overcome our natural weakness, our disordered and selfish passions, what belongs to God in us will be withdrawn from the sanctifying power of his love and will be corrupted by selfishness, blinded by irrational desire, hardened by pride, and will eventually plunge in the abyss of moral nonentity which is called sin. Sin is the refusal of spiritual life, the rejection of the inner order and peace that come from our union with the divine will. In a word, sin is the refusal of God's will and his love. It is not only a refusal to 'do' this or that thing willed by God, or a determination to do what he forbids. It is more radically a refusal to be what we are, a rejection of our mysterious, contingent, spiritual reality hidden in the very mystery of God. Sin is our refusal to be what we were created to be-- sons of God, images of God. Ultimately sin, while seeming to be an assertion of freedom, is a flight from freedom and the responsibility of divine sonship."

—Thomas Merton, *Life and Holiness*[195]

PART FOUR

Louie's Place

Interior of Merton's Hermitage, 2000; *Photo by Gerry Straub*

CHAPTER 29

Alone in the Woods

Merton's Table

Monday, August 28, 2000, 2:40 pm, North Hollywood. Great news: just received a letter from Brother Patrick Hart, informing me that the Abbot has approved my request to stay in Merton's hermitage for a week. I'll enter the hermitage on Sunday, December 3rd and will leave it on Sunday, December 10th.

Seven days, alone, in the woods, praying, and writing on the very table on which Thomas Merton wrote some of his masterpieces. The days will be long and quiet. The nights will be cold, dark, and lonely.

The Opened Doors

On Thursday, November 31, 2000, I traveled to Louisville, Kentucky. Early the next morning, Jonathan drove me to Gethsemani Abbey. I spent Friday and Saturday night in the monastery. On Sunday, because of the snow, I was driven to the hermitage in a small maintenance cart at noon.

Very early one morning before leaving for Kentucky, I sat in my library in California with a candle burning and a CD of chanting monks playing. I marveled at all the doors that had opened for me since that moment in the empty church in Rome where the reality of God broke through for a fleeting, furtive second. The opened doors allowed me to enter into the gritty world of some of the worst slums on earth as well as enter into the inner sanctum of some of the most sacred places on earth. In all these desperate and holy places, I learned about the struggle for physical survival and the struggle for spiritual growth. I learned that in my loneliness and longing I am not alone, that I am truly united with all of creation.

> *"February 24, 1965. Everything about this hermitage fills me with joy. There are lots of things that could have been far more perfect in way or the other—aesthetically or "domestically." But it is the place God has given me after so much prayer and longing—but without my deserving it. It is a delight. I can imagine no other joy on earth*

than to have such a place and to be at peace in it, to live in silence, to
think and write, to listen to the wind and to all the voices of the wood,
to live in the shadow of the big cedar cross, to prepare for my death
and my exodus to the heavenly country, to love my brothers and all
people, to pray for the whole world and for peace and good sense among
men. So it is "my place" in the scheme of things. That is sufficient."

—THOMAS MERTON, *THE INTIMATE MERTON*[196]

In her book *Thomas Merton: When the Trees Say Nothing, Writings on Nature*, Kathleen Deignan writes:

> Thomas Merton spent his whole monastic life listening for that secret pulsating in the heartbeat of creation, and wedded the forest so he could listen with absolute rapture and commitment as one would listen to a spouse, "for better, for worse, in sickness and in health, until death . . ." What he heard in the murmurings of the wilderness were "the sweet songs of living things" whose choirs he joined as a solitary monk offering a psalm of glory and thanksgiving on behalf of humankind.[197]

Eating in Silence

My stay at Gethsemani in December of 2000 was my third visit there that year. The first trip was a simple visit in May for a few hours, during which I had been given permission to photograph Merton's hermitage on a Sunday afternoon. In August of 2000, I spent four days doing research at the Merton Center at Bellermine University in Louisville. Before returning to Los Angeles, I spent the weekend at Gethsemani, spending two nights in the monastery. During the brief stay, I jotted down a few observations, all having to do with silence.

Prophets and Pudding

August 11, 2000, 6:25 pm, Gethsemani Abbey. Silence is observed in most areas of the monastery. Even in the dining hall, where I'm now sitting. I was near the end of a long line of retreatants filing past the buffet serving table. The guest house has thirty-one rooms, and all are occupied. Mostly women. As we picked up the plates and served ourselves, not a word was spoken. Dinner consisted of a grilled cheese sandwich, salad, and soup. And pudding for dessert.

Each table has a small sign on it saying: *Silence is spoken here.*

It seemed odd, unnatural. I wanted to speak. I recalled the raucous meals during the pilgrimage to Assisi. The sound of all our chattering was deafening. Back then, I often wished we could have eaten in silence. Tonight, I wished I could speak. I'm curious about all these "silent" people. Especially a guy who looks as if he is in his early sixties and who has a long—very long—beard . . . gray, untrimmed, wild. He looks like an Old Testament prophet. Or a Capuchin friar from the bone church in Rome. At a nearby table, a young woman in her early twenties silently eats her meal. Who are they? Why are they here? I could be eating with an angel. The pudding is good.

Communication seems essential to our nature—this silent world is hard. I miss the sound of my own voice. I notice people communicating through simple gestures.

"It is not speaking that breaks our silence, but the anxiety to be heard."

—THOMAS MERTON, *THOUGHTS IN SOLITUDE*[198]

At the foot of the Cross
words sink into silence
as I look up and ask,
for the love of God,
if I am ready
to follow Christ.

A Secret Message

Silent chairs. Silent tables.
Noisy forks. Noisy plates.
Perhaps someone is tapping out
a secret message in Morse code:
Do you know if
the Yankees won?

"We fill our lives with noise, from television to radio to stereo and
compact disc. Our culture says noise is necessary. We prefer noise because
it dulls our innate loneliness. We are uncomfortable with silence. Yet
only by cultivating silence daily do we begin to accept its many gifts."

—JOHN DEAR, *LIVING PEACE*[199]

Deadly Silence

Friday, August 11, 2000, 6:50 pm, Gethsemani Abbey. The silence is killing me. I think I'll call my sister. The "silence" silences small talk. But not the noise within.

> *"Simplicity clears away all the inessentials of existence and makes a life of genuine depth and meaning possible. When we remove the clutter from our lives, we become inwardly free to give ourselves to the mystical journey, to seek union and communion with the ultimate mystery. Simplicity of life allows us to become single-minded about the inner experience, and not waste our precious time and energy on useless efforts that only distract us."*
>
> —WAYNE TEASDALE, THE MYSTIC HEART[200]

Note: *All of that was just during a weekend . . . and the silence was unbearable. Now I was facing a week of silence and solitude inside Merton's hermitage. I hope I make it.*

CHAPTER 30

Hermitage Diaries

Paradise Is All Around Us

Friday, December 1, 2000, at 10:00 am, Trappist, Kentucky. Jonathan and I left for Gethsemani Abbey shortly before 7:00 am. Within minutes, dawn began to break through the winter darkness. The trees along the highway were all bare. The beautiful, bucolic rolling hills and farms of Kentucky delighted my sleepy eyes. The beauty of the sunrise illuminated the mystery of creation. Merton said sunrise was "the most wonderful moment of the day . . . when creation in its innocence asks permission to 'be' once again, as it did on the first morning that ever was." He went on to say: "Here is the unspeakable secret: paradise is all around us and we do not understand it."[201]

We arrived at the monastery shortly after 8:00 am. The monk at the front desk wasn't prepared for my arrival and couldn't find my name on any guest list. He made a call to someone and part of his comments made me smile: "There is a guy here who says he will be staying in Louie's Place." *Louie's Place* . . . the phrase rang with warmth and affection. Yes, I would be going to Louie's Place. Wow. (Louis was Merton's monastic name.)

Before Jonathan returned to Louisville, we had hot bowl of oatmeal and a cup of coffee in the dining hall. By 9:30 am, I was in Room 211, unpacking my bags.

Killing Birds and Eating Lunch

Friday, December 1, 2000, at 1:35 pm, Gethsemani Abbey. A few minutes before noon, Brother Patrick Hart knocked on my door. He invited me to join him for lunch in the back dining room where the lay staff eats and where talking is permitted. "This way we can kill two birds with one stone—talk and eat." Lunch consisted of fish, cabbage, and potatoes, with cream of corn soup. Brother Patrick told me he was editing the exchange of letters between Merton and Jean Leclercq, a Benedictine monk of the Abbey of St. Maur and St. Muarice in Clervaux, Luxembourg, and who is a monastic scholar and a professor at the Pontifical Gregorian University; the book will be published by Farrar, Strauss and Giroux.

Lunch and the conversation were delightful. We spoke about Murray Bodo, my book on St. Francis, my photo/essay book on poverty, and, most of all, this book (*Two Monks*), which seems to really intrigue the monk. He said that next weekend, Harold Talbott, a renowned American Buddhist who accompanied Merton on his final journey to Asia, would be at Gethsemani to give a talk to the monks on the eve of the anniversary of Merton's death. The event, closed to the public, will be held in the Chapter room in the monastery, and Brother Patrick invited me to attend. We also talked about my time at Christ in the Desert (a Benedictine monastery in New Mexico). Brother Patrick said that he would love to go there next year to celebrate his fiftieth year as a monk.

He said that guests who stay in the hermitage occasionally have a hard time with the solitude. He didn't think I would have any trouble, but he gave me a few words of advice. He also told me not to come to Mass; it is too early and too dark. "Stay in the solitude. Be still." However, he did recommend I come up to the monastery at least every other day for a good warm meal at noon.

Eating with Brother Patrick, whom I really like, and talking about the hermitage has heightened my sense of anticipation. Sunday cannot come quickly enough.

Can't Wait

Friday, December 1, 2000, at 6:20 pm, Gethsemani Abbey. Darkness came quickly, engulfing the monastery grounds during vespers. Evening meal: grilled cheese sandwich and soup. Eaten in silence. My only thought: I can't wait to get into Merton's hermitage.

An Open Ear

Saturday, December 2, 2000, at 6:10 am, Gethsemani Abbey. From lauds:

> *You do not ask for sacrifice and offerings.*
> *But an open ear.*
> *You do not ask for holocaust and victim.*
> *Instead, here am I.*

That, I suppose, is the theme for the week.

Moving Day

Sunday, December 3, 2000, at 9:15 am, Gethsemani Abbey. Today is the first day of Advent. A fitting day for me to enter the expectant silence of Thomas Merton's hermitage, which I'll be doing this afternoon. Brother Robert just knocked on my door. He is the monk assigned to take me to the hermitage. It snowed most of the night, and Brother Robert said the path to the hermitage is covered with a few inches of snow. He is going to take me in a pickup truck at 3:00 pm. He will have some food provisions for the week for me. When we get there, he'll check to insure there is sufficient drinking water and firewood. He said if I need anything else, he'd drive me to the little town of New Haven where there are stores in which I can pick up additional supplies. I'm getting very excited.

I went out after breakfast and did some photography. The dark, naked trees against the snow-covered rolling hills made the wintry landscape look like a Zen painting or line drawing. Simple, stark lines of graceful poetry on a white canvas. The little angel below my window has about two inches of snow on her head. The temperature is a chilly 31 degrees. The air has a hushed stillness to it.

Note: A year later, those photographs ended up in my film on silence and solitude, Holy Pictures.

The Real Deal

Sunday, December 3, 2000, at 9:50 am. Another knock on the door. It was Brother Patrick. He had the key to the hermitage—and some words of advice on living in solitude. Bursting with enthusiasm for my book (*Walking with Two Monks*), I showed him some of the text and how it was laid out. He said using the stuff of my life, like my sister's illness and my struggles with sin, was wonderful.

Brother Patrick went on to say Merton hated wasting time with cooking. I told him I didn't cook, plus I was very impractical. He reminded me to come up to the monastery at least every other day for a good meal at noon. As he sat in the chair in front of my window, the sun broke through the gray clouds and highlighted his white hair. You can see the joy in his eyes. He is the real deal.

A Flawless Dive

Sunday, December 3, 2000, at 2:40 pm, Gethsemani Abbey. I went to the library to "kill" some time while waiting for my ride to the hermitage. While browsing in some books, I came across a quotation I wanted to jot down in my notebook. After copying it, I got up to put the book back. I'd taken about a step or two, when I noticed my moderately expensive fountain pen rolling off the table. There was nothing I could do to stop it, and so I watched as the nib of the pen hit the floor. When I picked the pen up, the nib was bent backwards, rendering it useless. I'm very upset. I love writing with that pen . . . and I had planned on giving it a real workout during my week in the hermitage.

Louie's Place

Sunday, December 3, 2000, at 4:20 pm, Merton's Hermitage. I'm in. Over my head. A bit daunted by it all. I may be too stupid for this. I couldn't get a fire started. But I managed to fill the room with smoke. Not exactly like incense rising in the temple.

Brother Robert met me at the main entrance of the monastery at a few minutes before three. He was driving a small, diesel-powered cart with fat wheels for traversing the rough, snow-covered terrain. I tossed my bags on the back deck, next to a box of food provisions for the week. We squeezed into the tiny cab and headed off. The cart made a tremendous amount of noise. Still, I managed to tell Robert about my pen. He offered to try to find me another fountain pen; I told him not to bother. In less than ten minutes, we were parked alongside the hermitage porch. I noticed snow on the horizontal beam of the large wooden cross in front of the hermitage.

When we entered the hermitage, it seemed colder inside than it was outside, where the sun had been doing a good job most of the day. The thermostat near the front door indicated it was 48 degrees inside the hermitage. Brother Robert showed me where the two electric heaters were and where the barrel of drinking water was . . . but that was about it for instructions. The box of food he carried into the kitchen contained a dozen eggs, a half-gallon of milk, two loaves of bread (wheat and white), three apples, two onions, two tomatoes, a cantaloupe, a package of cheese (made by the monks), a can of apple juice, two cans of pork and beans, and a half a bottle of olive oil. Even Julia Childs would have a tough time rustling up a meal with those meager rations. He opened the cupboard and pointed out the cans of soup and fruit. I noticed the coffee brewer and coffee. Brother Robert opened the refrigerator, which contained a stick of butter, a jar of peanut butter, and some more eggs. I like eggs.

As the cart rattled its way down the path, I closed the hermitage door—and took a big breath. Now what?

Well, I figured I had better start a fire to chase away the chill. Fifteen minutes later, my hands and jeans were covered with thick, black soot, and I had nothing to show for my puny efforts. Some jerk in California can light a cigarette and toss the match out the window of a moving car and ignite a blaze that consumes thousands of acres, scores of homes, and takes days to extinguish, yet here I am with a box of wooden matches, dried and quartered logs, a box of scrap wood for kindling, and an old newspaper, and all I can manage to do is get myself dirty and fill the room with smoke. It is going to be a long week.

Well, with perseverance—and luck—I managed to get a fire started. I then turned my attention to the wood-burning stove in the far corner of the room. It reminded me of my days in Christ in the Desert. When you entered the church at four in the morning, the monks had all four furnaces fully ablaze, pumping out lots of heat. This should be easy, I thought. Wrong. After another 15 minutes and another layer of soot on my hands and pants, I finally got a fire started. Between the furnace, the fireplace, and the electric space heaters, the temperature in the main room had soared to a balmy 61 degrees. Who is going to keep the fires burning while I'm sleeping? That must be what the coffee is for.

Well, after all of that, plus making a pot of coffee, I'm doing what I'm here to do: sitting at Merton's table. Behind me, the fire is crackling. In front of me, beyond three large windows, a snow-covered meadow encircled by bare trees delights me. Off in the distance,

I can see the top of a small mountain. On the porch, just below my window, are two rows of stacked logs waiting to be consumed by Brother Fire to keep Brother Gerry warm.

I'm now going to put the dumb ballpoint pen down and go into Merton's little chapel and pray. For help. How did Murray Bodo do this?

Note: I love reading that. It lets me laugh at myself. Yet in my bumbling search for God, I see now a genuine seriousness. I couldn't light a fire, yet God had lit a fire in my heart, and I was burning with desire to know the unknowable.

The Sounds of Silence

Sunday, December 3, 2000, at 5:20 pm. This is hard. I can feel the aloneness. The sun is setting. Soon, darkness will embrace aloneness.

The temperature outside is 34 degrees; inside, 64 degrees. I just had two slices of toasted bread. Earlier, I took some photographs, interior and exterior. God, it is quiet. The furnace rumbles a little. The fireplace crackles a little. There is a little hum from the electric heaters. The sounds of silence.

In a little more than two hours, I've learned one thing: prayer is hard. Harder than starting a fire.

Twinkling Lights

Sunday, December 3, 2000, at 5:45 pm. I just made a cup of herbal tea. I turned around one of the big rocking chairs so it faced the front window. I turned out all the lights. I'm going to watch it get dark. On the distant mountain, about halfway up, I can already see a few twinkling lights.

Note: Years later, when I read this snippet from my hermitage diaries, a smile gently crossed my face as I recalled the sweetness of my "hermit" experience, which offered me the possibility of pausing to drink in the arrival of the night. Each day is filled with natural wonders we don't even see, which is why seeing God in everything is so foreign for us. Merton experienced the sacred throughout the natural world. We do not. If we did, we won't be facing an ecological disaster that is looming. We are blindly and thoughtlessly destroying creation.

It Is Dark

Sunday, December 3, 2000, at 6:20 pm. "It is dark. I am alone." Those were the first two sentences my fictional creation (and alter ego) wrote to his daughter, Kate, in my dreadful mess of a novel, *Dear Kate*. I had not thought of those lines in many, many years. When I penned them, the darkness and aloneness were creations of depression . . . and exhaustion from my futile search for God.

Tonight, once again, it is dark and I am alone. But this is different. I've found God. Well, not exactly. God found me . . . and I'm struggling to get to know God. All I know is God does exist. And God, I believe, is calling me to come closer—to stop loving from a distance, a safe distance from which I can still be myself. God says, "Give yourself up. Come to Me."

That is what this week is about. It's not about writing. It's about surrendering. It's about moving closer to God.

It is dark . . . and it is wonderful. I am not alone.

Note: My novel, Dear Kate, was a fumbling literary attempt to discover if there was a deeper meaning to life. Published in 1992, it was a dark, depressing epistolary novel about a man who had become so exhausted from his futile search for God that he elected to kill himself. The 479-page book was an angry scream at the Church. Critics called it a philosophical novel, which meant . . . no one bought it. It sold about 300 copies, fifty of which I purchased. The novel's protagonist is a Hollywood television producer and writer named Christopher Ryan, who said, "I'm going to start wearing one of those living-will dog tags instructing any passerby that if I show any signs of wanting to go church, they have my permission to pull the plug." Today the book stands as a testament that change is possible.

Pork and Beans and Poverty

Sunday, December 3, 2000, at 6:40 pm. I cooked a can of pork and beans for supper. It was accompanied by a slice of buttered bread. The room is nice and warm. As I ate my humble meal in front of the roaring fire, the simplicity of the scene struck me. The first word that entered my head was "poverty." As poor as the simple cinder block building is, as poor as my simple meal is, I am, in fact, dining in luxury in comparison to the impoverished people I've photographed in India and Kenya. I was driven here, handed the key to the house, and given a box of food. I have electricity, hot and cold running water, a toilet, a shower, a refrigerator, a stove, and an ample supply of firewood.

I'm so rich that I fail to see my own poverty. And my need for God.

Welcome to Los Angeles

Sunday, December 3, 2000, at 7:20 pm. The temperature outside has dropped to 28 degrees. Brrr. Inside . . . it is Los Angeles, a pleasant 74 degrees. Perhaps I put too much wood in the furnace.

About three hours ago, I figured I'd be going home on Tuesday because I felt so overwhelmed by the prospect of making it on my own in such primitive conditions.

I just had a brief moment of excitement. The kettle started whistling in the kitchen and, at that exact moment, a log rolled out of the fireplace. After dashing about, calmness has returned.

The Sound of Milk Steaming

Sunday, December 3, 2000, at 8:40 pm. Just said a rosary in Merton's little chapel. The furnace and the fireplace are doing great. I'm kinda proud of myself. It felt good to get them going. It is really dark outside. Can barely see the logs stacked outside the window. Very quiet. I unplugged the electric heaters. I'm sitting at Merton's table reading his books—and praying for insight into his thoughts.

I believe I'm exactly where I should be. Too bad there isn't a Starbucks within walking distance. I miss the sound of milk being steamed for a latte.

Note: Twenty years later, I look at that last paragraph, and I'm struck by the irony of how the first part speaks of contentedness, and the second part speaks of yearning for what I don't have. "Yearning" seems to pull us either forward or backward . . . but at any rate, out of being in the present.

Dancing Flames

Sunday, December 3, 2000, at 9:25 pm. Around 9 pm, I decided I'd go to bed. I put a big fat log in the furnace and turned out all the lights. The golden glow from the fireplace caught my fancy. I sat down in one of the large rockers . . . to enjoy the peaceful quiet and the dancing flames for a few minutes. While sitting in the nearly dark room, I noticed a picture of Merton on the wall near the doorway to the kitchen. It was taken by John Howard Griffin, and it depicts Merton at his table writing; he was wearing a coat—and I know why. As I looked at the picture, I couldn't help but think about Merton's dedication to his vocation as a writer. It must have taken great discipline to turn out so many words and books in this austere and demanding environment . . . and without a computer. He had to do everything himself. Keeping the fire going in the winter is no small feat.

This place is not comfortable. No easy chairs. No easy writing. I'm going to bed because my back is aching from sitting on a wooden chair for so long. But the very severity and austerity of the place freed Merton from trivial distractions and allowed him to keep a very fine focus on his work. And his prayer. That's what he did here: wrote and prayed. Being in his home is telling me something about the man.

I don't think of this place as holy ground—as some do, including a number of writers who have stayed here. Oh, for sure there is an aura of holiness within these walls—by virtue of Merton's life here and also because it has become a house of prayer for those who have been graced with the opportunity to partake of its solitude and silence. Each year, every monk at Gethsemani is given the chance to spend a week in this hermitage. The place is holy because God has visited a lot of people here. I pray for such a visitation myself. Lord, teach me to listen; open the ears to my heart.

As the Sun Rises

Monday, December 4, 2000, at 6:20 am. Woke up a few minutes before six. Temperature outside was 24 degrees; inside it was 56 degrees. There were still some hot embers in the furnace, so it was easy to get a fire started in it. But I had trouble starting a fire in the fireplace. It is still pitch-black outside. Coffee is brewing. I'll be able to say the morning office as the sun rises.

On December 4, 1964, Merton wrote: "In the hermitage I see how quickly one can fall apart. I talk to myself, I dance around, I sing. This is all very well, but it is not serious."[202]

Slowing Down

Monday, December 4, 2000, at 11:00 am. This morning, it suddenly dawned on me that I do everything too fast. I rushed around the hermitage like a cyclone this morning. Almost simultaneously, I started a fire, brewed coffee, said a prayer, made some toast, washed the dishes—it was all a blur. Meanwhile, the first rays of sunlight broke through the darkness without my noticing.

I eat too fast (and subsequently too much because I become stuffed before I realize I've had enough). I do everything too fast, as if I were rushing to a fire. My life seems to be ruled by "what's next" rather than the "now" of the present moment.

Monastic life slows things down. This week, I hope the hermitage teaches me how to slow down, how to do one thing at a time before rushing off to the next task. A moment cannot speak to you when you are racing through it.

> *"Let me seek, then, the gift of silence, and poverty, and*
> *solitude, where everything I touch is turned into prayer:*
> *where the sky is my prayer, the birds are my prayer, the*
> *wind in the trees is my prayer, for God is all in all."*
>
> —THOMAS MERTON, *THOUGHTS IN SOLITUDE*[203]

Note: More than twenty-one years after writing this entry inside Merton's hermitage, I'm spending a week of solitude inside my apartment in Fort Pierce. But I am far from still. During the last five days, I've been too busy to even take a short walk along the ocean. Instead of resting and renewing my body and soul after three weeks of insanity in Haiti, I'm editing this book (which means reliving painful memories) and dealing with pesky administrative chores. Seconds ago, near the end of the last chapter in an entry date May 6, 2020, I mentioned that I wanted to visit my eight-two-year-old sister in Upstate New York. Two years later, on May 31, 2022, I booked a flight from Fort Lauderdale to Albany, New York, to visit me sister, Regina, and her husband, Ronald, for the end of August. By the time I see her, she might not know me. She is now in the early stages of Alzheimer's disease. She sometimes does not know who her husband is. This is very sad, very painful. Her loving and kind life is slowly being erased. She still lights candles for me, still prays for me every day.

This book seems to be a collection of memories of the things I saw on my unique journey to God. Sitting alone in the early more stillness as huge puffy clouds roll in from over the ocean, I feel lost in a cloud of memories, trying to make sense of all I've seen and did since that moment in an empty Franciscan church in Rome when for a fleeting second, I felt that God was real and actually loved me. I've traveled far and wide since then . . . to get nowhere. The exorcism of my false self has not truly succeeded. Anguish and doubt still have much to teach me. My only relief in my inner torment is the realization that I've reached out with a loving hand to some whose struggles are far worse than mine. I would not change a thing.

Conversion must happen every day. There is always more inner work to do. I'm going to get back to work, back to editing this book . . . which I believe few will read. Even some people I love probably won't read it.

Birds Chirping

Monday, December 4, 2000, at 12:05 pm. While reading Merton's *Zen and the Birds of Appetite*, I became aware of the sound of birds chirping. I smiled.

Without listening, it is impossible to know God . . . or peace.

Birds Eating

Monday, December 4, 2000, at 1:20 pm. The birds have finally spotted the white bread on the snow. I put it out at seven this morning. Until the snow melts, I should feed them pumpernickel—that would be easier for them to spot.

The Big Wooden Cross

Monday, December 4, 2000, at 2:00 pm. While seated at Merton's table, if you look out the window, slightly to your right, you can see the big, wooden cross planted in the clearing. The cross was important to Thomas Merton, as it was to Saint Francis of Assisi and most saints.

A few minutes ago, I was reading Merton's *Thoughts in Solitude* and came across the following on the Cross:

> My Lord, I have no hope but in Your Cross. You, by Your humility, and sufferings and death, have delivered me from all vain hope. You have killed the vanity of the present life in Yourself, and have given me all that is eternal in rising from the dead.

Why should I want to be rich, when You were poor? Why should I desire to be famous and powerful in the eyes of men, when the sons of those who exalted the false prophets and stoned the true rejected You and nailed you to the Cross? Why should I cherish in my heart a hope that devours me—the hope for perfect happiness in this life—when such hope, doomed to frustration, is nothing but despair?[204]

A Big Black Bird

Monday, December 4, 2000, at 3:10 pm. A big black bird just landed on the lawn just beyond the porch and after gobbling down three pieces of white bread the bird scurried about picking up four or five more pieces until his mouth was stuffed and then flew off with his bounty. If he returns, I must talk with him about the virtue of sharing.

Solitude, Silence, and Sleep

Monday, December 4, 2000, at 3:50 pm. A little while ago I was reading Merton's *Thoughts in Solitude* when I feel asleep. Sound asleep. For about a half hour. When I awoke, I resumed reading. Within two pages, I came across this passage:

> We are like pilots of fogbound steamers, peering into the gloom in front of us, listening for the sounds of other ships, and we can only reach harbor if we keep alert. The spiritual life is, then, first of all a matter of keeping awake. We must not lose our sensitivity to spiritual inspirations. We must be always able to respond to the slightest warnings that speak, as though by a hidden instinct, in the depth of the soul that is spiritually alive.[205]

Same Date, Same Hermitage

Tuesday, December 5, 2000. Thirty-six years ago today, Merton sat at this very table in this hermitage and penned a few words about his inner and exterior life in this space:

> December 5 [1964]. In the hermitage, one must pray or go to seed. The pretense of prayer will not suffice. Just sitting will not suffice. It has to be real. Yet, what can one do? Solitude puts you with your back to the wall, or your face to it, and this is good. So you pray to learn to pray.[206]

> December 5 [1964]. Tonight it is cold again and as I came back up in the dark a few small snowflakes were flying in the beam of the flashlight. The end of an oak was still burning with small flames in the fireplace. [. . .] I came up with candles and with sugar for coffee. What greater comfort could a man want? Well, of course, I will be glad to get electric light. The question of light is an important

one. Not that I have anything against sister lamp here, chaste, quiet and faithful as she is; but she is a bit dim for serious reading. And yet, for centuries, no one had any more than this. St. Thomas Aquinas may have had much less good light than my lamp here. What am I complaining about?[207]

I have the electricity Merton was dreaming about when he penned the above entry in his journal. In another entry, written in the summer, he said it was so hot he had been perspiring over everything, adding it was hard to get any work done.

Brrr

Wednesday, December 6, 2000, at 7:50 am. Another very cold morning—24 degrees outside; 52 degrees inside. My fire-starting skills are improving. Got a really fine blaze started with just one match. I'm going to make eggs for breakfast.

Homeless

Wednesday, December 6, 2000, at 10:40 am. After breakfast, I sat quietly in front of the fireplace. The house was really cold, and I hadn't started the furnace, thinking I'd wait until later this afternoon. After meditating for about 20 minutes, a picture flashed across my mind: the interior of an abandoned building in the Kensington section of Philadelphia, where squatters had set fire to the staircase to keep warm during a bitter cold night. I had been in the building—and many more like it—while making the [first] documentary on the St. Francis Inn. One day, Fr. Francis Pompei, OFM, found a young man in the abandoned building. He was bundled up against the cold night. His name was Efrem, and he had been homeless for about a month. He said, "It is rough." A towering example of an understatement. Sitting alone in Merton's hermitage—living in "rough" conditions—I'm reminded of the plight of the poor who live in far, far worse conditions because of injustice and not out of seeking a "spiritual" experience. We cannot walk toward God and turn our backs on our suffering brothers and sisters at the same time.

Note: I remember once reading something Thomas Merton wrote about monastic poverty in which he snickered at the idea, saying something like monks can get pretty much what they wanted simply by asking . . . and that for Merton was hardly poverty.

Eggcellent

Wednesday, December 6, 2000, at 6:15 pm. Dinner was a bowl of cereal and a hard-boiled egg. Eggcellent.

The hardest thing about these first three full days in the hermitage has been the chair at Merton's table. I spend about eight to ten hours a day sitting on it, and it is very uncomfortable. Last night, I went to bed around 9 pm—not because I was tired, but because my back ached from so many hours on that chair that I simply had to lie down and stretch out. Today, I moved the folding chair from the chapel to the table. It seemed marginally better—for a while. After dinner, I was getting some firewood, and I spotted the "Bench of Dreams." Bingo! I took it inside, placed it in front of Merton's table, and—perfection! I'll be staying up late tonight, sitting on a bench of dreams writing on Merton's table.

Smoke Gets in Your Eyes

Wednesday, December 6, 2000, at 7:20 pm. I just managed to turn paradise into a smoke chamber. I screwed something up with the furnace and filled the room with thick smoke. I had to open all the windows and the door. There goes the pleasant 70-degree room I'd carefully nurtured. Perfect joy.

A Tiny Nibble

Wednesday, December 6, 2000, at 8:55 pm. I'm just playing hermit here. If that monastery wasn't down the hill offering me warmth, food, fellowship, and a phone whenever I needed it, I would be running like hell from here. I'm only getting a taste—a tiny nibble—of the solitude Merton desired and discovered.

School Days

Thursday, December 7, 2000, at 8:35 am. Woke up this morning at 6:30 am. The night here in this corner of the meadow is dark and quiet. I put extra logs in the furnace last night, and the room was a warm 65 degrees when I stumbled into it this morning. Outside, it was a brisk 33 degrees.

I'm settling nicely into hermitage life. I think it takes at least a full week to garner some insight into the value of the hermitage. This has been an education—and I have three full days, plus part of Sunday, left for classes.

$4.95

Thursday, December 7, 2000. I spent a few hours today reading Merton's *No Man Is an Island*. I bought the paperback edition I'm reading a long time ago . . . I know because it has a sticker price of $4.95 on it. What I found interesting as I read it, besides Merton's insights and his way of expressing himself, is the passages I'd highlighted with a yellow marking pen when I first read it, perhaps a dozen years ago (circa 1988). Back then, I caught a glimpse of what Merton was saying, but not enough of it to have any real impact on my life. Today as I read it, Merton's thoughts were jumping off the pages, and I was able to catch hold of them and apply them to my life. That is not to say that by next week, when I'm home in North Hollywood, I will not have forgotten. It simply means that progress along the spiritual road is slow, deliberate, and cannot be rushed. Each day, each season of our lives, hopefully adds a little more to our understanding and our ability to surrender more and more to God. This stuff is actually very simple, yet somehow, we've made it complicated. There seem to be so many options, so many ways to God—yet it all comes down to one basic truth that each of us needs to discover, embrace, and live.

Note: Reading that twenty years later, I more fully realize just how painfully slow progress along the spiritual road truly is. I've mostly been crawling since those words were penned. In truth, I've been resisting the deeper changes the Gospel requires of me, unwilling or unable to make the sacrifices required in order to give up or let go of things I know are not good for me. This is perhaps so because I've not spent enough time in prayer fueling the gift of faith that I was given.

Three Candles

Thursday, December 7, 2000, at 9:05 pm. I just spent the last half hour in Merton's chapel. I lit three candles and placed them on the altar. I lit some incense. I turned off the lights and stood at the altar facing the crucifix on the back wall. And I prayed.

I asked forgiveness for my sins. Then unexpectedly, I told God that I forgave [name deleted], saying I wasn't angry at him personally, but because I thought his teaching has harmed people. Then, I forgave [name deleted (a Catholic priest)] "for hurting me, deeply."

Then I said (to God), "And I am sorry for hurting You."

Then I laid my confusion over my future before the Lord, praying for guidance about a film I wanted to make. "God, perhaps you want me to forget this project and go serve the poor somewhere. Sometimes I think, Lord, that would be the best thing I could do. Dear Lord, please, give me the gift of prayer, teach me discernment. . . . Without Your help, how can anyone know anything about You? Please help me, Lord."

The time went by quickly. It was peaceful, reflective. There were no bells, no visions, no voices. Just a simple, quiet moment of surrender.

In this humble hermitage, the intimate and the ultimate meet.

Note: What caught my attention as I read this hermitage diary entry as the sun rose on November 24, 2020, was that I seemed to intuit that actually serving the poor was a better path for me than filming the poor. It took me fifteen years before I put down my camera and lived among the poor.

On June 9, 2022, as I sat in the predawn stillness and darkness of Haiti, I wondered: Is it better? I don't know. It certainly was harder and required far more sacrifice. I am feeling old, worn down by the relentless struggle. I want to leave Haiti and never come back. But I can't.

Haiti has become home, with all the complex implications of that simple statement of fact. My life could end today, courtesy of a bullet. I would not change anything. It was as it should have been . . . for me. We are all unique and all the same. Pick your path and keep walking, keep looking, keep listening. Most of all, keep loving. There is nothing else. Saint Thérèse of Lisieux said her in her autobiography: "There was to be no unclouded happiness this side of heaven." All is transitory and corruptible. Nothing on earth can completely satisfy us . . . which might explain our longing for the perfection of God. The material world is incapable of sustaining our happiness.

A Warming Trend

Friday, December 8, 2000, at 7:35 am. The week is flying by. Only two full days, plus Sunday morning, before I must leave. I think the week has given me some insight into Merton's love of solitude . . . and the importance of it in my own life.

Got up at 6:20 am today, the Feast of the Immaculate Conception. The monks will be celebrating the Eucharist at 10:30 am—we are on the Sunday schedule in honor of the Blessed Mother.

Managed to burn the tip of my index finger on my right hand while shifting a log around in the furnace.

I love the early morning light . . . and the promise of a new day. Temperature was 38 degrees when I got up—a warming trend!

> *"The first chirps of the waking day birds mark the 'point vierge' of the dawn under a sky as yet without real light, a moment of awe and inexpressible innocence, when the Father in perfect silence opens their eyes."*
>
> —THOMAS MERTON, CONJECTURES OF A GUILTY BYSTANDER[208]

Eating Goat-Milk Cheese

Friday, December 8, 2000. Thirty-four years ago today, in this very room, Thomas Merton entertained a very famous guest. Two days later, he documented the visit in his journal:

> **December 10, 1966.** Two days ago . . . Joan Baez was here—memorable day. . . .
> We came up to the hermitage and spent the rest of the time here. Played one side
> of her new record, 'Noel.' Lit a fire. Sat on the floor, talked. Grey rugs spread out.
> Sitting around, lying around.
>
> Joan sat on a rug eating goat-milk cheese and bread and honey and drinking
> tea, in front of the fire. Lovely!
>
> She is an indescribably sweet girl, and I love her. I know she loves me too—
> she said she had discovered prayer, in reading my books. . . . [209]

A Good Liberator

Friday, December 8, 2000, at 3:20 pm. The landscape I see out the window when I look up from Merton's table has a very calming influence on me. Merton said a landscape is a "good liberator" from all the harmful images we ingest each day. Contemplation is only effective when it learns to dispose of images, even good images, such as an icon of Christ.

A Hungry Lion

Saturday, December 9, 2000, at 7:05 am. Morning is ever so slowly breaking through the darkness of night. Silence. Only the sound of the coffee brewer gurgling away in the kitchen (making my second pot) can be heard. Temperature is 38 degrees. This is my last full day in the hermitage. I wish I had another week.

Last night as I lay falling asleep in Merton's bedroom, my thoughts drifted to the life of the man who lived here, the man whose life is the reason I'm here. I thought about his death. And mine.

Merton's life was a continuous struggle, especially his last dozen years at Gethsemani. I thought about all the mental and spiritual wrestling he did in this humble hermitage, and how the man poured his external and internal life out on pages covered with words carefully documenting every aspect of his life. His expansive mind and personality took everything in . . . and gobbled it up like a hungry lion. He entered fully into everything. He probed, poked, pushed, and badgered people and ideas. He was serious and funny. He was outgoing and reclusive. He was profane and personal. He loved freedom but practiced discipline. He lost his life in order to gain it. He had great intensity.

And then, suddenly, unexpectedly, he is electrocuted in a hotel room in Bangkok, Thailand. And he is gone. Or at least the "he" we saw and experienced is gone, taken from our midst. We are left only with a pile of paper, countless words on pages struggling to say: "I am."

Speculation as to where Merton would have gone or what he would have done had he not touched that wire is a useless parlor game played only for our entertainment or to support our theory of who he was. Even though it seems very likely that he would have left Gethsemani, in truth, we have no idea what course his life would have taken, just as he had no idea his last breath was seconds away.

Life is a struggle, a continual search for meaning. We live in exile. Each dawn brings us the chance to wake up to the true reality: the insubstantial, shadowy, false self must dissolve into God.

Farewell

Sunday, December 10, 2000, 6:20 am. Today is my last day in the hermitage. Later today, I'll leave Gethsemani Abbey; Jonathan will pick me up and take me back to Louisville.

On this date in 1941, Thomas Merton entered Gethsemani Abbey. On this date in 1968, Thomas Merton entered into eternal life. He was a month shy of his 54th birthday at his death, which occurred in Bangkok, Thailand.

On that fateful trip to the Orient, Merton departed from the airport in San Francisco. I love the way he described the wonder and exhilaration of the take-off.

> There was a delay getting off the ground at San Francisco: the slow ballet of big tailfins in the sun. Now here. Now there. A quadrille of planes jockeying for place on the runway. The moment of take-off was ecstatic. The dewy wing suddenly covered with rivers of cold sweat running backward. The window wept jagged shining courses of tears. Joy. We left the ground—I with a Christian mantra and a great sense of destiny, of being at last on my true way after years of waiting and wondering and fooling around.[210]

Note: I've spent many years "waiting and wondering and fooling around." Having survived a serious illness in Haiti during which I thought I was going to die, it is time for me to really get serious.

> *"The only way to enter that joy [the joy of the mystical love of God] is to dwindle down to a vanishing point and become absorbed in God through the center of your own nothingness."*
>
> —Thomas Merton, *New Seeds of Contemplation*[211]

Inward Stillness, Outward Peace

Sunday, December 10, 2000, at 7:40 am: When I'm centered on God, I'm not distracted by my wayward self and am more easily absorbed in the presence of God. One of the basic messages gleaned from the life of Saint John of the Cross is that inward stillness gives birth to outward peace. As we prepare for the birth of the Prince of Peace, we see few signs of outward peace in the world. During Mass, after the consecration, we symbolically give each other a sign of peace by shaking hands or exchanging hugs. It is the most real moment in the liturgy. One hand reaching out to another. But we quickly pull back, returning to our self-centered fortress that even God cannot penetrate.

Henry David Thoreau tells us that solitude brings us face-to-face with "the essential facts of life." Solitude is a meeting place . . . a place to meet ourselves and God. Solitude is a place where we can change and grow, a place where we can set new priorities. It's a place of new beginnings and also a great place to cure self-deception and put to death bad habits.

Solitude is also a school, a place where we can learn sensitivity, compassion and empathy . . . and truth. Solitude is ideal for reflection, self-examination, creation, purification, penitence, and prayer. For this reason, Thomas Merton writes, "Solitude is as necessary for society as silence is for language and air for the lungs and food for the body."[212]

By Merton's Grave

In the summer before my week in Merton's hermitage, I spent a weekend at Gethsemani Abbey. Before leaving, I sat in the shade under a tree that stands just a few feet from Merton's grave. I wanted to say goodbye to Thomas Merton.

Thank you, Father Louis, for leading me here. Words you faithfully penned so long ago have managed, by the grace of God, to speak to me. They gave me hope, even in my darkest days of unbelief and doubt. Thank you for sharing your journey, for throwing me—and countless others, also—a lifeline to God. Your desire to explore the bleak terrain of your soul combined with your great gift with words to create a lasting impression of a soul's journey to God. Thank you.

As I prayed, a woman walked nearby. She was looking at all the crosses that marked the graves of monks. She was looking for Merton's. I pointed it out. The woman was a bishop in the Episcopal Church. I thought that was very cool. We had a delightful conversation. She had been in Assisi just two weeks before the earthquake. She loved Saint Francis and Fr. Louis. Me too.

Before leaving the hermitage, I silently whispered this to Fr. Louis: "I do not know where this journey will take me . . . but as long as it takes me closer to God, I know it will be—what? . . . amazing, challenging, miraculous, fun, sad, and filled with light and darkness. But no matter where the next year takes me, the ups and downs, I pray that you intercede for me before the throne of God so that I may have the courage and grace to cling to Jesus at all costs. What attracts me to you and Saint Francis is how tenaciously, in your own highly individual ways, you followed Christ no matter where he led you. Thank you, Father Louis. Pray for me."

Merton's grave at Gethsemani Abbey; *Photo by Gerry Straub*

Note: As I read that prayer on June 17, 2022, I had the thought that prayer may have been answered. I have tenaciously clung to what I felt I should be doing, whether filming poverty or serving poor children in Haiti, despite all the obstacles I encountered and the litany of my mistakes I made. I did it all for Jesus, who helped my overcome my fears, doubts, weaknesses, and times of betrayal. It was all grace . . . amazing grace. I'm seventy-five and still standing, albeit a bit bent over, still serving, and, as you will read in the Afterword, still learning to love.

June 9, 2022, Haiti, 5:22 am. After finishing my final review of this section of the book, I went to the kitchen for another cup of coffee. When I returned to my office, the muted TV had images of the intense fighting in Ukraine. The war was already more than 100 days old. The slaughter of innocent civilians, including women and children, was hard to fathom. The world was riveted to the valiant effort off Ukraine to fight to maintain their freedom. But of late, we became weary of the coverage, as the cost of helping Ukraine with money and weapons to defend themselves began to have a negative impact on the global economy as gas prices skyrocketed. The horror of the brutal war in Ukraine was suddenly overshadowed by the slaughter of nineteen innocent children in an elementary school in Uvalde, Texas. Details had begun to emerge that illustrated the devasting power of the AR-15 assault gun. The kids had been blown to pieces. The impact of the bullets actually decapitated two children. Some kids could only be identified by their DNA.

If all that was not enough, the next day, on prime-time TV, televised hearings into the January 6, 2021, attack on the Capitol would begin. It was expected that the Congressional committee would provide new and compelling evidence that Trump was at the center of the insurrection designed to overthrow the government in order to void a valid election so he could remain in power.

A significant percentage of Americans, though still in a minority, continued to insist that weapons of war were not responsible for killing kids in schools and defended the right for eighteen-year-old kids to buy these deadly weapons; they resist reasonable and rational gun policy reform. The same people continued to claim that Trump won the election and that the invasion of the Capitol was not an "insurrection" but merely a protest.

Americans are deeply divided. Democracy is at risk. Things are falling apart. Homelessness is on the rise. New variants of Covid-19 are on the horizon . . . along with inflation.

We are collectively facing a global dark night of the soul. We are approaching the border of purgation, an intensification of the agony. We have drifted far from divine love. We need a radical transformation. The old structures of religion are no longer able to hold us together, to nurture and sustain us. Change is coming. It will be painful . . . and, hopefully, life-giving.

What we need most
in order to make progress
is to be silent
before this great God
with our appetite
and with our tongue,
for the language
he best hears
is silent love.
—Saint John of the Cross[213]

PART FIVE

Daily Journals from Haiti

Haiti, 2009; *Photo by Gerry Straub*

CHAPTER 31

Behind a Mask of Cheerfulness

How is it that for me the contemplative life has taken root in such a noisy, chaotic, violent place as Haiti?

I asked myself that question in July 2020.

A month earlier, during the Zoom launch of my new book, *The Sunrise of the Soul*, the host asked me a very direct question: "Are you a contemplative?" I said in response: "I'm a knucklehead." Why did I give such a flippant response? Perhaps saying I was a contemplative would have made me seem odder than I am. Still, my ministry for more than fifteen years was one of action. I was always on the move, filming poverty around the world and giving 250 multimedia presentations on poverty at churches and schools across the United States and in Europe. Now during my just over five years in Haiti caring for kids being choked by poverty I've been in perpetual motion, going from crisis to crisis. Yet at the core of my very active life, there was a contemplative spirit. Perhaps I already answered the question five years earlier in this journal entry written in a slum in Haiti:

May 2015. To be in Haiti is to be in the belly of the beast. In Haiti, the presence of God takes on the form of absence. It is the sign of Jonah writ large. In Haiti, human misery is raw and real. In Haiti, my false ideas and values were shattered into thousands of little pieces. In Haiti, I saw things in their utter nakedness. The cross was around every corner. The cross had no place to hide. I either closed my eyes to the cross, or I had to confront and embrace the cross. I saw clearly the pain and suffering of Christ, the pain and suffering of the human condition. In Haiti, there are no diversions, no false idols to avert my gaze from the misery. There was no place to turn . . . all I could see was the hiddenness of God, the apparent absence of God. In this void, I slowly and humbly prepared to approach the consciousness of God. In the absence of God, the presence of God awaits. Detachment, for me, seemed to be the path to wholeness.

In the slums of Haiti, I felt closer to God than I do at Sunday Mass in my home parish. In Haiti, I was detached from the world yet not attached to God. It was a place of dreadful inner anguish for me. I could neither believe nor not believe in anything. Yet, in Haiti, I felt God was hidden in the insignificant and the unassuming, like Christ hiding in a morsel of bread. The poor felt their own fragility and understand their dependency. Somehow, in Haiti, I felt the way to God was through the misery and nothingness of my false self. It was there that I saw more clearly my true self and my complete dependence upon God. It is there that I feel more tangibly God's love.

Love is a mystical force that pushes open the door to forgiveness and mercy.

In another journal entry discussing the agony of Mother Teresa, now Saint Teresa of Calcutta, I wrote:

December 4, 2015. Before Mother Teresa began helping the sick and dying in Calcutta, she had a profound inner experience of God. Her soul was flooded with light. Perhaps it was just a flash. It woke her up to a transcendent reality, which prompted her to abandon her previous expression of religious life. She followed her instincts and ended up on the desperate streets of Calcutta and became a channel of God's mercy. As she worked among the poor, tirelessly devoting herself to them, she never again experienced that flash of mystical insight. She entered the dark night of the soul . . . and never emerged from it. How she continued to tirelessly bring the Light of God's love and compassion to the sick and dying despite her own inner darkness is truly a mystery.

Perhaps in that original fleeting moment of revelation, Mother Teresa felt connected to everything, to everyone, but then after it, she felt disconnected from everything . . . even God.

I know the feeling.

In the early morning hours of July 23, 2020, I was in such a dark place, I wanted to be anyplace but Haiti. I wrestled with the thought that on my upcoming trip to Florida I simply not come back. The darkness was so bad, I harbored the faint regret that I survived Covid-19. I wasn't going to bother going to Mass at the Sisters. I mustered the strength to go for only one reason: Sr. Immacula's days in Haiti were dwindling down to a precious few before she returns to India. During Mass, I was completely disengaged from the ritual. At one point, I thought, *This is all bullshit.* Yet Fr. Tom's homily was interesting enough for me to jot down a few notes:

Without loving yourself, you can't love others.
If you don't love yourself, you don't believe in God's love for you.

Love must be three dimensional.
You must love yourself.
You must love others.
You must love God.

When all three dimensions of love are present, they create a synergy.
If one aspect of love is missing, love is not whole.

You can't love God without loving your neighbor.

By the time the Eucharist was being dispensed, I felt so alone and isolated that I didn't want to receive the Body of Christ. But I did. Back in my seat, I silently spoke a few disjointed words to Jesus.

At the end of Mass, I was tempted to duck out before the Sisters began their prayers after communion, which are very beautiful. I stayed. I mumbled half of the prayers. When the prayers ended, I wished there was a backdoor so I wouldn't have to walk past Fr. Tom and Sr. Immacula. Not that a backdoor would've been helpful as they were standing next to my car. Fr. Tom was cracking his usual jokes, poking fun at me and Sr. Immacula. Smiling was hard. But he clearly was in a hurry so the banter ended and he drove off. I was left facing Sr. Immacula. She asked, "How are you, Gerry?"

There was a long pause before answering. I guess I was calculating whether to just say "fine" and hit the road.

I said, "Not very good." The honesty felt good. Before she could say anything, I said, "I don't want to be here anymore."

She asked, "Is it the finances?" She knew our bank account was minus $13,000 thanks to $52,000 in credit card debt.

I said, "Actually, you were right. Some money has come in, enough to get us through August. But not enough to get us through September." In the previous five days, $48,000 had been donated by just four people.

She said, "More will come later."

I told her that when I was in Florida begging, I told many people, "My friend Sr. Immacula always tells me to trust in God, that God will provide."

She smiled, saying, "It is true."

I then told her that the financial hole I'm in is because an expected $100,000 donation in January donation never materialized because of the donor's illness. What I was saying was it would take nearly two dozen $5,000 donations to make up for that huge shortfall.

I said I was in a dark place, and not just because of the money woes. I said the problems are just overwhelming. I mentioned a few, including our inability to move some of the older kids to a good orphanage that could better serve them.

She said she would help find a suitable orphanage for some of our kids. She said there is one excellent orphanage run by Protestants. They give the kids a solid education and keep them until they are eighteen years old. I told her about two special boys at Santa Chiara: Isidore and Vanderson. I said they are both smart and creative. I can't give them the education they need. She said she would focus on finding a suitable place for them.

Then I spoke about the darkness that Saint Teresa of Calcutta endured for many years. I said, "I'm a bit like Saint Teresa. I had this flash of enlightenment and then nothing. I do not know how she endured the darkness for so long."

Sr. Immacula said, "Gerry, Mother told me, 'I hide the darkness behind a mask of cheerfulness.'"

Wow. I thought about how I am constantly joking . . . to hide my despair, to pretend all is fine?

I asked Sister, "Do you have dark days?"

She said, without hesitation, "Many. All the sisters have dark days."

I felt so close to Sr. Immacula at the moment. I said, "I'll really miss you."

She said, "Gerry, you must cling to Jesus. You must trust in God's love for you."

With each of our hands joined in a prayerful manner, we bowed to each other . . . and then I got in my car and drove home. As usual, I was mobbed by a battalion of toddlers. Peter and Clare followed me up to the second floor for a glass of mango juice. When they left, I tried to cling to Jesus as I got to work. A child needed to be taken to the hospital. A search for scarce diesel fuel was also on the agenda.

The darkness was slowly lifting.

Saint Teresa of Calcutta's Missionaries of Charity have that amazing and rare combination of utter groundedness and constant risk-taking that always characterizes the true Gospel. Yet, they can be overly dogmatic. (*Note: Once Sr. Immacula departed for India, it seemed she took all the joy of the place with her. I slowly scaled back my visits, offering the increasingly dangerous streets as an excuse. By the end of December 2021, I stopped going, as their dogmatic rigidity became unbearable. Still, they are doing great work on behalf of the poor.*)

God is with me . . . all of the time. Sometimes it gets too dark to feel God's presence, God's boundless love. Likewise, God is with you . . . always, everywhere.

I shared this with my friend Jonathan just after writing it. Within minutes, he wrote back saying, "You entered the school of your life, the overshadowing of God's mercy coming through from Immacula, praying with the sisters while your heart is turning to stone, going home to serve mango juice to your children. This is the 'gospel' in words but primarily showing relationships as contemplative moments, receiving 'God's' love every day."

When I read Jonathan's wise words, I realized that when Sr. Immacula spoke to me, it was as if God was speaking to me. The truth is, God is speaking to all of us all the time. Sadly, at least for me, I'm often not listening. Yet God, the All Merciful, keeps speaking.

I also shared it with Fr. Dumarsais, a Haitian who was ordained a priest in Florida and is the pastor of a parish not far from my home in Florida. He wrote: "I think it's beautiful and raw. That's life in Haiti. There's no elaborate plan and certainties. As you journey with Jesus on Holy Thursday Night after the meal, you are experiencing his own feeling of ineffectiveness and banal reliance on the Father. Remember you are on road to Emmaus: disappointments and discouragement are later crowned by joy and satisfaction. Keep on hoping!"

Note: No one can see the depths of their own poverty. Without words or thoughts, I must force myself to stand naked before God. Only then can I learn to say truthfully: "Blessed are those who know that they are poor." Coming face-to-face with my own total poverty is the only way to come face-to-face with God and find true enlightenment.

CHAPTER 32

Haiti 2015 Journals

The *Haiti Journal* officially began in December 2015. (Before then, I sent monthly reports to small select group of friends.) Through the present day, I've sent a journal entry to my friends and supporters virtually every day. Taken together, they would fill a dozen oversized books, as they document the daily struggles and offer spiritual reflections. The remaining pages of this book offer just a smattering of the spiritual reflections or entries that dramatically capture the harshness of life for the poor.

Possibility and Purpose

June 14, 2015. The Gospel for today (the 11th Sunday in Ordinary Time) was the familiar parable of the mustard seed found in the 4th Chapter of Mark's Gospel. Jesus compares the kingdom of God to "the smallest of all the seeds on earth," yet the insignificant mustard seed grows into "the largest of plants," whose branches attract all manner of birds and provide shade for all. The lowly mustard seed is very easy to overlook, yet it is filled with life-giving potential. In Haiti, mustard seeds abound, in the form of neglected and abandoned people who are being swept away by the ill winds of severe poverty. But each person, Jesus tells us, contains possibility and purpose. I can't help but think of all the small kids in Haiti who are not given a chance to grow into the person God created them to become. My prayer is that the Santa Chiara Children's Center becomes a place where those who are small and forgotten are given a chance to grow.

A Drop in the Bucket

July 6, 2015, at 6:35 pm. Around five in the afternoon, an intense thunderstorm rumbled through Peguyville, accompanied by Sister Lightening. Immediately, many people, including us, rushed to get empty buckets to catch the free water. They will use the water to wash floors and flush toilets . . . if they have toilets. One young woman stood on the roof of her building totally naked as she leisurely took a long shower.

But, for the most part, the rain only intensified the misery. The street vendors had to scramble for cover. Still, the rain cooled down what had been an intensely hot day. In this heat, it is hard to do anything. Most people in this slum do nothing. Most can't find jobs. The unemployment rate is estimated to be a staggering 60 percent, though accurate figures are hard to find or verify. Such widespread idleness breeds all kinds of problems. Many men pass the day playing cards or attending cock fights. I read that 80 percent of the population lives below the poverty line, and 54 percent of those people live in abject poverty. Every day is a struggle for survival. From my observation, most people work really hard to earn the little money they do. There is no such a thing, in the many slums at least, as enjoyable leisure time. Most of the poor are extremely uninformed about current events outside their own neighborhood; they know virtually nothing of world events, such as the tragic war in Syria that has killed over 300,000 people and left millions to flee their homes and live as refugees.

To give you a sense of just how deep and devastating the poverty in Haiti is, here are some statistics I unearthed during the early months of our mission in Haiti that shocked me and also let me know what we were doing was just a drop in the bucket in the face of overwhelming need.

+ In Haiti there is one doctor for every 15,000 people.

+ Poor sanitation and widespread poverty have led to young children being fifteen times more likely to die from diarrhea and pneumonia than from HIV/AIDS.

+ 1 out 4 children are moderately to severely malnourished.

+ 138,000 children die of preventable diseases each year.

+ 10% of children will die before their fifth birthday, largely from treatable diseases.

A Cruel Tyrant

July 6, 2015, at 9:40 pm. A little while ago, Orlane (the first child we served whose nickname is Baby) and I were a bit hungry. So, I made us each a ham and cheese sandwich on Syrian bread. The house was still hot, so we sat outside in the rain-cooled air, enjoying not only the sandwich but a pleasant evening breeze. Out of the darkness the little girl who lives next door in the unfinished building appeared. Her name is Sabine. She is ten years old. She is very thin. She wears the same frayed, oversized denim dress every day. She has no shoes. She is usually very dirty. She has never been to school. She cannot read or write. If all that wasn't bad enough, her father often beats her. Sabine frequently comes to our apartment, perhaps seeking refuge. I always joke with her and make her smile. We were nearly finished our sandwiches when Sabine came for a visit. I couldn't help but notice how she was watching us eat. I had Baby ask her if she was hungry. She said yes. I went into the house and made her a sandwich. I was sure the little girl never had Black Forest ham or cheddar cheese before. I folded it all inside a large piece of Syrian flat bread. What absolutely stunned us was how quickly Sabine devoured the sandwich. She practically inhaled it. It wouldn't have been possible for me to have eaten it any faster. We fed Jesus a ham and cheese sandwich.

Seeing What Jesus Sees

July 7, 2015. Yesterday's Gospel reading (Matthew 9:9–13) presents us with many possible lessons. The short passage tells how Jesus encountered a tax collector named Matthew. Tax collectors were people with extremely low reputations; they were seen as cheaters and thieves. Jesus had just two words for Matthew: "Follow me." And Matthew did just that. A few lines later, we read about Jesus sharing a meal in his house, and the Pharisees questioned, "Why does he eat with tax collectors and sinners?" Jesus, of course, had the perfect answer: "Those who are well do not need a physician, but the sick do . . . I did not come to call the righteous but sinners."

When people looked at Matthew, they saw a cheater and thief. God saw something very different. When people saw Paul, they saw a murderer. God saw something else. When people saw Peter, they saw a dysfunctional guy and a braggart. God saw something else. The most obvious lesson in the Gospel passage is that God looks beyond our idiosyncrasies, beyond our faults, beyond our misdeeds, and sees the beauty in the core of our being. Matthew was a social outcast, but he was not beyond the outreach of God. We often exclude people because we can't see past their surface weaknesses and proclivity for improper behavior. We label them and dismiss them. Rather than interpret scripture, we need to allow scripture to interpret us. God speaks to us through the scriptures, especially in the words of Jesus. God says in this passage that we need to be more aware of our insensitivity toward others, that God seeks mercy, not sacrifice from us.

The Eye of a Needle

October 10, 2015, at 8:50 pm. Long day. I'm tired. I'm distressed about the boy with the enlarged testicles; they looked really bad tonight . . . the swelling seemed worse than ever before.

I just looked ahead to the Gospel reading for tomorrow . . . it's a tough one from Mark, Chapter 10, in which Jesus told a man to "sell what you have and give it to the poor . . . and follow me." The man went away sad because he had many possessions. Jesus went on to say to his disciples that it is "easier for a camel to pass through the eye of a needle than for one who is rich to enter the kingdom of God."

All of us, even the poor, have too many possessions to truly follow Christ. When Jesus asks us to follow him, we are tormented when we look within ourselves and realize how much we must let go of in order to follow him who beckons us each day to walk further down the path of detachment and into the self-emptying love of God. Every day in Haiti helps me see more clearly just how rich I am and how much more I must let go of.

Blessed Communion

October 14, 2015, at 6:55 am. During my quiet time of reading this morning, I came across this cryptic jewel from the prolific theologian Walter Brueggemann: "What we are about is serious conversation leading to blessed communion."[214] You don't see much evidence of blessed communion in the little slice of Haiti where we spend our days. Even in America, I see more estrangement and division than communion. In his refreshingly open book *Notes from the Underground: The Spiritual Journal of a Secular Priest*, Fr. Donald Cozzens writes:

> I'm drawn to it like a magnet because if Christianity is about anything, it is about communion—communion with God, with family and friends, with creation, with mystery. It's the existential dimension of Jesus' Reign of God. We are held ... in an unspeakable unity with the whole of creation and its divine source. When I preach of communion and intimacy, I preach to ears that often know more alienation and estrangement than communion and intimacy, to ears that know more betrayal and heartbreak than the comfort of human solidarity.[215]

There are graced moments in Haiti when I feel real communion, real moments of unity within myself and my surroundings. Here the importance of the common good is crystal clear. I think authentic human intimacy happens more easily here. This stuff is all so hard to explain ... I just simply feel more alive here in Haiti. I even danced with Orlane in the kitchen last night.

The Baby Jesus

December 5, 2015. On the first Christmas Day, God not only became a human being, God became an infant human being. As a baby, Jesus needed to be fed, needed to be clothed, needed to be sheltered and protected. God as a baby was not only weak but totally dependent upon human help. As an adult, Christ said that whenever you feed the least of God's children you are feeding him. Because God is present within each of us, God still needs to be fed, which is why it is so important to learn to see Christ in the poor, because when you feed the poor, you are truly feeding Christ. God is still helpless, patiently waiting for us.

Christian compassion is rooted in the discovery of Christ in the suffering people of the world. Moreover, solidarity with the poor and the oppressed is the very essence of Christian mysticism. Still, when I see the vastness of the problem of global poverty, I feel absolutely helpless. But that feeling gives insight into the Good News, for "God's power working in us can do infinitely more than we can ask or imagine." (Ephesians 3:20) The power of God is the power of love, which invites, but never coerces. This love, whether we are conscious of it or not, is the longing of all our desire and restlessness. But that is such a hard truth to learn. I still harbor ungodly desires, and my heart is still often restless.

We need to ponder the infant Jesus lying powerless in the manger and wonder at the divine humanity we are all graced with. If we see ourselves as full of God's beauty as the infant Jesus was, we could no longer continue to hurt each other, and all acts of violence would cease to exist. God's outrageous love, manifested in the planned vulnerability of Jesus, would lead Christ to the cross that awaited him on Calvary and should lead us to embrace the vulnerability of love that is forever beckoning us.

Be Strong, Fear Not

December 7, 2015, at 4:15 am. Today's Gospel reading from Luke tells the story of the crippled man who was lowered through the roof of a building where Jesus was speaking. In biblical times, the blind and paralyzed were ostracized. They had no voice or power in society. Their infirmities were seen as punishments from God for human sin or as the result of evil spirits. To be disabled was to be seen as weak and inferior. Seeing the faith of the man and his friends, Jesus forgave his sins and healed him. This is what it is all about: trying to make whole what has been broken. Every day, we encounter many broken people as well as our own brokenness. Our Advent challenge is to come more fully into the presence of Jesus so he can heal us, restore our spirits, fill us with new hope, and give us the courage to heal others.

Fathering Hope

December 7, 2015, at 5:35 am. Why is it that being in Haiti is so good for me? It is a question I've pondered. My hunch is it's because here I get to step outside myself, outside my own sheltered, self-sufficient world. Essentially, all we are doing in Haiti is welcoming the strangers who come to our door. That happens to be very biblical, going all the way back to Abraham and Sarah, who graciously received three strangers. Their openness to others changed their lives to such a degree that Sarah became fertile at an old age. I think that in some way I need these kids to make me whole. They are giving me a bigger heart. Being in a foreign and therefore unfamiliar place tends to disperse my own inner loneliness and helps me see with new eyes. Without this challenge, I think I would've just withered away. Instead, in Haiti, I'm becoming more fertile, fathering hope in those who have none.

In America right now there is a rising movement that sees the other as a threat, a danger to our way of life. We set up social, economic, and legal barriers to keep the stranger out or to set them apart. Of course, both the Old and the New Testaments urge us to welcome the stranger. In biblical terms, the stranger was the foreigner fleeing oppression, war, or hunger in their own land. Today, many Americans want to kick undocumented migrants out of the country, even though most have been living here peacefully for years. They also want to stop desperate Syrian refugees fleeing terrorism from entering our country. At the root of all this is the reality that we are basically afraid of whatever is not familiar to us. The time I spent with Sufi Muslims in Turkey helped me see the beauty in Islam. The wonderful Muslims who hosted me and brought me to many mosques became my brothers. We shared with each other our faith and found a great deal of common ground. In fact, when I go back to California after Christmas, I'll be having dinner with one of my Muslim friends from Turkey who will be in Los Angeles.

A Beggar of Love

December 7, 2015. Haiti is a dark place, and it is tempting to say, as I have, that it is hopeless. But the Light did come into the world and the darkness cannot extinguish it—therefore, there is always hope, perhaps a timid and fragile hope, but hope exists whenever one person reaches out to another in a spirit of compassion and genuine human kindness. As the Leonard Cohen song proclaimed, it is the imperfection, the crack, the flaw in everything and everyone, that lets the Light in. Haiti is, ever so slowly, by God's abundant grace and the extraordinary kindness of countless volunteers, rising from the ruin of the earthquake. (**Note:** *Of course, by 2022, Haiti was teetering on the brink of anarchy. The gang's controlled the country, there was essentially no government, the unchecked violence turned barbaric, and any sense of hope was quickly vanishing.*)

In my book *Thoughts of a Blind Beggar*, I wrote that we are all blind beggars who need to hold outstretched, empty hands to God, who will give us a new vision and all that we need. Well, I think the truth is actually more fundamental, more profound than that . . . the truth is that God is also a beggar. God's powerful love for each of us is so great, so far beyond measurement that we, in our blindness, cannot begin to understand it. Yet when it comes to our loving God, God is powerless. Not only does God not push us, God even tolerates our indifference, our apathy, our detours, our revolts, our faults, failures, and sins. God's love includes the extravagant freedom to accept it or reject it. God desires our love. Yet, God does not interfere or manipulate, or coerce us into loving. God is a beggar of love, patiently waiting at the door of our soul.

With God, our isolated existence dies and we are born again into a great union of love where we freely enter into a nurturing, life-giving relationship with all of creation, especially with the stranger, the rejected, the isolated, the tormented and the marginalized, out of which arises a new earth, a new heaven, where prisons of poverty such as Cité Soleil no longer exist.

Go be a candle of hope, be a witness and manifestation of God's love by ending hunger and creating peace. Advent helps us look to the future with hope. But we cannot hope for a better future and remain indifferent to the suffering that currently surrounds us; otherwise, Christian hope is little more than pious escapism. We must act. Human goodness aided by divine help can overcome the dark forces that are holding so many people in a lethal bondage of poverty.

In light of the miracle of Christmas, we must become candles of hope, shining incarnate light on a world and a Church lost often in the dark. Because of the Incarnation, everything is now graced. Every breath we take matters. Every life matters . . . because every life contains divine potential. God is aware of every tear, every heartache, and every physical and emotional wound. God, a beggar of love, is waiting to transform our lives.

> *"The idea that some lives matter less is the root*
> *of all that's wrong with the world."*
>
> —PAUL FARMER, PHYSICIAN, ANTHROPOLOGIST,
> AND COFOUNDER OF PARTNER IN HEALTH[216]

Our Common Humanity

December 9, 2015, at 4:50 am. Suffering is a reality. To understand suffering is to learn compassion and forgiveness. Jesus makes it perfectly clear that compassion is to be our primary spiritual practice. My film *When Did I See You Hungry?*, which was narrated by Martin Sheen, contains this line: "Compassion is far removed from pity and sympathy. Compassion grows out of an awareness of our common humanity." I understand the truth of that statement much more today than I did when I wrote it more than fifteen years ago. There is a Buddhist dharma (teaching), which I came across recently, that captures the same idea: "The worst enemy of compassion is called sympathy. Sympathy feels so badly for that poor fellow, as if he were different from us in any way."

By actually living among the poor in Haiti after the earthquake, living in the same dreadful conditions as they did, I came to see myself in my neighbors. We really were no different; we shared the same common humanity. I meet the spirit of the broken Christ in the harsh, barren landscape of unjust poverty, in dark places where Christ still has no home.

You don't need to go to Haiti or Africa to experience the broken Christ. God is on a street corner, at the intersection of everyday life in your own neighborhood. If attentive, we can feel the divine presence in a gentle breeze as God passes by on the street, often in a distressing disguise, hoping for an encounter. In the ordinary moments of the day, the extraordinary loving presence of God is reaching out to us. We don't see or respond to the unjust suffering of the poor because we're distracted by a torrent of trivialities. Our lives are swept up in a perpetual hustle and bustle as we hurry here and there striving to make progress in our endless quest for more and more. On a deeper level, we are slow to compassion because we are quick to exploit others for our own gain.

As we prepare to celebrate the birth of the Prince of Peace, it is important to recognize that peace begins with compassion. As we grow in compassion, we are able to see more clearly the beauty of all life and we also increase our desire to transform everything ugly into something beautiful.

There is no doubt that there is a lot of ugliness in the world today. The news is filled with it. But I think there is actually far more beauty . . . if you really look you can see it. The headlines of the last few weeks, from Paris to San Bernardino, create a feeling of hopelessness. It feels as if the world is spinning out of control. Some politicians are quick to exploit the tangible fear in the air by creating deeper divisions in our society. Yet in this holy season of Advent, we are supposed to look to the future with hope . . . which is not easy. But we follow Jesus, and he lives outside the city of conventional thought, beyond the bounds of conventional wisdom . . . and Jesus says there is hope.

CHAPTER 33

Haiti 2016 Journals

Breathing Deeply Out of Both Lungs

January 3, 2016

> *"Our thought should not merely be an answer to what someone else has just said. Or what someone else might have said. Our interior world must be more than an echo of the words of someone else. There is no point in being a moon to somebody else's sun, still less is there any justification for our being moons of one another, and hence darkness to one another, not one of us being a true sun."*
>
> —Thomas Merton, Conjectures of a Guilty Bystander[217]

In his journals, Thomas Merton wrote: "I write to allow life to live itself in me. For me to write is to think and to live, [and] even, to pray." My dear friend Jonathan Montaldo said:

Writing eventually became one of Merton's major spiritual exercises. Writing became his way of breathing deeply out of both lungs. Writing journals was a significant dimension of Merton existing in and dialoguing with God. Writing journals gave flesh to his inner experiences. By writing journals, he documented God's epiphanies to him in ordinary daily life. By writing journals, he intended his writing to be an epiphany of himself to God. Writing journals for Merton was a way of praying that gave him access to a center in himself, to what he called it, *le point vierge*, a 'virgin point' where he would experience fleeting but unobstructed communion with God.

Through perseverance and tenacity, Merton transcended the limits and boundaries that separate, divide, quantify, and define existence on our material plane. He boldly dared to wander outside the coral of life, slipped into greener pastures, and found outside the bounds a freedom he had never known before, a kind of new world. He documents his inner journey in his journals and manuscripts. He fuses material and spiritual in the creation he brought forth. His writing was both a conduit to the holy and yet was from the holy.

Thomas Merton's writings never fail to teach me, to push me into new ways of seeing things, push me into thinking more deeply. I'm not sure why I've forced myself to document so thoroughly my post-conversion life and struggles, but I see how in doing so I was able to look back over the last twenty years of notebooks and slowly reach a better understanding of myself and the ways in which God may be working in my life. Each day offers us little epiphanies. Yet, all too often these little flashes of insight get blown away by the whirlwind of life. Jotting them down on paper gives them a chance at permanence, and over time they collectively open the door to a larger epiphany and, perhaps, a deeper, clearer understanding of our lives. I'm a long way from reaching the "virgin point" of which Merton wrote, but hopefully, in this year-long journal, I might take some baby steps in the right direction. It is my hope that my personal writings will help others who are lost in the darkness that shrouds so much of life today. Santa Chiara Children's Center is about more than the kids in Haiti.

The Unexpected Epiphany

The hallmark of Merton's prayer life was his ability to keep vigil in silence with his heart's eye on the horizon of the next moment. The next moment could reveal in light or in shadow the presence of the Beloved he so eagerly awaited. He kept his mind's eye open for the unexpected epiphany. Waiting without projecting his own needs into the next moment became a dark form of hope for him. Down through the ages, mystics of all faiths understood that silence is the place where time and eternity embrace.

The Fly and the Chicken

Monday, January 11, 2016, at 2:48 am. Woke up with some bad wheezing. This is getting tiresome. Took a few pumps of the maintenance inhaler. Not sure I can go back to sleep. Maybe I'll go hunt the one pesky fly buzzing around the computer. The chicken is so loud he sounds like he is under my desk. I tried to feed it some pudding yesterday, but he was not interested. Perhaps no one ever chased him with a spoon before. Between the fly and chicken, this will not be a silent night for contemplation.

In the spiritual life, we struggle to learn how to hear the deeper sounds beneath the ordinary noise of the day, how to see the interconnectedness of life in the chaos of the day. How is God speaking to us in the ordinary events of our own unique life? So many speak of knowing or doing "God's will," but such knowledge is a tricky proposition. I feel God has led me to Haiti, that somehow Haiti is part of God's will for me. But still there are doubts and questions . . . as well as other viable options. I suppose we all must learn how to live with the questions and to just simply follow what we believe is the movement of the Spirit. It takes practice, patience, and stillness to hear the still, small voice in the onrushing flow of the day. I often forget to ask myself a simple question each day: *What is God saying to me today?* Moreover, it is not easy to quiet the clamoring devilish voice that tries to lead me astray. Today it is so easy to follow a destructive path. Discernment on how to move forward with Santa Chiara Children's Center must be rooted prayer. It is often hard to know when to act and when to wait. In the spiritual life, there are no easy answers.

I love this quote from Henri Nouwen: "God speaks to us all the time and in many ways, but it requires spiritual discernment to hear God's voice, see what God sees, and read the signs in daily life." Only through daily prayer and checkering our days with short periods of stillness and silence can we slowly learn to read the signs of daily life.

As I typed that quote, I remembered something I wrote long ago, way back in my atheist days. In one of my two atheist books, I said something like: "I don't need to hear God's voice. I'd be happy just to hear him clear his throat." Back then, I needed to deny God to find God. I see now that what I was doing was throwing out all the old, even harmful ideas about God in order to find more expansive, more loving ideas of God. We like to put God into a box we can easily manage. The God I was introduced to as a child was a stern, judgmental, vengeful God who loved to dole out harsh punishments for menial acts of transgression. Does intentionally missing Mass on a Sunday deserve eternity in hell?

I think these journals are opening up a new way for me to move forward while at the same time reflecting on my past. The journals are forcing me to be more disciplined in my efforts to read the signs of my daily life.

A Safe Place

Monday, October 3, 2016. It is hard to calculate just how hard life in Haiti is for many women. The story I am about to share is, I fear, rather common. A woman named Olita brought her two kids, a nine-year-old girl and six-year-old boy, to Santa Chiara back in February. She lived in a nearby slum and was working as a domestic servant. She was unable to care for her children. The kids have been living at Santa Chiara since February. The mother visits them frequently. The man whom Olita worked for repeatedly harassed her. A few months ago, he attempted to rape her. She managed to flee the house. Olita was living with the father of her two kids. When she told him what had happened, the man said she was lying. He said she was having an affair with her boss. He called her "stupid" and hit her . . . and threw her out of their shack of a home. Suddenly, this poor woman had no job and no place to live. Since her life fell apart, she has been living with a cousin . . . and she continued to visit her children. This week, Olita told me about her situation. She wanted to volunteer at Santa Chiara. With so many kids still in diapers, we need all the help we can get.

One of our weaknesses is overnight staffing, especially on weekends. We asked Olita if she would like to live, at least temporarily, at Santa Chiara. She spent her first night here on Saturday. On Sunday morning, she was all smiles. She told me she would be thrilled to come to Delmas when we move. She is not even asking for any pay. She simply wants to feel safe and to stay close to her children. If this works out as we hope it will, I'll give her a small salary in hopes she can begin to save some money and become more independent. (**Note:** *As of 2022, Olita is still working at Santa Chiara; she is a joy-filled, hardworking woman.*)

Power Failure

Thursday, October 6, 2016. I woke up Wednesday morning at 4:00 am. I could see the light from the computer screen in the outer office and the fans were on, so I knew we still had power, which surprised me. I couldn't tell if power to the area had been restored or if we were still on the inverter's stored energy. Normally, I get right up, but yesterday, I lingered for about twenty minutes before rising. As is my early morning routine, I made a pot of coffee before going to the bathroom and brushing my teeth. Just as I was leaving the bathroom, the power went out. The apartment was thrust into darkness. My first thought was that I was glad I'd sent Wednesday's journal on Tuesday night . . . at least everyone knew we were OK. Then I kicked myself for not immediately getting up 4:00 am . . . because the coffee maker had not had the time to brew a full pot of coffee before we lost power. I was grateful I had at least a half a pot of coffee . . . but not so happy that it was not so hot. But then I realized how fortunate we were to have had electricity for so long, when all the other residents of Peguyville had not had power since late Tuesday afternoon and spent the evening stuck inside because of the rain but also in darkness.

The Dark Side of the Aftermath of the Hurricane

Wednesday, October 12, 2016. While many wonderful individuals and charitable organizations are rushing into Haiti to help the survivors of Hurricane Matthew, there are others who are using the storm for their own personal gain by scooping up displaced children and selling them.

During the last eighteen months, I have frequently mentioned in this journal how kids in Haiti are frequently sold by their parents into domestic servitude because the parents can't afford to care for the child. A child who has been sold into servitude is called a "restavec," a word that comes from the French *reste avec*, meaning "one who stays with." Restavecs are typically young girls who have been born into severe poverty. These children receive food and shelter in exchange for doing housework. Restavecs are usually treated badly; they will not receive any education and are often physically abused and sexually molested.

Tragically, the life of a restavec is often considered better than the alternative life of chronic, hopeless poverty, which is why some parents allow their children to become restavecs. We have one young girl living at Santa Chiara who was a restavec; she ran away from the family she was sold to and sought refuge with us. Haiti is a nation of 10 million people, and thousands of children are restavecs. Theirs is a hidden, harsh life. As poverty and political turmoil increases, so do the numbers of restavecs. A few years ago, in the aftermath of the earthquake that devastated Haiti, it was estimated that at least 150,000 kids, and perhaps as many as 500,000 kids, were sold into domestic servitude, where they were susceptible to beatings and sexual assaults.

Human traffickers prey on the ranks of restavecs. Hurricane Matthew has exacerbated the risks for kids displaced by the storm to be further victimized by human traffickers. The deadly storm killed over a thousand people in Haiti; it wiped way entire towns and villages. Children of families who lost everything, and those who were separated from their parents, may get sold into forced labor and be subjected to other atrocities because they're so vulnerable. It has been estimated that at least 2,000 vulnerable children have been separated from their parents by the storm. Some of those kids probably have been evacuated to orphanages. While Port-au-Prince was spared the blunt of the hurricane, the torrential rains and winds did damage many schools in the city, leaving many kids with nowhere to go each day. The schools where we are sending thirteen of our kids are opened and our kids are attending school. Of course, our classes at Santa Chiara were not interrupted by the storm.

What troubles me now in the aftermath of the storm is the reality that traffickers will use the storm to their advantage by approaching families who have lost everything and promising them a better future for their kids. This is exactly what happened after the earthquake . . . and in all probability it is happening right now.

Hurricane Matthew just accentuates the importance of the Santa Chiara Children's Center. I fully realize we can't respond to the overwhelming devastation in the western part of Haiti, but we can be a light in the darkness to the kids in our neighborhood in Haiti. I think many people from the rural, coastal areas, including countless children, who were displaced by the hurricane will migrate to Port-au-Prince. We need to be ready to serve them.

Like a River Flows

Note: In this journal entry, I looked back at our move into our third home in Haiti.

Saturday, October 29, 2016. Yesterday I had this thought: I could spend the rest of my life here, in this house in Delmas, 33. The thought took me by surprise, even though I have vaguely thought in the past that I would end up living . . . and dying . . . in Haiti. When we were cleaning up the old place before we surrendered the keys, I thought about our beginning in the apartment in the slum, with its three small rooms, a kitchen and one bathroom . . . and how we had at least a half dozen kids living with us. Then we moved up the street to what initially felt like paradise . . . we had space and security. Last December was truly an exciting time of transition, culminating in a big Christmas party with a staffer dressed up as Santa Claus and small gifts for all the kids.

It was the perfect location to put the vision of Santa Chiara to the test. We learned and we grew. The number of kids coming kept increasing . . . pushing us and the location to the limits. We made lots of mistakes. No one was really qualified to do what we were doing. I saw so many things that were wrong but had to patiently trust it will all work itself out in time. On moving day itself, I saw so many things that could have been planned better, but I thought to myself, *Shut up and stay out of the way . . . they will somehow get everything on the truck.*

One of my favorite authors is the Irish writer John O'Donohue, who died suddenly in 2008 at the age of fifty-two. He was a poet, a former priest, and a Hegelian philosopher. In one poem, he wrote:

> I would love to live
> Like a river flows,
> Carried by the surprise
> Of its own unfolding.

I have truly been surprised by the unfolding of Santa Chiara. I didn't always understand the unfolding as it happened. I just had to let go of my doubts, insecurities, and expectations, and simply trusted it was God's will for me to be in Haiti and so it would all somehow work out. Things have really moved fast. It hasn't been a gentle canoe ride down a lazy river; it was more like running white water rapids with not much control over the elements. But now we have maneuvered those crazy, unpredictable currents and have arrived at smooth stretch of the river.

I think the change of venue has given us a chance to revisit the vision of our mission. Besides the twenty-eight kids who lived with us in Peguyville, we had anywhere from twenty-five to forty-five additional kids coming every day. Many of those kids came before or after their school day. They ate, they played, they did crafts. While all the kids were poor, most of the kids who came for the day lived with one or both of their parents. The parents worked; some had decent jobs, but most did very menial work for low pay. The point I am making is that many of the "day kids" were not as impoverished as most of the chronically poor in Haiti. Their families were managing to survive, even if barely doing so. We in fact were, for those kids, a day-care center. The kids were not on the streets; they were in a safe, nurturing environment.

Here in Delmas, we have thirty-four kids living with us. These were truly the most vulnerable kids we served. They had nowhere else to be. Some of those "full time" kids had a loving mother or father, but they couldn't care for their child or children. Some kids simply were abandoned by their parents. It seems clear to me that not many of the day kids from Peguyville will come to Delmas. But those kids will be OK because they do have responsible parents. Our focus has to be the kids who are living with us. Yet we are not an orphanage. I want us to be much more than that. I do think that truly impoverished kids from the surrounding slums will find their way to our new place . . . where they will be welcomed to spend the day. I guess the point I am trying to make is that if all we did was care for the kids living with us, it would still be a great thing. I am not sure where this river named Santa Chiara is taking us.

Note: In time, we had seventy-two kids living with us. It was too many kids. We gradually and compassionately reduced the number not only to survive but also to better care for the kids who remained. By June 2022, we were fully certified by the agency of the Haitian government responsible for the social well-being of children to operate an orphanage.

A Very Long Day

November 5, 2016. On Friday morning, we arrived at Grace Children's Hospital at 8:30 am. Hundreds of people with sick kids were already in the large waiting room. We brought back Judline, Tamysha, and Kendy for the multiple tests they each needed. From the moment we entered the waiting area, I knew it would be a long day. I had no idea how long, how hard . . . or that we would be leaving with only two kids. Kendy has mild malnutrition, among other things. They gave us a supply of a super-enhanced peanut butter, which should turn his situation around. Judline had some very unexpected good news . . . but I need to wait until tomorrow to share some special news about Judline. Friday was all about Tamysha. Clearly, she was sick. She of course tested positive for HIV, which was no surprise.

The clinic and labs at the hospital are located in a series of small buildings, all with tin siding. Inside the main clinic there was a maze of examining rooms made of rough plywood. The doctor who eventually saw the kids was crammed into a small office inside a sea container. The place was chaos. All the tests were completed by noon . . . but we waiting until 2:30 pm to see the doctor, who examined all three children.

Tamysha was the last to be seen. I could see the concern on the doctor's face as he examined her. Her breathing was very labored. The doctor said she was very sick, and her condition was unstable. He said she had to be immediately admitted to the hospital. We left the sea container and walked to the children's ward of the hospital, which consisted of a large room jammed with rows of metal cribs. As we walked, the doctor said that if there was no open space, we would have to immediately take her to another hospital. Mercifully, there was an open crib. When the doctor began to work on her, Tamysha began screaming and would not stop. Once she was placed in the crib, the doctor gave us a list of prescriptions that had to be filled immediately and brought back to the hospital as soon as possible. We also had to bring back diapers and some special powdered baby milk.

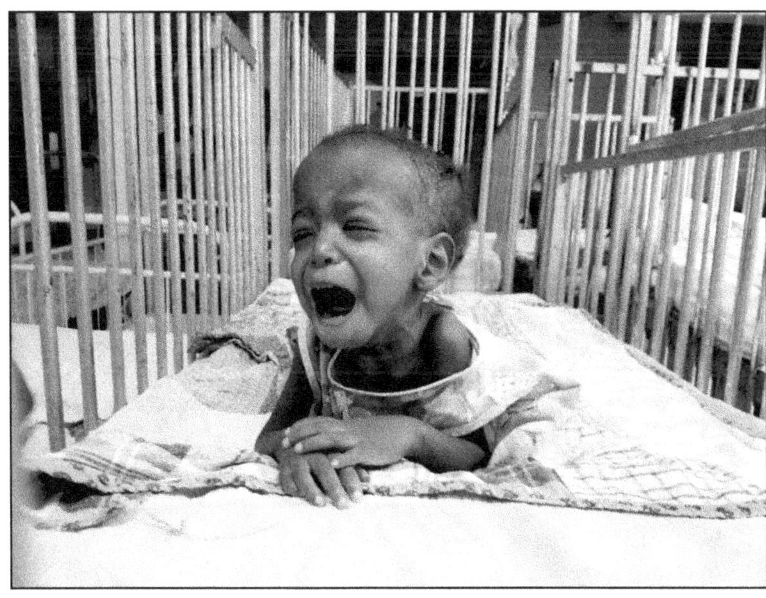

Tamysha at the hospital, 2016

We left the hospital at 3:30 pm . . . a full eight hours after we entered it. We had to go to two pharmacies to get all the prescriptions. It took nearly an hour to get back to the hospital. We are expected to visit Tamysha once a day . . . which of course we will do. Please keep Tamysha, and all our kids, in your prayers.

A Silent Symphony

November 23, 2016. Each morning we are awakened to the presence of God. When our hearts and minds are awakened by God, each morning becomes a silent symphony, each day is orchestrated according to the ways of harmony and peace and each moment becomes a sacramental moment where heaven and earth have the potential to meet. Our journey to God begins afresh each morning. If we begin the day in prayer, in God, then the day will flow out from God and lead us home to God.

O Lord, help me to renew
my innermost being.
I stumble and fall often.
My many failures
disappoint me.
But You never treat me
as I deserve.
You close your eyes
to my faults.
I trust in your endless
mercy and compassion.
But I need your help
to truly purify
my deepest being,
to create there
a more suitable chamber
for Your spirit to reside.

CHAPTER 34

Haiti 2017 Journals

Truly Free

May 22, 2017. If you truly believe deep in the core of your being that you came from God and that one day you will return to God, then you would be truly free to act as God would like you to act by being a manifestation of God's love. When you can look into the mirror and say with full confidence, "I am a child of God," you will no longer need to conform to the ways of the world, and you can bring God's love to those who are suffering.

I jotted those thoughts down a few days ago in the predawn stillness and silence while everyone on the second floor was still sound asleep.

Even though I spent a good chunk of my life in the hustle and bustle of network television in Hollywood and New York, I've always been attracted to monasticism. I find the lives of monks, both ancient and modern, to be very fascinating. From the Desert Fathers of early Christianity to Thomas Merton and Thomas Keating, monks, both Eastern and Western, never fail to attract my attention. For some time, I felt mysticism was most at home in monasteries. Of course, I loved that Saint Francis of Assisi said that the world was his cloister, choosing to be neither a monk nor a priest. More than a physical place, monasticism takes root in the heart.

I'm slowly beginning to see this slum in Haiti where I live as my cloister. While Santa Chiara is a busy, noisy place (can fifty kids be anything other than busy and noisy?), and I spend many hours either driving around an extremely chaotic city or inside dismal and dispiriting hospitals, I do manage to carve out many solitary hours where I sit alone in my office a floor above most of the activity. I recently wrote in this journal about my "linguistic loneliness" (not to be confused with eating linguine alone); my aloneness is deeper than the contours of language. I can't spend too much time downstairs . . . it is all too frenetic for me. I don't know how to respond to so many kids clinging to me. Most of the thirteen younger kids still in diapers are now walking . . . and falling. The really young, abandoned infants, like Kenja and Jerome, are still very fragile and in need of constant attention. It seems like countless things can go wrong. Moreover, I see so much I would do differently, but implementing the kinds of changes I'd like to see simply isn't possible at this time, as I have neither the staff nor the funding to make sweeping improvements. Despite all we've accomplished, and the lives we have saved or changed, we are still far from being what I would like us to be. Reality has a long way to go to catch up to the vision. But we have traveled far and are going in the right direction, albeit slowly. Patience is a virtue that I'm being forced to learn.

Mysticism, I'm slowly learning, is also at home in the nitty, gritty, and messiness of daily life, in the busy marketplace, in the towers of commerce, in the gutters of life. No matter where we are, from moment to moment, God is present, making each moment open to an ocean of possibilities. Through mystical eyes, we see the interrelatedness of all life and are therefore called to treat all life with loving-kindness . . . with the possible exception of mosquitos in Haiti. All of us, including people of all faiths, are called to become mystical mirrors of God's boundless love. The gravity of life can only be transfigured by love.

In my little one-room slum monastery, I see more clearly the contradictions of my own life. I see how easily I become confused . . . and depressed. But, paradoxically, I also see more clearly God's mercy. Merton said God's mercy "in no way depends on the approval of others," and the awareness of God's mercy is "a kind of liberation." I would say God's mercy is a taste of liberation. I know I am not truly free, that sin and personal weaknesses still have a grip on me. But their grip is nowhere near as strong as it once was. I can taste liberation. I can pray and continue to walk toward more full liberation. Meanwhile, it is a joy to help the kids become liberated from a cruel, often violent, prison of poverty . . . that we can give them a ray of hope and provide them a chance at the happiness of just being a kid, a place for them to learn and to run around and play without the fear of hunger.

Yes . . . the Santa Chiara Children's Center is also my monastery. Perhaps you might like to visit and play and pray with us. Call Brother Guest Master (that would be me) and schedule a visit. If you come, bring mosquito repellent.

Note: In the above journal entry, I mentioned a fragile infant named Kenja. Less than a month later, she was dead. The events surrounding her death filled up pages of the journal. I sent a very condensed news of the death to an array of people who did not receive the journal. In it, I wrote:

June 19, 2017, was an extremely tragic day at the Santa Chiara Children's Center. The day began with the death of a four-month-old infant girl. Her name was Kenja. She had been with us for two months. She was very sick when we received her. We took her to the hospital for treatment. She spent a week in the hospital and seemed to be on the road to recovery. But at three in the morning of June 19th, Kenja began crying. She had a fever and diarrhea. She eventually fell back to sleep. At 7:00 am, we began to get her dressed in preparation for taking her back to the hospital. When she had on new diapers and clean pajamas, the staff left Kenja in her crib in order to get ready to transport her to the hospital. A few minutes later, when we entered the babies' room, the infant was dead. Soon, her tiny crib was surrounded by kids crying as they looked at her lifeless body.

We had two of Kenja's older sisters living with us . . . in fact, they are still living with us. One was an eight-year-old girl named Bency. I was in the process of adopting her. She had lived with me as my daughter for more than a year. At the end of the day that Kenja died, Bency was abruptly dragged away by her deranged, drug-addicted monster of a mother who had beaten the girl badly before she had "given" me the child. The child was dragged away screaming. The mother lived in the dreadful Cité Soleil slum, in a one-room shack without electricity, running water, or a toilet. The walls were made of tin. The roof was a porous canvas. The floor was dirt. The girl I had cared for as my daughter would be living in deplorable conditions and would be subjected to daily beatings.

I knew that Kenja was with God. But Bency was in a horrific slum. At the time, I wrote: "I felt as if my heart had been ripped out of my body on that dreadful day. I have within me a profoundly deep emptiness. It is hard to focus on the fifty kids still living with us, twelve of whom are in diapers." A week or so later, the man who lived with the mother returned Bency to me.

Note: And so it has gone, from crisis to crisis, for more than five years. So much happens each day, it is hard to remember it all. This crazy, soap opera-esque journal stands as a historical record of trying to do as Christ would have us do, and that in doing so, we'll continually encounter the Cross at every turn. Staying faithful requires prayer, patience, and an array of supportive friends offering funds and guidance.

When I think that at this moment (August 6, 2020) our future is cloudy, I realize that for every day for more than five years our future has always been cloudy. We've been in worse financial shape. We've lived through horrendous tragedies, such as Tamysha's brutal removal and subsequent death, to having my own life threatened by a gang of protestors intent on setting my car on fire with me in it, to surviving my personal encounter with the nasty Covid-19 scourge that had me on oxygen twenty-four hours a day for seven straight days. Day in and day out, it comes down to one thing: Radical trust in God.

My heart still aches of the death of Tamysha. She was so malnourished when she was brought to us, she had to be hospitalized for a full month. Because she was the weakest among the weak, she was, for me, the heart and soul of Santa Chiara.

On the following page is a photo of her taken on the day she arrived [left] and a photo taken on the day I brought her home from the hospital.

From the day, I brought her home, she never stopped clinging to me. It took me two weeks to get her to smile, which happened on Christmas Day, 2016. It was the best Christmas present I'd ever received.

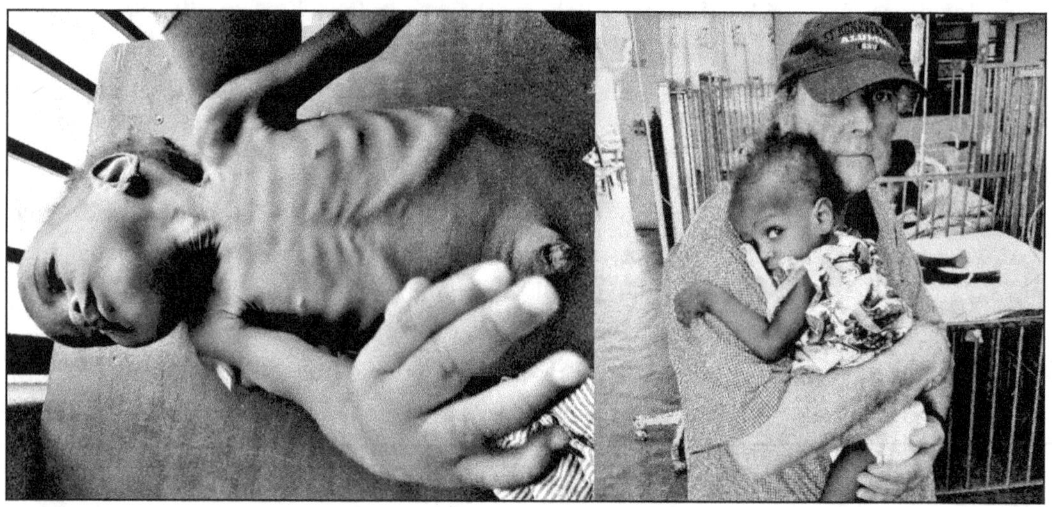

Tamysha and me in December 2016. May she rest in peace.

Masterpieces of God

August 31, 2017. If I am unable to see myself as a uniquely masterful creation of God and accept that reality, then it will be impossible for me to see and accept you as a masterpiece of God. I personally have not reached this point. There are many days, I don't really like myself. But on those days, I trust that God loves me anyway, just as I am, in my faithfulness and in my sinfulness. If I can see myself and you also as a masterpiece of God, it would dramatically alter the way I encounter you.

As a unique creation of God, I must strive to be faithful and committed to the truth that sustains and guides me. However, that truth can't dominate me or close me off to a deeper or more profound truth. The truth that I hold dear, the truth that shapes my behavior, can only expand by listening to others without needing to refute or belittle the truth they hold dear. The hope is that each of us, in our own God-created uniqueness, can discover a higher truth. Of course, as human beings, you and I must both realize that we each may make mistakes in our pursuit of the Truth. I can hardly believe all the misconceptions I had about God over the years.

As a Christian whose faith is rooted in the Trinity, I imagine God to be essentially relational. Therefore, it is imperative for me to relate to all whom I meet as I walk through life, whether or not we share common beliefs or hold entirely different beliefs. The point is to find unity where we can. And in those areas where unity is not immediately possible, let's give the other person the freedom to hold on to their own truth. When it comes to relating to people of a different faiths, charity is essential. In a democratic society, it is vitally important to respect and defend everyone's right to worship and praise God as they see fit.

Here is the bottom line: without peace among religions, there will never be peace among nations. Moreover, without honest, open dialogue, there will never be peace among religions. I think the survival of humanity is contingent upon people of different faiths learning to walk and work together. They must work together to build a just, merciful, and peaceful society. Otherwise, the haters and extremists will bring us to the brink of extinction.

All of Creation

November 13, 2017. All of creation flows from a good and loving God; therefore, all of creation is good. All of creation is an expression of God's love. Because God is the author of all life, we, along with all of creation, are brothers and sisters who are called by God to be one in cosmic harmony. All of humanity is connected to God and created to live in relationship. All humans were created to emulate the self-emptying love of God and to share God's love and mercy with each other, especially with those living on the periphery of society who are imprisoned by chronic poverty.

Note: As I typed those words, which I copied from the piece of paper I found last Thursday in the unopened box in my closet in Florida, I was tempted to add something to the first sentence: All of creation flows from a good and loving God; therefore, all of creation is good . . . except possibly for asparagus.

Of course, the addendum was an attempt to be funny. But giving the current dismal state of the world and the divisive state of American politics, it is not a time for humor, unless you happen to be a political satirist, which I am not. Living in harmony is a serious matter . . . and far from easy. People easily annoy us. Some of the kids living at Santa Chiara annoy me. Those are the very kids I need to work harder at to see the God-given goodness within them. There was one four-year-old little girl (who shall remain nameless) who really pushed all my buttons . . . she easily made my annoyance spill into anger. But one day, I decided to simply embrace her . . . and show her nothing but love. Within a short period of time, everything changed. Now when I see her, I can't help but smile. Her behavior has changed. I am not implying she is a little angel. But the fact that she knows I love her no matter her behavior has made her behavior better. Teaching the kids (and the staff as well) the way of nonviolence and living in peace and harmony is a top priority at Santa Chiara.

CHAPTER 35

Haiti 2018 Journals

Keep Hope Alive

July 12, 2018. In Haiti, hope is always delayed and often betrayed. To effectively serve the kids in my care, I must constantly struggle against the temptation to think my work is hopeless. The only way to disarm the destructive sense of hopelessness is prayer. My search for God has pulled me strongly in two opposite directions: to the impoverished kids in Haiti and to solitude. Balancing action and contemplation is essential in our humble, often-flawed efforts at following Christ and living the Gospel more fully.

Our singular aim as individuals, as communities, and as a Church is living out and being true to the Gospel. All of us, including the institutional Church, are not yet fully converted to Jesus, and we all remain in constant need of conversion. I believe the Beatitudes are the core of the teachings of Jesus and the primary pathway to authentic Christian discipleship that gives birth to a spirit of peace and nonviolence in which we extend mercy and compassion to all.

Hope is the wind in the sail of spirituality.

Mad Dogs and Swine

June 30, 2018. Tuesday's Gospel reading was from Matthew's account of the Sermon on the Mount. I'm still contemplating it. It contained this line: "How narrow the gate and constricted the road that leads to life. And those who find it are few." That line always reminds me of a film I made on peace and nonviolence with Fr. John Dear, the title of which was *The Narrow Path*. But I heard the Gospel on Tuesday in a different way. A few sentences earlier Jesus was telling his disciples not to give "what is holy to dogs or throw your pearls before swine." In a way, Jesus was testing the disciples. Jews at the time considered non-Jews to be mad dogs or swine. For them, those who believed differently from them were to be avoided. But Jesus turned this idea upside down.

During the liturgy, many consider the elevation of the host and then the chalice as the high point and most symbolic moment of the celebration. But perhaps the real essence is when the priest breaks the bread. When you break bread and share it with someone, it says you are welcoming them, making them, in essence, your sister and brother. Jesus understood this. In the breaking of the bread, Jesus is shattering all boundaries. He is saying everyone is your sister and brother, even those who worship God by a different name than you do, even your enemies.

Less than a century ago, in the name of nationalism, calling those who were different from you swine led to the extermination of millions of Jews. When I was growing up, my Catholic parish (St. Benedict Joseph Labré) was about thirteen blocks from our home. But just across the street from us was a small Baptist church. We viewed all Protestants as . . . I want to say "as seriously misguided," but that is far too diplomatic; we viewed all non-Catholic Christians as devils and contact with them should be avoided. Those were dark days. But the Light began to shatter the darkness when Pope John XXIII had a moment of revelation, a genuine epiphany, during a Good Friday ritual in the 1960s. It all but knocked him over. Some of his assistants actually thought he was sick. He immediately retreated to a private room and wrote a decree eliminating all negative language about the Jews from the liturgical life of the Church. Jews were no longer going to be referred to as "Christ killers." This bold, unprecedented moment led to Vatican II. The windows of the Church were thrown open and the Light flooded in . . . and Catholicism would never be the same again. The Spirit of God had moved . . . and is still moving.

Today, around the world, politics has become mean-spirited. The art of politics rests upon the idea of "give and take." Your side gives a little and you take a little from the other side. Jesus did not buy in to this premise. He told us to give without seeking or expecting anything in return. Many Americans today are calling our brothers and sisters from Central America and Mexico, who are fleeing poverty and violence with their children, thugs, rapists, murderers, and undesirable people who are breaking into our country to steal from us. Theirs is a politics of fear and division. They spread an endless stream of falsehoods. They say that millions are crossing the border illegally, when the truth is that the rate of undocumented migrants entering the United States has steadily declined over the last decade. The crime rate among undocumented migrants living in the United States is actually lower than the crime rate for citizens of our nation.[218]

We need to break down the walls of division and discover the humanity of the stranger through hospitality, even though they do not share our perspective and stories. When our hearts are ruled by love and we seek unity we will be on the road to peace.

In both my past ministry and the present ministry, I've steadfastly avoided making any political statements. I also avoid making any comments about social issues within the Church, such as married priests or women priests. My focus was solely on poverty. I never mention Democrats or Republicans. I never mention traditional or progressive factions within the Church. Only one of my films carried political overtones. *Endless Exodus* was about undocumented migrants. Produced in 2004, the film's focus was not political or social, because the film was really about the spirituality of migration, and our response to the plight of the migrants, many of whom died trying to cross the desert to get a job nobody really wants.

The film's goal was to shed light on the life of the poor in order to help the viewer better understand why they are forced to leave their homes and countries for a backbreaking, low-paying job in a foreign land whose culture is dramatically different from theirs. But it wasn't just a film about empathizing with migrants who only wanted a better life. The film parallels our own spiritual journey through our own desert of doubts and confusions, as the migrants teach us about sacrifice, fearlessness, and dedication in the face of grave circumstances. The film was not about a specific political agenda; it was about trying see the face of Jesus in the face of the undocumented migrant.

We so easily turn the "other" into an "enemy." What is happening along our southern border in separating parents from their children is disgraceful and immoral . . . and a violation of international human rights.

Yesterday, Today, and Tomorrow

July 2, 2018. Yesterday morning I woke much later than usual . . . at 4:50 am. I was tired. Everything within me wanted to just roll over and go back to sleep. I knew if I did, I would miss Mass with the Sisters at 6:30 am. I recalled how at the end of my two-hour presentation to the Sisters during their retreat week last month, I jokingly asked something along the lines of: "Are there days you just don't want to get up, days when you want to ignore the bell calling you to prayer?" Their laugher told me they do indeed have days like that.

Here in Haiti, there are days, even weeks, that seem just too overwhelming to bear. During those days, I need to cling to my anemic faith . . . but that is not always easy. Fear and doubts creep in. In yesterday's Gospel (from Mark) in which Jesus heals two people and raises a little girl from death, He says to a synagogue official: "Do not be afraid; just have faith." Jesus is always telling us that, yet we often find it hard to do. When I get down, I have to pause and really try to hear the voice of Christ say, "I was with you yesterday, I am with you today, and I will be with you tomorrow. Do not be afraid . . . things will work out, as they always have."

We don't always see the hand of God guiding us as we work through difficult times. During those times, we need to remember God's presence in the past and trust that God is still walking with us, still loving us, still wanting us to live life to its fullest. Whether we are aware of it or not, God is always working in the background to help us carry through the mission entrusted to us. Life is a journey, a long journey. There will be dark days, dark weeks. In those times, it is essential to believe in God's loving-kindness.

A Divine Space

July 6, 2018. The wellspring of all virtue is within us. There is a place deep within our souls where there is great love, kindness, mercy, and forgiveness. The primary goal of our lives is digging down to reach this divine space . . . and then share its fruits with all. This interior digging, in which we come face-to-face with our true selves, is a continuous act of transfiguration. When we reach this divine space, the mystics tell us, what has been invisible will become visible, what has been hidden will come into the Light.

Before this digging, this journey to our true center, begins we need to let go of our bondage to temporal and external things and focus on the universal hunger within all of us for deeper, interior and eternal truths that are beyond image and word, beyond all physical sensations. We must learn to hold the external and internal, the visible and invisible, the known and unknown in balance, which is not easy given our own vulnerable complexity. It is a solitary journey that is made easier when we walk in harmony with other seekers, friends on the spiritual path who are also comfortable living without clear answers.

This quest for the divine is quest for love. We need love. We hunger for love. Love is the oxygen of our souls. Love has a transfiguring power that changes water into wine, night into day, rigidity into softness, fear into courage, emptiness into fullness, estrangement into unity, clinging into sharing, poverty into sufficiency, exile into homecoming, negativity into sunrise. Sadly, we feed this hunger for love with all the wrong things, things that ultimately move us further away from life-giving love. To love is to be open to an Other. Love dismantles walls of separation. Love is the dawn of new understanding.

CHAPTER 36

Haiti 2019 Journals

The Eyes of Christ

January 5, 2019. Following Jesus requires a lot more than learning abstract ethical and moral principles; it requires a change in heart, a change in the way we look at life. A heart transformed by the love of Christ is a patient heart, a heart that takes the time to be still and to listen.

> To see
> with the eyes of Christ,
> is to see
> the beauty of all creation,
> to see
> the beauty within ourselves
> and within each other.

We are all in such a hurry, rushing from here to there, from this to that, an endless treadmill of movement going nowhere. Anxiety is as common as a cold. We are anxious about the future, our jobs, our relationships . . . we're anxious about virtually everything. Our anxiety breeds a drive to acquire more and more of everything. Nothing is enough. We want more of everything. More money, more prestige, more clothing, more contacts, better cars, bigger houses, faster computers.

In our endless movement, our constant rushing, we don't see our own loneliness, our brokenness. We are all wounded. But as our hearts become more transformed by the presence of Christ, we are able, in our weakness, to feel the love of God and to trust in the abundance of God's love.

> Our relentless drive to acquire more
> is fueled by our deep-rooted
> sense of scarcity,
> our inability to trust
> that God wants
> to give us all that we need.

Ordinary Time

January 15, 2019. When I woke Naïve up at 5:00 am yesterday, I helped her climb down the ladder from the top bunk. She does not like the top bunk. I put out my arms and said, "I'll catch you." I thought she said she had to pee. But when I embraced her, she was all wet. She tried to tell me she had peed in the bed. My nice clean T-shirt was wet with pee. And so, the day began.

When I left Santa Chiara, backing up slowly through the gate, I paused briefly to look at all the kids waving goodbye. I suddenly felt overwhelmed by the sensation that I lived with angels. So many of the staff, regrettably, are quick to classify a child as bad. But, in truth, God dwells within each child and so they are angels . . . who sometimes behave badly for a variety of reasons. It is easy to harshly judge a child. There are a few of our kids who can get under my skin. It is those kids that I have to embrace more firmly and find the good within them. Santa Chiara is a school of life for me.

A Bed of Roses

March 6, 2019. Tuesday's Gospel reading came from Mark and began with Peter telling Jesus: "We gave up everything and are following you." While Peter went on to become a great leader, in those early days, he was a bit dysfunctional and very human. He was like us. But what exactly did Peter give up . . . a rickety old boat? The subtext of what Peter was saying was "What am I going to get out of this?" What Peter wanted and what we all want is to be infinity loved just as we are.

Heaven is being loved fully by God and being totally aware of it. We know God loves us, but, like Peter, we really don't appreciate it.

What am I getting out of being in Haiti? I'm getting a chance to grow in the knowledge and awareness that God loves me. Moreover, I'm getting far more back than I gave up. I'm learning to be a better human being, learning to go deeper into prayer, learning to give love and receive love. In Haiti, I'm learning what it means to follow Christ. We want a bed of roses. Christ offers us the Cross. Following Christ requires sacrifice, requires putting to death countless things within us that betray our love of Christ.

For Love to Give Love

April 13, 2019. How sad, how tragically sad, that we allow ourselves to be ruled and controlled by our illusions and fears. And so, we live much of our lives in a prison of falsity. This is not God's plan for any of us. God wants us to know true peace and freedom.

We were created in the image of God, which is to say we were created to mirror the love of the Trinity by giving ourselves away, for life to give life, for mercy to give mercy, for compassion to give compassion, for peace to give peace, for love to give love.

Because we do not know our real self, our true nature, we live in darkness and doubt. Conflicts haunt us. We feel threatened. We build walls around ourselves for protection. In the depths of our being we feel isolated, alone, naked. Joy is fleeting. Bitterness grows in our uncultivated garden starving for sunlight. The goodness and creativity of God is unknown, hidden, in part, by our own brokenness, our own weakness.

Holy Thursday

April 18, 2019. In the Passover meal celebrated by Jesus, we begin to learn about true sacrifice and true servanthood. God is not interested in human or animal sacrifice. Nor is God interested in the sacrifice of fasting from certain foods on certain days. The sacrifice that God seeks is the letting go of all that is ungodly within us, the letting go of our ego, the false self that always puts ourselves first.

To "pass over" from an ego-centered life to a God-centered life, from a self-centered life to another-centered life, requires a sacrificial surrendering of all that binds us, all that needs to die, so we can walk freely into the mystery of God.

Suffering and sharing are the gateways to divine intimacy. And to become intimate with God means to become the humble and loving servant of all. By washing the feet of another, God's love moves from an abstract theory into a concrete reality.

Jesus came to be a servant, to sacrifice himself for us. We must do likewise, by sacrificing ourselves and serving others.

God is talking to us. God has always been talking to us. God will always be talking to us. God has been, is, and will be saying one word: Love.

In that love rests a profound truth: We are one. We just imagine (as Thomas Merton pointed out) that we are not one, that division exists within the human family. In God, there is unity. In the beginning, we were one. We are still one. We just need to recover our original unity. At the Last Supper, Jesus prayed that we all may be one. Communion needs to be a significant part of our spiritual syntax. To isolate ourselves from the world stifles our ability to sense the dignity of the divine image in human beings.

The road to salvation is a journey to wholeness. When people lack the basic necessities to sustain life—clean water, adequate nutrition, essential health care, electricity, and sanitation—it's hard to become whole. Survival is struggle enough. For the people in the slums surrounding us, their every waking moment is directed toward meeting their basic physical needs.

To see a woman squatting in rotting rubbish or in the street (as I often do) to urinate or defecate is an unthinkable indignity. In love, through love, and with love we must unite and eradicate such indignity wherever it is found. We are called to incarnate God's love. It really is that simple. If we have the will to do it, we will figure out how to do it, how to set the captives free.

The Passover liberation story of being freed from captivity has relevance for us today.

It tells us that we too can be freed from the oppressive forces that overwhelm and bind us, that we can be healed and transformed through a new life in Christ. The Last Supper was a Seder meal, the Jewish tradition that called to mind that rebirth, renewal, and transformation are possible, and that we are not stuck in the dark, cold, deadly energies that often hold us—and society—captive.

Passover and Easter can easily become empty celebrations of past victories and past resurrections of hope if we forget or ignore that widespread oppression is still very real in our day, as more than 2 billion people live in hopeless situations, struggling to stay alive on less than two dollars a day. In the United States, millions are without homes, jobs, and access to adequate health care, and even more have jobs that do not pay a living wage as a result of immoral social and economic policies that favor the rich and suffocate the poor . . . a draconian situation that is getting worse rather than better, with even darker days in store for the chronically poor.

When we embrace the ethos of global capitalism, with its emphasis of materialism and selfishness, we begin to look at the world through the lens of our own narrow self-interest (asking questions such as "What have you done for me lately?" or "What can you give me to satisfy *my* needs?") and thereby fail to see the holiness, the beauty, the uniqueness, and the commonality of all human beings. When we live for ourselves instead of living a life of service to others, we keep ourselves enslaved and powerless.

Becoming a Part of a Whole

April 20, 2019 (Holy Saturday). Haiti is seared with sadness. The poor are stuck in the long, lonely, dark Holy Saturday between the cross and the resurrection, enduring the immensity of waiting for something to change. In Haiti, the wealth of a few is built upon the poverty of many. The same is true in America. Wall Street gamed and inflated the housing bubble, stealing billions in the process while leaving millions of households in ruin, as countless Americans lost pay, jobs, homes, and savings. We need to return to the principle of the common good. We can't create a good society on a foundation of maximizing the profits of industry and business and maximizing the choices for consumers, especially when both profit and choice depend upon risky and unsustainable levels of corporate and personal debt. Allowing the common good to take primacy in our lives will help us to live well together and create social conditions that will allow everyone to more easily reach their full human potential.

We urgently need to move beyond our individual and nationalistic egos and see ourselves and our countries as part of a whole, each of us living gratefully and contributing to the entire human family, sharing and caring for each out of love.

None of us is entitled to anything. Yet God gives us everything. As angels of compassion, we need to commit ourselves to nonviolence and to growing in awareness of the needs of others as we increase our sensitivity to new and better possibilities of serving each other.

Mahatma Gandhi said, "I am a part and parcel of the whole, and I cannot find God apart from the rest of humanity."

The Ant Killer

July 2, 2019. Saint Francis's embrace of nonviolence was so total that he would not kill an ant. In fact, he praised their industriousness. I try to be a good Franciscan and emulate Saint Francis as best as I can. But I kill hundreds of ants a day. When I entered the kitchen yesterday morning, two areas of countertop had morsels of food the kids left and they were each surrounded by dozens of ants. I didn't say, "Brother and Sister Ants, enjoy your meal in peace." Not by a long shot. I zipped to my office and grabbed a spray can of insecticide. Within seconds, the countertop was a killing field.

Note: As I read this three years later, I wonder if any of us is truly nonviolent. I suppose Saint Francis exaggerated to make point. A few weeks ago in Haiti, I killed dozens of cockroaches as if it were a sport. I recall a story of Saint Francis admonishing the cook for soaking beans overnight in preparation for the next day's meal, telling the cook that Christ said not to think about tomorrow. Clearly, Francis was not the patron saint of calendar makers. But the point is to be present to the present moment. Life is littered with paradoxes.

CHAPTER 37

Haiti 2020 Journals

Love

July 31, 2020, Haiti. For more than twenty years, I've been thinking about and writing about love. Not the surface love we know and sometimes experience, a love too easily engaged and discarded. But the self-emptying love of Christ and the relatively few "saints" from all faiths who entered self-emptying love deeply and practiced it through extreme hardships and suffering. Our world has been wounded by violence and social exclusion of all kinds. Only through the power of vulnerable and naked love can we incarnate Christ's new creation. We resist fully embracing Christ's foolish way of love because we are reluctant to enter into an inconceivable mystery; we also fear the consequences of being in solidarity with all forms of poverty, which will cost us everything and demand some suffering on our part. Because radical love makes dangerous demands, we shun it. Before 1995, such a love was far beyond my consciousness.

For the last five years in Haiti, I valiantly tied to live this self-emptying love, but virtually every day I failed in countless ways large and small. Contemplating self-emptying love is easy and often inspiring, but to actually live it, live it fully, seems beyond my reach. I feel I've emptied myself of so much, yet, in reality, I've so much more that needs to be sacrificed on the altar of authentic love of God and all humanity. Just a few days ago, I tried to escape the stuffy, dusty confines of my office for a little fresh air. Within two minutes of sitting down on a bench at the back of the property, a staffer approached me and said, "Mr. Gerry, I have a problem." I didn't need him to tell me what his problem was. It was the end of his shift, and he probably needed money for the tap-tap ride home. He did. He needed about five bucks. I said OK, got up and went to my office for the money. I gave him ten 50-gourde bills. He thanked me. I decided to return to my office. I resented that "my time" on the garden bench had been interrupted. Instead of sitting and thinking about nothing, my head and heart were filled with the reality that I do not pay the staff enough and yet I need to cut their salaries during this time of financial crisis.

This was, of course, a very minor episode, but it nonetheless illustrates that I'm far from the kind of self-emptying love to which I aspire. Sure, I'm here in Haiti when I don't need to be, but each day, I put myself and my needs ahead of others and their serious needs.

I am comfortable; those around me are not. Yesterday morning as I drove in the predawn darkness to Mass, I passed a woman defecating on the side of the dirt road. It really disturbed me. She probably has no toilet, no toilet paper, no bathroom. I see countless heartbreaking things every day . . . and do not respond. On Sunday on the way home from the supermarket where I bought (with my personal credit card) an $18 bottle of Italian wine and a $20 bag of frozen peeled shrimp, I passed a woman with one leg who was dressed in rags. She was seated atop a concrete road divider. Traffic forced me to be driving slowly enough to have paused and put a little money in her outstretched hand. I did not.

Don't call me—or imply that—I'm a saint. I'm just a flawed guy trying to be less so, a guy trying to be more fully attuned to the consciousness of God at all times.

The kind of self-emptying, nonviolent love espoused by Jesus as manifested in a few heroic figures truly intrigues me. One such person, though never embracing Christianity, was a Jewish woman who died at the brutal hands of the Nazis in Auschwitz in 1943, one more victim of Hitler's fear-driven hatred. Her name was Etty Hillesum. As a young non-practicing Jewish woman, Etty was a philosopher and a seeker. Her intellectual attempts to understand the meaning of love eventually brought her to the heart of God . . . which totally transformed every fiber of her being. She became the love she had tried to understand.

The details of that remarkable journey of transformation were recorded in Etty's diaries and letters, many of which can be found in *Etty Hillesum: An Interrupted Life and Letters from Westerbork.* Even in the unthinkable horrors of the concentration camp, Etty could write: "I live in constant intimacy with God."[219] Before her incarceration, she wrote: "The jasmine behind my house has been completely ruined by the rains and storms of the last few days, its white blossoms are floating about in muddy black pools on the low garage roof."[220] Here are more entries from her diaries:

> There is a really deep well inside me. And in it dwells God. Sometimes I am there, too. But more often stones and grit block the well, and God is buried beneath. Then [God] must be dug out again.[221]
>
> But somewhere inside me the jasmine continues to blossom undisturbed, just as profusely and delicately as ever it did. And it spreads its scent round the House in which You dwell, oh God. You can see, I look after You, I bring You not only my tears and my forebodings on this stormy, grey morning, I even bring scented jasmine. . . . I shall try to make You at home always. Even if I should be locked up in a narrow cell and a cloud should drift past my small barred window, then I shall bring you that cloud, oh God, while there is still strength in me to do so.[222]
>
> This morning I said to Jopie, "It still all comes down to the same thing: life is beautiful. And I believe in God. And I want to be right in the thick of what people call "horror" and still be able to say: life is beautiful.[223]

In his book *Jesus and the Prodigal Son: The God of Radical Mercy,* Brian J. Pierce, OP, writes:

Etty's rootedness in God sets her free. Once she discovers the fountain of life-giving water, her heart expands to embrace the entire universe. Etty's love knows no boundaries. Writing in her diary, she says, "German soldiers suffer as well. There are no frontiers between suffering people, and we must pray for them all."[224] Etty's deep interior peace confounds those who live in a world void of any semblance of transcendence.[225]

Etty knew and lived the truth and beauty she discovered deep within her. Her horizon was so broad that even the horror of a concentration camp couldn't defeat her. In contrast, I'm easily unsettled by life's vacillations. I long for the inner stability and grandness that Etty knew. The road to that kind of inner peace is rough. It is the road Jesus traveled. We need to follow him for he showed us the way of radical love, a self-emptying love that gives everything away. Fr. Brian Pierce writes, "The crucified and dead body of Christ has been transformed into a gushing spring of life. This is what Etty Hillesum points to when she speaks of 'the really deep well inside me.'"[226]

Liminal Space and My Weeklong Sabbath

August 5, 2020, Fort Pierce, Florida. In some Christian circles you often hear the term "liminal space." Hard to define, the term has its origins in the word first coined by anthropologists: *liminality*. Liminal is rooted in the Latin word *limen*, which means threshold. I feel as if I'm at a threshold moment in my life, ready to make some kind of transition. My time alone in Florida this week is essentially a hermitage or retreat experience that will help me enter a liminal space. It is a time apart to ponder a possible transition . . . or a regeneration of my existing life in Haiti.

By coming apart and entering solitude, we have a chance to think deeply about the change and flow in our lives. It is normal and easy to lose energy in the fulfillment of tasks we love. When this happens, our spirit is crying out for transformation and regeneration. Often, old things must die for new things to be born. In liminal space, normal and familiar activities cease, so we can consider creative ways to make needed improvements. My week in Florida is a sacred pause between the darkness of winter and the sunshine of spring. I'm entering the mystery of the unknown . . . and prayerfully deciding which way to go.

On Sunday, I pulled from a bookshelf a book titled *The Sabbath* by Abraham Joshua Heschel. He was a Jewish rabbi and an internationally known scholar. He is one of my favorite spiritual writers. In his masterpiece *Man Is Not Alone: A Philosophy of Religion*, Rabbi Heschel wrote: "This is the meaning of life: To reconcile liberty with service, the passing with the lasting, to weave threads of temporality into the fabric of eternity."[227]

In *The Sabbath*, I came across a passage I had highlighted many years ago:

All week we may ponder and worry whether we are rich or poor, whether we succeed or fail in our occupations; whether we accomplish or fall short of reaching our goals. But who could feel distressed when gazing at spectral glimpses of eternity, except to feel startled at the vanity of being so distressed?

The Sabbath is no time for personal anxiety or care, for any activity that might dampen the spirit of joy. The Sabbath is no time to remember sins, to confess, to repent or even pray for relief or anything we might need. It is a day for praise, not a day for petitions. Fasting, mourning, demonstrations of grief are forbidden. The period of mourning is interrupted by the Sabbath. And if one visits the sick on the Sabbath, one should say: "It is the Sabbath, one should not complain; you will soon be cured." One must abstain from toil and strain on the seventh day, even from strain in the service of God.[228]

I'm not sure why I highlighted that passage the first time I read it. But when I read it on Sunday, it was the last phrase that struck me—to abstain . . . *even from strain in the service of God.*

I needed a Sabbath week.

We must have periods in which we lie fallow and restore our souls. A time consecrated with our attention, our mindfulness, honoring the quiet forces of grace and spirit that sustain and heal us.

On the Sabbath, the pressures of ordinary life are bracketed, and we give ourselves permission to stop, to shut down, to rest. Sabbath need not be an entire day. Sabbath may be an afternoon, a Sabbath hour, a Sabbath walk. Let us not allow restlessness to drive us into activity, but sit with it until it turns into quiet and solitude, and sheer delight!

Years ago, in an unpublished manuscript, I wrote: "Liberation is found in the stillness and silence of the Sabbath, where we are called to drop our burdens and rest in the Lord and be refreshed and renewed by God's unmerited and unrelenting grace." It is crazy to realize how I forget my own advice.

Sabbath is not merely a time to put down normal work activities; neither is it simply a time to just relax and play. Sabbath is a time for nourishing and healing. It is a time to be free from the slavery of busyness in order to be alone with God. We all need Sabbath time in our lives, even if it is just for a few minutes each day to regain our composure and set our bearings. Our very busyness can disconnect us from our deeper selves. Sadly, our culture despises silence . . . we are surrounded by all kinds of sounds. The sounds of commerce mute the sounds of nature. Not so long ago, phones were confined to our homes and workplaces; now they are in our pockets. Thanks to laptop computers, when we go on vacation, we take our work with us. Sophisticated technology has created a plethora of personal communication devices that feed us a steady stream of music and movies. These devices are so addictive it is extremely hard to unplug from them. Maybe the Sabbath is a time to unplug them for a day . . . and listen to something *Real.*

Man does not live by the smartphone alone.

The Hell of Isolation

November 16, 2020. Dante's *Divine Comedy* confronts our struggle to arrive at a place of human promise amidst human frailty, injustice, and loss. The poem takes us on a journey from the blinding isolation of Hell (*Inferno*) into the tranquility and open air of Mount Purgatory (*Purgatorio*).

> *"We walked along the lonely plain*
> *like one who returns to a path once lost,*
> *whose journey, till then, seemed meaningless."*
>
> —PURGATORIO, 1.118-20

Before I entered that empty church in Rome in 1995, my journey through life seemed meaningless. The path I was on took me to a place of despair. In a flash, I was brought back to "a path once lost." I caught a glimpse of the beauty of a life shared with God and all humankind. I wanted to walk down a path of mutuality and kindness, a path of human interdependence that encourages us to lift others out of the hell of alienation, despair, prejudice, and marginalization. To do so, I began my journey down poverty road. I was shocked by the dehumanizing conditions I witnessed.

What makes the Santa Chiara Children's Center so frustrating, besides my inability to communicate or understand a culture so enslaved to violence, is that I dreamed of it being a large, loving family. It is large, but it is far from loving. The petty bickering, the mean-spirited gossiping, the stealing, the self-centered quest for survival, and the apathy and disdain from the Haitian elite meld together to mitigate the sense of community I dreamed of creating. Ascending to the heavens of the blessed in *Paradiso* is not possible.

I'm feeling the hell of isolation. Hope is dying. But this is OK because it pushes me deeper into prayer. *Oh God, give me wisdom, give me strength, give me courage. Help me not to lose my temper.*

Things will not change in Haiti or the world as long as inhumanity remains profitable and justice remains indifferent. The culture of corruption in Haiti is crippling. If you have money, anything is possible, all doors open. If you are penniless, your life is a dead end.

I fell asleep in the recliner last night at 7:30 pm despite the loud music and fireworks outside my office window. I woke at 1:30 am. After realizing I'd not written today's journal, I wrote this. Things seem clearer in the dark of night. Afterward, I took a deep breath and tried to steel myself against the unknown terrors of the coming day. I knew I had to take a sick staffer to the hospital. I knew one of the women I banned from the Santa Chiara Children's Center on Friday had told another staffer she would be returning today to confront me. I dread her arrival. I do not want to let her inside. Not sure what I will do. Nor am I sure how I will deal with the apparent disinterest of one of the Center's leaders. I'm so tired of nothing ever getting done in a timely fashion. In Haiti, the name of the game is delay, delay, delay. *Progress* is an unknown word. The only thing that matters is that schoolgirls have ribbons in their hair. It is an absurd, undivine comedy.

Murmuring

November 17, 2020. When he wrote his monastic rule, Saint Benedict repeatedly warned against the corrosive effects of "murmuring," a form of complaining or grumbling, which can destroy community life. It has only been in the last few months that I've become aware how destructive the mean-spirited gossiping within Santa Chiara has been. The various cliques within Santa Chiara seem to relish dishing out rumors and innuendos meant to deepen the divisions within the organization.

One high-ranking staffer basically said most of the staff needs to be replaced. It is very hard to establish a spirit of unity within a population that thrives of gossiping and tearing down those in leadership roles. As to St. Benedict, a group of disgruntled monks secretly put poison in his wine. Benedict blessed the glass before he put it to his lips. It shattered, and the wine spilled to the floor. I better be more diligent in saying grace before meals. In our early days, someone tried to poison someone in leadership. The plot failed. I can't recall how it failed. I just had a hard time believing that poisoning someone was in the realm of possibility. A life isn't worth much in Haiti.

Looking Back to See Today More Clearly

Note: *This was written after a horrible week when a tsunami of problems washed over me. To compound the trouble, I didn't have the funds to make it through December. It looked hopeless and like time to give up.*

November 18, 2020. In Haiti, a day feels like, at least for me, a week. So much happens it is hard to process it all. Yesterday (November 17), as I sat in the silence of the Missionaries of Charity sisters' chapel before Mass, I scribbled a few scattered, unfiltered thoughts.

Tumultuous five days
So much lying
Easily agitated
Poor communications
Lots of misunderstandings
Frustration level high
Still . . . this is home
Must relax and recenter
Can't let go

Can't walk away
My Merton book is my retreat from the chaos
Writing it (and reading it) is healing
So easy to lose focus
So easy to succumb—or better put, to entertain—the pull to walk away

Before I left for the Missionaries of Charity, I was looking for a specific book when I came cross a black, blank book. I pulled it from the shelf. It was a book I carried with me in 2016 to jot down thoughts. A few pages into the handwritten notes, an entry written on January 28, 2016, arrested my attention. It was written in an empty church in South Pasadena, California. The piece was titled "Fade Out."

I don't want to make another film.
I don't want to write another book.
I don't want to give another presentation in a church or school.

I want to disappear.
Not disappear as in vanish. I just want to fade from public view.
I no longer need the attention that comes from being an author, a filmmaker,
  or a speaker.

After filming extreme poverty all over the world . . . I think I've encountered
  Christ with the poor in Haiti.

I want to write. I need to write. But I don't need publication. I like writing
  my Haiti Journal for the 83 people who want to receive my daily scribbling
  via e-mail.

I don't even want to maintain my blog anymore and checking on how many
  people visited each day.

I think I prefer Haiti to America. Haiti demands faith. There is no safety net.

Haiti is an invitation to let go, to surrender completely to trust, to be moved
  by love.

Haiti is where I can go deeper into the heart of love.

In Haiti, my familiar props are removed. It is me and God . . . and a sea of kids.

In Haiti, life is real and raw.

In a filmscript, at the end of a scene, the writer writes: FADE OUT.

Note: I liked this flashback because it captured where I was nearly four years ago. I fulfilled its promise: I have all but completely disappeared outside of the 180 people who now subscribe to my journal. And my love for the kids has deepened.

Violence

November 21, 2020. About a ten-minute drive from us is the Peace Hospital. I've spent endless hours in that hospital. It is filthy, chaotic, and overcrowded. One of our kids, a toddler, spent many weeks in the hospital. During my daily visits to see our kid, I got to know a little sick boy in the same ward. I was shocked to learn he had died overnight because his mother could not pay for the oxygen tank. I was so outraged at this that I found my way to the oxygen storage room in the bowels of the building. I got to know the man who delivered the oxygen to the patients. I told him to never deny a child oxygen because of lack of money. I asked him to deliver the oxygen, and I would pay for it on my next visit.

I spent so much time in the hospital, people knew me. The sick often asked me for help to pay for medicine. We haven't been to the hospital for some time, as I found better hospitals. Yesterday, violence broke out in front of the hospital. Lots of gunfire. A tap-tap driver was shot. Not sure if he was killed. Closer to us, within walking distance, there is a major intersection. More violence at this busy, always congested area. Another tap-tap driver was shot and killed.

I went up to Pétionville yesterday afternoon. There was some kind of police protest that had traffic tied in knots. Fortunately, I didn't encounter any shooting. Every time I leave Santa Chiara, I never know what will happen. Getting shot is always a possibility. This is a very dangerous time in Haiti. On November 18, the protests resumed in earnest. Most of the roadblocks of burning tires were confined to downtown, but some blockades were sprinkled across parts of Delmas. Two Haitian engineers were kidnapped. The thugs broke into their office and pulled them out. Haiti remains a dangerous place to be. Bad things can happen to anyone at any time. On the upside, it is a bit cooler at night. In Haiti, you hang on to any speck of good news.

Note: Shortly after I sent that journal entry, a reader from Ohio responded with this:

> Gerry, while your Journals break my heart, they are also stabilizers in an insane world. What looks like a problem around here becomes like a grain of sand on the beach when compared to Haiti. When I read, I am torn . . . thanking God that you are there doing such amazing things for your kids . . . then wishing you could come back to the States. You are the oxygen for SCCC just as you were for the guy in the oxygen supply room. Of course, your Oxygen is the Holy Spirit. How else could you continue?

Note: *A week later I was about to take a boy to the hospital for surgery when the hospital called saying they had to cancel the surgery because the doctor had been kidnapped. That happened on the heels of a Haitian priest being kidnapped; the kidnappers demanded a ransom of $80,000, which wasn't paid, and it was assumed the priest had been killed.*

Postscript: In early November 2020, I wrote in my journal that the fast-approaching Christmas would be my sixth Christmas in Haiti . . . and it would be the first Christmas I wouldn't be able to buy Christmas presents for all the kids because we simply did not have the funds. I didn't see how we could last until the end of the year. We needed a huge miracle. The world needs a huge miracle. (Someone donated money specifically for use to buy gifts for the kids.)

We are all connected. This is the great teaching of Saint Francis, who said we are all brothers and sisters sharing the same earthly home. On October 4, 2020, the feast of the poor man (*Il Poverello*) of Assisi, Pope Francis was in Assisi to sign his new encyclical, *Fratelli Tutti*. In it, the Pontiff wrote: "We need to think of ourselves more and more as a single-family dwelling in a common home." The essence of the encyclical is that we are all connected and that "I" must become "We." You might say Pope Francis adapted the famous prayer attributed to Saint Francis: Where there is individualism, let me sow solidarity. The Pope ends his encyclical with a reflection on Blessed Charles de Foucauld, who worked as a missionary among the poor and abandoned in the Moroccan desert. Pope Francis wrote: "Only by identifying with the least did he come at last to be the brother of all." Amen.

CHAPTER 38

Haiti 2021 Journals

Our Collective Hands

January 4, 2021. The pace of our planetary unraveling is accelerating. Global pandemic, raging wildfires, social injustice, racial discrimination, spreading poverty, and deepening divisiveness are clear and undeniable signs that our common future is headed for destruction and desecration of all that is good and sacred. We are all called to protect the most vulnerable among us while expanding the common good. The American Civil Rights activist Bayard Rustin said, "We need, in every community, a group of angelic troublemakers." We need them now more than ever before. Our common future is in our collective hands. If we do not stand up to hatred and injustice, it will continue to spread until life on earth becomes unsustainable.

"A Need Far Greater Than We Ever Imagined"

Note: I was tempted not to share this entry as I felt it might be seen as self-promoting. But at the end you'll read mention of this book. No matter what was happening, no matter how bad things were in Haiti, I never let go of the book, because it was a part of me.

January 6, 2021. On the flight to Florida on Saturday I was deeply concerned about the future of Santa Chiara. We did not have enough funds to make it to the end of January. I needed to receive at least $10,000 in donations before I return to Haiti next Monday. Now that I've processed all the mail, I found waiting for me at the post office, as well as the mail that arrived on Monday and Tuesday, I'm happy to report that since December 11 through yesterday, we received nearly $16,000 in donations. It takes $22,000 a month to operate Santa Chiara.

But today's mail touched me thanks to a handwritten note on the inside of colorful greeting card that carried a message to: **Believe** *. . . with God all things are possible.* The note read:

Dear Mr. Straub,

Your book *The Sunrise of the Soul* was given to me by our friend and neighbor, Louise. The book touched me deeply. I would read it during my hour of Eucharistic Adoration. The chapter on Contemplative Prayer was especially moving. Louise shared with us some of the moves you have made, two in which Dr. Tony Lazzara's work with the children in Peru is depicted. The children helping each other, and the extreme generous self-giving Doctor opened our eyes and our hearts to a need far greater than we imagined. Please accept our enclosed donation to help the children at the Santa Chiara's Center. We will send a separate donation to Dr. Tony Lazzara at the Villa La Pax Foundation in St. Petersburg, Florida.

Thank you for opening the consciousness of all those who are privileged to view your work. Thank you for unselfish gift of yourself to the children you serve. May God bless you always.

It was the last three sentences that brought a tear to my eyes. I opened the envelope while seated in my car in the post office parking lot. For many years, before Haiti became the focus of my life, my mission was to open people's eyes to the plight of the poor through my films and books and the need for viewers and readers do something to help reduce the suffering caused by severe, unrelenting poverty. I truly loved making the films, even though most people found them too hard to watch. Making films have given way to making sandwiches for kids in Haiti. I was touched that the sweet film I made about the awe-inspiring work of my friend Dr. Tony (*The Patients of a Saint*) still touched someone some fifteen years after it was produced.

While filming is a thing of the past, writing still occupies a good chunk of my time. Hearing that *The Sunrise of the Soul* touched a reader in Whitehall, Michigan, meant a lot to me. The book has many stories about the mission in Haiti. A few hours before going to the post office, I sent the manuscript of my latest book, *Reading Thomas Merton and Longing for God in Haiti,* to a potential publisher. I think it is the best thing I've done in my life . . . outside of being Papa Gerry in Haiti. (The publisher politely passed on the book.)

Meanwhile, a staffer informed me that he spent three hours on line at a gas station hoping to fill up the tank of his car but also a half dozen five-gallon jugs with gas. Before reaching the gas station, the gas station ran out of gas. He'll try again today, but his concern about the gas protests that are planned and that will further disrupt life. I may be walking to Santa Chiara from the airport on Monday.

The Notes of Grace

January 8, 2021

Life has become so
frenetic and fragmented
that
stillness and wholeness
have become
the impossible dream.

In stillness and silence
you can hear
the notes of grace
singing in the breeze.

Watching the Sunrise

January 10, 2021

A Silent Symphony

Before bed at night
surrender the anxieties
of the day
into the tender hands
of God's love.
Rest in peace;
arise in hope.

To bring to a new day
yesterday's pain and failures
is the easiest way
to darken the new day.

Every sunrise
is accompanied by
a silent symphony
of hope and peace
which can only be heard by
a surrendered heart.

Each Moment

We begin each day
without knowing
how it will end.
But in that very beginning
we see the promise,
see the road to fulfillment.

In Haiti, I often sit
on the balcony
in the predawn darkness
sipping coffee
and watching the sunrise
slowly and faithfully bringing
the fresh promise
of new hope.

The radiant hope of God's light
is truly present
at the dawn of each new day,
yet we are often
too sleepy
or too distracted
to see it.
Each moment
of the coming day
is a rebirth,
each moment
a Christmas miracle.

And each moment
presents us with
an opportunity
to become more Christ-like,
to respond to every person,
especially every poor or suffering person,
and to every situation,
with love and compassion.

Each moment
gives us
an opportunity
to be instruments
of grace and peace.
Each moment
offers us
an opportunity
to reject our
culture of death
and promote
a culture of life.
Each moment
presents us
a chance
to transform our hearts
and our society.

Each moment
gives us an opportunity
to be embraced by
the tenderness of God's love,
an abundant love
that is generously extended
to all beings
without exception.

All of creation is
one Holy Family,
which we,
in our pride and selfishness,
have torn asunder.
As God's children,
we are, as Paul says,
"holy and beloved,"
and we are called to express
"heartfelt compassion, kindness,
humility, gentleness, and patience"
in our relationship
with each other
and all of creation.

But we do not.
I do not.
But that is
the goal of our journey.
Each day
we need to
redirect our efforts,
check the maps
of our inner lives.
I do so by scribbling down
some of the avalanche of thoughts
that dot my days
and the meager periods of
stillness and silence
that I try to carve out of each day.
I record my scattered thoughts
primarily for myself.
I need them.
Desperately.
It is so easy for me
to forget the lessons
I have learned,
so easy to forget
the gentle whispering
I faintly and occasionally hear
in the stillness of
prayer and contemplation.

And, perhaps more shockingly,
it is often easy for me to forget
the pain and suffering
I've seen in the many horrific slums
I've filmed around the world
and that I see every day
here in misery-plagued Haiti.
I need to be constantly reminded
of the self-emptying love of Christ
which I am called to imitate
in my own halting, clumsy, limited way.

Stormy Seas

January 23, 2021

The following was in the journal of April 30, 2017. I came across it "accidentally" on Thursday evening. Thursday was a lousy day. It left me depressed and wanting to get as far away from Haiti as I could. The details are not necessary. By the end of the day, all the troubles had been resolved. Still, I was left with the residual pain and heartache of the day . . . and wanting to throw in the towel. Of course, I couldn't and wouldn't.

> Yesterday's Gospel reading featured the story of the disciples on a boat during storm when suddenly they see Jesus walking on the water, telling them: "Do not be afraid." Some days at Santa Chiara, I feel as if I am in a boat being tossed about by a turbulent sea. When I took a leap of faith and basically moved to Haiti to care for children in need, I had no idea of the storms we would face. But I had the assurance the disciples must have had when they saw Jesus coming with his calming words not to be afraid. I am convinced that Jesus looks within our hearts, sees the purity of our intentions, and simply says to come follow him. Following Jesus is all that we are doing, trusting he is with us and guiding us, no matter if Santa Chiara sometimes feels like a little boat being tossed about in a big sea. If we keep our eyes focused on Jesus, we will stay afloat. If we take our eyes off Jesus, we will sink. It really is that simple . . . and that hard.

Stormy days will come . . . and go. One came on Thursday, and I took my eyes off Jesus. My little boat took on water. I could only see my frustration and the faults of others. Mea culpa.

Note: Another really bad day came on June 9, 2022. I became dreadfully upset by hearing new details of my Haitian ex-wife's insane behavior and unfaithfulness. I became depressed, upset, and angry. Then I learned in specific details about the degree of thievery committed by her son. The tension and heartache mounted, and when it combined with my dangerous lack of sufficient rest, I exploded at a sixteen-year-old girl who refused to follow directions from two members of the medical staff. I later spoke harshly, even cruelly, to my adult "daughter," Orlane. I became very upset with myself. It was another emotionally draining lost day. Only this time, as you will soon read, there was someone to calm me down and sooth my wounded spirit. In the next entry, you will see that a year after this commentary in which I recognized I needed rest, I nonetheless did not learn how to rest.

Stop. Sit. Surrender.

February 12, 2021

> *"Just to be is a blessing. Just to live is holy."*
>
> —Abraham Joshua Heschel[229]

We need a new language—new words—for God. The judgmental, vindictive God of my youth was retired long ago. In a sense, I still need a new way of praying. You can't put new wine (the Spirit) in old skins (our humanity). After six stressful, nonstop, action-packed years in Haiti, scarred by violence and death, I had reached the point where I understood that I needed to do less, to even experience less, and find the courage to rest more. To simply sit and rest is, for me, very hard. But unless you are still, you can't really hear anything.

> *"Unless you can listen, you cannot hear."*
>
> —Yo-Yo Ma

Real prayer, transformative prayer, is letting the divine speak to you . . . not you speaking to the divine. You must stop to really hear. Sitting helps. Once we've stopped and are seated, we must surrender. Stop. Sit. Surrender. In time, the false you will be shaken and dissolve. During prayer, we need to be attentive to feel and understand what bubbles up within you. You bring to your prayer the wisdom of your life. For me, writing is a way of processing the thoughts that arise in prayer.

> My problem,
> and it is huge, is
> I have not given myself
> time . . . time to
> stop, sit, surrender,
> and heal.

To properly heal, I need to be more in touch with my deep self, my inner self, to encounter my true self, my original self, my inner child, who understands the divine that has been lost or buried beneath a mountain of busyness—both the irrelevant, frivolous busyness of modern life and the important busyness associated with work or ministry.

The deep self is the best of you; it is the you who is closest to God. When you hear your inner child, new ways of being, new ways of knowing the Beloved, will arise within you. Most of us are far from who we really are and have been so for far too long because we do not stop and listen to our deep self. We have forgotten our inner child, the little girl or little boy who was, according to Jesus, much closer to God than we are as adults. We have no relationship with our deep self. Our deep self is a stranger. Your inner child is innocent and removed from all your wounds, faults, and failures. We must find and embrace our inner innocence. This is contemplative prayer, falling in love with the stranger who is yourself. Merton invited us to enter the school of our own life so we can feast on our own life.

> *"My life is a listening; His is a speaking.*
> *My salvation is to hear and respond."*
>
> —Thomas Merton

To sit, to rest, is a prayer. It probably is a better form of prayer than rushing off to church each day. Recently, I realized that some days it is better for me not leave Santa Chiara at six in the morning to go to the Sisters and instead remain in silence, attentive to the silent voice of the Spirit. To walk in the woods or along the shoreline is a prayer. All of creation is a cathedral. Slow down. Look within. Listen to your inner child.

> *"Listening is the beginning of prayer."*
>
> —Mother Teresa

In stillness and silence, I understood how much grief I had been carrying. I had not cried over the many losses I endured, mistakes I had made, sins I had committed. All the loses, mistakes, sins pull us down unless they are transformed into something positive.

Rainer Maria Rilke speaks of the divine gravity that pulls us to a place where the divine rests. In this holy place, we begin to see life differently; we begin to see as the Beloved sees. We spend much of our time fighting this gravity that tries to pull us to an ancient place where we see things from different perspective. In time, you see the wonder of who you are. In this time, late as it is, I'm learning I need to let go of the fear I carry. My neurotic behavior when I travel was a manifestation of my fear things would go wrong, that I wouldn't be safe, that I'd lose my passport or forget my phone at a restaurant. Travel was so exhausting because I was in a state of constant panic. In Haiti, I worry about all the things that can—and do—go wrong. I worry about not being able to care for the kids, of running out of the money I need for food and medicine.

After twenty-five years since I let go of my former life and began to follow St. Francis down poverty road, I'm still learning that I need to let go of countless deep hurts, of unfulfilled dreams, of loves lost. I've been carrying too much baggage. I need to dump the stuff that has made my journey a constant struggle. I never reached my goal because I was carrying too much stuff that slowed me down, that led my down many cul-de-sacs of doubt and despair. I need to step beyond my fear, to take a risk to step out into the beyond, into the arms of the Beloved.

I first became a pilgrim in the late 1990s when I knew, deep inside, I had to travel to all the places in Italy that were important to Saint Francis of Assisi. Many thought I was crazy. They thought I was even crazier to spend so much time filming in the worst slums on earth. I had to do it. In Haiti, I'm still a pilgrim, still searching, still learning. We each need to make the journey that our lives beg us to make. Say yes to the journey of your life . . . even when you feel too old to start a new journey. I'm too old to be caring for little kids in Haiti. Covid-19 should have killed me in Haiti. I felt very close to death. I saw the love within some of the staff and kids who did not want to let me go. I didn't survive in order to just keep walking in the same manner, to keep carrying the same stuff, hauling the garbage of my life through slums of suffering. Changes within me had to be made. It was not too late to start afresh . . . again. Transformation is a continuum, not a one-time trick.

Michael Fish, a Benedictine Camaldolese priest, monk, and hermit who was born in South Africa, says—and I'm paraphrasing—scripture is God telling us Her story; prayer is us telling God the story of our life, the story of our day. Me: "Today, dear Lord, I was too tired to go to the doctor even though I knew the skin infection could cause me lots of trouble. Today, Lord, I was too depressed to fight the temptation to do something I knew would only make me feel worse. Today, Lord, I was too angry to be kind. Today, Lord, I was too self-centered to be compassionate. Today, Lord, I was too judgmental to be merciful. Today, Lord, I was too filled with doubt to love my young girlfriend. Today, Lord, I was too spiritually empty to live the Beatitudes. Today, Lord, my heart was too filled with violent, angry thoughts to follow the nonviolent Jesus. Dear Jesus, today I was too fearful, too preoccupied with nonsense, to see your face in the face of the homeless woman sitting on the side of the road after I had filled my car with food and wine from the supermarket while she was hungry and lonely." Mea culpa, mea culpa, mea maxima culpa.

Prayer leads you to the Presence. Come, let us pray. Words are not necessary. Just sit. Be still. Be open.

A Sense of Absence

February 13, 2021. In the beginning we were one. In time, we lost part of ourselves. We all have lost something. We each have a sense of absence, an inner emptiness and sadness, an inner ache. This is normal, part of the human condition. Much of the modern economy is based on empty promises that some product will fill that emptiness. We become addicted to things that don't fill our emptiness such as porn or alcohol or the internet. The sadness, the loneliness remains . . . and even intensifies. We are lost. And will remain lost until we understand our inner pain. You must name, embrace, accept, and dialogue with the pain and emptiness inside you.

The divine is inside us, but we look outside ourselves to soothe the pain within us.

Hafiz, the great Sufi mystic and poet, said: "Don't surrender your loneliness so quickly. Let it cut more deep. Let it ferment and season you as few human or even divine ingredients can."

Jesus is the searching God looking for us. Jesus knows where God is hiding.

Rainer Maria Rilke, the German poet, giving voice to God speaking to us, writes: "I am, you anxious one." Yes, God knows our inner anxiousness, our inner longing for something we don't know or can't find, our inner pain and despair. Rilke has God ask us a series of questions. Here is one:

> *Don't you sense me ready to break*
> *into being at your touch?*

God is always reaching out to us, waiting for a response from us. Knock and God will answer, in good time. I knocked for ten years before God opened the door just crack, enough for me to catch a fleeting glimpse of the Light.

Here is another:

> *Can't you see me standing before you*
> *cloaked in stillness?*

We can't see because we are not looking. Perhaps we are too busy . . . buying stuff and dreaming of things we can't have. That was me for most of my life. But God says, according to Rainer Maria Rilke:

> *I am the dream you are dreaming.*

Imagine, God is our real dream, the key to our original unity with God. God wants us. God longs for us. We are a part of God that God is missing. God wants to fully embrace us. Jesus told us this in the Parable of the Prodigal Son. Absolutely nothing we do can separate us from the love of God. This is truly amazing. And so unbelievable, we don't believe it. Until God touches and changes us when we invite Her into our unfulfilled lives, into our lonely existence, into the pain we can no longer carry, making us whole, holy, and lacking nothing of importance.

In Haiti, I am a pauper . . . and a beggar, begging for what my kids need. Yet within my poor exterior, I am a very rich man . . . as long as I keep my eye on God and trust fully in Her. The "devil" is in the distractions.

Creating the Change Needed

August 7, 2021. People around the word are struggling to cope with the emotional consequences of a year of grief and sequestrations . . . and plans and dreams that were blown to pieces by Covid-19. Covid changed everything for just about everyone. Besides nearly killing me, Covid has forced me to take two Covid tests every month in order to travel to and from Haiti; these tests cost money (in Haiti) and eat up about five hours every month. The biggest change in my life took me by surprise in an empty church in Rome back in March 1995. In a flash I went from being a questioning atheist to a believing Christian. But the "conversion" was not a clean break from my past. I did not go from sinner to saint . . . and still I am closer to the former than the later. I was a "new man" holding on to to some old ideas and assumptions.

Cardinal John Henry Newman, the nineteenth-century Anglican priest and philosopher who became an influential Catholic priest, said: "In another world it is otherwise, but here below to live is to change, and to be perfect is to have changed often." For some of us, even a small change in our lives feels like a catastrophic change. Most of us don't like change. We love our routines, and we're sticking to them. We want to hold on to continuity while changing. This is the challenge: not holding on while letting go. There was much about my return to Catholicism that bothered me (and still does), things that forced me to abandon the Church. No need to list them. On many Catholic beliefs and dogmas, I am still very much a "doubting Thomas."

So many people of faith, no matter their faith, have become aggressively fanatic and dogmatic . . . even cultic in nature. The current white supremacy movement reveals the paranoid nature of a cult that has an omniscient sense of who and what needs to be included and excluded; everyone in the cult is good, and everyone outside the cult is bad. When I see fanaticism in any form, I know something has gone horribly wrong. The world is currently awash in fanatics, and thanks to social media and campaigns of misinformation, the fanaticism is spreading like wildfire. But I digress.

I am still changing, still letting go of assumptions once held tightly. For me to follow Christ ever more closely, I need to recognize and create the change needed in me that will make that possible. This is my ongoing challenge.

CHAPTER 39

Haiti 2022 Journals

The Plague of Intolerance, Prejudice, and Hate

> *. . . when speech is in danger of perishing or being
> perverted in the amplified noise of beasts, perhaps it
> becomes obligatory for a monk to try to speak.*
>
> —Thomas Merton, Seeds of Destruction[230]

Note: *The following was never posted a Journal entry. On the last day of reviewing the final editing of this book—September 2, 2022—I wrestled with adding a new piece that I had written a week earlier that I felt belonged in this book. My intention was not to a add another angry, divisive voice to the political noise following the FBI's removal of classified, top-secret files from the former president Donald Trump's home and country club in Palm Beach, Florida. My aim was not to throw more gas on the fire. I wanted to bring Merton's voice into the analysis of Trump's potential to destroy democracy with his repeated lies and irrational behavior and his disgraceful support of the violent insurrection at the Capitol on January 6, 2021. There is legitimate concern that if Trump is prosecuted for the illegal removal of sensitive, secret documents from the White House and his refusal to return them that it will incite a bloody rebellion. I look at all this turmoil from a spiritual, not political, perspective. Sadly, Christianity also has a long, dark history of violence, prejudice, and domination that is in direct conflict with the teachings and spirit of Jesus.*

There was a Merton quote earlier in this book in which the monk spoke about editing his best-selling first book and his need to tailor his work to meet the expectations of a wide variety of readers . . . including the people his superior was afraid to offend. For more than twenty years, I have steadfastly refrained from sharing in my books, films, or talks any political views when it comes to Church or State for fear of offending anyone. I want to keep the focus on the poor. Helping the poor, I felt, was not a Left or Right issue. Since Trump's surprising election victory in 2016, I confess to being surprised how some people who supported both my film ministry and my ministry in Haiti leaned so far to the political Right in both Church and State life. I heard dreadful remarks about President Biden and Pope Francis. I remained silent, not wanting to deflect attention from my humble efforts to help the poor. Merton had no such need to restrain his opinion of the state of global and national politics. At the last possible second, I elected to include the following.

Donald Trump started a mass movement based of fear and loathing of a minority group. He demeaned migrants and made them scapegoats for the widespread anger felt by many Americans who believed their chance of having a meaningful life was slipping away. White Nationalism, infused with hatred and vitriol, became Trump's path to the White House. He spoke overtly racist and violence-inciting language from the Oval Office. To hang on to an office he lost in a free and fair election, the narcissistic, egotistical former president incited a mob of his followers—many wearing para-military attire—to engage in violent revolt that perpetrated acts of domestic terrorism and insurrection against democracy that left five people dead. In the aftermath of the chaos, President Trump called the domestic terrorists "great patriots" and said they were "special." On September 1, 2022, Trump said if he ran for president in 2024 and won, he would pardon all the Capitol rioters who had been sentenced to jail.

Thomas Merton foresaw and addressed all of this in an essay entitled "Christianity and Totalitarianism" in his book *Disputed Questions.* He wrote:

> A mass movement readily exploits the discontent and frustration of large segments of the population which for some reason or other cannot face the responsibility of being persons and standing on their own feet. But give these persons a movement to join, a cause to defend, and they will go to any extreme, stop at no crime, intoxicated as they are by the slogans that give them a pseudo-religious sense of transcending their own limitations. The member of a mass movement, afraid of his own isolation, and his own weakness as an individual, cannot face the task of discovering within himself the spiritual power and integrity which can be called forth only by love. Instead of this, he seeks a movement that will protect his weakness with a wall of anonymity and justify his acts by the sanction of collective glory and power. All the better if this is done out of hatred, for hatred is always easier and less subtle than love. It does not have to respect reality as love does. It does not have to take account of individual cases. Its solutions are simple and easy. It makes its decisions by a simple glance at a face, a colored skin, a uniform. It identifies an enemy by an accent, an unfamiliar turn of speech, an appeal to concepts that are difficult to understand. He is something unfamiliar. This is not "ours." This must be brought into line—or destroyed.
>
> Here is the great temptation of the modern age, this universal infection of fanaticism, this plague of intolerance, prejudice and hate which flows from the crippled nature of man who is afraid of love and does not dare to be a person. It is against this temptation most of all that the Christian must labor with inexhaustible patience and love, in silence, perhaps in repeated failure, seeking tirelessly to restore, wherever he can, and first of all in himself, the capacity of love and which makes man the living image of God.[231]

Note: Those two paragraphs illustrate why I was hooked on reading Thomas Merton and why reading the monk was an essential part the transformation of my life, going from a self-centered Hollywood television producer consumed with my own power and pleasure to a guy living a hidden life in a slum in Haiti trying to live the self-emptying love of Christ in spite of my continual failure to do so.

Flashback: A Wounded Healer

January 16, 2022. It is hard to believe, but the following journal entry was posted just three days short of exactly six years ago. It was posted on Tuesday, January 19, 2016, at 4:45 am. We were in the first full month of our second home in Peguyville. The day before there was an electrical fire in the power lines outside our gate that left us without electricity for thirteen hours.

> The fan was still on when I woke a few minutes ago. That's a good sign. Yesterday was a bit odd with the prolonged blackout. When the power outage first ended, I immediately went into the apartment to check my e-mail. It was really a hot and exasperating day. I needed to cool off a bit in front of the fan. The day had its moments of tensions, as some of the children were not on their best behavior. One child spoke in a disrespectful manner to their mother, and a staffer strongly admonished the child. I didn't fully approve of her tone, which sounded too harsh. I felt someone was stealing food. For me, every day is littered with irritating moments. The mess in the refrigerator always triggers unkind thoughts. The point I'm struggling to make is that yesterday I was especially edgy. I felt powerless to pull myself out of a little funk . . . which even electricity couldn't have helped. Even the calmest staffer seemed on the threshold of frustration. Perhaps I was just tired . . . or felt imprisoned in this enclosed space. It was in this context that I took refuge in the quiet of the office, seated near the cooling breezes of the fan.
>
> One of my e-mails was the automatic posting of my blog. I am embarrassed to admit I don't know how to even log into my own blog if I am away from my home library in Burbank. Before leaving for Haiti for these two weeks, I preset a spiritual reflection to be posted every three days. Because I was stressed for time, everything I set to be posted came from old material, stuff I had written long ago. Suddenly I was into recycling. I opened the blog posting. It was titled "The Messiness of Life." It was as if I had read it for the first time . . . or more precisely as if someone else had written it, someone really cool like Nouwen or Merton. It hit me like a ton of bricks.
>
>> We live in a world that is filled with pain. The planet is covered with people who are overwhelmed by suffering. Wars, monstrous acts of terrorism, famines, economic injustice, chronic poverty, drug addiction, diseases, and natural disasters are killing people every day. We are

impotent when it comes to making the pain go away. Life is hard and messy and painful. Hurt abounds and hope is in short supply. Jesus did not clean up every mess or relieve all the pain He encountered. Jesus simply told us to take the pain and the mess of our lives and place them before God. Even then, the answers to the riddles of our lives are not always perceivable or even obtainable. Jesus teaches us to live with the questions, to live with the pain. Peace, He suggests, is found in faith. God is bigger than we are; and we, in our weakness, need to lean on the strong arm of God. Cures and answers may not come to light, but faith, hope, and love changes who we are and how we deal with the messiness and pain of life.

I really can't fix all the problems at the Santa Chiara Children's Center. Yesterday, I felt as if this entire venture was on the verge of collapse. I felt I had taken on an insurmountable task. There were just too many problems, too few people helping, too many divergent personalities, not enough resources. And step outside the gates and there is a world of hurting in the midst of whirlwind of chaos, pollution, filth, and people screaming at each other. The noise is relentless. Yesterday, I wanted to be anyplace but here. Last night, I just wanted to left alone, wanted to crawl into a hole and cover it. I did not even want to have our nightly *Three Stooges* screening. It was late, everyone was tired, Baby was sick. I canceled the screening. The girls seemed very disappointed, adding they said they didn't have that many more nights to see Moe, Larry, and Curly. I was busy trying to post yesterday's journal entry, hoping I could send it before there was another power failure. As soon as I sent it, I announced we could watch one episode. Baby and Lysa were very excited. Within five minutes, the room was filled. We actually watched two of the old, short films produced in the 1930s. The second film was loaded with crazy mayhem as the Stooges totally ruined a classy dinner and turned an elegant home into a disaster area. They roared with laughter. Even young Laura, who just turned four, laughs at the slapstick stupidity. In one of the films, Curly asked Moe to hand him a "rooster bar." Moe said it was a "crowbar." Curly said, "Well, roosters crow don't they."

This morning, I woke up thinking about yesterday's blog posting. I knew I had to immediately read it and absorb it . . . and listen to what it was telling me. I need to take my doubts, confusions, and frustration and place them before God. I can't do Santa Chiara without God. I must live with the endless questions without hardly ever having any good answers.

Here is the takeaway: Life is messy. I am weak. God is strong. Pray and keep working.

God really is not asking me to be productive or even successful. God is asking me to be faithful. I just glanced at the burning St. Clare candle I bought yesterday. I thought of all the hours I spent inside the Basilica of Santa Chiara in Assisi on my knees before the San Damiano Crucifix . . . the very one that Saint Francis knelt before in the abandoned, dilapidated Church of San Damiano located on the hillside below the ancient town of Assisi during a confusing time in his life. I fervently prayed back then for some sense of direction in my life, some real purpose. I sometimes lose track of the journey I've been on over the last twenty years, with all its twists and turns, all the exhilarating moments and all the moments of disappointments and crushing despair, especially during my final months at the San Damiano Foundation, which were deeply painful. Yet, here I am in Haiti surrounded by wounded kids, doing my best to be (to use a Nouwen term) a wounded healer, even though I can't even heal myself.

Reading this account six years after it was written was extremely poignant. The problems, tensions, frustrations, and irritants keep rolling along, day after day, year after year. Thanks to my sense of fatigue after seven years of relentless eruptions of problems, I am easily knocked off center. My own hypersensitivity turns even the most insignificant problem into a destructive force from which I want to flee. Every day is a struggle to stay hopeful.

The Night Sings of Death

January 26, 2022. An added benefit from my daily walks is that I get a closer glimpse into the lives of the poor. While my surrounding neighborhood is very impoverished, it is a far cry from the bigger slums such as Cité Soleil. The houses are sturdier and more secure; still, they are basically cinder-block construction with few amenities. Most nights are spent in darkness. The stench in the streets comes from dumped fecal material as there is no indoor plumbing. But at least some of the roads are paved. While walking, you see the harshness of life for the poor.

The poor in Haiti are faced with continual threats to their well-being and survival. Dangers and tribulations abound. Just staying alive is very stressful. The night sings of death. Sunrise brings a fragile hope that will be dashed before the sun is high in the sky.

If I were magically transported to living in one of the homes I pass in my walk, I would not last very long. My simple second-floor apartment is a palace compared to the homes I see as I walk. I have a refrigerator, a microwave, and a TV—yet, I dream of air-conditioning and hot water. The staff brings me jugs of water, fills my propane tank, and the guys make sure I have uninterrupted electricity. These things are far beyond the reach of the poor I encounter on my walks. I can see the hunger in their eyes. I can see the threadbare clothing they wear. I can see their exhaustion.

In following the example of Saint Francis of Assisi and Jesus, I wanted to be one with the poor. I may be living among the poor, but I am not one of the poor. I am not fully sharing their anxiety, hardships, and suffering. I'll be getting on a plane on Friday for a week on a beautiful island off the eastern coast of Central Florida. This is beyond the reach of

99.9% of my neighbors. Even my wife will face an uphill struggle to get a visitor's Visa to occasionally come to Florida with me.

I wish I could do more. Yesterday, was Peter Francis Straub's fourth birthday, which helped me realize I am doing all I can. He came to us on the second day of his life. His mother left him in the garbage. He went from the trash to being a treasure, a tangible sign of hope. I went downstairs early yesterday to see Peter before he left for school. I brought my professional Canon Camera and in less than thirty minutes I took 236 photographs. The kids went wild. They get truly excited to have their pictures taken; they tug at me to see them. I walked with them to school. Over the next few days, I'll share the best of the photographs. The kids are irresistible. Whenever I feel down about my life in Haiti, all I need to do is hang out with the kids for an hour and I feel much better.

I wrote the above yesterday morning. A few hours later, a journal reader wrote about his reaction to reading Sunday's long entry. He said reading it brought tears to his eyes. He went on to say:

> Years ago, you wished/longed to truly understand poverty, and you realized to gain that understanding you knew you had to live with the poor. Perhaps then you didn't fully understand that to live with them is to suffer with them, but not to suffer in the same way, but rather to suffer in the unique way only you could suffer because of all you are and were, all you have witnessed and experienced in your life. Isn't that kind of the Merton way? Now you know the true nature of poverty because of the deep pain, anguish. and suffering (and betrayals) you have experienced. That you have reacted badly at times reveals your humanness. That you and SCCC have prevailed reveals your innate goodness, strength of character, and a true longing (I believe) to live the selfless and sacrificial life in imitation of Christ and St. Francis.

The Risen Life

February 1, 2022. The great English artist and mystic Caryll Houselander suggested that we lead a Risen Life, that is "a life of love, love that creates, love that fills up the measure of each life with joy. Love that is light and peace. Love that forgives and heals and sustains, that makes us one. Love that gives life to the world and beauty to life. Love that is food and clothing and water for thirst. Love that is bread."[232]

It is the love given to us by God, a love that God wishes we embrace for ourselves and give to one another. It is Easter Love that animates the Risen Life.

Note: Those words come at the end of a film I made in Honduras in 2012 featuring the work of the Medical Missionaries of Mary, a congregation of sisters founded in Ireland a century ago whose members are mostly doctors and nurses. The film was titled Rooted in Love.

In one month and a day we will enter the season of Lent, which is a time to refocus our lives on the Resurrection. The following is also from the narration of *Rooted in Love*:

The crucified and transfigured Christ's message of love
compels us to judge no one, to exclude no one;
moreover, it requires us to help others to carry their cross,
fully sharing in their pain and suffering.

Mother Teresa said,
"The poor anywhere in the world
are Christ who suffers.
In them, the Son of God
lives and dies.
Through them,
God shows his face."

Individuals and governments have the ability
to use their power
to either dominate or serve.
We certainly know how
Jesus used his power.

Note: I am powerless to change anything . . . but myself, which is why I always need Lent. Still, I can use what little talent and influence I have to help the abandoned kids in Haiti carry the unfair crosses of their innocent lives. To do this, I in turn need help from all the wonderful people who generously give me the resources needed to keep the kids safe and loved in a very dangerous and unloving environment.

I'll bring this last part of the book to a close with two short poems from my book A Journey to Meekness.

A Silent Symphony

Before bed at night
surrender the anxieties
of the day
into the tender hands
of God's love.
Rest in peace;
arise in hope.

To bring to a new day
yesterday's pain and failures
is the easiest way
to darken the new day.

Every sunrise
is accompanied by
a silent symphony
of hope and peace,
which can only be heard by
a surrendered heart.

Genesis

We live in
a constant state
of genesis,
always changing,
always evolving,
always being born anew.
Today we begin again.
This very moment
is pregnant
with new possibilities
for growing
in God,
with God,
through God.
Today is
a new creation.

Gerard Thomas Straub
A
Journey
to
Meekness
PRAYER POEMS & REFLECTIONS

My Unbelief

The novelist Graham Greene once said to a Spanish priest, "I don't believe my unbelief." Wow. That perfectly expresses my state of being in my atheist days. I couldn't believe in God. But I so dearly wanted to believe. My doubt was like a parched desert. There was no nourishment, no comfort, no solace. Just dryness and thirst. Doubt, I see now, is part of faith. Graham Greene's acceptance of Catholicism was tepid, but he felt he "must always keep a foot in the door" of the Church. Greene's priest friend said to him, "I don't believe in God, I touch him." Another wonderful summation of faith.

In Haiti, I often sense the presence of God. I feel on a deep level that God is leading me, providing for me, and protecting me. When I look at a suffering Haiti, especially old people and kids, I feel I'm looking at them the way God sees them—that is, with mercy, compassion, and kindness. I have a hard time saying "no" to a person in need. Of course, I'm in need.

When my ministry was making poverty films, I often joked, "I make films no one wants to see with money I don't have." Now I care for kids no one wants with money I don't have. I call that faith. Belief is not part of the equation.

The opening line of his novel *The End of the Affair*, Graham Greene writes: "A story has no beginning or end: arbitrarily one chooses that moment of experience from which to look back or from which to look ahead."[233] My story began late in life. I was forty-eight years old when I sat down in an empty church in Rome. I didn't enter the church to pray. I simply was looking for a quiet, cool space to sit and rest, as I absorbed the beauty of the sacred space. Without warning, an empty church and an empty man became a meeting place for God to mysteriously slip into my life. In that transformative moment, I went from doubting the existence of God to knowing on a deep level that God was real and that God loved me. In a flash, everything changed.

I'd been drawn to Italy in 1995 by the life of Saint Francis of Assisi. While I didn't believe in God, the lives of the saints greatly attracted me and sparked my imagination. I wanted to understand how Saint Francis could believe that poverty was our highest calling. I followed Saint Francis by writing about Saint Francis. In following him, I eventually had to walk down poverty road. Returning to the faith of my youth wasn't easy. So much about the Catholic Church really bothered me. The Church's attitude toward celibacy for priests, their suppression of women, their rejection of gays, and their shunning of divorced people was going to eventually spell doom for it—growth is not possible when you turn your back on large swaths of humanity. Yet, my brain seemed wired for Catholicism. While I was naturally enticed by Buddhism, I felt that as I moved toward God, I had to stick with what I knew, which is Catholicism. I pretty much ignored the hierarchy of the Church, though I was encouraged by the life and witness of Pope Francis, who embraced simplicity, comforted the poor, cared for creation, and defended liberation theology and its preferential option for the poor. Inside the Vatican, however, there was significant force of prelates who opposed him at every turn.

The message of Jesus and the example of Saint Francis convinced me that growing closer to God required letting go of all that I had thought was important to me. That was scary. The saints walked away from everything, leaving family, friends, and jobs to embrace a radically new way of living. I didn't think I had the bravery of Dorothy Day or Óscar Romero. I could film the poor, but living among the poor was a bridge too far to cross. Until I did.

To understand Saint Francis's love of poverty, which made no sense to me, I traveled to a slum in Philadelphia to spend time with Franciscan friars who served the homeless. It was an eye-opener. The humble soup kitchen, the St. Francis Inn, dramatically changed my life, my point of view, and put me on a course to the worst slums in Africa, Central and South America, the Caribbean, Mexico, the Philippines, and India. Poverty Road made me into the person I was created to be. I became a wounded healer.

On December 30, 2020, 3,882 Americans died from Covid-19, which the highest single day death toll since the pandemic reached our shores. As the world has been brought to its knees by Covid-19, it is clear that we are living in a loaves-and-fishes moment. The need is overwhelming. But there are only a few loaves of bread and a few small fishes to feed a hungry world. This common need pushes us to accept the common good, to look out for the weakest among us, to strive for the health of the whole.

Calcutta, India, October 28, 1999; *Photo by Gerry Straub*

Individualism is dying. A new reality is slowly, painfully being born. Love your neighbor. It is that simple, that hard. Your neighbor is not just the family living next door to you. Your neighbor is everyone. Your home is all of creation. All members of the animal kingdom are your sisters and brothers. The key to this new reality is mercy and forgiveness. I'm learning to forgive myself, which makes it easier to forgive others, including those who have hurt me the most. We are all children of the living God. We are all united in a bond of love.

The pace of our planetary unraveling is accelerating. Global pandemic, raging wildfires, social injustice, racial discrimination, spreading poverty, deepening divisiveness, and mass killings are clear and undeniable signs that our common future is headed for destruction and desecration of all that is good and sacred. We are all called to protect the most vulnerable among us while expanding the common good. Our common future is in our collective hands. If we do not stand up to hated and injustice it will continue to spread until life on earth becomes unsustainable.

Christopher Pramuk writes in his book *At Play in Creation: Merton's Awakening to the Feminine Divine*, "Sophia is the *eros* of God become one with all creation, the love in God that longs for incarnation from before the beginning. She is the co-creativity of God, always inviting, never compelling, coming to birth in us when we say yes to [what Thomas Merton calls in his January 30, 1960, letter to Abdul Aziz] 'the dawning of divine light in the stillness of our hearts.'"[234,235]

While my young boy's dream of being a missionary priest in China went unfulfilled, its essence has become my reality as I live, serve, and hope to end my journey in Haiti. Mentored by Saint Francis of Assisi and Thomas Merton, my life today is truly blessed. Yet, I still need to further close the gap between what I've been "preaching" in my books and films and my own longing flesh by living increasingly more deeply and more compassionately, moment by holy moment, among my children who have adopted me in Haiti.

About the Author

Gerard Thomas Straub is a former documentary filmmaker and the Founder and President of Pax et Bonum Communications. He has written and directed 23 documentary films in such poverty-stricken nations as India, Kenya, Uganda, Jamaica, Haiti, Brazil, Peru, Honduras, El Salvador, Mexico, and The Philippines. His film work was featured in articles in *The New York Times* and the *Los Angeles Times*; he was also featured on the PBS show *Religion and Ethics Weekly*. Gerry is an accomplished photographer; a film featuring his photography was narrated by Martin Sheen. His photo/essay book on global poverty, *When Did I See You Hungry?*, was published in 2002. Gerry's striking black & white photography from the book were exhibited in the art gallery attached to the Cathedral of the Assumption in Louisville, Kentucky, and published in *The New York Times, The National Catholic Reporter* and *Sojourners* magazine. Pax et Bonum Communications published Gerry's most recent book, *A Journey to Meekness,* in 2021.

Mr. Straub had a long and distinguished career as a network television producer and executive in New York and Hollywood; he produced dramatic television series that have aired on CBS, NBC, and ABC.

An award-winning author, Gerry has written nine books, including a novel. His book *The Sun & Moon Over Assisi* was named the "Best Spirituality Hardcover Book of the Year" in 2001 by the Catholic Press Association. A revised and updated edition of the book was published in 2015. His book *The Loneliness and Longing of Saint Francis,* which was a winner in the Spirituality category of the 2015 Association of Catholic Publishers' "Excellence in Publishing Awards." His book, *Hidden in the Rubble,* published by Orbis Books in 2010, is based on his experience in Haiti during the aftermath of the horrific earthquake that killed over 300,000 people. Tom Roberts of the National Catholic Reporter said of the book: "Gerry Straub is a story-teller with a camera. In an era when news has become so atomized and fast-paced it is almost impossible to get a sense of the whole, Straub engages two great risks. He takes us to see what much of the world would rather ignore, and he does it slowly and reflectively. The risks pay off here in a kind of meditation on Haiti that is simultaneously brutally frank and filled with the hope of religious imagination." His book, *The Sunrise of the Soul,* was published by Paraclete Press in the summer of 2020.

Gerry has written essays, poems, and reflections which were included in five published books. "Falling Silent" was published in *Bridges to Contemplative Living with Thomas Merton: Advent and Christmas,* which was edited by Jonathan Montaldo & Robert G. Toth and published by Ave Maria Press in 2010. "A Hollywood Option for the Poor" was published in *The Preferential Option for the Poor beyond Theology,* which was edited by Daniel G. Groody, CSC and Gustavo Gutiérrez, OP and published by University of Notre Dame Press in 2014. "What We Are" was published in *Messengers of Hope: Reflections in Honor of Thomas Merton,* which was edited by Jonathan Montaldo and Gray Henry which was published by Fons Vitae Press in 2015. Gerry's poem, "I Hand It All to You," was published in *A Maryknoll Book of Poetry: Beauty, Truth, and Goodness from Around the World,* which was published by Orbis Books in 2014. Three short reflections were published in *A Maryknoll Book of Inspiration: Readings for Every Day of the Year,* which was published by Orbis Books in 2010. *Notre Dame Magazine* has published three essays written by Gerry, one of which was on Vincent van Gogh. They also published an article about Gerry's orphanage in Haiti.

Gerry also taught a course on television writing and directing at the Pontifical Gregorian University in Rome, Italy. In addition, he has spoken at more than 250 Catholic churches, high schools, and universities across the United States, as well as in Canada, France, Italy, and Hungary, as well as a Jewish temple in Los Angeles. He gave a retreat for the Missionaries of Charity in Haiti; he also gave a multi-media presentation to the Trappist monks of Gethsemani Abbey in Kentucky. In April of 2012, the School of Communications at Illinois State University named Gerry as the recipient of their annual Documentary Voice of Conscience Award. During the award ceremony, the school screened Gerry's film *Mud Pies & Kites,* which was set in Haiti during the horrific aftermath of the 2010 earthquake. In November of 2013, Gerry was the President of the Jury at the Faludi International Film Festival in Budapest, Hungary; the film festival is run by the Jesuits. He has been awarded three honorary doctorate degrees in recognition of his work on behalf of the poor. Gerry is a Secular Franciscan.

Gerry lives primarily in Port-au-Prince, Haiti where he operates the Santa Chiara Children's Center, which is a home for 50 abandoned and displaced kids, a dozen of whom are still in diapers. Gerry has a small apartment in Vero Beach, Florida where he spends one week a month.

ABOUT GERRY'S STUDY PARTNER

Jonathan Montaldo is a writer, editor, and retreat presenter. His renditions of Thomas Merton's writing include *A Year with Thomas Merton; Dialogues with Silence: Merton's Prayers & Drawings; Choosing to Love the World;* and *Thomas Merton In His Own Words.* He co-edited *The Intimate Merton: His Life from His Journals* with Brother Patrick Hart of Gethsemani Abbey. He edited the second volume of Merton's private journals, published in seven volumes, under the title *Entering the Silence* (1945–1959).

Jonathan served as director of the Thomas Merton Center at Bellarmine University, the largest archive of the writer's work from 1998–2001. He was Associate Director for the Merton Institute of Contemplative Living in Louisville, Kentucky, for which he created *Bridges to Contemplative Living with Thomas Merton,* a ten-booklet resource for small group dialogue. In tandem, he served as the director and retreat master for Bethany Springs, the Merton Institute's Retreat Center one mile from Merton's Abbey of Gethsemani.

He narrated five audiobooks of Merton's work including *New Seeds of Contemplation* and *No Man Is An Island.* He is the Co-General Editor with Gray Henry of Fons Vitae's nine volumes presenting Merton and World Religions and edited *We Are Already One, Reflections on Thomas Merton's Centenary, 2015.* He currently writes a monthly reflection on a Sunday Gospel for the online English edition of *L'Osservatore Romano.*

Endnotes

1 Mirabai Starr, "Dazzling Darkness," *Oneing* 10, no. 1, *Unveiled* (Spring 2022): 83, 87–88.

2 Thomas Merton, *Run to the Mountain: The Journals of Thomas Merton* Volume One 1939–1941, Edited by Patrick Hart, O.C.S.O. (HarperSanFrancisco, 1995), 227.

3 Thomas Merton, *New Seeds of Contemplation* (New York: New Directions, 1961), 78.

4 Thomas Merton, *A Vow of Conversation*, ed. Naomi Burton Stone (New York: Farrar, Straus, Giroux, 1988), 109.

5 Thomas Merton, *A Vow of Conversation*, ed. Naomi Burton Stone (New York: Farrar, Straus, Giroux, 1988), 106.

6 Thomas Merton, *Entering the Silence: Becoming a Monk and Writer, The Journals of Thomas Merton*, Volume 2, 1941–1952, edited by Jonathan Montaldo (New York: HarperCollins, 1997), 202.

7 Mary Oliver, *New and Selected Poems*, Volume 1 (Boston, MA: Beacon Press, 1992), 94.

8 Thomas Merton, *The Seven Storey Mountain: An Autobiography of Faith* (San Diego, CA: Harcourt, Brace and Company, 1941), 111.

9 Thomas Merton, *Conjectures of a Guilty Bystander* (New York: Doubleday, 1966), 188.

10 Thomas Merton, *Monastic Observances: Initiation into the Monastic Tradition*, Volume 25, ed. Patrick F. O'Connell (Collegeville, MN: Liturgical Press, 2010), 80.

11 Thomas Merton, *Dancing in the Water of Life: Seeking Peace in the Hermitage*, The Journals of Thomas Merton, Volume Five, 1963–1965, Edited by Robert E. Daggy (San Francisco, CA: HarperSanFrancisco, 1997), 114–115.

12 James Baldwin. "Letter from a Region in My Mind," *The New Yorker*, November 9, 1962, https://www.newyorker.com/magazine/1962/11/17/letter-from-a-region-in-my-mind, Accessed August 27, 2022. Published in the print edition of the November 17, 1962, issue.

13 Thomas Merton, *Passion for Peace: The Social Essays*, ed. William H. Shannon (New York: Crossroad Publishing, 1997), 174–175.

14 Thomas Merton, *Seeds of Destruction* (New York: Farrar, Straus, and Giroux, 1964), 25.

15 Thomas Merton, *New Seeds of Contemplation* (New York: New Directions, 1961), 21.

16 Thomas Merton, *Choosing to Love the World*, ed. Jonathan Montaldo (Boulder, CO: Sounds True, Inc., 2008,) 105.

17 Vatican Radio, "Pope urges priests to have hearts of mercy and compassion," 2014-03-06 13:42:22, http://www.archivioradiovaticana.va/storico/2014/03/06/pope_urges_priests_to_have_hearts_of_mercy_and_compassion/en1-779136, Accessed August 27, 2022.

18 Patrick Hart, OCSO, ed., *Run to the Mountain: The Story of a Vocation*, The Journals of Thomas Merton, Volume One, 1939–1941 (San Francisco, CA: HarperSanFrancisco, 1996), 497.

19 William H. Shannon, ed., *The Hidden Ground of Love: The Letters of Thomas Merton on Religious Experience and Social Concerns* (New York: Farrar, Straus and Giroux, 1985), 10.

20 Thomas Merton, *The Asian Journal of Thomas Merton*, Edited by Naomi Burton, brother Patrick Hart & James Laughlin (New Directions, 1973), xxviv.

21 William H. Shannon and Christine M. Bochen, eds., *Thomas Merton: A Life in Letters* (New York: Harper One, 2008), 188.

22 Thomas Merton, *New Seeds of Contemplation* (New York: New Directions, 1961), 78.

23 Merton, *New Seeds*, 76–77.

24 Thomas Merton, *Thoughts in Solitude* (New York: Farrar, Straus and Giroux, 1958), 79.

25 Merton, *Thoughts in Solitude*, 79.

26 Thomas Merton, *The Climate of Monastic Prayer* (Collegeville, MN: Cistercian Publications, 1973), 122–123.

27 Thomas Merton, *Meditations, December 23–30, 1941* (Columbia University Library, Mark Van Doren Collection, unpublished), 2, http://merton.org/ITMS/Seasonal/25/25-4Montaldo.pdf.

28 Thomas Merton, *Dialogues with Silence: Prayers & Drawings*, ed. Jonathan Montaldo (San Francisco, CA: HarperSanFrancisco, 2001), ix–xiv.

29 Thomas Merton, *Contemplation in a World of Action* (New York: Doubleday & Company, 1971), 142.

30 Thomas Merton, *The Seven Storey Mountain: An Autobiography of Faith* (San Diego, CA: Harcourt, Brace and Company, 1941), 108.

31 Merton, *Seven Storey Mountain*, 110.

32 Merton, *Seven Storey Mountain*, 113.

33 Thomas Merton, *Seeds of Destruction* (New York: Farrar, Straus and Giroux, 1964), 310.

34 Thomas Merton, *No Man Is an Island* (New York: Harcourt Brace Jovanovich, 1983), 260.

35 Quoted in *A Retreat with Thomas Merton* by Esther de Waal (Canterbury Press, 2011), 40, and quoted by David Stendl-Rast, OSB, in "Recollection of Thomas Merton's Last Days in the West" published in Monastic Studies (Pine City, New York, Mount Saviour Monastery, 1969).

36 John Kirvan, *God Hunger: Discovering the Mystic in All of Us* (Notre Dame, IN: Sorin Books, 1999), 155.

37 *Pico Iyer, The Art of Stillness: Adventures in Going Nowhere* (New York: TED Books (Simon & Schuster), 2014) 12.

38 Thomas Merton, *The Sign of Jonas* (Orlando, FL: Harcourt, Inc., 1981), 89.

39 Gerard Thomas Straub, *The Sunrise of the Soul: Meditations on Prayerful Stillness, Silence, Solitude, and Service in the Spirit of St. Francis of Assisi* (Brewster, Massachusetts: Paraclete Press in association with Pax et Bonum Communications, 2020), 98

40 Paul Tillich, *The Shaking of the Foundations* (Wipf and Stock; Reprint edition, 2012), 150.

41 Thomas Merton, *No Man Is an Island* (New York: Harcourt Brace Jovanovich, 1983), 12.

42 Georges Bernanos, *The Diary of a Country Priest* (New York: Macmillan Co., 1965), 123.

43 Thomas Merton, *Conjectures of a Guilty Bystander* (New York: Doubleday, 1966), 77.

44 Thomas Merton, *Contemplation in a World of Action* (New York: Doubleday & Company, 1971), 69.

45 Thomas Merton, *The Inner Experience: Notes on Contemplation* (San Francisco, CA: HarperSanFrancisco, 2004), 58.

46 Thomas Merton, *New Seeds of Contemplation* (New York: New Directions, 1961), 3.

47 Thomas Merton, *A Search for Solitude: Pursuing a Monk's True Life*, The Journals of Thomas Merton, Volume 3, 1952–1960 (San Francisco, CA: HarperSanFrancisco, 1996), 45.

48 Thomas Merton, *Choosing to Love the World*, ed. Jonathan Montaldo (Boulder, CO: Sounds True, Inc., 2008), 3–11.

49 Thomas Merton, *New Seeds of Contemplation* (New York: New Directions, 1961), 3.

50 Merton, *New Seeds*, 136.

51 Ruth Burrows, *Interior Castle Explored* (London, U.K.: Sheed and Ward, 1981), 65.

52 Or N. Rose, ed., trans., *God in All Moments: Mystical and Practical Spiritual Wisdom from Hasidic Masters*, (Woodstock, VT: Jewish Lights, 2004), 115.

53 Thomas Merton, *The Hidden Ground of Love*. Letters, Volume 1. William H. Shannon, editor. (New York: Farrar, Straus and Giroux, 1985), 157–158.

54 Thomas Merton, *Turning Toward the World: The Pivotal Years*, The Journals of Thomas Merton, Volume 4, 1960–1963 (San Francisco, CA: HarperSanFrancisco, 1997), 331–332.

55 Thomas Merton, *Thoughts in Solitude* (New York: Farrar, Straus & Giroux, 1958), 79.

56 Merton, *Turning Toward the World*, 87.

57 Karl Barth, *The Epistle to the Romans* (London, U.K.: Oxford University Press, 1968), 33–34.

58 Thomas Merton, *The School of Charity* (New York: Farrar, Straus & Giroux, 1990), 31.

59 Thomas Merton, *The Seven Storey Mountain: An Autobiography of Faith* (San Diego, CA: Harcourt, Brace and Company, 1941), 419.

60 Thomas Merton, *Disputed Questions*, (New York: Farrara, Straus and Cudahy, 1960).

61 Henri J. M. Nouwen, *Love, Henri: Letters on the Spiritual Life*, ed. Gabrielle Earnshaw (New York: Convergent, 2016), 9.

62 Robert Kennedy, *Zen Gifts to Christians* (New York: Continuum, 2004), 119.

63 Kennedy, *Zen Gifts*, 120.

64 First published in 1965 by New Directions. Edited by Thomas Merton, the book presents a selection of Gandhi's writings that reveal his essential beliefs on non-violence.

65 Thomas Merton, *New Seeds of Contemplation* (New York: New Directions, 1961), 23.

66 Dalai Lama, *The World of Tibetan Buddhism: An Overview of Its Philosophy and Practice* (Boston, MA: Wisdom Publications, 1995), 63.

67 Art Perry, *The Tibetans* (New York: Viking Studio (Penguin Putman, Inc.), 1999), 140.

68 Michael Casey, OCSO, *Toward God: The Ancient Wisdom of Western Prayer* (Liguori, MO: Liguori/Triumph, 1996), 122–123.

69 Anne Lamott, *Traveling Mercies: Some Thoughts on Faith* (New York: Pantheon Books, 1999), 22.

70 Robert Baker and Gray Henry, eds., *Merton & Sufism: The Untold Story* (Louisville, KY: Fons Vitae, 1999), unnumbered page.

71 Naomi Burton, Brother Patrick Hart, and James Laughlin, eds., *The Asian Journal of Thomas Merton* (New York: New Directions Publishing, 1973), 308.

72 Thomas Merton, *Conjectures of a Guilty Bystander* (New York: Doubleday, 1966), 144.

73 Roger Haight, *Jesus Symbol of God* (Maryknoll, NY: Orbis Books, 1999) 333.

74 "Declaration on the Relation of the Church to Non-Christian Religions Nostra Aetate Proclaimed by His Holiness Pope Paul VI on October 28, 1965," Documents of the Second Vatican Council, Vatican, accessed August 18, 2022, https://www.vatican.va/archive/hist_councils/ii_vatican_council/documents/vat_ii_decl_19651028_nostra-aetate_en.html.

75 Thich Nhat Hanh, *Living Buddha, Living Christ* (New York: Riverhead Books, 1995), xiii.

76 Thich Nhat Hanh, *Living Buddha, Living Christ* (New York: Riverhead Books, 1995), 87.

77 Thich Nhat Hanh, *Living Buddha, Living Christ* (New York: Riverhead Books, 1995), 91.

78 Hanh, *Living Buddha, Living Christ*, 93.

79 Hanh, *Living Buddha, Living Christ*, 95–96

80 Hanh, *Living Buddha, Living Christ*, 100–101.

81 Hanh, *Living Buddha, Living Christ*, 105–106.

82 William Apel, ed., *Signs of Peace: The Interfaith Letters of Thomas Merton* (Maryknoll, NY: Orbis Books, 2006), 25.

83 Antoine de Saint-Exupéry, *The Little Prince*, English translation (Harcourt, 2000), 70.

84 Christian Salenson, *Christian de Chergé: A Theology of Hope* (Collegeville, MN: Liturgical Press, 2012), 57.

85 Naomi Burton, Brother Patrick Hart, and James Laughlin, eds., *The Asian Journal of Thomas Merton* (New York: New Directions Publishing, 1973), 313.

86 Thomas Merton, *Zen and the Birds of Appetite*, New Directions; Later prt. edition (January 17, 1968).

87 Thomas Merton, *When the Trees Say Nothing: Writings on Nature*, ed. Kathleen Deignan (Notre Dame, IN: Sorin Books, 2003), 35.

88 William Apel, ed., *Signs of Peace: The Interfaith Letters of Thomas Merton* (Maryknoll, NY: Orbis Books, 2006), 125.

89 Thomas Merton, *New Seeds of Contemplation* (New York: New Directions, 1961), 31.

90 Martin Buber, *The Way of Man: According to the Teaching of Hasidism* (New York: Routledge Classics, 2002), 10.

91 John O'Donohue, *Anam Cara: A Book of Celtic Wisdom* (New York: HarperCollins, 1997), 202.

92 Thomas Merton, *Seeds of Contemplation* (New York: New Directions, 1949), 36.

93 Thomas Merton, *The Inner Experience: Notes on Contemplation* (San Francisco, CA: HarperSanFrancisco, 2004), 49.

94 Thomas Merton, *No Man Is an Island* (New York: Harcourt Brace Jovanovich, 1983), 108.

95 Thomas Merton's Japanese Preface to *Thoughts in Solitude*.

96 Thomas Merton, *Conjectures of a Guilty Bystander* (New York: Doubleday, 1966), 144.

97 Walter Brueggemann, *Theology of the Old Testament: Testimony, Dispute, Advocacy* (Fortress, 1997).

98 Thomas Merton, *Soul Searching: The Journey of Thomas Merton*, Edited by Morgan C. Atkinson with Jonathan Montaldo (Collegeville, Minnesota: Liturgical Press, 2008), 23.

99 Naomi Burton, Brother Patrick Hart, and James Laughlin, eds., *The Asian Journal of Thomas Merton* (New York: New Directions Publishing, 1973), 306.

100 Antonio Spadaro and Pope Francis, *My Door Is Always Open: A Conversation on Faith, Hope and the Church in a Time of Change* (Bloomsbury in Association with La Civiltà Cattolica 1994), 97.

101 Kieran Kavanaugh, *John of the Cross: Doctor of Light and Love* (New York, Crossroads Publishing, 1999), 144.

102 Thomas Merton, *Learning to Love: Exploring Solitude and Freedom*, The Journals of Thomas Merton, Volume Six, 1966–1967 (San Francisco, CA: HarperSanFrancisco, 1998), 335.

103 Thomas Merton, *The School of Charity* (New York: Farrar, Straus & Giroux, 1990), 31.

104 Rabindranath Tagore, *Fireflies* (New York: Collier Books, 1976), 203.

105 Barack Obama, *A Promised Land* (New York: Crown, Random House, 2020), 65.

106 Thomas Merton, *No Man Is an Island* (New York: Harcourt Brace Jovanovich, 1983), 52.

107 Anne Lamott, *Traveling Mercies: Some Thoughts on Faith* (New York: Pantheon Books, 1999), 134.

108 Abraham Joshua Heschel, *Moral Grandeur and Spiritual Audacity: Essays*, edited by Susannah Heschel (New York: Farrar, Straus and Giroux, 1996), 225

109 Thomas Merton, *No Man Is an Island* (New York: Harcourt Brace Jovanovich, 1983), 164.

110 Madeleine Delbrêl, *We, the Ordinary People of the Streets* (Grand Rapids, MI/Cambridge, U.K.: William B. Eerdmans Publishing Company, 2000), 100.

111 Rabbi Michael Lerner, *The Politics of Meaning* (Cambridge, MA: Perseus Books, 1977).

112 Thomas Merton, *Dancing in the Water of Life: Seeking Peace in the Hermitage*, The Journals of Thomas Merton, Volume Five, 1963–1965 (San Francisco, CA: HarperSanFrancisco, 1997), 254.

113 Thomas Merton, *Entering the Silence: Becoming a Monk and Writer, The Journals of Thomas Merton*, Volume 2, 1941–1952, edited by Jonathan Montaldo (New York: HarperCollins, 1997).

114 Thomas Merton, *The Literary Essays of Thomas Merton*, ed. Br. Patrick Hart, OCSO (New York: New Directions, 1981), 218.

115 Thomas Merton, *The Asian Journal of Thomas Merton* (New York: New Directions, 1973), 329.

116 Abraham Joshua Heschel, "Dissent," in *A New Hasidism: Roots*, eds. Arthur Green and Ariel Evan Mayse (Philadelphia, PA: Jewish Publication Society, 2019), 174–175.

117 Thomas Merton, *A Search for Solitude: Pursuing a Monk's True Life*, The Journals of Thomas Merton, Volume 3: 1952–1960 (San Francisco, CA: HarperSanFrancisco, 1996), 70.

118 Thomas Merton, *Dancing in the Water of Life: Seeking Peace in the Hermitage*, The Journals of Thomas Merton, Volume Five, 1963–1965 (San Francisco, CA: HarperSanFrancisco, 1997), 232.

119 Ronald Rolheiser, "Private Integrity," Lifeissues.net blog, updated June 9, 2020, accessed August 18, 2022, https://www.lifeissues.net/writers/ron/ron_458.html.

120 Thomas Merton, *Thoughts in Solitude* (New York: Farrar, Straus & Giroux, 1958), 48.

121 Anthony Padovano, *The Human Journey* (New York: Image Books, 1984), 96.

122 Thomas Merton, *Seeds of Contemplation* (New York: New Directions, 1949), 59.

123 Thomas Merton, *Disputed Questions*, (New York: Farrara, Straus and Cudahy, 1960), 196.

124 Naomi Burton Stone and Brother Patrick Hart, eds., *Love and Living* (New York: Harcourt, 1985), 43.

125 Michael Paul Gallagher, *Into Extra Time: Living Through the Final Stages of Cancer and Jottings Along the Way* (London, U.K.: Darton, Longman and Todd, 2016), 68.

126 Thomas Merton, *The Inner Experience: Notes of Contemplation*, Edited by William H. Shannon, (HarperSanFrancisco, 2003), 15.

127 Thomas Merton, "Hagia Sophia," in *Emblems of a Season of Fury* (New York: New Directions, 1963), 68–69.

128 Thomas Merton, *New Seeds of Contemplation* (New York: New Directions, 1961), 21.

129 Ruth Burrows. *Ascent to Love: The Spiritual Teaching of St. John of the Cross* (Dimension Books, 2006), 47.

130 Merton, *New Seeds*, 2.

131 Merton, *New Seeds*, 12.

132 Merton, *New Seeds*, 1e.

133 Peter Maurin, *The Forgotten Radical Peter Maurin: Easy Essays from the Catholic Worker* (Fordom University Press, 2020), 46.

134 Hans Urs van Balthasar, *Light of the World: Brief Reflections on the Sunday Readings*, trans. Dennis D. Martin (San Francisco, CA: Ignatius Press, 1993).

135 Thomas Merton, *The Asian Journal of Thomas Merton* (New Directions, 1973), 341–342.

136 Gerard Straub, *The Sun & Moon Over Assisi* (Phoenix, Arizona: Tau Publishing, 2015), 334.

137 Ross Labrie, *The Art of Thomas Merton* (Texas Christian University Press, 1979), 14.

138 Labrie, *The Art of Thomas Merton*, 15.

139 Thomas Merton, *Conjectures of a Guilty Bystander* (New York: Doubleday, 1966), 19.

140 Milan Kundera, Slowness (Harper Perennial, 1997).

141 Igumen Chariton, comp., *The Art of Prayer: An Orthodox Anthology* (London, U.K.: Faber and Faber, 1997), 46.

142 Thomas Merton, *No Man Is an Island* (New York: Harcourt Brace Jovanovich, 1983), 193.

143 Erasmo Leiva-Merikakis, *Fire of Mercy: Heart of the Word: Meditations on the Gospel According to Saint Matthew Vol. 1* (San Francisco: Ignatius Press, 1996).

144 Daniel O'Leary, *Horizons of Hope* (Dublin: Columba Books, 2021), 129.

145 O'Leary, *Horizons*, 130.

146 Ilia Delio, Keith Douglas Warner, and Pamela Wood, *Care for Creation: A Franciscan Spirituality of the Earth* (Cincinnati, OH: Franciscan Media, 2008) 131–132.

147 Bruce Epperly, *Walking with Francis of Assisi: From Privilege to Activism* (Cincinnati, OH: Franciscan Media, 2021), ix, 8–9, 4–5, 12.

148 Mirabai Starr, "Dazzling Darkness" *Oneing* 10, no. 1, Unveiled (Spring 2022): 83, 87–88.

149 Thomas Merton, *Run to the Mountain, The Journals of Thomas Merton*, Volume One 1939–1941, Edited by Patrick Hart (HarperSanFrancisco, 1995), 227.

150 Thomas Merton, *The Inner Experience* (San Francisco, CA: HarperSanFrancisco, 2003), 138.

151 Thomas Merton, *Monastic Observances: Initiation into the Monastic Tradition*, Volume 25, ed. Patrick F. O'Connell (Collegeville, MN: Liturgical Press, 2010), 83–84.

152 Max Picard, *The World of Silence*, trans. Stanley Godman (Chicago: Henry Regnery, 1977), 251.

153 Robert Ellsberg, ed., *Dorothy Day: Selected Writings* (Maryknoll, NY: Orbis Books, 2001), xxxv.

154 Bruno Barnhart, *The Future of Wisdom* (Continuum, 2007).

155 Bruno Barnhart, *Sacred Simplicity* (Paulist Press, 1999), 49–50.

156 Barnhart, *Sacred Simplicity*, 90.

157 Rowan Williams, *A Silent Action: Engagements with Thomas Merton* (Louisville, Kentucky: Fons Vitae, 2011), 12.

158 Thomas Merton, *Conjectures of a Guilty Bystander* (New York: Doubleday Publishing, 1966), 156–157.

159 Thomas Merton, *A Search for Solitude: Pursuing a Monk's True Life*, The Journals of Thomas Merton, Volume 3, 1952-1960 (San Francisco, CA: HarperSanFrancisco, 1996), 182–183.

160 Naomi Shihab Nye, "Kindness," in *Words Under The Words: Selected Poems* (Portland, OR: The Eighth Mountain Press, 1994).

161 Mary O'Driscoll, OP, ed., *Catherine of Siena: Passion for the Truth, Compassion for Humanity* (Hyde Park, NY: New City Press, 1993).

162 Thich Nhat Hahn, *Going Home: Jesus and Buddha as Brothers* (New York: Riverhead Books, 1999), 164.

163 Dietrich Bonhoeffer, *Meditations on the Cross* (Louisville, KY: Westminster John Knox Press, 1998), 46.

164 Found in *A Silent Action* by Rowan Martin (Louisville, Kentucky: Fons Vitae, 2011), 34.

165 Thomas of Celano, *The Francis Trilogy of Thomas of Celano* (Hyde Park, New York, New City Press, 2004), 91.

166 James Finley, *Merton's Palace of Nowhere: A Search for God Through Awareness of the True Self* (Notre Dame, IN: Ave Maria Press, 1978), 30.

167 Finley, *Merton's Palace*, 30.

168 Thomas Merton, *The Way of Chuang Tzu* (New York: New Direction, 1965), 35–36.

169 Thomas Merton, *New Seeds of Contemplation* (New York: New Directions, 1961), 34.

170 Thomas Merton, *The Inner Experience* (San Francisco, CA: HarperSanFrancisco, 2003), 24.

171 Elie Wiesel, *Messengers of God: Biblical Portraits and Legends* (New York: Simon & Schuster Paperbacks, 2005), 30.

172 Ilia Delio, *The Hours of the Universe* (Orbis Books, 2021), 240.

173 Thomas Merton, "Hagia Sophia," in *Emblems of a Season of Fury* (New York: New Directions, 1963), 61.

174 Quoted in the *Jerusalem Post*, May 7, 2020.

175 Thomas Merton, *A Search for Solitude: Pursuing a Monk's True Life*, The Journals of Thomas Merton, Volume 3, 1952–1960 (San Francisco, CA: HarperSanFrancisco, 1996), 20.

176 Thomas Merton, *The Way of Chuang Tzu* (New York: New Directions, 1965), 115.

177 Thomas Merton, *Turning Toward the World: The Pivotal Years*, The Journals of Thomas Merton, Volume 4, 1960–1963 (San Francisco, CA: HarperSanFrancisco, 1996), 87.

178 Thomas Merton, *Learning to Love: Exploring Solitude and Freedom*, The Journals of Thomas Merton, Volume Six, 1966–1967 (San Francisco, CA: HarperSanFrancisco, 1998), 355.

179 Boniface Ramsey, *Beginning to Read the Fathers* (New York: Paulist Press, 1985), 77.

180 Edward Kaplan, "To Keep the Pain Awake," *The NICM Journal* 2, no 2 (Spring 1977): 63–73.

181 Thomas Merton, *Faith and Violence* (Notre Dame, IN: University of Notre Dame Press), 145–146, 164.

182 *The Sayings of the Desert Fathers*, translated with a foreword by Benedicta Ward, SLG, Preface by Metroploitan Anthony (Cistercian Publications, 1984), 178.

183 John R. Donahue, *The Gospel in Parable* (Fortress Press, 1990), 126.

184 John Drury, trans., *Poverty of Spirit* (Paramus, NJ: Paulist Press, 1968), 26.

185 Abraham Joshua Heschel, *I Asked for Wonder*, Edited by Samuel H. Dresner (New York: Crossroad Publishing Company, 2001) 88.

186 Etty Hillesum, *Etty Hillesum: An Interrupted Life and Letters from Westerbork* (New York: Henry Holt and Company, 1996), 157.

187 From a homily delivered on Fed. 17, 1980, Quoted in the *National Catholic Reporter* on April 7, 2010.

188 Naomi Burton, Brother Patrick Hart, and James Laughlin, eds., *The Asian Journal of Thomas Merton* (New York: New Directions Publishing, 1973), 306.

189 Thomas Merton, *Life and Holiness* (New York: Image, 2014), 88

190 Carlo Carretto, *Letters from the Desert* (Maryknoll, NY: Orbis Books, 1972), 130.

191 Thomas Merton, *Contemplative Prayer* (New York: Image Books, 1996), 48.

192 Teilhard de Chardin, Quoted in "A New Level of Thinking about Creation" by Ilia Delio published in the Global Siters Report on May 11, 2015.

193 Thomas Merton, *No Man Is an Island* (New York: Harcourt Brace Jovanovich, 1983), 215–216.

194 [citation to come?]

195 Thomas Merton, *Life and Holiness* (New York: Image, 2014), 12–13.

196 Thomas Merton, *The Intimate Merton*, ed. Patrick Hart and Jonathan Montaldo (San Francisco, CA: HarperSanFrancisco, 1999), 238.

197 Thomas Merton, *When the Trees Say Nothing: Writings on Nature*, ed. Kathleen Deignan (Notre Dame, IN: Sorin Books, 2003), 23.

198 Merton, *Thoughts in Solitude*, 89.

199 John Dear, *Living Peace* (Doubleday, 2001), 27.

200 Wayne Teasdale, *The Mystic Heart* (Novato, California: New World Library, 1999), 151.

201 Thomas Merton, *Conjectures of a Guilty Bystander* (New York: Doubleday, 1966), 131–132.

202 Thomas Merton, *A Vow of Conversation*, ed. Naomi Burton Stone (New York: Farrar, Straus, Giroux, 1988), 108.

203 Thomas Merton, *Thoughts in Solitude* (New York: Farrar, Straus & Giroux, 1958), 94.

204 Merton, *Thoughts in Solitude*, 29.

205 Merton, *Thoughts in Solitude*, 39.

206 Thomas Merton, *A Vow of Conversation*, ed. Naomi Burton Stone (New York: Farrar, Straus, Giroux, 1988), 109.

207 Thomas Merton, *A Vow of Conversation* (New York: Farrar, Straus, Giroux, 1988), 110.

208 Thomas Merton, *Conjectures of a Guilty Bystander* (New York: Doubleday, 1966), 131.

209 Christine Bochen, ed., *Learning to Love: Exploring Solitude and Freedom*, The Journals of Thomas Merton, Volume Six, 1966–1967 (San Francisco, CA: HarperSanFrancisco, 1997), 167.

210 Naomi Burton, Brother Patrick Hart, and James Laughlin, eds., *The Asian Journal of Thomas Merton* (New York: New Directions Publishing, 1973), 4–5.

211 Thomas Merton, *New Seeds of Contemplation* (New York: New Directions, 1961), 182.

212 Thomas Merton, *No Man Is an Island* (Harcourt, Brace, Jovanovich, 1955), 247.

213 Roy Campbell, trans., *The Poems of St. John of the Cross* (New York: Random House, 1960), 25.

214 Quoted in Fr. Donald Cozzens, *Notes from the Underground: The Spiritual Journal of a Secular Priest* (Maryknoll, NY: Orbis Books, 2013).

215 Fr. Donald Cozzens, *Notes from the Underground: The Spiritual Journal of a Secular Priest* (Maryknoll, NY: Orbis Books, 2013), 57

216 Paul Farmer and Gustavo Gutierrez, *In the Company of the Poor: Conversations with Dr. Paul Farmer and Fr. Gustavo Gutierrez* (Orbis Books, 2013).

217 Thomas Merton, *Conjectures of a Guilty Bystander* (New York: Doubleday, 1966).

218 *Washington Post*, June 19, 2018; NPR, May 2, 2018; A study by the University of Wisconsin-Madison issued on 12/7/2020; On 6/27/18 FactCheck.org demolished Trump's false and misleading claim the illegal migrants caused an increase in violent crime.

219 Etty Hillesum, *Etty Hillesum: An Interrupted Life and Letters from Westerbork* (New York: Henry Holt & Co., 1996), 44.

220 Hillesum, *An Interrupted Life*, xx.

221 Hillesum, *An Interrupted Life*, 97.

222 Hillesum, *An Interrupted Life*, 179.

223 Hillesum, *An Interrupted Life*, 226.

224 Brian J. Pierce, OP, *Jesus and the Prodigal Son: The God of Radical Mercy*, (Maryknoll, NY: Orbis Books, 2016), 156.

225 Pierce, *Jesus and the Prodigal Son*, 167.

226 Pierce, *Jesus and the Prodigal Son*, 168

227 Abraham Joshua Heschel, *Man Is Not Alone: A Philosophy of Religion* (New York: Farrar, Strauss and Giroux, 1976), 296.

228 Abraham Joshua Heschel, *The Sabbath* (Farrar, Straus and Giroux, 1995), 30.

229 Abraham Joshua Heschel, *Moral Grandeur and Spiritual Audacity: Essays* (Farrar, Straus and Giroux, 1997), 264.

230 Thomas Merton, *Seeds of Destruction* (New York: Farrar, Straus, and Giroux, 1964.

231 Thomas Merton, *Disputed Questions*, (New York: Farrar, Straus and Cudahy, 1960), 132–134.

232 Caryll Houselander, *The Risen Life* (New York: Scepter Publishing, 2007), 11.

233 Graham Greene, *The End of the Affair* (New York: Penguin Books, 1999), 7.

234 Christopher Pramuk, *At Play in Creation: Merton's Awakening to the Feminine Divine* (Collegeville, MN: Liturgical Press, 2015), 5–6.

235 William H. Shannon, ed., *The Hidden Ground of Love: The Letters of Thomas Merton on Religious Experience and Social Concerns* (New York: Farrar, Straus and Giroux, 1985), 46.